I0901480

Irish women's writing, 1878–1922

MANCHESTER
1824

Manchester University Press

Irish women's writing, 1878–1922

Advancing the cause of liberty

Edited by Anna Pilz and Whitney Standlee

Manchester University Press

Published by Manchester University Press
Altrincham Street, Manchester M1 7JA
www.manchesteruniversitypress.co.uk

British Library Cataloguing-in-Publication Data
A catalogue record for this book is available from the British Library

Library of Congress Cataloging-in-Publication Data applied for

ISBN 978 0 7190 9758 4 hardback
ISBN 978 1 5261 2711 2 paperback

First published 2016

Typeset by Out of House Publishing
Printed in Great Britain
by TJ International Ltd, Padstow

Contents

Figures

Contributors

Aurelia Annat completed her D.Phil. with the History Faculty, University of Oxford, on 'Imaginable Nations: Constructions of History and Identity and the Contribution of Selected Irish Women Writers 1891–1945'. Subsequently she was research assistant for Dr Michael Biggs at the Department of Sociology (Oxford), investigating Irish republican and British suffragette hunger-strikers in the early twentieth century. She currently teaches modern British history at Trinity College, Oxford.

Lauren Arrington is Senior Lecturer at the Institute of Irish Studies. She studied in the United States, Ireland, and the UK. Her monograph, *W. B. Yeats, the Abbey Theatre, Censorship, and the Irish State: Adding the Half-Pence to the Pence*, was published in 2010. Recent publications include essays on Irish Modernism and anti-imperialist discourse. Her most recent book is the biography *Revolutionary Lives: Constance and Casimir Markievicz* (2015).

Naomi Doak completed her Ph.D. in the Faculty of Languages and Literature at the University of Ulster in 2006. She has published several articles and chapters on Ulster Protestant women writers, including 'Assessing an Absence: Ulster Protestant Women Authors, 1900–60', in M. Busteed, F. Neal, and J. Tonge (eds), *Irish Protestant Identities* (2008). She is currently employed as a tourism, culture, heritage, and arts development officer at Belfast City Council.

Heidi Hansson is Professor of English Literature at Umeå University, Sweden. Her main research interest is women's literature, and she has previously published in the fields of postmodern romance, nineteenth-century women's cross-gendered writing, Irish women's literature, and northern studies. Among her works on Irish topics are the study *Emily Lawless*

1845–1913: Writing the Interspace (2007), the edited collection *New Contexts: Re-framing Nineteenth-Century Irish Women's Prose* (2008), and *Fictions of the Irish Land War* (2014), edited together with Professor James H. Murphy.

Margaret Kelleher is Professor of Anglo-Irish Literature and Drama at University College Dublin. She has published widely in the areas of nineteenth-century literature, Famine studies, women's writings, and cultural studies. Professor Kelleher is President of the International Association for the Study of Irish Literatures, Chair of the Irish Film Institute, and a member of Science Europe's Humanities Committee. Her current project is a cultural history of the 1882 Maamtrasna episode from the perspective of nineteenth-century language change.

Jane Mahony is a Ph.D. student in the School of English, Trinity College Dublin. Her thesis draws on the perspectives of book and publishing history, aligned to archival research, to offer a fresh contribution to Irish literary history in the period 1885–1922, placing Irish literary actors of the period within a more global sense of the field of book production and distribution. She was previously Marketing Controller at Cambridge University Press and Managing Director of Pickering & Chatto Publishers Ltd., London.

Patrick Maume is a native of Cork and a researcher with the Royal Irish Academy's *Dictionary of Irish Biography*. He is a graduate of University College Cork and Queen's University Belfast, lived in Belfast for many years, and takes an interest in Ulster history and culture. He has published many papers on nineteenth- and twentieth-century Irish political, media, and literary history as well as a monograph on early twentieth-century nationalist political culture and biographies of Daniel Corkery and D. P. Moran.

Lia Mills writes novels, short stories, essays, and reviews. She has worked on several public art commissions and as an arts consultant. Her third novel, *Fallen*, was published in 2014. She teaches aspects of writing, most recently at the Irish Writers' Centre and at University College Dublin, where she was previously a teaching and research fellow with a particular focus on the work of Irish women writers. She lives in Dublin.

James H. Murphy is Professor of English at DePaul University, Chicago. He is both a literary and political historian of nineteenth-century Ireland. His political studies include *Abject Loyalty: Nationalism and Monarchy in Ireland* *during the Reign of Queen Victoria* (2001) and *Ireland's Czar: Gladstonian Government and the Lord Lieutenancies of the Red Earl of Spencer, 1868–1886* (2014). His literary work includes *Irish Novelists and the Victorian Age* (2011) and the editing of *The Oxford History of the Irish Book*, vol. IV: *The Irish Book in English, 1800–1891* (2011).

Ciaran O'Neill is Ussher Lecturer in Nineteenth-Century History at Trinity College Dublin. His research interests focus on elites and elite education, Ireland and the transnational, and public history. He has also developed an interest in literary history and has published articles on the Irish schoolboy novel. O'Neill is the author of *Catholics of Consequence: Transnational Education, Social Mobility and the Irish Catholic Elite, 1850–1900* (2014) for which he won the James S. Donnelly Prize in 2015. Since 2014, he has been President of the Society for the Study of Nineteenth-Century Ireland.

Eve Patten is Professor of English at Trinity College Dublin, where she lectures in nineteenth- and twentieth-century British and Irish literature. Her publications include *Samuel Ferguson and the Culture of Nineteenth Century Ireland* (2004), *Imperial Refugee: Olivia Manning's Fictions of War* (2012), and *Ireland, West to East: Irish Cultural Connections with Central and Eastern Europe* (2014, co-edited with Aidan O'Malley). She is currently working on a study of English writers and Ireland, 1910–45.

Anna Pilz is an Irish Research Council Postdoctoral Fellow at the School of English, University College Cork. Pilz's doctorate focused on the dramatic works of Lady Gregory, and she has published articles in *New Hibernia Review* and *Irish Studies Review* as well as book chapters on the playwright's literary output and class politics. Her current monograph project focuses on the symbolism of trees in Irish literature.

Whitney Standlee lectures in English literature and cultural studies at the University of Worcester. Her research interests include late nineteenth- and early twentieth-century Irish women's writing and women's contributions to popular culture after 1880. She has published on the politics of Irish women's writing, Land War fiction, and the Irish *Künstlerroman*. Her monograph, *'Power to Observe': Irish Women Novelists in Britain, 1890–1916* (2015) was the winner of the 2013 Peter Lang Young Scholars Competition in Irish Studies.

Kieron Winterson completed his doctoral studies under the supervision of Dr Frank Shovlin at the Institute of Irish Studies, University of Liverpool, in 2008. That research looked at the representation in Irish poetry of the

Great War in the context of the long nineteenth century. In addition to Katharine Tynan, he has written on Winifred Letts and Alice Cooke and is currently pursuing an interest in mythography. He has worked for the Open University since 2009.

Mai Yatani is a Ph.D. candidate at Trinity College Dublin, working under the supervision of Professor David Dickson and Dr Ciaran O'Neill. She took both her BA (2008) and MA (2010) at the University of Tokyo. Her research interests include the history of reading, history of books, history of women, urban history, and history of science in modern Ireland.

Foreword

WHY does academic criticism matter? And why does a collection like this, with a clear focus on work by women at the turn of the last century, have particular value? Is it not enough to know about and study the exalted few Irish writers who are recognised as important and universally relevant, those with international appeal and reputation – the ones I don't even have to name because your mind, reading this, is already filling in the blanks?

Well, no. It's not enough – and not just because our notions of what is significant, important or relevant change over time. It matters because the historically assumed non-existence or scarcity of Irish women writers is untrue. It matters because assumptions about their lack of value or relevance are wrong. It matters because when we look at Irish literature across the centuries but exclude women and other writers who don't conform to – or who write in direct opposition to – our notions of what is appropriately 'Irish', the shape and developmental trajectory we assume for it bears little resemblance to its actual shape. Worse, the texture is entirely missing. Without connective tissue, the body of a literature can't breathe let alone grow or be coherent. It will eventually die. And it matters because the apparent vacuum is a deprivation for writers as well as readers of the future. How much time is lost when we need, not only to reinvent the wheel, but to reimagine it?

It's like coming across the ruined wall of what was once a town. If a brick is enough for you, there's no more to be said. But if it's depth, colour, and movement you're after, if it's life you want – with all its mess, argument, and contradiction, its soaring pleasures as well as its crushing defeats – a single wall won't satisfy you, it will only sharpen your appetite.

I should declare bias, here. I started writing when I was a child, before my imagination got the news that it was supposed to be gendered. When I wasn't reading, I was inventing worlds in my head and on paper, drawing maps of places I didn't know enough to call fictional. Speaking, I'm embarrassed to admit, lines of dialogue, whether I was alone or not. Writing was something I always wanted to do, but I didn't know a writer was something a person like me could *be*. There are as many internal and personal reasons for that sense of a lack of entitlement as there are writers they inhibit. There are practical obstacles, which have been extensively and capably discussed elsewhere. What's relevant here is the unnameable absence that amounts to ignorance, the not-knowing that there are models, exemplars, and solutions to hand.

Reading dismantled my internal barriers, block by suffocating concrete block. I came to women's studies in the 1990s and read my way to the blindingly original insight that I wasn't the first, I wouldn't be the last, I wasn't the only writer who had to chisel her own path to the printed page. Finding your own way is part of the necessary apprenticeship a writer undertakes, but it helps when the path is lit and broadened by those who've travelled it already. I'm a slow learner, but it finally dawned on me that no one would give me permission or invite me to write. Equally, no one could stop me except myself. If I wanted it, I had to step up and claim it, learn how to do it word by word, deal with the fallout later. Authority requires agency and by definition no one else can give it to you or do it for you. It really is that simple. It's that hard.

Reading the work, the lives, journals, and letters of writers of any age, gender or background helps us to understand what writing is, what it means to those writers, what challenges they had to overcome to do it, their intentions, ideas, failures, neuroses, joys. The words of women writers had specific power for me because so many of my personal obstacles and taboos were rooted in gender and 'loyalty', that great universal silencer. Whether to family or individuals, to peer group, church or state, loyalty will trip us up and blind us every time. In a country steeped in contested memory and identities, those things are highly charged. It would be simpler to lapse into brooding silence instead of raising awkward questions, but where's the satisfaction in that? The more questions we pose, the more we learn.

My first novel, *Another Alice*, was written as a counter-narrative to a lot of white noise and nonsense that was being bandied about at the time, on the airwaves and in print, about women and sexual violence. The novel took shape in my mind in 1992, a bad year to be a woman in Ireland; it was the year of the X case and several other high-profile cases of rape and murder. I wanted to give a character space from which she could answer back, tell her own story in such a way that readers would enter it with her and hear what she had to say. For me, writing the novel explored questions about ownership of a story, who gets to tell it and how. It's a matter of choosing, defining, and inhabiting a narrative space.

Those issues returned in force with my most recent novel, *Fallen*, which is set before and during the Easter Rising in Dublin (1916). I started with a simple – and, significantly, a neutral – question: What would it be like to step out of your house one day and find your city overtaken by forces you don't recognise or understand?

What I knew of the Rising was the received and cherished account that amounts to the foundation myth of the Irish state: On Easter Monday 1916, while the Great War convulsed the world, a group of Irish men and women took over key buildings and civic spaces in Dublin in the name of an Irish republic that didn't yet exist. It took six days of street fighting and siege for the British Army – which included thousands of Irishmen – to force a surrender. The rapid execution of sixteen of the leaders of the Rising turned public opinion against the British and set us on the path that ultimately led to independence. It's a story we love, with good reason.

The trouble with iconic and well-loved stories is that their surface is so smooth, so perfectly glossed, that they're difficult for a writer of fiction to penetrate. When I found my way inside the available narrative space, the story I loved and thought I knew about the Rising became something else entirely. The story that wanted me to tell it was other than the one I started with; it revealed itself slowly and against the resistances, conscious and unconscious, of my own previous relationship with it. My angle of entry was such that I found I had to rearrange the lines, bend them to new shapes that would accommodate the uncomfortable realities. For example: not the sixteen dead leaders my mind naively retained as a toll, but 442 people dead, more citizens than rebels and British Army put together. I'd be lying if I said I didn't have moments of unease about all this, a return of those ghosts of entitlement, ownership, loyalty. But I also had the comfort of knowing I was neither the first Irish, nor the first woman, writer to experience such qualms or to write against the conventional grain.

When I began to research and read the work of turn-of-the-(last)-century Irish women writers, first as an MA student and later as a teaching and research fellow at University College Dublin, I was genuinely shocked that they occupied such a blind spot in our literature. I think what actually shocked me most was my own previous willingness to accept not just their absence but, effectively, their non-existence through my own lack of curiosity. As if only women of our time have ever cared about questions like equality, freedom, self-actualisation, art, survival, ambition, faith, or justice. The omission was unthinking rather than deliberate, but it amounted to betrayal just the same. I knew about the token few, of course – Edgeworth, Somerville and Ross, Bowen, O'Brien – but except for the latter, I had an inherited expectation that their work could have no particular value or relevance to contemporary Ireland and may even be in some way inimical to it. It's shaming to admit to such intellectual laziness on my part, but it's true, so I must.

I did what I could to make up for it. I'd spend the next ten years reading, teaching, and writing about women writers of that generation, the generation whose work this book addresses so comprehensively. I came to love and value them, not just for their work, or for their approach to the stories they told and the worlds they depicted, but for what I came to know of their writing lives, how they were received, what happened to them later. My world and time are so different that we might as well inhabit separate planets, but what struck me was how much more we have in common than the artificial – and perceived – divisions that separate us. Here were the models and exemplars I'd been missing, without knowing enough to know I needed them. Now, when I write, I feel their solid presence at my back, the ground of a ghostly tradition underfoot. Collectively, they have the bracing effect of *Get on with it, or get out of the way.*

Fiction's great strength is empathy. Or maybe I mean that empathy is what makes fiction possible. It might even be the actual, osmotic mechanism that draws a reader into the world behind the lines and enlarges our understanding of the complexity of human experience. It expands our sense of possibility, but only if we read variously and with an open mind – this is another reason why critical essays asking a wide range of questions of a broad selection of writers matter.

The challenge for writers is to *write* variously and with an open mind. The most crucial decision for any story is what narrative position(s) to occupy. This choice determines everything that follows: the story's shape, its bias, its atmosphere; where the light falls, where the shadows deepen; and what it all might mean, on its own terms and for a reader.

The work of academic criticism is not a million miles away from creative writing, but it leans instead towards creative reading, generating worlds of discussion and argument along with flashes of brilliant illumination. The extent and quality of a novel's life depends on the alert, discriminating, and continuing attention of readers. Critics act as a conduit between fictional and actual worlds. It is an act of immense generosity to bring a critical intelligence to bear on someone else's work, to immerse yourself in it; to enlarge, promote, and help to extend its life through discussion, introducing the work to new readers in new contexts and, crucially, passing the conversation on through the generations.

If literary history matters at all, if culture and context matter at all, then attentive engagement with the work of women writers, as in the essays presented in this volume, is vitally important. Otherwise we are left with a false sense of a series of giant leaps rather than something organic, various, evolving; a literature that people of previous generations were reading, writing, and talking about; a world that is dynamic not static, alive and not dead, still waiting to be explored.

Books like this one tell us that despite the doomsday predictions – the death of the author, the death of the book – there is a new generation of readers, academics, and critics who care enough about the texture and fabric of literature to devote their own creative, thoughtful energy to keeping the conversation going, to keeping the work alive.

Lia Mills
Dublin, March 2015

Acknowledgements

THE editors wish to express their thanks and gratitude for the support they received in the early stages of this project from Mervyn Busteed, Sophie Cooper, John Wilson Foster, Roy Foster, Eimear McBride, Lucy McDiarmid, Nicola Morris, Frank Shovlin, Karen Steele, Julie Anne Stevens, Elizabeth Tilley, and Diane Urquhart. We would like to thank Margaret Kelleher for her enthusiastic response to our endeavour, and we owe to her an all-important alteration to the book title. Thanks to Claire Connolly, Margaret Kelleher, and Diane Urquhart for reading through and commenting on drafts of the 'Introduction'. Special thanks are due to Lia Mills for taking the time to write such a wonderful Foreword, which eloquently expresses why the writers with which this volume is concerned, and the research the volume contains, are so very important. We extend our thanks to Berni Metcalfe from the National Library Ireland in assisting with the acquisition of the image of the 1910 'poster' from the *Irish Independent* and to Jonathan Martin at the Irish Newspaper Archive for granting us permission for reproduction. We are grateful also to Martin Doyle, Michael Ruane, Irene Stevenson, and especially Dearbhla Kelly for granting us permission to reproduce the 2015 Irish Writers Poster from the *Irish Times*.

Margaret Kelleher wishes to thank Maura Farrelly, Deirdre Wildy, and their colleagues from Special Collections, Queen's University Belfast (QUB), as well as Norah Perkins at Curtis Brown Ltd, for their permission and assistance in quoting from the Somerville and Ross Archive, QUB. Anna Pilz acknowledges her gratitude to Colin Smythe on behalf of the heirs of Lady Gregory for copyright permission to quote from Lady Gregory's manuscripts and letters. Thanks to Norah Perkins at Curtis Brown Ltd for their permission to quote from the Wilfrid Scawen Blunt Papers. Finally, special thanks to Isaac Gewirtz on behalf of The Henry W. and Albert A. Berg Collection of English and American Literature, The New York Public Library, Astor, Lenox and Tilden Foundations for permission to quote from the Lady Gregory collection of papers.

Introduction

Anna Pilz and Whitney Standlee

In her foreword to this volume, Lia Mills recollects her own experiences in the 1990s of finding an Irish women's literary tradition where she once believed none existed and highlights the great excitement she felt – both as an academic and as an Irish female author – at this discovery. That the process of unearthing and acknowledging this neglected and imperative aspect of Ireland's literary landscape continues to be a work in progress three decades later is evidenced most visibly in prevailing popular conceptions of Irish literature. There is, for instance, a well-known poster of Irish writers that showcases, against a sepia background, the names, brief biographies, and photographs of twelve authors who are seen to stand as testament to the quality of Irish literature: J. M. Synge, Flann O'Brien, Oliver Goldsmith, Jonathan Swift, Samuel Beckett, W. B. Yeats, Brendan Behan, Oscar Wilde, Patrick Kavanagh, James Joyce, Sean O'Casey, and George Bernard Shaw. This specifically gendered accumulation of the country's literati is not altogether surprising: Irish writing has often been conceived in the popular imagination and conceptualised in academic scholarship as a male phenomenon. Although academic interest in redressing the gendered imbalance in literary history has gained conspicuous pace since the 1990s, Irish literary studies for many years lagged well behind its American and English counterparts in challenging such preconceptions.[1]

For the more general Irish (and international) reading public, the process of supplanting the image of an all-male literary contingent has been even slower. The relative obscurity of Irish literary women came prominently to the fore in the spring of 2015, when Martin Doyle, Assistant Literary Editor of the *Irish Times*, embarked on a project to put 'Irish women writers back in the picture'.[2] In the process, Doyle solicited articles from forty Irish writers, critics, and academics, collated the responses, and culminated the project by unveiling an alternative, female-only version of the poster. Framed as 'a pastiche or palimpsest of the original to celebrate Ireland's long, rich and diverse tradition of woman writers', it was described as representing a 'sample of the best female Irish writers in the English language'. Speaking of the finished work, Doyle admitted that the results were purposefully biased 'towards the past in order to chart a tradition dating back centuries, not decades'.[3] In concept, therefore, this project offered a confrontational counter-narrative to what had been conceived, portrayed, and promoted as *the* Irish literary tradition.

Doyle's claim that the sample chosen substantiated the long history of women's writing is, however, open to question. In format, the 2015 version of the poster simply replaced the twelve original images with those of a group of females whose names and works were just as (or *almost* as) familiar as the men who preceded them: Maria Edgeworth, Lady Augusta Gregory, Edith Somerville and Violet Martin ('Martin Ross'), Kate O'Brien, Elizabeth Bowen, Molly Keane, Mary Lavin, Maeve Brennan, Edna O'Brien, Jennifer Johnston, Eavan Boland, and Anne Enright (see Fig. 0.1). Of these, the work of only four – Edgeworth, Gregory, Somerville, and Ross – predates the twentieth century, with three-quarters of the women represented having begun their careers in or after the late 1920s.[4] Instead of evidencing a long and varied tradition of women's writing, the *Irish Times* poster, like its predecessor, offered the reading public a selection of writers as noteworthy for the gaps in Irish literary history it revealed as the spaces it filled.

This volume is a project to fill in at least some of those gaps; to recognise and acknowledge that there have been far more women writers, with far more diverse identities, than popular manifestations of literary history have acknowledged. This book focuses on the political engagement, both direct and oblique, of texts written by Irish women during the pivotal historical period between 1878 and 1922. Over the course of these decades, Irish women entered the literary marketplace in conspicuously large numbers, a development in publishing that has tended to elude the academic gaze but did not escape the notice of a number of high-profile contemporary commentators. On being introduced to the Irish writer Hannah Lynch in the mid-1880s by his mother Speranza (herself a poet), for example, Oscar Wilde declared that 'young Irish geniuses' such as her were 'as plentiful as blackberries' at that time.[5] This abundance was made more publicly apparent in 1891, when the *Daily Graphic* remarked upon the degree to which Irish women were asserting their influence on the publishing industry: Irish fiction was, just then, 'practically in the hands of Irish women', the paper suggested.[6]

Existing academic studies tend to confirm these types of assessments, more often collaterally than overtly. Of the approximately 700 writers listed in Stephen J. Brown's *Ireland in Fiction* (1916), at least 200 are women,

Figure 0.1 Irish Writers Poster, *Irish Times* (7 March 2015).

the vast majority of whom authored texts in the four decades immediately prior to the volume's publication.[7] More recently, both John Wilson Foster and James H. Murphy, in their seminal studies of nineteenth- and early twentieth-century Irish literature, have brought renewed attention to the contributions made by women writers to the literary landscape of the era. Murphy notes that of the 150 novels on which his study is based, male and female authors are represented in almost equal numbers and draws explicit attention to the 'prominence of women novelists, somewhat against the general trend which tended to favour men'.[8] Even a purposefully brief study that focuses primarily on canonical works of literature such as A. Norman Jeffares' *Pocket History of Irish Writers* (1997) – all of 170 pages – makes space for no fewer than thirty-one women writers, more than a third of whom were publishing their texts between the years 1878 and 1922. Of the twelve women of that period to whom Jeffares refers, ten – Katharine Tynan, Jane Barlow, Alice Milligan, Ethna Carbery, Dora Sigerson Shorter, Susan Mitchell, Eva Gore-Booth, Nora Hopper, Alice Furlong, and Mary Devenport-O'Neill – were involved in literary revivalism, all of them names that would have been intimately familiar to many readers in their day.

The sheer number of women who might have been included in these pages means that this is not – could not possibly be – a comprehensive volume. The following chapters, grounded in archival research and the exploration of periodical culture, offer compelling indications of the reasons for the proliferation of Irish women writers between the years 1878 and 1922. Each demonstrates that these authors had reasons to write which were not always, or not *only*, economic.

The period under investigation begins in the year in which the Intermediate Education Act was passed (1878). The social reforms set in motion by this Act (and later developments that extended them up to and including, of course, universal suffrage) allowed women to emerge in the public sphere on an unprecedented scale. This was a momentous period marked by extremes of debate and conflict around issues as varied as the University Question, the Woman Question, suffragism, the Land War, the Boer War, Revivalism, Parnellism, Home Rule, the Ulster Covenant, Orangeism, the temperance movement, the Repeal of the Contagious Diseases Acts, the First World War, the Easter Rising of 1916, the Anglo-Irish War of 1919–21, Partition and the formation of both the Irish Free State and Northern Ireland in 1921, and the advent of the Civil War in 1922. To suggest that these were the only political issues that mattered, though, is to minimise the imaginative achievements of women during these decades.

The contributors to this volume consider the ways in which Irish women, officially disenfranchised through much of the era, felt inclined and at liberty to exercise their political influence through unofficial channels.[9] The chapters investigate their responses to, expressions of, and dialogue with a contemporary politics that included the topics of education, cosmopolitanism, language, Empire, economics, philanthropy, socialism, the marriage 'market', the publishing industry, readership(s), the commercial market, and employment. What emerges is an intricate study of how women writers used their work to advance their own private and public political concerns through astute manoeuvrings both in the expanding publishing industry and against the partisan expectations of an ever-growing readership.

An Irish women of letters' banquet and a toast to the King

THE complexity of the political landscape negotiated by women writers can be glimpsed in turn-of-the-twentieth-century alternatives to the modern *Irish Times* women writers' poster. An illustration published in the *Irish Independent* on 3 May 1910 affords, for instance, one intriguing correlative. Taking up most of a page in that day's paper was a composite of eleven photographs of some of the most famous Irish writers of the era, including Alice Stopford Green, Katherine Cecil Thurston, Alicia Adelaide Needham, Lady Gilbert (Rosa Mulholland), Edith Somerville, 'Martin Ross', Hon. Georgina O'Brien, Dr Annie Patterson, Mrs Power O'Donoghue, L. T. Meade, and Mary Costelloe (see Fig. 0.2).[10] The article that accompanied these pictures, headlined 'Lights of Literature', informed readers of a banquet, hosted by the Corinthian Club, which was about to be held at Dublin's Gresham Hotel in celebration of Irish women of letters.

Detailed reports about the event were publicised widely in leading newspapers in the days that followed, and these often drew attention to those women who had been invited but failed to attend. The *Irish Independent* was among the papers which noted that an 'interesting souvenir of the function was distributed' – one that contained photographs and autographs of those who 'found it impossible to be present'. Among their number were Katharine Tynan, L. T. Meade, Eva Gore-Booth, and Lady Gregory, all of them among the most well-known Irish writers of either sex at that time.[11] The absence of so large and high-profile a contingent is curious, and we might conjecture that those who stayed away did so due to some precognition or foreknowledge of the political factionalism that came to mark the event. Whatever the reasons, press reports suggest it turned out to be a politically divisive affair.

Alice Stopford Green, a historian and nationalist, delivered the evening's opening keynote on the subject of historical impartiality by querying

THE IRISH INDEPENDENT, TUESDAY, MAY 3, 1910.

Lights of Literature.

Irish Women who will be entertained in Dublin to-night.

The Corinthian Club, Dublin, will to-night entertain at a Banquet in the Gresham Hotel a number of Irish ladies distinguished in the world of Art and Literature. We reproduce photos of a number of the ladies who will be present.

Miss Alicia Adelaide Needham.

Mrs. Alice Stopford Green.

Mrs. Katherine Cecil Thurston.

Hon. Georgina O'Brien.

Lady Gilbert.
Photo by Elliott and Fry.

Miss Edith Œnone Somerville.
Photo by Lafayette.

"Martin Ross."

Dr. Annie Patterson.

Mrs. Power O'Donoghue.

Mrs. L. T. Meade.
Photo by G. Vandyk.

Miss Mary Costelloe.

MRS. ALICE STOPFORD GREEN, was born at Kells. Her father was Archdeacon of Meath. She is a distinguished historian, and amongst her latest works are "The Making of Ireland and Its Undoing."

LADY GILBERT (ROSA MULHOLLAND) is the authoress of numerous novels and two books of poems. She is a daughter of Dr. Mulholland, of Belfast, where she was born.

MRS. L. T. MEADE was born at Bandon, Co. Cork, in which county her father was a Rector. She wrote her first book when she was only 17, and is one of the most prolific and popular writers of fiction.

MRS. KATHERINE CECIL THURSTON, who is also a Cork lady, is the author of many brilliant novels, including the famous "John Chilcote, M.P."

MISS EDITH ŒNONE SOMERVILLE is a daughter of the late Lieut.-Colonel Somerville, of Drishane, and a granddaughter of Charles Kendal Bushe, Chief Justice of Ireland. She has studied art in Paris and London, has exhibited (in oils) in London and Dublin, and is a member of the Water Colour Society of Ireland and the Women's International Art Club. In collaboration with her cousin "MARTIN ROSS" (Miss Violet Martin, of Ross, Co. Galway), she has written many notable books and magazine articles. She was Master of the West Carbery Foxhounds, 1903-8.

MISS ALICIA ADELAIDE NEEDHAM is a gifted composer, most of whose beautiful compositions are familiar to the Irish people. She has composed hundreds of songs, ballads, and lyrics, including 100 songs for the American public schools. She was the first and only Lady President Royal National Eisteddfod of Wales, and has had conferred on her a Welsh Bardic title signifying the Harp of Ireland. She won the £100 prize for the best Coronation song in 1902.

MRS. POWER O'DONOGHUE is the youngest child of the late Mr. Charles Lambert, Castle Ellen, Athenry, and is the wife of Dr. Power O'Donoghue, Mus. Bac. She is a regular contributor to many of the leading American journals and the London periodicals. In addition, she has written several successful novels and works on horsemanship for ladies, which latter are accepted as standard authorities on the subject. She has owned and trained several famous horses, and was a regular follower of the hounds until she met with an accident in the hunting-field.

DR. ANNIE W. PATTERSON, Mus.Doc., is a Scholar and Organ Gold Medallist, R.I.A.M., and is widely known as a Professor of Music, lecturer, and composer. She was the originator of the "Feis Ceoil" movement. A native of Lurgan, she resides at present in Cork. At the time she received her degree of Mus. Doc. she was the only lady in the world who had attained such a distinction, except Queen Alexandra, whose degree was honorary.

THE HON. GEORGINA O'BRIEN, daughter of Lord O'Brien of Kilfenora, Lord Chief Justice of Ireland, has given evidence of the possession of literary gifts of a high order, especially as a writer of short stories.

MISS MARY COSTELLO, a Dublin lady, is the author of many stories and miscellaneous contributions, marked by ability and grace of style, to the Press. She is also a playwright, her production, "The Hireling," being considered a gem.

Figure 0.2 'Lights of Literature', *Irish Independent* (3 May 1910).

the very possibility of either political neutrality or parity in relation to Ireland: 'I suppose we may accept it that the words partial and impartial in Irish affairs have a recognised technical meaning. Impartial means a strong bias to Imperial and English interests; partial signifies a special regard for the special interests of Ireland (laughter).' Discussing negative English attitudes towards every race and class in Ireland, she moved on to suggest that the Irish *en masse* had been constructed by their British rulers as a people incapable of governing themselves and touched on a variety of political arguments – including the promotion of cosmopolitan over nationalist interests, which she believed had served to divert the attention of the Irish people away from the welfare of their country. Any Empire desiring loyal citizens, she concluded, must allow its peoples to come into the fold of imperialism willingly: 'with the spirit of freemen, and bring their language [and history] with them'.[12] The tenor of these opening remarks is broadly nationalist but also ameliorative, and, combined with the touch of humour that evidently inflected the speech, Stopford Green's rhetorical strategies suggest she was promoting a broader and more inclusive version of politics to and for Ireland than was allowed for by prevailing nationalist and unionist binaries.

The setting and the predispositions of the hosting organisation, however, provided a much narrower political framework. The presence of the Lord Chief Justice and the Lord Lieutenant, both of whom gave the concluding speeches on the night, indicated official British government sanction (at least of the Gladstonian Liberal variety) of the event. The Lord Chief Justice's speech was particularly telling in terms of evoking a sense of the Corinthians' political purpose in hosting the banquet: the (apparently nationalist) 'demon of political and sectarian dissension', he stated, would find 'no foothold' in the club. The evening closed with a toast to the King, and thus was punctuated on a note of loyalist bias that appears, with hindsight, to have been designed to defuse any hint of anti-loyalist sentiment (such as Stopford Green's) which might have arisen over the course of the evening.[13]

A correspondent writing in the *Freeman's Journal* noted as much by suggesting that 'for gatherings such as that of the Corinthian Club an Irish Nationalist is supposed to be non-existent, just as in former times a Catholic had no existence in the eyes of the English law'.[14] This commentator speculated that a propagandist ploy was at work in the staging and running of the Irish women writers' banquet: that, by promoting political harmony in a discordant setting, the Corinthians and the government officials who represented them were attempting to occlude the complexity of political divisions among those present. The event and the reporting on it affords us a microcosmic view of the fraught political moment into which Irish women writers were thrust, and indicates that – both on this particular evening and in their careers more broadly – they were expected to contend with and confront a political landscape which left little room for political interests outside of or in between nationalism and unionism.

Advancing the cause of liberty

During the period under consideration, Irish women made only gradual (and sometimes short-lived) gains in their access to official political channels with their admission to the local government franchise and the association of some female political associations (such as the Primrose League, the Women's Liberal Federation, and the Ladies' Land League) with mainstream parties from the 1880s and 1890s.[15] Yet women's political interests regularly transcended factionalist politics. To fully comprehend the richness and complexity of women's texts, therefore, a more wide-ranging definition of the term 'politics' is required: one that abandons the tendency to prioritise nationalist or unionist agendas to include a more Aristotelian conception of politics that engages in the process of 'obtaining the ends of civil society as perfectly as possible'.[16]

The subtitle of this volume paraphrases a passage from the constitution of the nationalist women's organisation Cumann na mBan (The Irishwomen's Council) which professes its mission to 'advance the cause of Irish liberty'. The term 'Irish' has been deliberately omitted from our subtitle as a signal of intent to liberate the idea of freedom from the concept of Irish nationhood and, in the process, to open up political agendas that include educational reform, the family, commercialism, language, religion, suffrage, and cosmopolitanism.[17] As Heidi Hansson has noted, 'Women writers have been censured as being uncommitted to the important questions of the day, while in fact they were engaged with creating a different literary-political scene that included women's private experience.'[18] As women, these writers were distanced from the official political process and the cronyism that often accompanied it and were, as a result, better able to recognise, and more at liberty to highlight, the difficulties of straightforward definitions or easy divisions between Irish people and the various factions with which they were aligned. When Katharine Tynan portrayed one of her characters overhearing the cries of 'Votes for Women and Loose Shoes!' on a London street, for example, she pointed to both the suffrage and rational dress movements in which she herself was interested.[19] While the political significance of the campaign for women's suffrage both then and since has been widely acknowledged, the similarly controversial rational dress movement has been all but forgotten in the intervening years. Yet it was founded on the belief that women's constricted clothing not only reflected but intensified their social and professional limitations. Adherents such as Tynan therefore argued against any type of dress that impeded women's physical movements or tended to injure their health. In placing these two issues in close narrative proximity to one another, Tynan offered (and continues to offer) readers both a glimpse of the blurring of the boundaries between public and private that marked women's lives and some indication of the diversity of political issues in which women were invested. Other female authors, like M. E. Francis, were likewise writing that certain concerns, including those as serious as the white slave trade, had 'suffered from the fact of having been labelled from the beginning "a woman's question" ', suggesting in the process that men, and an all-male government, paid little or no attention to those issues that impacted primarily on women.[20]

Unwilling to alienate potential readers, women writers often professed a lack of interest in or tangential association to the politics of national government. Katherine Cecil Thurston once confessed in an interview 'that from her childhood she [had] been interested in politics, but at the same time she [was] of the opinion that a woman ought not to take the prominent place in party politics which some members of the gentler sex at times arrogate to themselves'.[21] Yet even here, in a statement that acts as a form of *apologia* for overstepping the boundaries of womanhood, the process of acknowledging a certain antagonism towards women's contribution to party politics does not negate the potential to engage in politics of another kind. Thurston's contemporary, Emily Lawless, meanwhile pointed to the close relationship between cultural revivalism and partisan politics when she stated that she was 'not *anti-Gaelic* at all so long as it is only Gaelic *enthuse* and does not include politics', indicating in the process an awareness of the threat to her own landowning class that Revivalist movements might pose.[22] This chimes with Lady Augusta Gregory's statement that she was 'not working for Home Rule', but 'preparing for it'.[23] Such proclamations suggest a desire – ultimately unsuccessful – to create clear differences between the realms of culture and politics at a time when such distinctions were unsustainable. In many cases, the personnel associated with cultural organisations including the Abbey Theatre, the Irish Agricultural Organisation Society, or the Gaelic League immersed themselves in both cultural and political milieus, allowing for a constant exchange and melding of ideas in which women could and did participate.

Events in Ireland from the mid nineteenth century played their part in bringing women writers into prominence. The post-Famine socio-economic changes from the 1850s onwards, accompanied by alterations in agrarian practices, created drastically altered circumstances for many women. The reduction in domestic industries and the shift from tillage to pastoral farming resulted in decreased demand for farm labour detrimental to employment opportunities for women. In this regard, Irish women were significantly more disadvantaged than their British counterparts, with the numbers of women employed in Ireland having dropped from 641,000 in 1881 to approximately 430,000 by 1901.[24] Unsurprisingly, these circumstances contributed to the processes that saw Irish women dominate the outflow of migrants to America from the 1880s onwards and during the 1890s outnumber their male counterparts to Great Britain.[25] Social trends account for the relatively young profile of those who migrated: between 1855 and 1914, 44 per cent of those leaving Ireland were between twenty and twenty-four years of age; the average age for women leaving the country was twenty-one.[26]

The preoccupations of Irish women writers of the late nineteenth century reflect the changes they witnessed, experienced, and confronted. Although issues of migration, land ownership, and marriage prospects affected the agrarian and working classes most profoundly, with increasing class tensions and the adoption of social practices which had the effect of pitting sibling against sibling and female against female, Irish women, regardless of class, often found their ambitions and options curtailed. The volume's opening two chapters by Patrick Maume and James H. Murphy reflect and illustrate women's coming to terms with the shifting politics of a rapidly changing socio-economic environment. Writing about Charlotte Riddell and Rosa Mulholland respectively, Maume and Murphy focus their analyses on themes of land management, inter-class relations, and marriage prospects. Their narrative preoccupations with women's struggle to achieve economic stability refract these authors' own experiences of attempting to remain commercially viable during a period of transformation in the fortunes not only of Irish women but also, as these chapters demonstrate, of women in the publishing industry.

For ambitious women, a lack of access to marriage and employment meant seeking out alternatives for their own subsistence. The most dramatic and positive impact on the lives of women in this regard came through a new level of access to formal schooling. In Britain, a women's educational reform movement began in earnest in the 1840s and gained momentum in the decades that followed. By the 1860s, the Schools Inquiry Commission was being pressured by women's rights campaigners into conducting an investigation into girls' schools, and the resulting report, published in 1867–68, was both scathing in its condemnation and impossible to ignore. Girls, it concluded, were not being 'taught intelligently or in any scientific manner'.[27] When the organised women's movement became increasingly prominent over the course of the 1870s, so too did the demands for access to equal and higher educational provision for females.

In Ireland, meanwhile, the Intermediate Education Act (1878) provided for the partial funding of secondary education. A crucial point in the reform of education, it granted all Irish women, irrespective of religious or political affiliation, the right to sit for public competitive examinations. But certain gendered and class-based inequities remained. Of those presenting for the intermediate examinations in Ireland at the turn of the century, only 15 to 25 per cent were girls, and, as Ciaran O'Neill has argued, the system remained elitist despite the reforms that had been introduced.[28] Yet the improvements in women's literacy over the course of the century were striking: by 1911, census records confirmed that 97.8 per cent of Irish women could read and write, compared with 26.8 per cent in 1841.[29] Likewise, the numbers of women enrolled in the arts-degree programme of the Royal University, Dublin, were slowly increasing: whereas there were only nine women on such programmes in 1884, enrolment climbed to thirty-three by 1893 and to sixty-one in 1900.[30] Along with the growing professionalisation of women's lives that accompanied education came a degree of female literary agency and a tendency for women to use their texts as a means of blurring the spheres of the public and private, the political and the cultural.

The debates that arose around the subject of female education brought to the fore a concern for the well-being of adolescents of both sexes and an attendant upsurge in literature for the young in which the prerogatives, advantages, and detriments of education were explored and tested. The chapters in this volume by Heidi Hansson and Whitney Standlee deal with the subject of children's education as it is portrayed in the juvenile works of Emily Lawless and L. T. Meade respectively. Hansson's analysis identifies the points of tension between Lawless's critique of regulated education and a recognition of its necessity in developing a type of citizen capable of dealing with the effects of an increasingly modernised and conflict-ridden Irish society. Standlee meanwhile distinguishes a more optimistic strain of thought concerning girls' schooling in Meade's texts, in which education offers the opportunity for females to form powerful intrasexual alliances.

Katherine Cecil Thurston's 1908 novel *The Fly on the Wheel* reflected the preoccupations of her society by explicitly linking a new form of fluidity in Irish class and social relations to women and their altering educational priorities:

> A century ago the rich Irish trader, the manufacturer, even the lawyer or doctor – unless by chance he could produce a pedigree – held little place in the social scheme; but to-day his granddaughters flaunt it with the best in the world of sport and the vaster world of education. True, the entry to these pastures is through a gate that still stands barely ajar and hangs upon rusty hinges, but

> there is incentive in the thought of a forced passage. . . . for this, the mother of a large family stints and saves to educate her daughters abroad.[31]

Rather than exalting nationalism, ruralism, and Revivalism, many Irish women writers such as Thurston used their texts to analyse and dissect the discontents of a newly educated middle-class Irish female population. It comes as little surprise that there is a cosmopolitan and international component to Irish women's literature at this juncture. Ambitious Irish women who wanted or needed to earn a living through their writing required access to the major publishing houses, the vast majority of which were located in London.

The Ulster writer Beatrice Grimshaw was one woman who pursued her literary ambitions in various environments, both urban and rural, outside of Ireland. Grimshaw was an astute negotiator of the publishing market, and, as Jane Mahony and Eve Patten confirm in Chapter 5 (which analyses her commercial success) found ample outlets for her travel writing. Whereas Grimshaw can be placed in the midst of a whole range of Irish women writers who used the city and its networks as a springboard for career mobility and to develop transnational profiles, other women writers also explored distinctively cosmopolitan sensibilities in their texts. Ciaran O'Neill and Mai Yatani compellingly demonstrate in Chapter 6 the magnetic pull that the urban exerted on a number of Irish women, who, in writings that reflected their own experiences of the city, constructed a range of counter-Revivalist narratives.

While all the authors here wrote as individuals, they also occasionally claimed allegiance to a particular group or cause. These types of writers *represent* particular political ideas on the one hand and were interpreted as *representative of* particular political ideas on the other. The two do not, however, necessarily go hand in hand. As cultural nationalism gained pace in the aftermath of Charles Stewart Parnell's death in 1891, the discussions surrounding what constituted a national literature for Ireland came to prominence. Writing about Ireland thereafter came to be seen as writing on behalf of Ireland, with attendant consequences. Alongside the diversification of society along religious, socio-economic, gender, and political lines came the question of who had the 'right' to write for the nation.

The project of the Irish Literary Revivalists, spearheaded by W. B. Yeats and Lady Gregory, was viewed by some as producing the type of writing which, to borrow Yeats's phrase, was 'for Ireland's not for England's use'.[32] Their Anglo-Irish Protestant backgrounds, however, rendered them unsuitable in the eyes of a different segment of Irish society, as evidenced by D. P. Moran, who proclaimed in the *Leader* that 'Irish Ireland is Catholic Ireland. Catholic Ireland is Irish Ireland.'[33] Some prominent

Revivalists were thus trapped in a purgatory of simultaneous insider and outsider status by the standards of a sizeable majority of their contemporary readership (and theatre audiences). Such interpretations, however, failed to take into consideration that there might be multiple gradations of politics that included positions in between or outside of nationalist/unionist, Irish/English, and Catholic/Protestant binaries. Margaret Kelleher persuasively argues in her chapter on aspects of bilingualism in the work of Somerville and Ross for 'more dynamic models of linguistic change in Irish cultural studies': ones which can account for more complex negotiations between varying ideological positions. In the subsequent chapter, Anna Pilz considers these types of negotiations by focusing on the relationship between Lady Gregory and her audience(s) in relation to *fin-de-siècle* Jacobite thought. By analysing the favourable response to Gregory's play *The White Cockade*, she illustrates that questions of representation were more nuanced than have previously been acknowledged and that elitism rather than denominational allegiances impeded a more widespread success for the Abbey.

Existing ideas concerning the boundaries and limits of Irish factionalism could also be challenged by the effects of an increasingly mobile society. Moving away from the family home has always offered unique challenges to women, but making the move to England, which was necessitated by the careers of many Irish writers, could carry with it additional challenges to familial and national loyalties. For some of these women, migration to England led to a questioning of their existing political values; for others, a reinforcement of them. These extremes made their way into women's texts and are placed under scrutiny in the chapters written by Kieron Winterson and Naomi Doak. Winterson interprets Katharine Tynan's altering political views as an extension and reflection of her changing political and personal contexts, and Doak delves into the life and works of the Ulster writer F. E. Crichton to demonstrate the ways in which familial loyalties informed and strengthened Crichton's unionism following her expatriation to England.

The period in the teens and early twenties that encompassed the Easter Rising, the enfranchisement of a significant number of Irish women, and the Irish Civil War is a much-charted history that requires no further elucidation here, but the chapters written by Aurelia Annat and Lauren Arrington remind us that there were more than two sides to the debates that surrounded all of these events. These two closing chapters challenge preconceptions that there was a continuum of political thought even among those women who were closely associated with cultural revivalism and political nationalism. As Senia Pašeta asserts in her study of Irish nationalist women, 'the "Irish Revolution" of the early twentieth century contained within it multiple demands for liberation'.[34] In chapters that verify such contentions, Annat and Arrington offer important reconsiderations of the ways in which Ella Young, Eva Gore-Booth, and Constance Markievicz pursued literary endeavours which were more accurate reflections of their personal imperatives than homogenised mainstream movements could encompass.

Then and now

THE chapters assembled in this volume offer compelling evidence that the study of Irish women's literary works within their historical, socio-economic, and political contexts is vital to gaining a fuller understanding of the literary history of Ireland. What we can glimpse clearly in these pages is the sense of the political immediacy of these women's texts, and the fame and popularity enjoyed by so many of them attests to the widespread appeal of that immediacy. In analysing what and why these women wrote, and how their texts were received, all of our contributors offer striking challenges to preconceived ideas about women's involvement in the public sphere, and in the process raise new questions about the connections between then and now.

By viewing these women's texts more closely and by placing them more thoroughly in their relevant historical contexts, we can see that their era and ours have many things in common. Women writing around the turn of the twentieth century were struggling through times of economic and social crisis, writing amid contentious and tense political moments, advocating and contemplating rights of access to education and opportunities for equality, and battling in a highly competitive literary marketplace. Which Irish woman writer in our own time – post-Celtic Tiger, post the referendum on marriage equality, in the midst of discussions of statistics on women in leadership roles, and in an age where Irish literary women are again in the vanguard of publishing – could not but find things in common with those Irish women writers of a century ago? How many Irish literary women being lauded and showered with awards today might, like them, be relegated in importance a century from now because the moment for their messages is deemed to have passed? By recognising the many connections between their past and our present, and by acknowledging that there is indeed a long established and important legacy of women's writing in Ireland, we can also begin to acknowledge the dynamic ways in which women have used and can continue to use literature to advance the cause of liberty, in all its complex and challenging forms.

Notes

1 Arguably, the debates surrounding the publication of the three-volume *Field Day Anthology of Irish Writing* in 1990 with its paucity of Irish women writers prompted and inspired subsequent projects of rediscovery and re-evaluation. See, for instance, Patricia Coughlan and Tina O'Toole (eds), *Irish Literature: Feminist Perspectives* (Dublin: Carysfort Press, 2008); Elke D'hoker, Raphaël Ingelbien, and Hedwig Schwall (eds), *Irish Women Writers: New Critical Perspectives* (Oxford: Peter Lang, 2011); Alexander G. Gonzalez, *Irish Women Writers: An A-to-Z Guide* (Westport, Conn.: Greenwood Press, 2005); Patricia Boyle Haberstroh and Christine St Peter (eds), *Opening the Field: Irish Women, Texts and Contexts* (Cork: Cork University Press, 2007); Heidi Hansson (ed.), *New Contexts: Re-framing Nineteenth-Century Irish Women's Prose* (Cork: Cork University Press, 2008); Heather Ingman, *Irish Women's Fiction: From Edgeworth to Enright* (Dublin: Irish Academic Press, 2013); C. L. Innes, *Woman and Nation in Irish Literature and Society, 1880–1935* (Athens, Ga.: University of Georgia Press, 1993); Lisbet Kickham, *Protestant Women Novelists and Irish Society, 1879–1922* (Helgonabacken: Lund University, 2004); Kathryn Kirkpatrick (ed.), *Border Crossings: Irish Women Writers and National Identities* (Tuscaloosa, Ala.: University of Alabama Press, 2000); Theresa O'Connor (ed.), *The Comic Tradition in Irish Women Writers* (Gainesville, Fla.: University Press of Florida, 1996); Ann Owens Weekes, *Irish Women Writers: An Uncharted Tradition* (Lexington, Ky.: University Press of Kentucky, 1990).

2 Martin Doyle, 'Putting Irish Women Writers Back in the Picture', *Irish Times* (23 February 2015). Available at www.irishtimes.com/culture/books/putting-irish-women-writers-back-in-the-picture-1.2113897. Accessed 27 April 2015. The poster was included in the edition of 7 March 2015. Note that this was not the first such attempt. In 1999, Mary Shine produced an Irish Women Writers poster. Available at www.irishtimes.com/culture/books/i-loved-your-irish-women-writers-poster-here-s-one-i-made-earlier-1.2135621. Accessed 27 April 2015.

3 Martin Doyle, 'Portraits of the Artists as Women', *Irish Times* (7 March 2015). Available at www.irishtimes.com/culture/books/portraits-of-the-artists-as-women-1.2129106. Accessed 18 April 2015.

4 Even in the articles written by academics and literary experts, only seven writers with works that predate the 1920s emerge.

5 Katharine Tynan, *Twenty-Five Years: Reminiscences* (London: Smith, Elder & Co., 1913), p. 150.

6 'Irish Fiction', *Daily Graphic* (5 October 1891). Quoted in Gifford Lewis (ed.), *The Selected Letters of Somerville and Ross* (London: Faber & Faber, 1989), p. 178.

7 Stephen J. Brown, SJ, *Ireland in Fiction: A Guide to Irish Novels, Tales, Romances, and Folk-lore* (Dublin and London: Maunsel & Co., 1916).

8 James H. Murphy, *Irish Novelists and the Victorian Age* (Oxford: Oxford University Press, 2011), p. 18.

9 Partial enfranchisement for British women over the age of thirty who met defined standards for property ownership was achieved in 1918. The franchise was extended to those Irish women between twenty-one and twenty-nine years of age by the Irish Free State government in 1923. Voting rights on a parity with men were not granted to their counterparts in the United Kingdom until 1928.

10 'Lights of Literature', *Irish Independent* (3 May 1910), p. 7.

11 'Famous Irish Women', *Irish Independent* (4 May 1910), p. 5.

12 'Famous Irish Women'.

13 'Famous Irish Women'.

14 'Impartial', 'To the Editor of the Freeman's Journal', *Freeman's Journal* (6 March 1910), p. 5.

15 A bill was issued in 1892 enabling women to be elected as Poor Law guardians in Ireland and thus allowing them access to the official arena of local politics. In 1898, the Local Government Act granted Irish women local franchise.
16 John Ogilvie (ed.), *The Imperial Dictionary: English, Technological and Scientific*, 2 vols. (Glasgow, London, and Edinburgh: Blackie & Son, 1859), vol. II, p. 416.
17 See R. F. Foster, *Modern Ireland, 1600–1972* (Harmondsworth: Penguin, 1989), p. 485.
18 Heidi Hansson, 'Introduction: Out of Context', in Heidi Hansson (ed.), *New Contexts: Re-framing Nineteenth-Century Irish Women's Prose* (Cork: Cork University Press, 2008), pp. 1–15, at p. 4.
19 Katharine Tynan, *Heart o' Gold; or, The Little Princess: A Story for Girls* (London: S. W. Partridge, 1912), p. 240.
20 M. E. Francis, *The Story of Mary Dunne* (London: John Murray, 1913), p. 282.
21 'The Making of a Novelist', *Ladies' Realm*, 17 (1904–5), 655–8, at p. 658.
22 Edith Sichel, 'Emily Lawless', *Nineteenth Century and After: A Monthly Review*, 76:449 (1914), 80–100, at p. 87.
23 Lady Augusta Gregory, Diary entry for 16 December 1898, in James Pethica (ed.), *Lady Gregory's Diaries, 1892–1902* (Gerrards Cross: Colin Smythe, 1996), p. 195.
24 Joanna Bourke, *Husbandry to Housewifery: Women, Economic Change, and Housework in Ireland, 1890–1914* (Oxford: Clarendon Press, 1993), p. 2.
25 See Mary Lennon, Marie McAdam, and Joanne O'Brien, *Across the Water: Irish Women's Lives in Britain* (London: Virago, 1988), p. 21.
26 David Fitzpatrick, *Irish Emigration, 1801–1921* (Dublin: The Economic and Social History of Ireland, 1985), p. 8.
27 June Purvis, *A History of Women's Education in England* (Milton Keynes: Open University Press, 1991).
28 Ciaran O'Neill, *Catholics of Consequence: Transnational Education, Social Mobility, and the Irish Catholic Elite, 1850–1900* (Oxford: Oxford University Press, 2014), pp. 167, 16.
29 O'Neill, *Catholics of Consequence*, p. 167.
30 F.S., 'The Irish University Question as Affecting Women', *Westminster Review*, 159:6 (1903), 610–24, at p. 612.
31 Katherine Cecil Thurston, *The Fly on the Wheel* (New York: Grosset & Dunlap, 1908), p. 3.
32 Roger McHugh (ed.), *W. B. Yeats: Letters to Katharine Tynan* (Dublin: Clonmore & Reynolds, 1953), pp. 102–3.
33 *The Leader* (29 June 1901), p. 282.
34 Senia Pašeta, *Irish Nationalist Women, 1900–1918* (Cambridge: Cambridge University Press, 2013), p. 16.

1

Works, righteousness, philanthropy, and the market in the novels of Charlotte Riddell

Patrick Maume

THE literature of the *fin de siècle* coexisted with that of older writers, who show how earlier literary tropes and cultural debates continued to influence the later period. The novels of Charlotte Riddell indicate that long-standing debates about the possibility of regenerating the Irish land system survived into the era of the Land War and the New Woman. Her references to a wide range of nineteenth-century Irish writers and her reimagining of contemporary events such as the murder of Lord Leitrim (1878) and the land agitation in Donegal reflect not only her own inability to turn her literary success into financial security but also a perceptible ambivalence on her part. This ambivalence is between a sense that the project of reforming Ireland through British capital directed by political economy has proved overambitious and a conviction that its opponents have nothing better to offer than self-indulgent fantasies represented by Charles Lever's glorification of aristocratic paternalism or nationalist idealisations of the peasantry which ignore their improvidence and failure to accumulate capital. Riddell falls back on a tacitly Protestant-inspired belief that individual virtue takes precedence over external works and that Ireland's well-being can only be secured through personal moral regeneration. This chapter compares her two Irish-set novels of the 1880s and her portrayal of Irish littérateurs negotiating the commercial constraints of London society and its literary market in the semi-autobiographical *A Struggle for Fame* (1883) with her earlier portrayal of a conflict between honest industry and aristocratic improvidence in *The Earl's Promise* (1873) to show how her exploration of these themes reflects late Victorian self-questioning of earlier eras' hopes for political economy or aristocratic regeneration.

Riddell was born Charlotte Elizabeth Cowan in Carrickfergus in 1832, the younger daughter of James Cowan, former sheriff of Co. Antrim, and his Liverpool-born wife Ellen Kilshaw. After her father's death in 1850, she and her mother lived in genteel poverty at Dundonald in north Down before moving to London in 1855. Her mother died in 1856, and in the following year Charlotte married Joseph Hadley Riddell, a civil engineer and patent agent. She subsequently became a professional writer, initially publishing under pen names (notably F. G. Trafford), and, after 1864, as Mrs J. H. Riddell. Through her husband's involvement in City schemes to exploit technical patents, Charlotte became acquainted with City finance, and the City often featured prominently in her fiction.[1] Unfortunately, however, his speculations and the debts of his relatives swallowed up Charlotte's literary earnings from her most successful years in the 1860s and 1870s. When Joseph Riddell died in 1881, he left Riddell childless and financially insecure, and her poverty was exacerbated by the fact that he had over the course of their marriage pledged her literary copyrights as collateral for his debts.[2] Riddell later defended her husband's actions, asserting that he was well-meaning and exploited, and the influence of his experiences on her fictional themes is evident in her repeated characterisations of men who suffer unjust accusations or support parasitic extended families.

Riddell moved between rented houses in the City and in the country just outside London. After her husband's death, her urban residences became humbler and her suburban dwellings further from town. She rarely returned to Ireland but kept in touch with friends there; a tour of Donegal and western Ulster in 1885 produced a novel, *The Nun's Curse* (1888). From the mid-1880s, her fortunes were affected by the decline of the three-volume novel and serial publication. Her ability to adapt to the changing publishing scene was diminished by age and breast cancer. In a reflection of the author's own financial circumstances, Glenarva Westley in *A Struggle for Fame* is told by a hostile publisher, 'I can see very clearly what the result of your career will be. You'll have to appeal to the Royal Literary Fund, and we'll see then whether you like their terms better than mine.'[3] From 1901, Riddell became the first author paid a pension (as distinct from one-off grants) by the fund.[4] She died in 1906 in Middlesex.[5]

Charlotte Riddell may seem incongruous among *fin-de-siècle* Irish women writers. Her first novel appeared in 1856, and she favoured such mid-Victorian genres as the sensation novel, with elaborate inheritance plots and ghost stories *à la* Sheridan Le Fanu. Indeed, Riddell's novels are often set some decades before their publication, in the world of her youth or her parents' maturity (one recurring theme is contempt for the artificial girlishness in dress and manner projected by Regency fashion), and she uses hindsight to reflect on how the problems of the time when she writes developed out of the earlier society which she remembers. Although she was still writing during the final two decades of the century (her last novel appeared in 1902 and some of her more successful works had one-volume reprints c. 1900), she derived no benefit from them due to the sale of the copyrights.

Riddell was a prolific commercial novelist whose works fit the Jamesian dismissal of Victorian novels as 'loose baggy monsters'.[6] Frequently, she inserts moralising interjections, often with the aid of scriptural quotations, to steer readers' responses. In her writing technique, she began by devising an ending and worked towards it so that plot elements abruptly vanish and seemingly major characters fizzle into insignificance as she runs out of space. Plot summaries can be misleading, since characters important in the overall structure may only appear summarily, while apparently less central or less sympathetic characters are explored in greater depth.[7]

Nevertheless, Riddell is a significant figure in the late Victorian Irish novel because her commercial approach led her to address new literary fashions and struggle to adopt established – often exhausted – literary tropes to changing situations.[8] This chapter analyses some underlying themes of Riddell's work. In particular, it considers her relationship to the Irish national tale genre, established in the early nineteenth century. Furthermore, it outlines Riddell's engagement with the tension between 'improving' economic rationalisation and supposedly pre-capitalist modes of landlordism as presented by earlier writers such as Maria Edgeworth and Charles Lever and raised anew by Gladstonian reform. It establishes the discourse between rationalist visions of human perfectibility through socio-economic reform and the traditional evangelical view that without inner faith such reform amounted to mere 'works-righteousness', whereby external accomplishments would be hollow without a corresponding inner moral transformation. And, finally, it elaborates on Riddell's negotiations with the moral ambiguities of philanthropy, Victorian concerns with social status, and attitudes to the 'fallen woman'. It principally analyses her four Irish novels – *Maxwell Drewitt* (1865), *The Earl's Promise*, *Berna Boyle* (1884), and *The Nun's Curse* – alongside *A Struggle for Fame*, with its 'Micks on the Make' in London literary circles. Some earlier works are included here to place her later novels – the primary focus of the chapter – in the context of her oeuvre and of ongoing contemporary debates over the problems of Victorian Ireland.

Riddell, the Irish national tale, and the limits of Edgeworthian rationalism

A DESCRIPTION of Riddell's character Gorman Muir in her novel *Berna Boyle* provides evidence, both conspicuous and subtle, of her connection to Irish literary antecedents:

> The man [Gorman Muir] was nearly eight-and-twenty, yet romance was as strong in him as in a schoolboy. He devoutly believed in Tom Burke of Ours

> and the doings of Charles O'Malley [novels of military life by Charles Lever]. 'The Collegians' [by Gerald Griffin] woke a responsive echo in his soul – and he could sing the song, 'A place in thy memory, dearest' [also by Griffin], with such mournful pathos that old ladies wept, and at the same time with such seductive tenderness that young ladies felt they could almost have gone off with him on the spot.... 'The Charge at Fontenoy' [ballad by Thomas Davis] thrilled his very soul. He felt more than half-rebel when he read the short and stirring story of that gallant, if mistaken band of 'United Irish' gentlemen who paid the penalty of their lives for their patriotism; but when he turned back the page of Irish history to the siege of Derry he felt he saw written there a grander narrative still ... He was one left over, as it might seem, by mistake from a generation long dead and gone, and yet with a love of pleasure and a capacity for settling to no work, and a thorough enjoyment in idleness which is the proud possession of the nineteenth century.[9]

Her novel *A Struggle for Fame* likewise confirms these associations by tacitly rewriting a text from the first nineteenth-century wave of Irish romantic antiquarianism, Lady Morgan's national tale *The Wild Irish Girl* (1806). Riddell's protagonist Glenarva, brought up as a vigorous tomboy on a remote sea shore by a dispossessed and enfeebled father, echoes Lady Morgan's similarly named heroine Glorvina. Yet where Glorvina's ancestors were dispossessed by conquest which can be reversed through a reconciliatory marriage, Glenarva is impoverished through her father's partnership in a failed bank and abandons sublime provincial isolation for the wider commercial world of London. Once there, she discovers that readers are tired of Irish stories: 'If Lady Morgan or Miss Edgeworth, or Banim, or Carleton, were to return to life and offer an Irish story ... they would have none of it.'[10] Glenarva thus relocates a story based on Co. Antrim memories to the Yorkshire seacoast, of which she knows nothing; with longer residence in England and marriage to an Englishman, she adopts London and Home Counties settings in her mature work.[11] Riddell herself set novels in Ireland throughout her literary career, but these appeared at periods of increased English interest in Ireland: *Maxwell Drewitt* may capitalise on interest provoked by the Fenian movement, *The Earl's Promise* responds to the Irish reforms of Gladstone's first government, and *Berna Boyle* and *The Nun's Curse* are linked to Irish land agitation of the 1880s and Ulster unionism.

Although Riddell touches the romantic sublime in describing landscapes, her attitude to the Irish literary tradition is determinedly commonsensical and anti-romantic, expressed by vigorous critical dialogue with earlier Irish writers familiar to an English readership. In *The Nun's Curse*, the weak but well-meaning landlord Terence Conway is engaged to the fashionable, self-righteous and cold-hearted heiress Philippa Dutton. While Philippa delays the wedding, Terence in Donegal encounters the disreputable horse-dealer Daniel Walley, whose manipulation of Terence by introducing him to the local shooting, fishing, and whiskey punch may comment on 'rollicking' literary celebrations – as in the early novels of Charles Lever – of a feudal bond supposedly cemented by shared participation in alcohol and the wild sports of the west. Terence thus comes into contact with Walley's daughter Grace, whom he seduces and impregnates. Terence's unsuccessful attempts to shake off Grace and her father, before and after his disastrous marriage to Grace at the insistence of the jealous Philippa, are punctuated with ironic references to Thomas Moore's Irish Melody 'Lesbia Hath a Beaming Eye', which contrasts the artificial charms of fashionable 'Lesbia' with an idealised peasant girl, 'gentle, bashful Nora Creina'.[12]

Two authors are particularly relevant to Riddell's treatment of Ireland. The first is Maria Edgeworth, whose critique of Irish land management is echoed in more forcefully capitalistic ways in Riddell's work. Riddell insisted on rationalist moral reform and responsible estate management, lending encouragement to later schemes to solve Ireland's problems by restructuring her agrarian system on the basis of clear title, rationalised holdings, a commercial society based on wage labour, and regeneration through outside investment. These schemes were more expressly capitalist than Edgeworth's, who displayed a certain unease about completely replacing personal quasi-feudal loyalties by the cash nexus. Riddell, whose City connections led her to emphasise the distinction between venture capitalist and manager, is more akin to later projectors than to Edgeworth, and her belief in original sin leads her to distrust the Edgeworthian belief that humanity can be made perfect through rational education. Nevertheless, the childishly irresponsible landlord families in *The Earl's Promise* and *The Nun's Curse* – who blithely and irrationally squander vast resources and are outwardly affable towards tenants whom they exploit, riven by family quarrels, and doomed to inherit collaterally rather than by father–son descent – echo the proprietors of Edgeworth's *Castle Rackrent*.

Moral realism and the 'fallen woman'

A MAJOR difference between Edgeworth's and Riddell's reformism is that Edgeworth believes in human perfectibility through reason while Riddell takes a more pessimistic attitude, influenced by Protestant belief in the insufficiency of good works without inner faith. Riddell's incidental references to religion indicate moderate Low Church Anglicanism, with the insufficiency of Catholicism self-evident, Nonconformity and ultra-evangelicalism plebeian and 'pharisaic', and Anglo-Catholic ritualism fashionable self-indulgence by moral lightweights. These dismissals are as much on social as on religious grounds: the Catholic parentage of Maxwell Drewitt and Barney Kelly in *A Struggle for Fame* and the disastrous mixed marriage of Terence Conway are primarily social degradation, and passing references to Catholic priests among their own community are surprisingly favourable.

Riddell often portrays outwardly esteemed individuals who may perform beneficial and lasting works but who are nonetheless amoral or evil, suffering a fatal moral flaw that vitiates their positive achievements.[13] This is clearly related to Riddell's attraction to the sensation novel, with its fatal secrets, and the Le Fanuvian ghost story, where attractive and often well-meaning protagonists by secret sin give evil forces irresistible power over them. Barney Kelly, the second protagonist of *A Struggle for Fame*, fits this pattern – though he gets away with it. The Protestant son of a mixed marriage, with an alcoholic Catholic father, he courts the local landlord's spinster sister until he is told that her income depends on her brother's consent to her marriage and is paid to leave for London. Starting as a travelling actor and assisted by self-denial (from prudence rather than moral conviction), Barney makes a journalistic career, deserting former friends who are no longer useful. He maintains correspondence with his former inamorata, and, when she is left an heiress, he marries her, using her wealth to become a social and literary lion.

Barney forms an ugly contrast to Glenarva, whose career he successively sabotages and revives with articles in literary reviews (neither of them undertaken from artistic or benevolent motives). He, however, never actually breaks the law or any formal obligations: his wife remains blissfully unaware of his mercenary motives and appears happier than under any conceivable alternative circumstances; despite her talents and virtues, it is Glenarva's lack of foresight that has contributed to her downfall. Barnaby may even be a vehicle for Riddell to offload her own hopes, resentments, and ambitions, which, if given to Glenarva, might have made her less sympathetic to Victorian readers. Barney's career seems to bear out his cynical suggestion that the best thing England could do for Ireland would be to 'throw her over', since the English are not so reckless as to risk enough capital in Ireland to transform the Irish economy.[14] It is better, the text suggests, to make the Irish fend for themselves than to remain idle in the hope that rich patrons might do something for them. This perhaps is Riddell's epitaph on the post-Famine hope of political economists – after land agitation, agrarian violence, and the Gladstonian Land Acts –that simplified land title and marketised land management would attract British investment and make Ireland prosperous.

The other side of Riddell's critique of external success is the confidence in inner rectitude irrespective of outward appearances seen in the heroine of *Berna Boyle*. Underlying one of the more striking features of Riddell's novels is an emphasis on the possibility of the 'fallen woman' regenerating herself. This is somewhat anachronistically optimistic for the Victorian era and stands in contrast to widespread stereotypes including the view that such women were either misled innocents who must spend the rest of their lives in sorrow and penitence, like Dickens's Emily in *David Copperfield* after her seduction by Steerforth, or irredeemable degenerates of whom any infamy could be expected. Riddell's 1870 novel *Austin Friars* centres on Yorke Forde, cast-off mistress of the title character, who goes into business (and is more successful than her former lover), is reconciled to the husband whom she deserted, and who, after his death, marries her business partner whose long-standing love, even after he knew her story, freed him from evangelical pharisaism.[15] 'Fallen women' feature in her Irish novels as well. Even though Maxwell Drewitt's discarded lover, Judy Ryan, has concealed her past from her husband, her disreputable brother's insistence that it renders her unfit to associate with her husband and their children is presented as hypocritical, and instant forgiveness and reconciliation are offered by her deceived husband.[16] In *The Earl's Promise*, Daniel Brady offers his wife the ultimate insult of sharing the house with a servant living as his mistress, but this servant is genuinely sympathetic to the wife and tries to do her best for the children of the marriage, and is allowed to attain respectability through marriage to, and emigration with, a husband who knows her past.[17] Berna Boyle's attitude to Gorman Muir's dissipation (including her eventual forgiveness) can thus be seen as resting on rejection of the double standard based on the possibility of redemption for both sexes.

Grace Walley, in *The Nun's Curse*, a much more conventional Magdalene figure whose slow death from tuberculosis helps to redeem her husband, is an exception to this pattern. Here Riddell's privileging of inner integrity over external honour is embodied in a different character. In *The Nun's Curse*, the apparently shocking advice of the Church of Ireland cleric Mr Malet to Terence Conway – that his obligation to the plebeian and illiterate Grace Walley does not extend to marriage – is presented by Riddell as a bracing dose of realism, rejected only by sentimental hypocrites. Malet later comes to respect Grace's virtues, chiefly her unrequited love for her husband; nevertheless, both he and Riddell reiterate that his advice was correct, and his integrity is underlined when Terence spitefully awards a rich parish promised to Malet to a less deserving candidate.

Falling feudalism: Riddell's critique of Charles Lever's 'rollicking'

RIDDELL's second sparring partner is Charles Lever, whose novels were the most widely read expression of a Tory male-adolescent celebration of a fantasy pre-Famine Ireland, with landlords and tenants joined in a quasi-libidinal 'rollicking' lifestyle of drunken hedonism and masculine (often military) bravery which was threatened by grasping exploitative upstarts and rationalistic English doctrinaires in unholy alliance with O'Connell.[18]

Maxwell Drewitt, the most lightweight of Riddell's Irish novels, centres on an outwardly virtuous young man whose father was disinherited for marrying a Catholic (Maxwell is brought up Protestant) and who intrigues ruthlessly to regain the estate from his uncle and cousins. The uncle is a financially reckless aristocrat familiar from Edgeworth and Lever, and Riddell includes an election scene of a type common in the latter, with Maxwell backing an English Whig against the incumbent Tory favoured by his uncle. Unlike Lever, however, Riddell is unsparing on the devastating results of the uncle's extravagances and moral evasion, while the Whig businessman later invests to save Maxwell's surviving relatives from the worst effects of his intrigues. Both Edgeworth and Lever portrayed their villains as mere exploitative rack-renters, but Maxwell is a genuine reforming landlord whose enterprise (backed by capital obtained through mercenary marriage and assisted by shrewd speculation in the Encumbered Estates Court) creates fertile farms from Connemara rocks. Although the dying Maxwell realises material achievement is not enough, the reader has too much access to his feelings to see him as simply malign like Edgeworth's Jason Quirk or the adventurer threatening Lever's Knight of Gwynne.

The most expressly counter-Leveresque of Riddell's Irish novels is the one most neglected by critics: *The Earl's Promise*.[19] It is sometimes suggested that the central weakness of Irish nineteenth-century literature is the absence of a realist novel of social analysis on the model of *Middlemarch*, and *The Earl's Promise* initially seems like an attempt at such a novel. The opening chapters seem to promise an overview of Irish landed society hastening towards the Famine, depicting varying social grades from the honest Presbyterian tenant farmer and paterfamilias Amos Scott, through the unscrupulous squireen Daniel Brady (wife-beater and land-grabber), the small landlord General Riley and his son John, and the county magnates, the Earls of Glendare and Marquess of Ardmorne. It focuses on a nascent seaside resort inhabited by well-to-do retirees and ladies of gossip and leisure in an unnamed Ulster county. The predominance of Presbyterians and its location in 'the southern part of the county' suggests Antrim. The village name Ballylough, ludicrously changed to 'Kingslough' in tribute to George IV, suggests Carnlough in Co. Antrim, but the place seems more closely modelled on Riddell's hometown Carrickfergus.

The reckless Glendares resemble the Chichesters (Marquesses of Donegall), although they are consistent Whigs whereas the Chichesters were usually Conservatives. Descended from the brother of the Lord Deputy who oversaw the Plantation of Ulster, the Chichesters held vast estates in Antrim, Down, and Donegal, including the town of Belfast. In the eighteenth century they were absentees; the second Marquess (1769–1844) returned to Belfast to escape creditors and let much of his estate on long leases at nominal rents in return for immediate payments which he squandered. His debts and the Famine forced his heirs to sell most of their estates in the early 1850s.[20]

Riddell's description of the rents exacted from the Glendare tenants might come from the most fervent tenant-right agitator, and she – unlike many Irish novelists of left and right who presented land-agents as the real villains of the land system – emphasises that the Glendares force their agents to tighten the screw on the tenants, who blame the agents while blessing the Glendares' personal distribution of a small fraction of what they bleed from the tenants.[21]

The novel's central character is Grace Moffat, heiress to a retired Northumbrian businessman living in Kingslough. After refusing a proposal of marriage from John Riley, who leaves to make his fortune in India, Grace seeks to remedy Ireland's sufferings: she relieves beggars of dubious character, criticises landlordism, and admires O'Connell.[22] Her father is cynical about philanthropy and political reform and utters home truths about Grace's protégés.[23] Although Mr Moffat is criticised for his inactivity, Riddell presents Grace as foolishly naïve.[24] She remarks that Grace sees only the failings of landlordism and not those of the tenants, which include widespread improvidence and dishonesty. The novel suggests that the working classes had demanded living wages irrespective of employers' circumstances, that such views caused Ireland to lose what she can never regain (the Established Church), and that after various 'political doctors' tinkered with Ireland, the 'latest and rashest surgeon' (Gladstone) was so disastrous that nothing similar would be tried for a long time.[25]

Much of the plot is driven by a visit to Kingslough by the Glendares, who are seeking to retain their traditional parliamentary seat by crowd-pleasing gestures, including sending Lady Glendare to bathe regularly at the resort although she hates sea-bathing.[26] The Glendares are contrasted with their sober Orange-Evangelical Tory rival, Lord Ardmorne, who is not loved as they are although he pours capital into the county while the Glendares drain it.[27] The character of Lord Ardmorne is based on the Evangelical Tory, and conspicuously frugal, third Marquess of Downshire who in the 1830s displaced the Chichesters from the parliamentary seat for Riddell's native Carrickfergus. (Ardmorne extracts the virtuous Rileys from the machinations of Daniel Brady, who buys the mortgage on their seashore estate which he recognises as ideal for holiday villas.) Furthermore, the Glendares are also contrasted with the Presbyterian tenant Amos Scott, compared to the quiet and relatively uncelebrated heroism of the Apprentice Boys of Derry, and despised by sentimental admirers of the Stuarts (with whom the Glendares, sharing their personal charm and self-destructive folly, are equated).[28] Riddell declares that Britain owes her continued possession of Ireland to the loyalty of Ulster Presbyterians in the O'Connell era, even though these solid folk are reviled by sentimental Britons who think Roman Catholicism very fine for other people, particularly Celts.[29] While the Glendares visit Kingslough, Amos Scott seeks a renewal of his lease. He meets the Earl out riding and pays his money for a verbal commitment (the 'Promise'). Amos does not get a receipt, the Earl forgets and dies, Daniel Brady buys the reversion of the lease, and the Scotts are reduced to penury.

Tenant-right politics of a type familiar in post-Famine Ulster appear in Kingslough with an ambitious young doctor called Hanlon (a social climber from a petit-bourgeois family aspiring to gentility), and Amos Scott is arrested for murdering Daly.[30] Instead of this apparent agrarian murder precipitating the long-presaged social collapse, it is manslaughter committed for personal reasons by Hanlon. With the acquisitive grabber dead and Hanlon and the dispossessed Scotts emigrating, the forces of disruption are banished (the Scotts downgraded from emblem of the Ulster Protestant community to victims of individual misfortune). Although we are told the Famine will precipitate the Glendares into the Encumbered Estates Court, the novel ends with a purely private resolution as Grace marries her returned colonial suitor and revivifies the Riley fortunes by constructing the holiday villas planned by Brady.

Berna Boyle, Riddell's nearest approach to an Ulster regional novel, is set in Dundonald. Its description of the village at the junction of the Newtownards and Comber roads, the Norman motte and the Church of Ireland church nearby, is still recognisable though its rural setting is now absorbed by Belfast suburbia; the straggling row of cottages (demolished in the 1930s) will be recognised by readers of Agnes Romilly White's novels *Gape Row* (1934) and *Mrs Murphy Buries the Hatchet* (1936), both set in 1890s Dundonald. In *The Earl's Promise*, Belfast is unmentioned, but the characters of *Berna Boyle* regularly make their way to Belfast. One of the novel's driving forces is the desire of Richard Charles Vince, an upwardly mobile Belfast businessman, to keep his horrendous cousin, Mrs Boyle (widow of a West of Ireland gentleman who died before he could clear his debts and provide for his wife and daughter) from pestering him by consigning her to a Dundonald cottage. The eponymous heroine is the daughter whose fierce integrity makes her insist on remaining with her mother when wealthy relations are willing to help her but not her dreadful parent. Mrs Boyle repays Berna with accusations of selfishness, denunciations of her late husband, and hare-brained assertions to all and sundry of her rightful social status and youthfulness.

The cottage is rented from Hewson Muir, a prosperous and enterprising Presbyterian farmer – not a paragon of pastoral virtue like Amos Scott but a man of dubious character married three times: first for love and ambition to the daughter of a landed family who cast her off; second, for economic advantage to a scrimping shrew who left a hard-working and brutally utilitarian daughter; finally due to casual sexual attraction to a promiscuous vagabond who left him with a flighty daughter. Gorman Muir, his son by the first marriage who has been brought up by a maternal uncle, returns to the paternal homestead after being falsely accused of trying to seduce his uncle's young wife (although he seduced other women). Gorman falls in love with Berna and sets up as a horse-dealer to be near her. He takes a farm from which a previous tenant has been evicted. The real-life Co. Down arson wave of the late 1840s, which involved burning of farmers' hay-ricks by mysterious incendiarists, is introduced in a manner – involving attacks by the family of an evicted tenant on their supplanters – reminding contemporary readers of the Land League agitation, but the attackers are defeated with implausible ease in a single incident involving shotgun cartridges loaded with salt.[31]

Berna remains obdurate, and Gorman sinks into dissipation. Although the novel ostensibly celebrates Berna's unyielding integrity, the reader is given more access to Gorman Muir's fluctuating thoughts than to Berna's, and it is implied that her stubbornness is partly responsible for Gorman's dissipation. Gorman is persuaded by his father to abduct Berna in the mistaken belief that she will go willingly. Once kidnapped, Berna tells Gorman that although she is at his mercy and the abduction has compromised her reputation, she will never marry him. The reason for this refusal, she explains to Gorman (and the reader) in a manner startlingly frank by nineteenth-century standards, is that she saw him with a prostitute on the Ormeau Road. He is therefore responsible for the woman's social destruction and his own degradation. The novel is hastily wrapped up in summary Leveresque fashion. A repentant Gorman returns Berna to her home, enlists in the army, and redeems himself by Crimean War heroism. Wealthy relatives reunite him with Berna (her mother fortunately dead); she relents and marries him, whereupon Gorman receives legacies from his repentant uncle and maternal grandparents.

Maxwell Drewitt and *The Nun's Curse* stand in the same relationship within Riddell's oeuvre as *The Macdermots of Ballycloran* (1847) and *The Land-Leaguers* (1884) within Anthony Trollope's works, the comparison of earlier and later novels implying an author moving from sympathy with those defeated by modernisation to rage at the prospect of its defeat.

Maxwell Drewitt is based on the assumption of the 1850s and 1860s that post-Famine Irish agriculture had undergone permanent and beneficial transformation, albeit at profound moral cost. The 1880s land agitation called this achievement into question. Maxwell's damnation is accomplished through his marriage to a rich older woman when a younger and poorer woman is pregnant with his child; the crowning folly of Terence Conway in *The Nun's Curse* is marriage to his plebeian lover. (Like the similar seduction/pregnancy plot of Trollope's *An Eye for an Eye* [1878–79], both these ill-starred relationships might perhaps be seen as allegories of the Anglo-Irish Union.)

The Nun's Curse, set predominantly in the immediate post-Famine period, is a Land War novel. The view that it evades the issues of the Land War is mistaken, because it reflects mid-Victorian controversies over Donegal landlordism still invoked by both sides in the Land War.[32] On the pro-landlord side, the improving Gweedore landlord Lord George Hill (1801–79) is cited repeatedly as an example by Terence Conway and his improving Scottish agent Mr Stirling. Like Lord George, Stirling succeeds with improved farming methods but finds his tenants unwilling to follow suit. Riddell explicitly attributes this to laziness and fecklessness which shows that peasant proprietors without the stimulus of rent would not be more productive.[33]

The novel opens with the widely celebrated death of Marmaduke 'Duke' Conway, a Donegal landlord who crowned a misspent life by evicting tenants en masse during the Famine from hatred of humanity in general and his heir in particular. In his final malevolent act, Duke leaves his personal assets to a remote relative so that the heir to the entailed estate lacks the capital to develop it. Duke's behaviour reflects a curse from a nun hunted with hounds by an ancestral Conway: namely, that while Conways own the estate there will be division between father and son, husband and wife, owner and heir.

Duke combines the worst features of several notorious Donegal landlords. The location of his estate near Dunfanaghy, with his arbitrary behaviour and clearances, suggest the third Earl of Leitrim (1806–78), whose hostility to tenant right, random eviction of independent-minded tenants, extensive rent-raising, and general quarrelsomeness were unpopular even among landlords and officials, and whose murder provoked the same type of rejoicing that accompanies Duke's natural demise.[34] Whereas most Famine-era clearances were driven to some extent by economic necessity (Leitrim's later clearances were partly motivated by fear of a new Famine), Riddell emphasises that Duke was wealthy enough to have supported his tenants throughout the Famine and sent them to their deaths purely from spite. Duke's clearances are not, however, presented as purely destructive.

Riddell disingenuously remarks that the clearances eliminate customary rights, ensuring that new tenants start on a *tabula rasa*. She thus evades the customary argument for tenant right.

Riddell explicitly states, however, that Duke and his predecessors did not seduce their tenants' womenfolk, whereas it was widely alleged (though also disputed) that Leitrim used his power to rape Donegal women under threat of eviction and that his assassins were relatives or lovers of these victims.[35] Terence's seduction of Grace Walley is described as placing him lower than previous Conways, yet not so low as the crimes attributed to Leitrim, for it is emphasised that Grace succumbed willingly. As we shall see, the novel reimagines the shooting of Lord Leitrim in another manner.[36]

At the behest of Philippa, who invokes his moral duty to improve the estate, Terence Conway rejects advice to rid himself and the estate of the curse by selling to a better-capitalised owner and paying debts he has contracted to a Jewish moneylender. Much of the second volume describes the efforts of Terence's agent and legal adviser to renegotiate the moneylender's extortionate terms, to find an investor to underwrite land improvement, and to recruit new tenants at a reasonable rent. These efforts are nearly defeated by Terence's gormlessness in holidaying when his presence is needed and ignoring legal documents, but his friends succeed: Terence promptly entangles himself with Grace Walley.

Terence's central betrayal, however, is not of Grace but of his hard-working and deferential coachman Pat Corrigan, Grace's fiancé. In a display of pseudo-benevolence, Terence offers to assist an immediate marriage, hoping to deceive Pat into thinking that he is the father of Grace's child, but Grace tells Pat the truth. Pat reproaches Terence and goes to another part of Donegal to earn money to emigrate. He visits soon after the birth of Grace's son to say goodbye to his lost love and ask Terence to be kind to her; his visit coincides with the near-fatal shooting of Terence, and, despite Terence's publicly expressed belief in his innocence, Pat is convicted of attempted murder. After Grace's death, it transpires that the assassin was her father Daniel Walley, seeking to gain possession of the Conway estate through his infant grandson; the attack on landlordism is thus presented not (as in the pro-tenant narrative) as the work of a noble peasant avenging genuine grievances but perpetrated by a self-seeking parasite ambitious to become a landlord himself. Pat dies before he can be released – like the central character of Emily Lawless's Land War novel *Hurrish* (1886), victim more of agitators' violence than of landlord misdeeds. Daniel Walley kidnaps his grandson and brings him up to be a Catholic priest.

A coda shows the estate in the 1880s. Terence, still conscience-haunted, has atoned for his misdeeds and has developed genuine moral fibre through suffering. He has made a happy second marriage with Audna

Malet, daughter of the benevolent local Church of Ireland rector, and the schemes initiated by his advisers and assisted by wise investment of a legacy have made the estate prosperous. The nun's curse re-emerges when Terence's priest son becomes a demagogic land agitator (probably based on Fr James MacFadden of Gweedore), motivated by personal resentment because the expiry of the entail allows his father to exclude him from inheriting the estate.[37] The transformation of an initially anti-landlord novel into an *apologia* for enlightened landlordism is complete.

Charlotte Riddell is an interesting and uneven writer, not a great novelist. Despite serious literary aspirations, she was trapped by financial constraints and never quite escaped the restrictions of her Victorian literary genres. But she was a shrewd, idiosyncratic social observer, and her interrogation of the literary conventions established by earlier Irish novelists helped to indicate their breakdown and clear the way for the fresh start of the Irish novel. More work is needed to indicate how attitudes to social class, philanthropy, and gender relations in her British novels compare with her Irish fiction, but her supposed indifference to Irish politics is exaggerated. She paid little attention to specifically *constitutional* politics but was clearly interested in one of the burning questions of nineteenth-century Irish politics, so often echoed in earlier nineteenth-century Irish novels: namely, how the Irish land system could be restructured for general economic advantage. Despite her criticisms of traditional Irish landlordism and her religiously inspired scepticism about how far social reform might go in producing lasting happiness, Riddell ultimately favoured rationalised and commercialised landlordism over Leveresque feudal nostalgia or peasant proprietorship because she saw Ireland, like Britain, as bound up in the growing web of commercial society to an extent that no political change could alter, but her failure to depict a convincing resolution of her characters' personal and social problems along these lines reflected the honesty, as well as the limitations, of her literary vision.

Notes

1 Riddell has been referred to as the novelist of the Victorian City. E. F. Bleiler, 'Introduction', in E. F. Bleiler (ed.), *The Collected Ghost Stories of Mrs J. H. Riddell* (New York: Dover Press, 1977), pp. v–xxii. See also Margaret Kelleher, 'Charlotte Riddell's *A Struggle for Fame*: The Field of Women's Literary Production', *Colby Quarterly*, 36:2 (2000), 116–31, at p. 119; James Gregory, 'Rev. of *Guilty Money: The City of London in Victorian and Edwardian Culture, 1815–1914*'. Available at www.history.ac.uk/reviews/review/771#author-response. Accessed 21 April 2015.

2 Emma Dale, 'Irish Stories Are Quite Gone Out', in Charlotte Riddell, *A Struggle for Fame* (Dublin: Tramp Press, 2014), pp. v–viii.

3 Charlotte Riddell, *A Struggle for Fame* (Dublin: Tramp Press, 2014), p. 396.

4 Rolf Loeber, Magda Loeber, and Anne Mullin Burnham, *A Guide to Irish Fiction, 1650–1900* (Dublin: Four Courts Press, 2006), p. 1116.

5 For biographical data, see Loeber et al., *A Guide to Irish Fiction*, pp. 1115–27; Kelleher, 'Charlotte Riddell's *A Struggle for Fame*', pp. 116–31; Robert Lee Wolff, 'Two Irish Novels by Mrs. J. H. Riddell', in Charlotte Riddell, *Maxwell Drewitt*, 3 vols. (New York: Garland, 1979), vol. I, pp. v–ix; S. M. Ellis, 'Mrs. J. H. Riddell: The Novelist of the City and of Middlesex', in S. M. Ellis (ed.), *Wilkie Collins, Le Fanu and Others* (London: Constable, 1931), pp. 266–335.

6 Henry James, 'Preface', in *The Tragic Muse*, 3 vols. (New York: Charles Scribner's Sons, 1908), vol. I, p. x.

7 *A Struggle for Fame* stands out because its plot is well integrated and fully worked out.

8 For fuller discussion of the commercial side of her career, see Kelleher, 'Charlotte Riddell's *A Struggle for Fame*'.

9 Charlotte Riddell, *Berna Boyle: A Love Story of the County Down* (London: Macmillan & Co., 1900), pp. 86–7.

10 Riddell, *A Struggle for Fame*, p. 122. William Carleton was still alive when the novel is set.

11 The placename 'Ballyshane' suggests the Glens of Antrim.

12 Charlotte Riddell, *The Nun's Curse*, 3 vols. (New York: Garland Press, 1979), vol. II, pp. 220–2, 249, 259; vol. III, pp. 11, 49, 166, 181, 202, 306. The lyrics of 'Lesbia Hath a Beaming Eye' are available at www.bartleby.com/337/1006.html. Accessed 21 April 2015.

13 Charlotte Riddell, *A Rich Man's Daughter* (London: F. V. White, 1897), p. 55.

14 Riddell, *A Struggle for Fame*, pp. 14–16.

15 Charlotte Riddell, *Austin Friars* (London: Tinsley Brothers, 1870).

16 Charlotte Riddell, *Maxwell Drewitt*, 3 vols. (New York: Garland, 1979), vol. III, pp. 145–57.

17 Charlotte Riddell, *The Earl's Promise: A Novel* (London: Hutchinson, n.d.), pp. 351–6, 371, 373–5.

18 Patrick Maume, 'Music-Hall Unionism: Robert Martin and the Politics of the Stage-Irishman', in Peter Gray (ed.), *Victoria's Ireland: Irishness and Britishness, 1837–1901* (Dublin: Four Courts Press, 2004), pp. 69–80; Patrick Maume, 'Containing Granuaile: Grace O'Malley in Two Nineteenth-Century Novels', *New Hibernia Review*, 19:1 (2015), 98–114. For a more complex analysis of Lever's relationship to the 'rollicking' tradition, see James H. Murphy, *Irish Novelists and the Victorian Age* (Oxford: Oxford University Press, 2011), pp. 71–91.

19 In comparison, *Berna Boyle* combines an outwardly Leveresque framework with a critique of the Lever hero based on individual moral commitment.

20 Compare Glendare's bilking his heir over granting leases and disentailing land in Riddell, *The Earl's Promise*, pp. 152–3 and 157–8 with the second Marquess: W. A. Maguire, *Living like a Lord: The Second Marquess of Donegall* (Belfast: Appletree Press, 1984), pp. 62–3 and 74–84.

21 Riddell, *The Earl's Promise*, pp. 25–6, 29–30.

22 Riddell, *The Earl's Promise*, p. 215.

23 Riddell, *The Earl's Promise*, pp. 204–18.

24 Riddell, *The Earl's Promise*, pp. 94–5.

25 Riddell, *The Earl's Promise*, pp. 183–4, 312, 343–4.

26 Riddell, *The Earl's Promise*, pp. 73–4, 85, 140–3. Lady Donegall's canvassing as the Chichesters struggled to retain the Belfast seat in 1832 drew comment. Maguire, *Living like a Lord*, p. 92.

27 Maguire, *Living like a Lord*, pp. 90–1, 92–5; and Riddell, *The Earl's Promise*, pp. 305–6. Compare also Ardmorne's electoral gains by purchasing a local estate in *The Earl's Promise*, p. 71, with Downshire's purchase in Maguire, *Living like a Lord*, pp. 93–4.

28 Riddell, *The Earl's Promise*, p. 29. For a representation of the Apprentice Boys as quiet Protestant heroes, see Riddell, *Berna Boyle*, pp. 86–7. Philippa Dutton's moral superficiality is displayed when visiting Derry; she despises the Apprentice Boys and admires James II. Riddell, *The Nun's Curse*, vol. I, pp. 186–7.

29 Riddell, *The Earl's Promise*, pp. 97–8.
30 Riddell, *The Earl's Promise*, pp. 168–9, 177–86.
31 Riddell, *Berna Boyle*, pp. 167–70. During the 1840s arson wave, two sisters who claimed to have shot an arsonist were hailed as heroines until they were discovered to have faked the incident. For samples of contemporary newspaper coverage, see *Tablet* (3 February 1849), p. 69, and *Tablet* (17 February 1849), p. 102.
32 Contemporary *Athenaeum* review quoted in Murphy, *Irish Novelists in the Victorian Age*, pp. 6–7.
33 See Sophia Hillan, *May, Lou and Cass: Jane Austen's Nieces in Ireland* (Belfast: Blackstaff Press, 2011); Breandán Mac Suibhne, 'Agrarian Improvement and Social Unrest: Lord George Hill and the Gaoth Dobhair Sheep War, 1856–60', in William Nolan, Liam Ronayne, and Mairead Dunlevy (eds), *Donegal: History and Society* (Dublin: Geography Publications, 1995), pp. 547–82.
34 James Quinn, 'Clements, William Sydney', in James McGuire and James Quinn (eds), *Dictionary of Irish Biography*, 9 vols. (Cambridge: Cambridge University Press, 2009), vol. II, pp. 579–80; A. P. W. Malcolmson, *Virtues of a Wicked Earl: The Life and Legend of William Sydney Clements, Third Earl of Leitrim* (Dublin: Four Courts Press, 2008).
35 Riddell, *The Nun's Curse*, vol. III, pp. 53–4.
36 Lord Leitrim is not the only model for Duke. Duke has some of his own sheep killed to justify evictions and get innocent men transported. These actions reflect accusations about John George Adair (1832–85) over the 1861 Glenveagh evictions, and Duke is likewise associated with the vices of the court of George IV in a manner reminiscent of the Conyghams. See W. E. Vaughan, *Sin, Sheep and Scotsmen: John George Adair and the Derryveagh Evictions* (Belfast: Ulster Historical Foundation, 1983).
37 Breandán Mac Suibhne, 'Soggarth Aroon and Gombeen-Priest: Canon James MacFadden (1842–1917)', in Gerard Moran (ed.), *Radical Irish Priests, 1600–1970* (Dublin: Four Courts Press, 1998), pp. 149–84.

2

'She's nothin' but a shadda': the politics of marriage in late Mulholland

James H. Murphy

THE prolific Irish novelist Rosa Mulholland (1841–1921) was a woman of the upper-middle-class. Like other women of her era, her social position can be triangulated by the professions of the men in her life: her father was a Belfast doctor; her husband, Sir John Gilbert, was a renowned Dublin historian; and her brother-in-law, Lord Russell of Killowen, was Lord Chief Justice of England. She was a devout Catholic and a prominent member of the literary circle that formed around Fr Matthew Russell, SJ, brother of Lord Russell and editor of the *Irish Monthly*. Finally, she was a feminist, though in her fiction her feminist concerns were often mixed with those of her class agenda. In addition, radical feminist solutions are often aired in her work, although Muholland tends to retreat from fully endorsing them. Nonetheless, there is an almost campaigning urgency in much of her fiction in the cause of women's advancement, energised for much of her career by a progressive optimism. This chapter focuses on two late novels, *The Return of Mary O'Murrough* (1908) and *Norah of Waterford* (1915).[1] Here the realism that accompanied the optimism of her earlier work gives way to a pessimism concerning the relationship between gender and economics as women struggle for happiness in a world where erotic love and marriage are tied in with material security.

This contrasts with her early work. *Dunmara* (1864), for example, concerns the struggles of a young woman artist in London. Mulholland herself had been encouraged to pursue a career as an artist by Sir John Everett Millais before Dickens helped to launch her career as a novelist.[2] In *Dunmara* there is a world of career possibility for young women, albeit those with means. 'What an independent person you are. A female doctor! What a strange idea', exclaims the heroine Ellen when a fellow art student tells her of her real ambition.[3] The other student's response to such surprise is one of restlessness with the status quo:

> I am perfectly sick of the life we girls have to lead. It is nothing at the best but dressing, and dancing, and flirting; and flirting, and dancing, and dressing, I said I would not submit to it ... Why should not a woman give herself to a high calling, as well as a man? Why should she not work the powers she has got?[4]

In the end, however, the novel resiles from such a complete feminism for something that marries new freedom with traditional responsibility. Ellen settles for this view of things:

> I don't think any woman is justified, or that she is studying her own interest, when she ignores the smallest, humble charities and duties of life. In the comparison with man, she puts herself at a disadvantage, for shine as she will, she can never arrive at the masculine summit of intellectual power ... I think it is well with the woman who, having sterner inspirations given by Providence for a purpose, can turn on the instant from easel, chisel, or pen, not disgusted and reluctant, but gladly, cheerfully, to do even such common-place things as tending a sick bed, or cleaning a child's stocking. Even the most isolated life has need of such calls. Obedience to them entails increase of liberty, and for those who live among their kind they are never ceasing.[5]

The novel ends with Ellen securely located in family life rather than what the novel implies might otherwise be an isolating independence.

Mulholland's *Marcella Grace* (1886) is a key novel of the Land War of the 1880s. One of the effects of the Famine of the 1840s was to reduce the diversity of rural Irish life. The class of small farmers, with several dozen acres, became a dominant component. The priority of these farmers was to consolidate and extend their holdings, as the subdivision among several heirs of holdings on which the abundant potato crop could be grown was one of the reasons why famine, disease, death, and emigration had been the results when that crop had failed in the 1840s. Now there could only be one heir, usually a male, and marriage to a woman with a dowry was a principal means by which the farming family's capital or land might be increased.

When agricultural conditions worsened again in the late 1870s, Irish tenant farmers were ready and, through the Land League, mounted a campaign to reduce rents and have rent arrears cancelled. The Land War was a conflict that in some respects lasted for several decades, though its first phase in the years around 1880 resulted in decisive legislative concessions by the government. Within a decade the way was open for Irish tenants to become owners of their farms on the strength of government loans to buy out the landlords. The land struggle of the 1880s was accompanied by various forms of active and passive resistance. Boycotting, attacks on landlords and their agents, intimidation, and cattle maiming were tactics employed by some that caused outrage in Britain. Thus the Irish Land War generated its own fictional genre, mostly for a British market, with novels analysing its causes, depicting its progress, and prognosticating its solution. Some of these novels were noteworthy for the prominence of women in them as active participants, though this was often taken as a symptom of a dangerous social dislocation caused by the conflict.[6]

The Land War provides not only the immediate setting of Mulholland's 1886 novel. The economic and social mores it helped to reinforce are also the basis for the two later novels that are the central concerns of this study. Consonant with its author's class and religious background, *Marcella Grace* does not favour tenant ownership but advocates the development of a Catholic gentry with greater sympathy for tenants to replace the discredited Protestant one. Its eponymous heroine is a vigorous young woman from a Dublin working-class background who finds herself turned into a landlord and becomes a successful one, though she retreats to the domestic sphere when the man she marries, Bryan Kilmartin, is cleared of false accusations and can resume his public role.[7]

She learns upon her arrival at her estate that a rumour is circulating that she is 'a furious radical woman who had spoken to platforms about woman's rights and walked about the country in a jacket like a man'.[8] In a similar fashion, her husband's waywardness is attributed to a disruption in the settled order of gender relations in the person of his mother:

> The fact that there was a mother in the question was mentioned in all the papers and the 'Press Association' discovered that the said mother was six feet high, with a masculine voice, and had been implicated, while Bryan was still a child, in international outrages abroad, when she had escaped from pursuit disguised as a man.[9]

There is thus a nervous unease in the novel around gender roles, an awareness of the mechanisms by which they are sustained. In the end, though, as with *Dunmara*, there is a retreat from a more radical feminist analysis, and Marcella returns to the role of wifely supporter of her restored husband. Though Mulholland's novels often advocate relatively advanced views concerning the role of women, she ultimately baulks in this particular text at allowing Marcella Grace's exercise of power to continue.

The middle years of Mulholland's career are full of narratives of poor young women struggling against adversity. They tend to be stories of urban women and the vagaries of Victorian morality but inasmuch as they are about poorer women they are closer to the late novels of rural women that are the principal focus of this chapter. *Onora* (1900), *Nanno, a Daughter of the State* (1898), and *The Tragedy of Chris* (1903) are about respectability and the causes and consequences of its loss.[10] *Onora*'s exploration of the tension between the affective and economic dimensions of marriage anticipates Mulholland's later novels. In it a servant girl leaves her employers when she concludes that the young head of the family would imperil its position if he were to marry her, as he wishes, rather than a rich girl who has returned from America. In *Nanno*, an unmarried mother abandons her child in pursuit of a new life, though ultimately her conscience prevents her from marrying while concealing her past. *The Tragedy of Chris* contrasts the lives of two girls from equally disadvantageous backgrounds, one of whom sinks into vice while the other attains respectability, in an obvious defence of the notion that one's state in life reflects one's moral choices. *Gianetta: A Girl's Story of Herself* (1889) concerns that most contentious aspect of the relationship between landlords and tenants, the eviction of tenants from their farms.[11] Like the later novels it has a rural setting, but it is more concerned with the public politics of the land than Mulholland's late-career work. It is, in fact, an indictment of the cruelties of evictions and as such was the cause of controversy when the Sheffield School Board in England bought 200 copies as prizes. *Father Tim* (1910) combines stories of rural and urban poverty with an optimistic view of the salutary effects of a strong religious faith.[12] Throughout, these novels urge the possibility of individual probity for women in the face of a difficult world. Heidi Hansson has seen *A Fair Emigrant* (1888) as essentially positive in its view of the possibility of progress in spite of the apparent intractabilities of Ireland's economic position. She argues that the novel's position is that 'the country only needs the clear-sightedness of the returning exile to prosper'.[13]

The returned exile, a common figure in Mulholland, is a trope that is present in the two novels considered in this chapter. Here, however, in a pessimistic turn in Mulholland's later fiction, the exile returns only to encounter (or, rather, generate) a hostile environment as she struggles with the distorting effects on romantic love created by the politics of Irish economics. This is a world which is not specifically identified in either novel but which in general is the world of the land struggle of the late nineteenth century. It was a world, as has been noted, where the fear left by the Famine meant that farmers were ever eager to assure the security of their land. To exist in such a world men must marry for dowry money to ensure the continuing solvency of their farm holdings.

The Return of Mary O'Murrough is swathed in religious piety. It is set in rural Kerry and typical of a Mulholland novel of old. Father Fahy, the parish priest, offers sound advice to all parties on the way to make the best out of a difficult life. He laments the destructive effects of emigration, and the narrative parodies popular British misunderstandings of the Irish situation, as when support for Shan Sullivan, a man falsely accused of cattle maiming, is interpreted as advocating criminal atrocities:

> What would be done, it was asked, for a people who sympathised with the most cruel and dastardly outrages, led by priests who gave countenance and encouragement to criminals? This miscreant, taken with the blood of the poor dumb animals on his hands, and his knife at his feet, having perpetrated a crime more revolting than many a murder of a human being, was applauded as a hero, and his just punishment would be regarded as a martyrdom.[14]

At its deepest levels, however, the novel itself offers a surreal account of the economics and affectivity of marriage through which its female characters must navigate their way.

The novel opens with an uncompromising account of the dilemmas of marriage in a rural Irish community blighted by emigration and in which the possession of a small farm offers the only hope of economic survival for the family. By the time in which the book is set, farmers in Ireland had set their sights on becoming owners of land rather than tenants. The Land War of the late nineteenth century had begun as an organised campaign among tenants to secure more rights against landlords during the agricultural slump of the last quarter of the century. It had ended with schemes that allowed tenants to borrow money to buy out their farms. In the novel, the harshness of this world is conveyed by the arrangement of 'the cabins of the poorest of the population [which] stand here and there, this way and that way, their gables set against the coldest wind, their bushes gathered round them, and their turf-stacks erected like barricades against an enemy'.[15]

The opening chapters are dominated by the figure of Mrs Dermody, who 'was a hard woman in regard to the tight grip she kep' of the half-dozen acres that Matthias [her late husband] left her'.[16] When she married, her husband had no land, and Mulholland never makes it clear how the couple acquired it. Nonetheless, Mrs Dermody is intent that neither of her daughters, Anne Bridget and Bess, is going to make the same mistake of marrying into poverty if she can help it. She has already frustrated Anne Bridget's attempts to marry for love, though as a result and because of the passage of time Anne Bridget is now less beautiful and thus less marketable than she once was. Bess, meanwhile, has been keen on Miles Donohoe, who has no land. Mrs Dermody's ambitions are fixed on Pether Flynn, whom she sees as industrious and a 'thrifty owner of a thriving farm'.[17] The varying attractiveness of the two daughters means that Pether Flynn would be prepared to marry the desirable Bess without a dowry, even though she is said to be 'comely rather than beautiful', but would require one to marry the now less attractive Anne Bridget, who is said to have had a beauty 'that vanishes after a very few years'.[18] Miles's father voices a contempt for this whole mentality as he confronts Mrs Dermody:

> An' what would y' want with grand-childher, you that has heifers an' pigs an' chickens to come afther y'? What would y' want with the young cratures of humanity? For myself, I'm glad that I have boys an' girls; an' if I was your daughter Bess, I'd rather go to America an' marry a young man that was there before me, than to lave myself in your han's to make little o' my life.[19]

In fact, Mrs Dermody is in some ways the greatest victim of the whole situation. She herself married for love not money, but she is, as one character describes her, 'like many's the mother that has one law for yourselves an' another for your childher'.[20] Eventually, her financial ambitions repel even Pether Flynn: 'Sure it's her that has the hungry eye on my bits of grass and my two-three sheep an' cows. It's better for me to keep out of her way!'[21]

What happens when personal attraction is not mapped onto economic logic? This is the case with beautiful Mary O'Murrough who loves Shan Sullivan but has no dowry. His father vetoes the marriage until she has money, forcing her to work in America for years. Remarkably, it is the women in the novel who are required to make the most strenuous exertions for economic betterment by emigrating. One minor character thus laments that she must go because her lover is 'spanchelled by the leg where he is' on the family farm.[22] His rather sheepish comment on the situation is '"God's a hard God! … You to be goin', an' I to be stayin"!'[23]

The solution to the economic-affective dilemma in the novel – marry a beautiful woman – seems logical but for the fact that beauty fades. The men, not unnaturally from their point of view, want to marry sooner rather than later so as to extract maximum value in terms of enjoying their wives' youthful beauty. This arises in the case of the young couple, Bess Dermody and the dubious Miles Donohoe, whose reliability is open to question. Bess wishes Miles to work hard so that they can afford to marry. He argues that marrying her would give him the incentive to work more steadfastly: 'It's good wages I could earn if it was you I was earnin' for, but when I think I'm not goin' to get you, asthoreen, the impliments drops out of my hands.'[24]

It might appear that female attractiveness functions, albeit evanescently, as a form of capital in something of the same way as do the products of the land: like a perishable crop, beauty diminishes with age. However, the position is a little more complex than this. That beauty will fade is inevitable and is accepted by men, so long as they have been able to enjoy their women at least for a period when they are perceived to be highly desirable. And, after all, women will still have their domestic skills, which will have grown in a compensatory fashion as beauty diminishes. Miles Donohoe's father certainly believes this to be true. 'Look at my Meg. D'ye think she's the same young girl that she was whin I courted her? Why need I care if her beauty's gone? Was she as wise a woman, an' as good a wife, in the beginnin' as she is at the end?'[25]

The main plot in the novel concerns the fact that when Mary O'Murrough returns, with money, it is discovered that she has lost her beauty, and Shan finds her repulsive. Beauty, however, exists in a space between the physical appearance of the woman and the erotic imagination of the man. Mary's appearance before her departure is mediated to the reader through Shan's intense fantasies of her, though these are more reminiscent of what would become the recognisable tropes of heterosexual female popular romantic fiction, positioning men in stirring settings, than they are of the more body-specific genre of male pornography. Shan's erotic imagination is so strong that he speaks to the absent Mary:

> The soft blue eyes o' you, and the lovely black hair, with a shiny wave in it like the little waves in the lake undher the Gap o' Dunloe whin the sun does be hittin' into the shadda! An' the two dimples in them round cheeks o' yours, a body would make y' laugh if it was only to see them runnin' in an' out. Who has the white teeth y' have, Mary, an' the rose of a mouth what could say the pleasant words?[26]

Things go further in Shan's imagination, and he believes he can actually glimpse Mary: 'Under this mystic tree he could see Mary standing where the ground is thick sown with reddish and purple seeds, falling from the network of spreading branches overhead, and forming a carpet, smooth, delicate, sumptuous, which Mary would scarcely dare to tread upon.'[27] The most telling aspect of this seeing of Mary is its association with the fecundity and sexual charge of the reddish and purple seeds (to which we shall return later).

That women's beauty is a function of the male erotic imagination may to some extent explain the otherwise surreal reception Mulholland contrives for Mary on her return home. It is as if Shan's erotic imagination has been projected onto the entire population. No one at all recognises her. When she introduces herself to Mrs Dermody, the latter replies that 'I only knew one of that name, but she was a beautiful girl, and very young. Nobody could ever forget her.'[28] Tellingly, Mrs Dermody goes on to describe the returned Mary as a shadow, less real than the more strongly present Mary of the male imagination which has been imposed on the general imagination of the community by being constantly alluded to. Mary's own experience of sacrifice causes her to urge Bess to marry without delay, even in the face of the disapproval of her mother and Fr Fahy.

The narrative evinces an almost sadistic propensity to indulge in Mary's drama of rejection. She has to face the horror of the local community at her altered appearance. 'Mary O'Murrough's come home, an' nobody would know her. Her good looks is all wrecked, an' she's nothin' but a shadda.'[29] Eventually, they adjust to her altered appearance, but then she has to meet

Shan, whom she has been prevented from seeing because he is in jail for the cattle-maiming, and face his revulsion: 'Not my Mary O'Murrough that went away to America. She must be dead, an' it's somebody that's come in her place!'[30] She appears unreal to Shan as he continues to inhabit his fantasy construct:

> Shan was staring over her head, and away beyond her at the distance, across the years, looking at the vivid picture never obliterated, never faded by a line or a tint, of a face that had been the companion of his fidelity, a countenance rounded in loveliness, blue eyes running over with laughter, dimpled cheeks the colour of the wild hedge-roses. That was Mary O'Murrough who went from him, and he had been told that she had come back to him. Who was this worn woman weeping before him, who had taken her name and was claiming her identity?[31]

She has brought him £300, 'her earnings for Shan, the price of his future welfare, of her lost beauty, and of her youth outlived'.[32] Mary is fully cognisant of the reality of the situation. She is, we are told, 'wildly aware that a weird and awful thing had happened; that they two who had lived apart in vivid life and faith so long were stricken by incredible death of the heart in the moment of their meeting'.[33] However, the fact that Shan is in difficulties is the one thing that keeps her engaged with him, as she tells him when she eventually plucks up the courage to visit him in jail:

> If it wasn't that you're where y' are and in trouble, if you were walkin' the fields of Killelagh, meetin' me with that look on your face, I would run for the boat an' go back to where I come from at once, without drawing a breath. But even if your heart's as cold to me and as fast shut as the prison gates, I couldn't turn my back on y' till I see you out of it.[34]

Shan, who is soon exonerated from the crime he is charged with, determines to offer to marry Mary out of a sense of duty and after an admonishment from Fr Fahy. 'Each of you kept a glorified picture of the other vividly before the mind, loved it, worshipped it, made a companion of it', Fr Fahy tells him. 'But now that you find the glorified picture of youth marred by time and toil, is your heart to become hard and faithless? Will God not be angry if you now cast this faithful woman off?'[35]

Shan's coldness to Mary remains unacknowledged in the nationalist excitement occasioned by his release from jail. He comes to associate Mary with his unjust imprisonment. 'A worn woman with an anguished countenance had come into his life in her place, had brought her tears into his prison to make part of the tragedy that had trampled out the joys and the hopes of his life.'[36] Indeed, Shan thinks that in marrying the faded Mary he might be being unfaithful to the true Mary of his erotic imagination.

Shan finds, at least temporarily, a replacement for Mary in a fifteen-year-old girl. 'Shan looked at her, and saw that her eyes were big and soft, and her hair yellow like the furze-blossoms.'[37] Then, in an extraordinary but fleeting moment, the inequity of the situation becomes apparent to him as he glances in a mirror. 'It was a hard, bitter face that he had seen, accidentally ... A woman might well dislike it.'[38] At no point, however, does the narrative register Mary's reaction to his physical appearance.

A Mulholland novel had to have a happy ending. Even she, however, finds it hard to bring about a convincing alteration in Shan's attitude to Mary – though this does occur and they marry after he races to the boat to prevent her emigrating again. Mary's singing voice and eyes remain reminders of her past self. As for her countenance, '[i]t was not such a very pale face now; there was a sweet touch of colour on cheeks and lips, and the thin contours were rounded into something like the winsome curves of old. The dark, smooth hair had broken away into ripples about the forehead, and the breeze blew a light ringlet across the blue of her eyes.'[39] Mary's care for Shan's father – those domestic qualities that men generally accept as a substitute for beauty when the latter fades – endear him to her. Mulholland unbelievably even suggests that Mary's beauty is somehow replenished, though she shows an understandable sheepishness about asserting it:

> Another miracle which was believed to have happened was the return of Mary's youth. The sad lines had disappeared from her face, her rounded cheeks had regained their carnation tint, and her eyes, which had always kept their flower-like blue, shone again, full of light, like the eyes of a girl of twenty.[40]

Again, however, the link between Mary's supposedly renewed physical condition and the talk about it being miraculous might also gesture towards the general recategorising of Mary's appearance now that she has become desirable to Shan once more.

The novel, however, veers at the end from the surreal assertion of Mary's restored position to a more sobering critique of marriage as endured by its female characters. Female erotic attraction is, for heterosexual males, of course linked with fertility and fecundity – those seeds strewn at Mary's feet in Shan's vision. Mary duly becomes pregnant, but the infant dies in childbirth, and Mary and Shan remain infertile thereafter. Meanwhile, Bess and Miles marry and go to America where they have children, although these will be American children. The novel ends with one character uneasily declaring that 'it is not our fault if there never will be childher more round the rings of Killelagh'.[41]

There is a topical political dimension to the novel, but this centres around an unjust police force and the need for Home Rule which remained the pressing nationalist demand at the beginning of the twentieth century.

There is no explicit critique of the economics of rural Irish society, though of course in highlighting the economics of marriage and emigration there is a strong implicit criticism of these practices. The structure of society is in some respects seen as a given, but it is one in which women are burdened with almost impossible expectations in terms both of economics and physical attractiveness. The net result is the bleak prospect of general sterility facing a society so erotically charged as to be describable only in surreal terms rather than those of conventional realism.

Norah of Waterford, by contrast, is an apparently realist novel, though with significant disturbing and counterbalancing fabulist elements within it which again focus on the interface between beauty and economics. The story is quite similar to that of the previous novel, except that here women have considerably more agency. Joe Aherne is a farmer with debts to the landlord and to the money lender (gombeen man), Rogan. He has to support his mother and orphaned nieces and owes money to his brother, and Mulholland comments that, 'At thirty years of age Joe had found himself in possession of the farm, the money-getting capabilities of which were lessening every year.'[42] He must marry for money but falls in love with the farm servant, Norah Fitzgerald, whose family have recently been evicted. The novel also embraces a standard tone of regret at the deleterious effects of emigration. Several characters express this point of view. Norah's mother puts the case mildly: 'my heart is sore seein' all the fine girls goin' out of the country'.[43] A priest puts the position more forcefully: 'an Irish girl like you is better half-starved at home than earning good wages in New York'.[44]

Unlike in *The Return of Mary O'Murrough*, physical attractiveness in this novel seems to inhere in individual appearance, and both men and women are subject to appraisal. Thus Joe's own physical appeal is in play in the novel:

> 'She's like myself', he thought, 'and still it's odd, for there's not a feature in our faces alike, and she's fair an' comely, while I'm a black, hard chap.' He reflected then that he would rather see a laughing, thoughtless girl who wouldn't show a man his own cares as if in a looking-glass.[45]

Here, blackness connotes a sullen reserve. Norah's appraisal of Joe's appearance is achieved by a comparison with his brother:

> Garrett came in from the farmyard and sat down in his place. He was slight and rather handsome, fair in complexion, with a good unthinking countenance. He had the look of a man who would resemble his sisters. Joe, on the contrary, struck one as a distinct individual like nobody but himself.[46]

Norah thus interprets his reserve as an attractive distinctiveness. Attractiveness here contains an element of assessment of character. Unlike the fantasies in *The Return of Mary O'Murrough*, the sense of how a person might or might not cope with the world is here figured as a factor in how attractive they are to others. This is reflected in the circumstances of Joe's acknowledgement of his love for Norah. At one point he sees her looking beautiful in the distance and walks towards her enchanted, rather as Shan Sullivan might have done with Mary O'Murrough. But he then returns to reality and acts gruffly towards her. It is only when he saves her from drowning that he declares his love.

Norah is, however, left in no doubt about economic priorities. These are brought home to her by Joe's sister, Anty, who in addressing the issue alludes to a residual terror of the potato famine that powered the need for farmers to assure the security of their land: 'There isn't the man born would marry a girl without money. And sure, why would they? Do I want to come into a man's house like a famine or a potato blight?'[47] Indeed, in this case, Joe does have an alternative in the person of Sabina Doolan. She occupies something of the position of Mary O'Murrough in the previous novel, although she is presented as a character of revulsion rather than sympathy. Like Mary, she has returned from America with money, but her money has been inherited rather than earned. She has been away longer than Mary, thirty years, but she now wants to marry and has the economic means to achieve her wish: 'she has come home', we are told, 'to buy a husband'.[48] Knowing that beauty and economics are ideally combined in an Irish peasant marriage, she tries to simulate youth through her apparel. The result is presented as a grotesquerie in this initial description of Sabina:

> This person was a woman of middle age, not to say elderly, hard-featured, and weather-tanned, dressed studiously in girl-fashion, and assuming the manners of seventeen. Her coarse dark grizzled hair was tied in a bunch behind, and allowed to fall loose on her back, looking, indeed, more like the tail of a horse than a maiden's tresses. A hat, piled with artificial flowers, was perched jauntily on her head, and a light much-betrimmed cape fluttered airily about her shoulders. She had not learned the art of more or less successfully feigning youth, and the result of putting her undisguised elderliness into a setting of girlish dress and manners was strange, if not grotesque.[49]

Whereas Mary O'Murrough comes to accept the unpalatable truth that she is no longer attractive and is rewarded, somewhat bizarrely, by a return to a form of beauty and marriage, Sabina rebels against facial reality and, indeed, appears to believe that she is somehow young. This makes her the object of what is presented as justified ridicule in the novel, whereas Mary O'Murrough had been the recipient of pity.

Joe is caustic about Sabina.

> 'She starved for years out in New York, and worked hard for bare life, and now, when all's over, she finds herself on a sudden with a pocketful of money. It would be all very well if she didn't want to go back about forty years and be a girl again.'[50]

He sees the sad irony in her arrival coinciding with Norah's potential departure. 'It's a nice kind of a world, with you to be goin' and she (indicating Sabina) to be comin' to us!'[51] Yet Sabina represents a hope for Joe's economic rescue. 'Sabina would make Joe miserable, but her money would save the farm and the family from ruin.'[52] Another young farmer, in a more prosperous position, seems to offer Norah hope concerning her desirability. 'What's gold to a pair of eyes like yours? What's silver to the kind of a smile you have? Och, be my sowl, all the houses an' cows in the world couldn't buy the laugh I heard out o' you a while ago.'[53] But she knows that the best thing for her to do is to emigrate to America. This is in spite of the fact that if anything her feelings for Joe are growing stronger:

> The conviction that she could never be his wife without ruining him gave her a kind of horror of herself for having crossed his path. She loved Joe with the woman's love that will grow the greater for a man because of some disadvantage he labours under or some misfortune that is pursuing him; the selfless mother-love central in the best of woman-nature, the sweetest and most indestructible instinct in the whole of humanity.[54]

At this point, going to America is no longer 'an escape but a martyrdom'.[55] Yet she knows that Joe is unrealistic in his determination to reject Sabina's interest and to marry her. He tells Norah, 'I love you even if I'm ground into the earth with trouble, and wrecked with ruination.'[56] Joe's mother, however, is all too clear about the ultimate fate of human feeling in urging him to marry Sabina. 'She isn't young, an' she isn't handsome, but what great differ does all that make when the heart is crushed out of you?' Joe has a very different view: 'I never knew the heart was alive in me till you brought Norah here.'[57]

That Norah and Joe's relationship may be a form of miscegenation is referenced by the parallel story of Norah's crippled and consumptive brother, Declan, who, because she encouraged his writing, loves Miss Lilla, daughter of the landlord at the Castle. Norah sees his situation with clarity:

> 'I wish you wouldn't be thinkin' so much about her. She's the landlord's daughter, and as high over our heads as the trees is above the daisies. She's years older than you, and she took to you through kindness when the boys was worryin' you tryin' to take your crutch from you.'[58]

Her kindness to him, though, merely acts as a form of soothing as he faces his death. Norah's mother puts Norah's own situation starkly to her daughter when she asks, 'Why did God Almighty give ye such a purty face of your own, my daughter? You to have the face an' her [Sabina] to have the cash.'[59]

This remark is in fact the hinge for the rest of the novel as the text turns in ghoulish and fabulist directions and as attention moves from Joe and Norah to Sabina. Joe's sister, Judy Neary, contrives to restructure reality in such a way as to dissolve Joe's refusal to marry Sabina, albeit with somewhat comic results. In this world, Sabina is truly young and beautiful. It is a version of reality that Judy seeks to reinforce in Sabina's mind in the hope of bringing a farm-saving marriage with Joe closer to reality:

> My, Sabina, but you do look fresh and young, and why wouldn't you, not like an old woman of thirty like me, with four children on her shoulders. Goodness, what a head of hair you have, an' mine full of grey. An' I declare I do think, if it's fair to say it, you're not more than two or three years younger nor myself, Sabina Doolan![60]

However, Joe's mother reacts with revulsion to Sabina's appearance. She tells her so directly. 'It could not be you. Oh no. Bad as it is, it couldn't. Anty said she was no beauty, but still an' all the Almighty wouldn't send Joe such a ransom as that would come to.'[61] Judy attributes these comments to Joe's mother's propensity to see beauty as ugliness, which is the result of her illness and for which specific medication has been prescribed. That Sabina's attitude to all this might itself be parodic is signalled by her remark that, 'Sure I wasn't born before I left, accordin' to what you said to me.'[62] Judy's reshaping of reality entails proposing to Sabina on Joe's behalf, arranging the wedding, and making the news of it known locally – all without Joe's knowledge. She allows Joe to discover what is happening through someone else in the hope that the arrangements will appear so fixed and inevitable as to prevent him from objecting. However, he confronts Judy and Sabina and declares that Norah is the only person he will ever marry.

It is at this point that Sabina comes into her own. She admires Joe for sticking to Norah, and it turns out that her principal motive for marrying Joe is not a form of romantic desperation but gratitude to his family because his grandfather had helped her mother at a point when her family farm was in difficulty. Her desire to marry him therefore has arisen solely from her wish to help him financially, and, in a startling challenge to men having the initiative in deciding such matters, she declares that she is the one who finds him physically repulsive: 'I'll tell the truth, I don't like your black face, nor the swing of your stick.'[63] Once again, these are not merely physical attributes. A black face here connotes anger or malice, and the stick speaks for itself. Sabina's concerns are really about the possibility of an abusive and violent relationship in marrying Joe, and when Joe reassures her that she need not be afraid of his stick, she says that, although she dislikes it, she is confident she would be able to counter the violence of any man.

Next, in a horror to fabulist reversal, Sabina transforms herself from witch into fairy godmother. Mulholland draws on the looking-glass trope so common in fairy tales and on the trope of the secret persona. This trope was common in the renewed Gothic of the turn of the century and is epitomised in the hidden portrait that bears the marks of ageing and moral depravity in Oscar Wilde's *The Picture of Dorian Gray* (1891) and in the monstrous character of Edward Jekyll wherein evil propensities are revealed in R. L. Stevenson's *The Strange Case of Dr Jekyll and Mr Hyde* (1886). Ironically, the monstrous persona has been apparent from the beginning in the form of the Sabina who has attempted to present herself as a young girl. Thematically, it is her attempt to fuse economics with beauty, but, as with its literary predecessors, it is a very male solution to what is here a female problem. Sabina has the economic capital and is pretending to herself most of all that she has the beauty and fertility of a young woman. The result is the grotesque figure that is the object of revulsion and derision. What occurs towards the end of the novel is that Sabina abandons that grotesque fusion and replaces it with the complementary alliance of youthful beauty and aged power found in fairy tales of young women and their fairy godmothers.

In order to effect this transition, Sabina has first to abandon her fantasist self-projection and acknowledge the reality, which she does with the aid of a looking glass:

> Sabina barred her door, and walked up to a looking-glass which with great complacency she had nailed up on her kitchen wall a few months before. She had spent many a half-hour arranging her hair and her ribbons and trying to believe at least a few of the flattering things that people said to her. Now her mood was changed, and she shook her clenched fist at the image she saw reflected in the glass.
>
> 'You fool', she said. 'You great she-ass; you disgusting old idiot. If you had ever had a grain o' sense in you you wouldn't have been listenin' to the rubbitch that was said to you, for nothin' in the world but to get han's on the bit o' money was left you!'[64]

She proceeds to dress appropriately as an elderly woman and, in another gesture to the fairy tale, plans to open a shop to sell apple cake to children. She also becomes Norah's fairy godmother by giving her half her fortune so that Norah can marry Joe and save the farm. Consonant with the less sentimental side of the fairy-tale genre, her motivation includes both pleasure at doing a good deed in settling her moral debt to Joe's family and delight in the discomfort all of this will cause to Judy and the gombeen man Rogan.

Norah of Waterford ends in an apparently triumphant fable of women's cooperation, but it is a cooperation that meets the demands of the still grim world of Irish rural economics. Earlier, in the more realistic part of the novel, Norah encounters little but opposition from other women, desperate to secure their own economic positions, in her attempts to win happiness with Joe. For all its exuberance then, *Norah of Waterford* shares the pessimistic prognosis of *The Return of Mary O'Murrough* concerning the position of women (and indeed of men) in rural Irish society. Each gestures towards the downward trajectory of what had once been Mulholland's progressive optimism concerning women and land in Ireland.

Notes

1 James H. Murphy, *Catholic Fiction and Social Reality in Ireland, 1873–1922* (Westport, Conn.: Greenwood, 1997), pp. 69–71; John Wilson Foster, *Irish Novels, 1890–1940: New Bearings in Culture and Fiction* (Oxford: Oxford University Press, 2008), pp. 177–8.
2 James H. Murphy, *Irish Novelists and the Victorian Age* (Oxford: Oxford University Press, 2011), pp. 245–6.
3 Rosa Mulholland (Lady Gilbert, Ruth Murray), *Dunmara*, 3 vols. (London: Smith, Elder, 1864), vol. III, p. 34.
4 Mulholland, *Dunmara*, vol. III, p. 35.
5 Mulholland, *Dunmara*, vol. III, pp. 37–8.
6 James H. Murphy, *Ireland: A Social, Cultural and Literary History, 1791–1891* (Dublin: Four Courts Press, 2003), pp. 124–33; Heidi Hansson and James H. Murphy, 'The Irish Land War and Its Fictions', in Heidi Hansson and James H. Murphy (eds), *Fictions of the Irish Land War* (Oxford: Peter Lang, 2014), pp. 1–18.
7 Murphy, *Catholic Fiction*, pp. 20–1, 44–7; Murphy, *Irish Novelists*, pp. 175–6, 178, 181–4.
8 Rosa Mulholland, *Marcella Grace: An Irish Novel*, ed. James H. Murphy (Washington, DC: Maunsel, 2001), p. 126.
9 Mulholland, *Marcella Grace*, p. 146.
10 Murphy, *Catholic Fiction*, pp. 31, 32, 35; Murphy, *Irish Novelists*, p. 160.
11 Murphy, *Catholic Fiction*, p. 41.
12 Murphy, *Catholic Fiction*, pp. 16, 54.
13 Heidi Hansson, 'From Reformer to Sufferer: The Returning Exile in Rosa Mulholland's Fiction', in Michael Böss, Irene Gilsenan Nordin, and Britta Olinder (eds), *Re-mapping Exile: Realities and Metaphors in Irish Literature and History* (Aarhus: Aarhus University Press, 2005), p. 100.
14 Rosa Mulholland, *The Return of Mary O'Murrough* (London: Sands, 1909), p. 114.
15 Mulholland, *The Return of Mary O'Murrough*, pp. 1–2.
16 Mulholland, *The Return of Mary O'Murrough*, p. 4.
17 Mulholland, *The Return of Mary O'Murrough*, p. 11.
18 Mulholland, *The Return of Mary O'Murrough*, pp. 29, 28.
19 Mulholland, *The Return of Mary O'Murrough*, p. 20.
20 Mulholland, *The Return of Mary O'Murrough*, p. 21.

21 Mulholland, *The Return of Mary O'Murrough*, p. 59.
22 Mulholland, *The Return of Mary O'Murrough*, p. 87.
23 Mulholland, *The Return of Mary O'Murrough*, p. 90.
24 Mulholland, *The Return of Mary O'Murrough*, p. 24.
25 Mulholland, *The Return of Mary O'Murrough*, p. 133.
26 Mulholland, *The Return of Mary O'Murrough*, pp. 41–2.
27 Mulholland, *The Return of Mary O'Murrough*, p. 45.
28 Mulholland, *The Return of Mary O'Murrough*, p. 127.
29 Mulholland, *The Return of Mary O'Murrough*, p. 132.
30 Mulholland, *The Return of Mary O'Murrough*, p. 157.
31 Mulholland, *The Return of Mary O'Murrough*, p. 158.
32 Mulholland, *The Return of Mary O'Murrough*, p. 136.
33 Mulholland, *The Return of Mary O'Murrough*, p. 161.
34 Mulholland, *The Return of Mary O'Murrough*, p. 158.
35 Mulholland, *The Return of Mary O'Murrough*, p. 191.
36 Mulholland, *The Return of Mary O'Murrough*, p. 214.
37 Mulholland, *The Return of Mary O'Murrough*, p. 220.
38 Mulholland, *The Return of Mary O'Murrough*, p. 225.
39 Mulholland, *The Return of Mary O'Murrough*, p. 227.
40 Mulholland, *The Return of Mary O'Murrough*, pp. 264–5.
41 Mulholland, *The Return of Mary O'Murrough*, p. 282.
42 Rosa Mulholland, *Norah of Waterford* (New York: P. J. Kenedy, 1915), p. 27.
43 Mulholland, *Norah of Waterford*, p. 7.
44 Mulholland, *Norah of Waterford*, p. 54.
45 Mulholland, *Norah of Waterford*, p. 18.
46 Mulholland, *Norah of Waterford*, p. 19.
47 Mulholland, *Norah of Waterford*, p. 38.
48 Mulholland, *Norah of Waterford*, p. 42.
49 Mulholland, *Norah of Waterford*, pp. 62–3.
50 Mulholland, *Norah of Waterford*, p. 65.
51 Mulholland, *Norah of Waterford*, p. 68.
52 Mulholland, *Norah of Waterford*, pp. 66–7.
53 Mulholland, *Norah of Waterford*, p. 69.
54 Mulholland, *Norah of Waterford*, p. 123.
55 Mulholland, *Norah of Waterford*, p. 127.
56 Mulholland, *Norah of Waterford*, p. 118.
57 Mulholland, *Norah of Waterford*, p. 135.
58 Mulholland, *Norah of Waterford*, p. 34.
59 Mulholland, *Norah of Waterford*, p. 145.
60 Mulholland, *Norah of Waterford*, p. 150.
61 Mulholland, *Norah of Waterford*, p. 153.
62 Mulholland, *Norah of Waterford*, p. 155.
63 Mulholland, *Norah of Waterford*, p. 191.
64 Mulholland, *Norah of Waterford*, p. 219.

3

Nature, education, and liberty in *The Book of Gilly* by Emily Lawless

Heidi Hansson

Representations of childhood in late Victorian and Edwardian writing often reproduce a Romantic philosophy where the child is understood as possessing a freedom of spirit and contact with the senses that has been lost to adults. This has repercussions on the spaces the child occupies as well as the activities described, with the child frequently depicted in natural surroundings that stimulate imagination and play. Such a notion of childhood characterises, for example, R. L. Stevenson's *A Child's Garden of Verses* (1885) where positioning the child in a literal and metaphorical garden suggests both a natural affinity between childhood and nature and an Edenic innocence.[1] It continues in a slightly different form in what has been termed the 'Nesbit tradition', a variety of children's literature inspired by the work of Edith Nesbit that typically takes place in the holidays, outdoors and without parental interference, with Arthur Ransome one of the most well-known adherents.[2] A range of other discourses and emotions contribute to the image of the child in the period, some of them with quite contradictory effects. Among these are nostalgia, educational debates, political developments, the increasingly destabilised gender contract, and larger cultural and literary trends such as New Woman writing, dandyism, *fin-de-siècle* aestheticism, embryonic modernism, and, in Ireland, the Celtic Revival and the Irish Literary Renaissance. Attitudes to children in the period 1880–1920, at the heart of what has been termed the 'Golden Age of Children's Literature', are consequently far from monolithic.[3] A particular source of ideological friction seems to be a perceived incompatibility between the idea of the child as fundamentally free and the role of education, understood as school or parental control, as restricting this natural liberty and potential. A common solution in children's literature is to set the story outside the real world, in the country, in a dreamland, or simply outdoors, where education can be removed to the distant future and located outside the boundaries of the tale. A more unusual approach is the one taken by Emily Lawless in her only children's novel, *The Book of Gilly: Four Months Out of a Life* (1906), where experiencing nature and formal education are identified as contrasts from the outset and their respective validity as routes to knowledge and self-definition interrogated.

In recent years, growing interest in children's conditions and experiences has led to the emergence of childhood studies as a distinctive field of research. In Ireland, this has manifested among other things in a special double issue of *Éire-Ireland* in 2009, with most of the contributions focusing on poor or mistreated children. This selective bias is typical also of literary representations, where advantaged children are not accorded much attention unless they are temporarily dispossessed or otherwise challenged. The child as metaphor has also received some interest, in the Irish context particularly as part of nationalist rhetoric, also predominantly representing images of poor children although the idea of the child as the country's future also exists.[4] *The Book of Gilly* was published in 1906, the same year as Nesbit's *The Railway Children*, and shares the idyllic conception of childhood, the absence of parents, and the predominantly open-air setting with this novel and other works in the Nesbit tradition. This is where the similarities end, however. Politically, Nesbit and Lawless were worlds apart, with Nesbit a member of the Fabian Society and Lawless considerably more conservative as a unionist and anti-suffragist. While Nesbit addressed a predominantly middle-class audience, Lawless wrote, if not for an aristocratic audience, at least about a privileged child. Nesbit's stories stimulate the imagination and are important precursors to present-day fantasy, whereas Lawless's work primarily engages the intellect. Although *The Book of Gilly* was marketed as a 'tale for young people', it speaks to an adult audience in at least equal measure.[5] The main character's upper-class status, together with the fact that the book is not easily categorised as a story for children, are probable reasons why the novel has not been the subject of critical attention, and it is perhaps significant that one of the few contemporary mentions of the book is primarily concerned with speculating on the possible real-life identity of the main character: 'It should not be difficult to identify the original of "Gilly".'[6]

Lawless's political conservatism means that it is easy to regard her literary output as equally unadventurous. She should certainly not be recovered as a New Woman writer or a budding modernist, and her works are infused with a residuary Victorianism in style, ideology, and subject matter that needs to be acknowledged. In her treatment of the interaction between humans and nature, Lawless, however, partly adheres to turn-of-the-century visions of a defunct social world reborn through an embracement of natural desires and feelings that chime with both *fin-de-siècle* aestheticism and modernist primitivism. An empirical approach based on temporary coincidence rather than political or artistic commitments destabilises the persistent identification between the metropolis and the literary avant-garde and makes it possible to detect that in this respect, *The Book of Gilly* is very much a product of its time. In more social terms, the novel has a great deal to offer as a contribution to Edwardian education debates inside and outside Ireland. The descriptions of the child characters illuminate the close relationship between education, class, and gender politics at the same time as the interaction between children suggests that hierarchies based on age and capability are equally important, which works to destabilise the class and gender contracts produced through schooling. The teacher characters in the novel embody contrasting educational philosophies, realised as the conflict between nature as an object of study and as a source of metaphysical knowledge. These rational and imaginative models expand to represent English and Irish systems of knowledge production, with the relative value of these approaches shifting throughout the text.

The Book of Gilly constitutes one of Lawless's most elaborate treatments of the relations between a stale social world and the healing potential of nature. When his father, the part-Irish Lord Dunkerron, accepts a government appointment in India, the eight-and-a-half-year-old Gilly – short for Lord Macgillicuddy – is sent to the island Inishbeg off the Kerry coast to 'get to care for the old places, and to do so while his little brain is still malleable'.[7] The conflict between nature and formal education is immediately introduced, with Lady Dunkerron asking whether Eton and the bogs are to be considered irreconcilable, and Gilly's father replying, 'More or less. Eton gives a set of its own to a boy's mind, as you very well know.'[8] Eton was the alma mater of Lawless's brother Valentine, later the fourth Lord Cloncurry, who attended between 1850 and 1858, and the choice of institution is offered unquestioningly, despite the hint of criticism in Dunkerron's comment. As the most prestigious and most obviously upper-class public school in Britain, Eton motions to Gilly's future place in society and is present as both implicit negative contrast and inevitable educational yardstick throughout the text.

An important educational movement in Ireland between 1887 and 1924 was the Fireside Club, engaging young people in pursuits intended to advance cultural nationalism. The club's ideas were diffused first through an addition to the *Freeman's Journal* called the *Irish Fireside*, then through a newspaper column, attached to the *Weekly Freeman*. The material was edited under the name 'Uncle Remus' by Rose Kavanagh, and after her death by Hester Sigerson.[9] In time, local branches of the club were formed. To promote an interest in the Irish language and the pre-colonial past as well as a love of nature were central aims, but the club also encouraged more general life skills such as self-sufficiency and self-respect in order to prepare the Firesiders for future leadership roles. The club members were stimulated to educate themselves, which can be seen partly as a resistance to English-based school systems, partly as an expression of faith in children's innate capacity. It is unlikely that Lawless would have supported the nationalistic outlook of the Fireside Club, but there are echoes of its de-Anglicising educational aims in Lord Dunkerron's criticism of narrow-minded understandings of knowledge: '"There are some two or three notions knocking about the universe besides those of Eton and – this place [London]."'[10] Lawless's depiction of Gilly as open to the teachings of nature and the knowledge to be gained through interpersonal encounters but resistant to that transmitted in schoolbooks is oddly in tune with the educational ideology of an organisation whose political objectives she would have rejected.

His father's purpose in sending Gilly to Ireland is then to allow him to develop a different mindset from that fostered in London, where 'everything we do here; everything we touch, and plan, and think about, down to our very dreams, is for the most part purely machine-made'.[11] Jaded city culture is set against the wonder and curiosity inspired by nature. The denunciation of metropolitan society in the novel is a logical continuation of Lawless's ecological thought, articulated in several journal articles focusing on how the advances of modernity endanger the natural landscape.[12] It is also evidence of an ambivalent attitude to contemporary celebrations of Celtic mythology and the Irish West – like those circulated through the Fireside Club, for example – that she embraced in terms of nature but whose social and political implications she rejected. In a letter to her cousin Horace Plunkett about the Irish theatre, she explains, 'I am not *anti-Gaelic* at all so long as it is only Gaelic *enthuse* and does not include politics.'[13] The contrast between enthusiasm for the Celtic past and its relevance for Irish politics in the present has its parallel in the perceived differences between the educational philosophies under scrutiny in the novel. Lord Dunkerron conveys the fundamental doubleness of Lawless's position when he argues for the necessity of liberating Gilly from the constrictions of the machine society, yet acknowledges that the

> machine exists; it's there, and has got to go on. It's all quite right and proper, and what this country requires. More-over, no one knows better than I do that it's just the want of that sort of stiffening which has been the ruin of Ireland; which has kept it for all these centuries in its own little backwater.[14]

England thus takes on the quality of mind-numbing but effective and necessary progress while Ireland becomes a pre-modern utopia, unable to govern itself but idealised as a source of mind-opening creativity and physical and spiritual renewal.

Gilly's sojourn in Ireland is framed as temporary even in the subtitle: *Four Months Out of a Life*. The story is bracketed by his departure from and return to England, which means that while Inishbeg is located outside reality and on the margins of modernity, it is not completely separated from the modern world. The fact that there is a tenuous attachment to the centre allows the island to be conceived as a space where metropolitan culture can be critiqued. The bog, in particular, functions as a symbolic opposite to London, with Gilly stating before his return to the city at the story's end: 'Some fellows do think a heap of London, I believe, but I don't. 'Tisn't like a bog, you know, not like a weal [real] out-and-out good bog.'[15] Besides condensing the nature–culture opposition that runs through the work, the bog is connected to childhood, the freedom of the outdoors, and, significantly, Ireland as a space of alternative possibilities.

The conflict between freedom and education in literature often takes the form of a temporary resistance to growing up that is eventually dissolved as the necessity to adapt is acknowledged. The primary example is J. M. Barrie's *Peter and Wendy* (1911), possibly known to Lawless in its stage version from 1904, where the children leave Neverland for the mundane but real world at the end. As Dieter Petzold notes, those children's classics from the late Victorian and Edwardian period that 'show the clearest wish to believe in the child's essential freedom also reveal an intriguing complexity which is due to their awareness of the dialectics of personal freedom and moral obligation'.[16] *The Book of Gilly* communicates the same problematic. As modernity's Other, the Kerry island becomes a dreamscape or Neverland that is temporarily accessible to the child but can only hold nostalgic value for the metropolitan adult. Ireland may be eminently compatible with the state of innocent childhood but lacks the potential entailed in the idea of growing up. The future prospect of responsibility and duty functions as a reminder that childhood will end, symbolised by a return to England and eventually Eton after the reprieve of the holidays. The demarcation of liberty in time and space serves as a recognition of the inevitable end of childhood and, with it, the pristine natural world. Apart from corresponding to the recurrent opposition between Romantic visions of the child as fundamentally free and education as constraining that freedom, this Arcadian loss connects to *fin-de-siècle* concerns with the passing of an old world order. What remains problematic is that the sense of dispossession relies on an awareness that the child will eventually become an adult and take its place in society, whereas the periphery is neither capable of nor desired to become part of the modern world but is stuck in a state of perpetual childhood.

Initially, the connection between childhood and nature is explored through the spatial hierarchies set up in the text. Inside the house, conventional adult–child relationships obtain, with the housekeeper Mrs Brown in charge. The same is true of social categories, with Gilly announced as the 'Earl of Shannagh' when he enters the living room of his mainland neighbour, Sir Maurice, but addressed as Gilly, 'small shaver', and 'Master Macgillicuddy' in the garden.[17] Interaction between children and between classes takes place in the open air, and, as Gilly's conversations with the Irish gardener Moriarty demonstrate, such communication is conducted on equal terms, with Moriarty accepting Gilly's arrival in the garden 'as the most natural thing in the world'.[18] Social hierarchies are dismantled outdoors, which makes it possible for Sir Maurice's undergardener to treat Gilly as a thief after finding him among the cucumber frames, but order is restored indoors with 'Master Gilly sitting, as a lord should, in a grand arm-chair'.[19] The house is subject to visual control with what goes on inside perfectly visible to the gardener's grandson Tim Moriarty from his vantage point up in a tree, but Tim invisible to Gilly looking out from the inside.[20] When Gilly's tutor Mr Griggs arrives at the island, one of his first acts is to reserve an unused bedroom as 'his own and his pupil's eating-room' and redefine 'the dining-room, henceforward to be known as the schoolroom'.[21] The one exception to these spatial regulations is the book room, which is positioned at the far end of the cottage, an extension to the original building that juts out over the ocean where the 'sea seemed to be not only below, but actually inside that room' and everything is tainted 'the colour of old moss when it has grown pale in the shade'.[22] As a place of learning and imagination, the library is a hybrid space between inside and outside, symbolising the power of art to transcend material limitations.

Except for the book room, the house is constructed as a place to escape from, and, as in most children's literature from the period, the outdoors is the place of adventure and freedom.[23] Inishbeg offers mind-expanding possibilities, and Gilly's first two days abound 'in incident, and in incident of a type calculated not a little to enlarge [his] previous stock of ideas' and streaking 'his horizon with more lights than months, perhaps years, in his Brook Street nursery would ever have set there'.[24] His solitary exploits underscore the inside–outside dichotomy as crucially connected to the freedom of the mind. The island is first introduced as an entirely natural world, inhabited by starfish, limpets, mussels, crabs, and prawns, and represented as primordial: 'It was like the beginning of the world over again! First zoophytes, then echinoderms, then shell-fish, then crustaceans.'[25] In this natural environment, the child is the ruler, with Inishbeg explicitly constructed as a colonial space, 'a playground which is [Gilly's] by right', 'his island', 'his *kingdom*'.[26] Roaming the island constitutes a process of 'general emancipation' explicitly contrasted with an outlook 'restricted to the four walls of a town house, varied by walks in the London parks'.[27] Outdoors there is 'liberty! Here was comparative independence; here, too, was something else – something which he had as yet hardly begun to take in – a new sense of ownership; of possession.'[28] The outdoors confers a measure of self-governance on the child, but one effect of the explicitly colonial rhetoric is to partially undermine the symbiotic bond between childhood and nature since the persistent focus on ownership prefigures a future relationship based on power and control. It would be too far-fetched to interpret the relation between the English boy and the Irish landscape as an unspoken support of the Union, but it is clear that any liberation is reserved for the human child, with Gilly's sense of freedom based on the illusion that the land is under his control. This sense of entitlement appears only in relation to the physical space, however, and there is no corresponding superiority in connection with Irish characters.

The country appears 'rather in the light of an agreeable variation of playground' also for adult visitors such as Gilly's mainland neighbour, Sir Maurice O'Sullivan.[29] All the English characters, in fact, have merely temporary relationships with Ireland. Inishbeg may be Gilly's birthright, but he is only there for a holiday visit. The housekeeper Mrs Brown and the nurse 'Hemma' both long to go back to what they consider civilised life in England, and, as house-bound and class-bound, they are the characters most alienated from Ireland and its sensual influences. Mr Griggs regards the Irish marine world as an object of study, but the results of his research are to be presented elsewhere, and for the convalescing Oxford student Phil Acton, Ireland is 'Dr. Kerry', a 'health resort'.[30] For characters willing to let go of their preconceptions – as the servants and the tutor are not – the landscape is nevertheless capable of inspiring love. This is its effect on Acton in particular:

> Without a drop of Irish, far less of Celtic, blood – to his own knowledge – in his veins, the taste, sentiment, fascination – call it what we will – of this South-Irish landscape had come to mean to him what as a rule only one landscape, and that a native one, comes to mean to a man in the course of his lifetime. It had stolen into his breast; had nestled, or had seemed to him to nestle into his very bones. It affected him with a sort of topsy-turvy home-sickness; he felt as if he had been waiting for it all his life, and that it had come home to him at last.[31]

South Kerry affects the senses and causes physical sensations, but its power cannot be integrated in a rational paradigm. It follows, then, that its benefits are experiential, emotional, and at least to some extent irrational, qualities also ascribed to the child and the artist. Again, there is an accord between the idea of the child and the idea of Ireland that is immensely attractive but whose downside is that it does not include the possibility of development and growth. Formal education, at Oxford in Acton's case and initially at Eton for Gilly, is where preparation for adulthood and responsibility takes place.

Whereas the rather thin plot of the novel is organised chronologically, the thematic level operates on a binary structure. The conflict between childhood liberty and educational restraint is mainly addressed through the contrasting characters of Griggs and Phil Acton and the divergent understandings of knowledge they embody. Throughout the text, metaphysics and emotion are contrasted with positivist science and empirical inquiry, denounced by Acton as inhibiting in their detached approaches to knowledge: 'Rotten materialism! Rotten conceit! Rotten anything that could make a man suppose all earth, and sea, and sky were able to be summed up, packed away and settled by a handful of trumpery formula.'[32] Acton represents spirituality and sensitivity in the novel and functions as the main example of how moral and physical health is bound up with the natural environment. He has come to south Kerry to recuperate after an accident that prevents him from taking part in physically demanding activities and is implicitly compared with his burly cousin Sir Maurice, whose primary interests are golf and fishing, as well as with the sturdy Griggs. In contrast to these characters, Acton has 'a thin whitish face, almost like a girl's face' and is feminised through his friendship with a child.[33] He is a belated aesthete, 'a born beauty-lover' with a profound faith in humanist forms of knowledge:[34]

> That elf or puck which hovers over beauty, which points towards mystery – which is quite capable of discovering the former even where it is practically invisible – was never far from his elbow ... To cheat life – if by any means such cheating could be accomplished – of some of its prose was with him the first, the most spontaneous of instincts.[35]

Together with his physical shortcomings, Acton's artistic-aesthetic leanings suggest an uncertain sexuality that can be connected to the gender games of the late nineteenth century. His character thus provides some foundation for relating *The Book of Gilly* to both *fin-de-siècle* cultural positions and the gender anxieties they fuelled. In this light, his advocacy of alternative ways of knowing becomes an example of the revolts against old dogma, and his insistence on the spiritual dimensions of knowledge and the importance of the inner life connects to late nineteenth-century concerns with psychology and psychoanalysis. Representations of children, although rarely included in investigations of *fin-de-siècle* literature, fit the patterns of literary aestheticism surprisingly well. Discussing children's classics by writers such as Richard Jefferies, Kenneth Grahame, and J. M. Barrie, Dieter Petzold pinpoints some striking parallels:

> the child as presented by these authors can be seen as a metaphor for the artist: he, too, likes to see himself as an outsider in bourgeois society; exempt from moral obligations (at least according to the aestheticists' credo); looking with a wondering but dispassionate eye, if not with downright contempt, at the quotidian doings of businessmen and shopkeepers; creating worlds of make-believe which seem more real, or at least more beautiful and exciting, than reality.[36]

Through their 'quaint ... alliance' and their belief in the value of the alternative knowledge produced by experiencing the natural world, Gilly and Phil Acton emerge as manifestations of aesthetic ideals that Lawless would probably not have consciously advocated, but that she was nevertheless responsive to.[37] At the same time, she recognises the limitations of a humanist educational ideal by continuously pitting it against empirical observation and ultimately Eton as Gilly's future school.

A significant subgenre of children's literature is the school story, usually set at an elite public school, charting the exploits over a term or a year of a group of children or young adults. The prime example is Thomas Hughes's Rugby novel *Tom Brown's School Days* (1857), where several of the genre characteristics are laid down, such as camaraderie, bullying endured and defeated, excelling in sports, and the importance of gentlemanly behaviour. The purpose of education is represented as identity formation and socialisation, especially in terms of class and gender as in the school depicted in Kipling's *Stalky & Co* (1899) where future colonial administrators are fostered. Book learning is a minor theme, but a recurrent topic is children's resistance to the repressive effects of teaching, in Kipling's novel realised as anarchic rule-breaking, including and transformed into a cheerful acceptance of the inevitable punishment that restores the hierarchical relationship between teacher and pupil. The earliest Irish schoolboy novels – the schoolgirl variety is rare if it exists at all in the early period of the genre – appeared in the late 1890s and are modelled on their British counterparts, although later examples reveal a more Irish cultural heritage with Cúchulainn the explicit or implicit model for schoolboy behaviour.[38] While not a schoolboy novel, *The Book of Gilly* exemplifies the transitions of the genre by straddling the English and Irish types through its acknowledgement of both the educational needs of the imperial project and the importance of an Irish cultural influence.

The debates between Phil Acton and Mr Griggs condense the epistemological enquiry in the novel, i.e. the subtheme of what constitutes knowledge and by what means knowledge is produced. Acton's voice is privileged and Griggs generally emerges as insensitive and unsympathetic. The issue of class is introduced as a significant factor, with Acton studying at Oxford and Griggs a product of Leeds and Melchisedec College, Indianapolis.[39] The hierarchy between these seats of learning supports Acton's position, but the outcome is not entirely clear, not least since Eton as a kind of feeding institution for Oxford and Cambridge is singled out from the start as restricting the mental scope of its pupils. The web of connections between childhood, liberty, nature, imagination, and Ireland on the one hand and adulthood, responsibility, city life, objectivity, and England on the other further complicates the picture. The initial dichotomy between 'the machine society' and the natural world runs through the work, but so does the idea that although humanism is the more attractive choice, it is not practical in the long term. The literary precursors of Griggs and Acton are 'the Sancho Panzas, with a sound grip on reality but no ideals, and the Don Quixotes, with the instinct of ideals, but without any decent hold on reality'.[40] As far as biographical criticism can be applied, it could be claimed that both men correspond to sides of Lawless herself, as the author of emotion-infused poetry and fiction as well as an ardent observer of moths, marine life, and plants.[41] The characterisation of Griggs and Acton as well as the philosophical drift of the text is much affected by the fact that neither of the knowledge systems represented is the incontestable winner.

Griggs is described as an 'Avatar of the modern world, an embodiment of the scientific spirit, newly alighted upon one of the waste places of a darkened and unregenerate Past'.[42] He regards Ireland as a backwater with no energy or drive towards progress, aligned with Lord Dunkerron's understanding that entering the machine society is necessary to ensure Ireland's place in the modern world, but without his love for its sensual appeal:

> When I see a place without the most elementary sign or appearance of life; with no stir or go of any kind; no fresh blood; no i-deas; no trade or resources – 'cept a few wretched pigs perhaps and bullocks – no push, no enterprise, and what's more, no desire for any of these things, then if the word 'rotten' doesn't suit that place, all I can say is I'm very imperfectly acquainted with the resources of the English language.[43]

Griggs's only reason for accepting the position as Gilly's tutor is that it will give him time to pursue his research into a species of diving beetles, and he conceives knowledge as a competition: 'The way those Germans cut us out at every point is sickening, sir – simply, I tell you, sickening.'[44] Griggs's method is painstaking observation, note-taking, and description, but his understanding of knowledge does not include theoretical development or radical reorientation, nor is he concerned with investigating what cannot be seen: 'his standpoint was essentially that of the scientific positivism of some forty or fifty years ago. Physiology for him covered the whole ground.

Psychology was not.'[45] His positivist outlook translates into a teaching method based on stuffing Gilly's head with as much knowledge as it can hold with the help of 'perfectly well-meant shovings, rappings, and snubbings' that have the unwanted and for Griggs unexpected effects of causing 'his pupil's mental petals to shut up as tightly as those of a May flower under an unlooked-for snap of cold'.[46] Being taught by Griggs primarily manages to crush Gilly's self-confidence: 'That Mr. Griggs really considered him to be a semi-idiot – too stupid to understand the simplest things he felt convinced, and writhed humiliatingly under the conviction.'[47] The learning process, as Griggs understands it, is a 'prickly and pebbly path' that it is not the teacher's task to make smoother, and he admits no difference between pupils:[48]

> A boy, let me tell you, sir, is a boy in exactly the same sense in which a cat is a cat, or a bull is a bull. And if it hadn't been that it was part of the bargain – the marquis, y' understand, barring corporal punishment – I'd have made that sweet, pretty pet of yours hop handsomely time and again! That's what he wants, and every boy wants, 'specially a dreamy-witted little beggar like that, with his head so high in the air that half the time he doesn't know whether it's a grammar or the multiplication table that has been put into his fingers![49]

Acton, in contrast, believes in individual differences. His model of teaching is Socratic and based on dialogue and intellectual exchange, and, in a heated argument with Griggs, he attacks the soul-destroying effects of undifferentiated approaches to teaching:

> You have had the luck to get hold of a rather exceptional little bit of human organism, and you promptly set to work with all your might and main to force it into the same iron-ribbed groove that has already had the spoiling of thousands; to make it, in other words, assimilate precisely the same number of pounds of solid pabulum [sic] that you would supply to every tough-stomached, bullet-headed young Briton, and then you wonder that the result is not satisfactory![50]

Unlike Kipling's schoolboys or the characters that populate the schoolboy stories, Gilly never accepts his tutor's authority with anything resembling trust or deference. Through her descriptions of how he pours his '[q]uestions, ideas, wishes, dreams, fancies, projects, ambitions' into Phil Acton's ears, together with the accounts of Gilly's exploration of the island, Lawless presents education as primarily a function of interaction, with a person or with nature.[51] The strongest and most explicit support in the text is then for Acton's view, but, despite Griggs's generally unsympathetic character and behaviour, there is occasional support for his position too, both through his overall association with the 'machine society' that is necessary for progress and in the way his teaching methods contribute to socialisation in terms of gender:

> How Gilly would have fared had he been left, say for a year or two, under the sole charge of a Mr. Griggs it is not easy to predict. That he needed a certain amount of hardening, by way of alternative to the atmosphere of petting which otherwise surrounded him, may be taken as undeniable.[52]

In the end, Griggs's robust masculinity is at least partly figured as a prerequisite for adult life and England, whereas Acton's feminised aestheticism becomes a manifestation of Ireland, valued for its potential to stimulate the mind, to preserve the curiosity of childhood, and as an expression of liberty but ultimately insufficient as a preparation for modern life.

When it comes to gender roles, there is consequently some discrepancy between what is actually stated in the text and what the work conveys. In the *Times Literary Supplement* review of the book, Lawless's characterisation of Gilly is praised as 'real' precisely because he is a less than exemplary model of heroic boyhood:

> Miss Lawless does not so arrange his surroundings that in every chapter he shall be shown up against them, a hero and a paragon. He cries; he even kicks his nurse (and the reader wishes he could kick too); he is rather frightened the first time he is put on a horse; and when a drunken old Irishman throws stones at him, he does not quell his assailant with a glance nor stand his ground with all the courage of his Crusader ancestors; he slips out of range into safety.[53]

The unarticulated contrasts in the review suggest that what the *TLS* reviewer describes as 'a little babyish' also entails a failure to live up to the expected gender norms.[54] A certain degree of heroism seems to be a required attribute of manliness, in the novel as well as in the review. To this end, assuming a protective role in relation to women (or girls) is represented as a necessary part of male adulthood, so that when Gilly comforts his little sister when she has nightmares, this act is figured as his first 'step forward along the road towards manhood'.[55] Despite his shortcomings as a teacher, Griggs is one of the characters in the story incarnating the conventional masculinity that it is implied Gilly must eventually attain, which partially redeems his teaching methods. The housekeeper Mrs Brown makes clear that it is exactly the kind of criticism and punishment later practised by Griggs that is required for Gilly to become a man:

> And as for me forgetting the difference between a little gentleman an' a little lady, or as for me not remembering that boys will be boys, why it's not a thing I've ever done in my life, never! Hoften an' hoften I've said, when they've been making a fuss over some little haccident or another 'Don't you go for to be a cry-baby', I've said, 'for I won't put up with it, not if it's ever so! You ain't a-going to be a little lady, sitting all day with your 'ands in your lap, an' never having to take a cross word, no, nor a blow neither! How will you ever learn to be a hofficer in the harmy if you're a-going to make a fuss like that over every little 'urt!'[56]

The idea of character-building through toughening is embedded in the public-school culture looming at the end of Gilly's summer reprieve. Apart from the more or less sanctioned bullying practices common at boarding schools, athletic sports was one of the activities serving this purpose. At Eton, Valentine Lawless was one of the pupils instrumental in setting up the 'Eton Beagles' towards the end of the 1850s as a distinctly upper-class sporting choice.[57] Hunting was understood as the continuation of a chivalric ideal and a remedy for degenerate tendencies and eminently preferable to any kind of scholarly activity. In this environment, 'all but the most practical forms of intelligence were considered effeminate'.[58] Adding Etonian sporting ideals to the mix of the valorised humanist attitude to life embodied in Phil Acton and scrupulous empirical investigation coupled with cramming embodied in Griggs radically complicates the issues of both educational philosophy and gender formation in *The Book of Gilly*. In this context, Acton's feminine-coded ideals emerge as unsustainable.

Evading the demands of the gender contract is thus only temporarily possible for boys, and largely regarded as a function of childhood. Gender-bending is, however, slightly more possible for girls. The primary example in the text is Babs Kennedy, the daughter of a land agent who has fallen on hard times. Babs is 'mistress of the house and its ruler' and in charge of the family's money.[59] Together with Acton, she represents gender instability in the novel, if not as a typical example of a New Woman, so at least by sharing some of her characteristics, such as freely speaking her mind, dressing in unrestrictive clothes, and engaging in physical activities. Babs's figure is 'straight, still rather boyish', and she is physically superior to Gilly and her brothers, described as 'the man of the party, if energy and self-assertion are the tests of manhood. She could ride, run, fish, sail a boat, and swim, moreover, against any one of them; do everything, in short, in the way of masculine accomplishment except shoot.'[60] Unlike the New Woman, Babs is not interested in pursuing learning, however, but takes a practical view that makes her reject formal education as a waste of time:

> Her education, she said, was her own affair, and she intended to learn useful things and not useless ones. Considering that the useless ones in question included nearly every branch of ordinary information, and quite every ladylike accomplishment, it will be seen that Babs had at least the courage of her opinions.[61]

Given that the novel's main character is a boy, women's education is obviously not a central concern, and there is no alternative understanding of its main purpose than to produce a 'lady'. In the case of Babs Kennedy, this process would give her the polish of what she dismisses as 'useless' information but rob her of the outdoor pursuits that liberate her from a restricting gender role. The dichotomy between useless and useful knowledge parallels the Acton–Griggs controversy in the text, this time privileging Griggs's position and implicitly supporting the view voiced by Lord Dunkerron in the opening pages that Ireland needs to enter the 'machine society' to be able to cope with the demands of modernity. Rejecting formal education, at the same time, is a prerequisite for the momentary power and autonomy Babs enjoys. Her freedom is connected to the outdoors, however, and her life is confined to Kerry.

The portrait of the main character in *The Book of Gilly* builds on the Romantic idea of an instinctive affinity between the child and the natural world. Regulated education, in the form of positivist science or boarding-school codes of conduct disrupt this symbiosis, with loss of liberty and a certain closing of the mind as its negative results. Humanist lore, on the other hand, can acknowledge both the virtue of a childish openness to new experiences and unfiltered encounters with nature as valid routes to knowledge. A corresponding critique of modernity and progress can be found in much children's literature from the late Victorian and Edwardian period, as well as in varieties of *fin-de-siècle* writing and early modernism. What is distinct about Lawless's novel is the struggle between this affirmation of childhood, nature, and Ireland and a reluctant acknowledgement that, in the end, the mindset this produces is not sufficient for the demands of the modern world. Although Irish politics only obliquely enter the work, this conclusion seems more informed by unionist political considerations than either educational philosophy or aesthetic movements.

Notes

1 Jean Webb, 'Conceptualising Childhood: Robert Louis Stevenson's *A Child's Garden of Verses*', *Cambridge Journal of Education*, 32:3 (2002), 359–65, at p. 360.

2 Marcus Crouch, *The Nesbit Tradition: The Children's Novel, 1945–1970* (London: Ernest Benn, 1972), pp. 15–17, 142.

3 Dieter Petzold, 'A Race Apart: Children in Late Victorian and Edwardian Children's Books', *Children's Literature Association Quarterly*, 17:3 (1992), 33–6, at p. 33.

4 For a discussion of child imagery in journalism, see Margot Gayle Backus, '"The Children of the Nation?" Representations of Poor Children in Mainstream Nationalist Journalism, 1882 and 1913', *Éire-Ireland*, 44:1–2 (2009), 118–46.

5 'Books for Boys and Girls', *Manchester Courier and Lancashire General Advertiser* (7 December 1906), p. 9.

6 'Library Gossip', *Western Times* (20 November 1906), p. 7.

7 Emily Lawless, *The Book of Gilly: Four Months Out of a Life* (London: Smith, Elder, 1906), p. 9.

8 Lawless, *The Book of Gilly*, p. 3.

9 Ríona Nic Congáil, '"Fiction, Amusement, Instruction": The Irish Fireside Club and the Educational Ideology of the Gaelic League', *Éire-Ireland*, 44:1–2 (2009), 92–3; Matthew Russell, 'Irish Writers of the Nineteenth Century', *Irish Monthly*, 27:314 (1899), 423–6, at p. 423.

10 Lawless, *The Book of Gilly*, p. 4.
11 Lawless, *The Book of Gilly*, p. 6.
12 Emily Lawless, 'Iar-Connaught: A Sketch', *Cornhill Magazine*, 45:267 (1882), 319–33; Emily Lawless, 'In the Kingdom of Kerry', *Gentleman's Magazine*, 252:1817 (1882), 540–53; Emily Lawless, 'Notes in the Morbihan', *National Review*, 4:22 (1884), 492–503.
13 Edith Sichel, 'Emily Lawless', *Nineteenth Century and After: A Monthly Review*, 76:449 (July 1914), 80–100, at p. 87.
14 Lawless, *The Book of Gilly*, p. 7.
15 Lawless, *The Book of Gilly*, p. 283.
16 Petzold, 'A Race Apart', p. 33.
17 Lawless, *The Book of Gilly*, pp. 100, 37.
18 Lawless, *The Book of Gilly*, pp. 55–6.
19 Lawless, *The Book of Gilly*, pp. 95, 104.
20 Lawless, *The Book of Gilly*, p. 105.
21 Lawless, *The Book of Gilly*, pp. 152, 153.
22 Lawless, *The Book of Gilly*, p. 71.
23 Lawless, *The Book of Gilly*, p. 18.
24 Lawless, *The Book of Gilly*, p. 16.
25 Lawless, *The Book of Gilly*, p. 15.
26 Lawless, *The Book of Gilly*, pp. 8, 12, 67. Italics in original.
27 Lawless, *The Book of Gilly*, p. 90.
28 Lawless, *The Book of Gilly*, pp. 62–3.
29 Lawless, *The Book of Gilly*, p. 46.
30 Lawless, *The Book of Gilly*, pp. 283, 206.
31 Lawless, *The Book of Gilly*, p. 179.
32 Lawless, *The Book of Gilly*, pp. 253–4.
33 Lawless, *The Book of Gilly*, p. 34.
34 Lawless, *The Book of Gilly*, p. 112.
35 Lawless, *The Book of Gilly*, pp. 180–1.
36 Petzold, 'A Race Apart', p. 35.
37 Lawless, *The Book of Gilly*, p. 112.
38 Ciaran O'Neill, 'The Irish Schoolboy Novel', *Éire-Ireland*, 44:1–2 (2009), 147–68, at pp. 148–9.
39 Lawless, *The Book of Gilly*, p. 162.
40 Lawless, *The Book of Gilly*, p. 181.
41 Articles illustrating Lawless's passion for naturalist study are, for example, Emily Lawless, 'An Addition to Mr. Birchall's List of "The Lepidoptera of Ireland"', *Entomologist's Monthly Magazine* (3 January 1867), 187; Emily Lawless, 'A Dredging Ground', *Nineteenth Century: A Monthly Review*, 10:53 (1881), 131–41.
42 Lawless, *The Book of Gilly*, p. 169.
43 Lawless, *The Book of Gilly*, p. 247.
44 Lawless, *The Book of Gilly*, p. 158.
45 Lawless, *The Book of Gilly*, p. 180.
46 Lawless, *The Book of Gilly*, pp. 161, 185.
47 Lawless, *The Book of Gilly*, p. 172.
48 Lawless, *The Book of Gilly*, p. 243.
49 Lawless, *The Book of Gilly*, p. 244.
50 Lawless, *The Book of Gilly*, pp. 243–4.
51 Lawless, *The Book of Gilly*, p. 184.
52 Lawless, *The Book of Gilly*, p. 185.
53 'Two Little Peers', *Times Literary Supplement* (14 December 1906), p. 417.
54 'Two Little Peers', p. 417.
55 Lawless, *The Book of Gilly*, p. 133.
56 Lawless, *The Book of Gilly*, pp. 75–6.

57 A. C. Crossley, *The Eton College Hunt: A Short History of Beagling at Eton* (Eton: Spottiswoode, Ballantyne, 1922), pp. 1–5; J. A. Mangan and C. McKenzie, 'Privileged Education, Hunting and the Making of Martial Masculinity', *International Journal of the History of Sport*, 25:9 (2008), 1106–31, at p. 1115.
58 Mangan and McKenzie, 'Privileged Education', p. 1117.
59 Lawless, *The Book of Gilly*, p. 224.
60 Lawless, *The Book of Gilly*, pp. 226, 225.
61 Lawless, *The Book of Gilly*, p. 224.

4

Girls with 'go': female homosociality in L. T. Meade's schoolgirl novels

Whitney Standlee

THE juvenile fiction written by the Irish novelist L. T. Meade (Elizabeth Thomasina Meade Toulmin Smith, 1844–1914) was extensive and diverse in both substance and reach. Sales records for her novels, a number of which continued to be reissued decades after their initial publication and which sold in the tens of thousands, confirm that her work appealed across temporal, geographical, religious, and even gendered boundaries.[1] Evidence of her widespread popularity occasionally comes from unexpected quarters, including the segments of Vladimir Nabokov's memoir *Speak, Memory* (1946) which deal with his aristocratic upbringing. In the fourth chapter of his book, Nabokov recalls that although his childhood was passed exclusively in his native Russia, the influence of English culture was everywhere apparent. His family, he suggests, had a 'traditional leaning toward the comfortable products of Anglo-Saxon civilization', including 'Pears soap', 'Golden Syrup', and 'fruitcakes, smelling salts, playing cards, picture puzzles, striped blazers, [and] talcum-white tennis balls'.[2] Admitting that he learned to read English even before Russian, he remembers with affection the various tales from England that his mother read aloud to him at bedtime, some of them by Dickens, others about knights and damsels in distress. Only two of these, however, does he recall in any detail: Florence Montgomery's 1869 work *Misunderstood* and *Beyond the Blue Mountains*, a novel by L. T. Meade which was first published in 1893. Although he describes the latter work as 'shamelessly allegorical', Nabokov writes of it with undisguised enthusiasm, referring to Meade's central characters by name and asserting that it 'contained enough exciting details to make one forget its message'.[3]

That Nabokov remembers with such fondness a writer whose personal circumstances were vastly dissimilar to his own and whose readership consisted largely of English schoolgirls is not, however, altogether surprising. During her long career, which spanned the period from the publication of her first novel in 1866 until her death nearly fifty years later, Meade's publishing success was extraordinary. She began writing novels while still living at home with her parents in rural Co. Cork. In 1875, she followed her career to London, having heard what she referred to as the 'murmurs and whispers' of the movement for the emancipation of women even from those 'remote shores of the Atlantic-bound coast of Ireland' in which she was raised.[4] A little over a decade later, she had already forged a substantial network of working relationships which act as testament to her professional prominence. Perhaps most notable in this regard is her tenure at *Atalanta*, the magazine she edited from 1887 to 1892. Aimed at girls in their pre-teen and teenage years, *Atalanta* remains remarkable in part for evidencing Meade's ability to attract high-profile contributors including H. Rider Haggard, Frances Hodgson Burnett, Christina Rossetti, and Grant Allen.[5] In exercising her editorial influence, she did not neglect to also and consistently promote and mentor her fellow Irish authors and artists: the work of Edward Dowden, M. E. Francis, Elinor Sweetman, John Butler Yeats, and Katharine Tynan all featured in *Atalanta*'s pages.[6] Her knowledge of the publishing industry was such that, in the late 1880s, it was to Meade that W. B. Yeats turned when seeking out advice about issuing his first volume of poetry. Yeats remarked in a letter to Katharine Tynan that he had spoken to Meade concerning her own experiences of publishing a novel by the method he was contemplating (subscription) and had been reassured by what he learned from her: 'Mrs. Mead[e] of *Atalanta* once did much the same, she says, which comforts me.'[7]

She was best known in her lifetime for her schoolgirl novels, and it is in this subgenre that her literary legacy is most readily evidenced. Hints of either her direct or oblique influence on the generation of female authors who followed her into the arena of writing stories about and for school-aged girls can be traced in the work of authors ranging from the noted schoolgirl novelist Angela Brazil, who, while still in school herself, was awarded the mark of 'highly commended' on an essay she submitted to *Atalanta* magazine's 'Reading Union', to L. M. Montgomery, whose characterisation of a wilful but kind-hearted protagonist in her *Anne of Green Gables* series of novels (1908–39) owes at least some of its debt to Meade's own Annie Forest, the heroine of the first novel she set in a school, *A World of Girls* (1886).[8]

The author of more than 280 works of fiction, Meade wrote primarily for an emerging independent readership of newly educated (or about to be educated) girls who were for the first time choosing books for themselves rather than having books prescribed to them by adults for their moral edification. Polls of schoolgirls' reading preferences confirmed her status as the most popular living novelist among young female readers at the turn of the twentieth century. She came first in a survey conducted by *Girl's Realm* magazine in 1899 to find their readers' favourite author, and, in a poll of high-school girls conducted by the suffragist Alice Zimmern in 1901, Meade was the sole living writer to be ranked in the top five.[9] Adult commentators, however, were often less than enthusiastic about her literary output. In 1906, the *Saturday Review*, while acknowledging that Meade was then 'The Queen of Girls' Book Makers', was moved to speculate on the reasons for her popularity and launched a scathing attack not only on the subject matter and literary merit of her work but also on her own morality:

> How is Mrs. Meade possible? Here is a person who year after year plants her stories on the public with as much regularity and in about the same bulk as an army contractor supplying shoddy shoes to the Government ... The explanation apparently is this. Parents do not care what books they buy; girls do not care what they read; so Mrs. Meade is able to slip in between, and need not care what she writes. Very evidently she does not care.[10]

After going on to assert that 'it would be too much to expect us often to undergo the torture of dwelling on Mrs. Meade's work', the *Saturday Review* proceeded to discuss four of her recently issued novels, taking her to task for producing what it incorrectly assumed were texts for girls that explored adult themes and which, they suggested, were marked by an 'insinuation of more terrible things' than those to which she overtly referred.[11] The article spawned a series of letters from a number of Meade's supporters and a rebuttal from the author herself, but the magazine remained decisively vitriolic towards her and her work. By 1929, just fifteen years after her death, her literary reputation had declined so steeply that all of her texts were placed on a list of books 'Not to Be Circulated' by libraries because they lacked literary or moral merit.[12]

It is in its capacity to act as a counterpart to and reflection of the development of female identities in the decades that bookended the turn of the twentieth century that Meade's schoolgirl fiction has been studied by academics since the 1980s. Her body of work initially came under intense scrutiny from scholars, particularly those feminist critics in the vanguard of researchers into girls' and women's popular fiction, for what was viewed as its lack of alternative or radical depictions of female autonomy: Mary Cadogan and Patricia Craig suggested in 1986, for instance, that Meade's 'progressiveness' was limited to depictions of girl characters who host clandestine cocoa parties in their bedrooms, and in 1991, Kimberley Reynolds branded Meade's work anti-feminist.[13] Sally Mitchell was among the earliest researchers to begin the process of rehabilitating Meade's reputation when, in 1989, she used the example of her work as the 'first step in discussing the creation of girlhood' as a separate and distinct form of childhood than that experienced by males – one that 'had its own interests, values, ... language, customs, and literature'.[14] More recently, Helen Bittel has argued that the ability to read 'against the grain' of Meade's often incongruous outcomes was the modality for rebellion in her girl readers.[15] Bittel suggests that, rather than being written for an inert and uncritical female readership, Meade's novels include sudden and jarring changes of literary tack as a means of targeting and engaging the active and discerning girl reader. This type of reader, she suggests, would have interpreted as unlikely and unfair the events by which girl characters in these stories are returned or coerced into normative feminine roles and thus would have viewed these outcomes as troubling and undesirable. At the same time, such endings served to reassure parents that her novels promoted 'wholesome' values. In doing so, Meade's works, with some complexity, both appealed to the radical sensibilities of the nascent 'new girl' reader and appeased her parents. Academic studies have since continued the process of revaluing her work in a supplementary vein by focusing either or both on its relationship to the New Woman movement of the 1890s and in a specifically Irish political and feminist context.[16]

Alongside this growing body of research into her work has emerged an ever-expanding network of histories of women's education and women's literary careers that aid in contextualising her contribution to the development of a literary tradition written not only by but specifically *for* females. Some comprehension of what Sarah Wadsworth refers to as 'the segmentation of the juvenile fiction market by gender', for instance, is important to gaining a fuller understanding of Meade's literary innovations and their import.[17] Wadsworth acknowledges that boys were identified as a distinct category of readers well before girls because it was assumed that, while the market for boys' books was inclusive of girls, the opposite was not the case. In other words, girls might read and enjoy boys' books, but boys would not do the same with books intended for girls.[18] The success of Louisa May Alcott's *Little Women* (1868–69), a novel that focused its attention primarily on the close bonds forged among four sisters and whose central female character transforms from tomboyish adolescent girl to successful working woman over the course of the narrative, signalled that the market for a new type of aspirational adolescent literary heroine existed.

Meade acknowledged that her own works were written in contravention of the stern moralising of books such as Mary Martha Sherwood's *The History of the Fairchild Family* (1818) that she had known as a child and instead to and for the type of girl she had longed to be:

> The culture of the mind, as far as girls were concerned, was not thought highly of in my youthful days. I had a passionate love for story-books, but was not allowed to read any, except a book full of horrors, called, 'The Fairchild Family'. This book being calculated to strike awe into the breast of any unfortunate child who perused it, was considered salutary and therefore allowable. I recall, even now, with a certain thrill, some of its scenes. A girl disobeyed her parents – punishment came swift and in an awful guise – she was burnt to death. Another little girl greedily devoured some plum jam – she had a fever in consequence, which nearly cost her her life.[19]

Her works were not, however, devoid of their own moralising: her career began in earnest with the publication of several distinctly didactic social-problem novels. Always a meticulous delineator of reading trends, she had in the mid 1870s used the highly popular (and highly sensationalist) work of the journalist James Greenwood as the basis for her first mature work, *Lettie's Last Home* (1875), a novel concerned with baby farmers in East London, and went on to tackle the problems of lack of access to health care by the London poor in *Great St. Benedict's* (1876), and the plight of London's street children in her first large-scale commercial success, *Scamp and I* (1877). It is therefore no coincidence that her first schoolgirl novel appeared in the same year that Edward G. Salmon, writing in the popular periodical *Nineteenth Century*, called for more appealing girls' novels which had a similar energy (or 'Go', as Salmon described it) to boys' books. Seeming to channel an embryonic feminism that would eventually emerge in its fullest form as the 1890s New Woman, Salmon asserted that girls' books needed to 'conform to the electric influences of the times'.[20] Perhaps Meade heeded Salmon's call, or perhaps she came to the same conclusions at the same time he did because such was the *Zeitgeist*. Whatever the reasons, *A World of Girls* is undeniably a novel about schoolgirls with 'Go' – who sleep in hedgerows, have midnight picnics in violation of school rules, and rescue younger children kidnapped by Gypsies.

Meade's own discussion in an article in the *Academy* in 1903 set out her theories that stories that appeal to girls must be distinct from, but equally adventurous to, those for boys:

> It is a common saying that girls like boys' books best. Now, I do not agree with that statement. I think the girl honestly enjoys her own book, written for herself. She wants plot, plenty of it, peril, a keen sense of danger, real tangles in the life of her heroine and adventure and movement to any extent.[21]

Concurrently, she identified the 'great enthusiasm' of her girl readers as 'their longing for girlish friendship' and her mission on their behalf as a project 'to fight with them and for them to the end of the world'.[22] She thus positioned herself as an advocate for a community of adolescent females who she recognised as separate in their tastes from, but equal in their craving for intrasexual bonds and communities to, their male counterparts.

In her working and personal life, Meade enacted her advocacy for such bonds in the relationships she forged with fellow females. She was among the members and served on the managing committee of the Pioneer Club, an all-female pro-suffrage organisation initiated 'with a view to furthering all movements to the advancement and enlightenment of women'.[23] Her acquaintances and friends included the Pioneer's controversial founder Emily Massingberd, who described the club six months after its founding in 1892 as a democratic, mutually supportive female community:

> Here we have no social distinctions, we all meet together on the common ground of sisterhood ... We are of all creeds and politics, of different professions and of no professions, although most of us 'do' something, but united together in the desire to promote the advancement of women's interests.[24]

In the wake of Massingberd's untimely death in 1897, Meade penned a novel, *The Cleverest Woman in England* (1898), whose central character, Dagmar Ollofson, is the leader of a women's organisation, the 'Forward Club', which promotes female suffrage and rights for working women. The text is detailed in its descriptions of the challenges that such a position carries with it and offers a poignant commentary on the death of Ollofson and the devastating effect her loss has on her followers:

> She was one of the pioneers in a great movement; and although her life ceased when her work was hardly begun, there are still some women in London who remember her, and can never forget her ... who but for her would not have dared to break through the thraldom of the narrow walls of old prejudice, and those women still in memory hear her voice, and touch her hand.[25]

Written several years after the height of the New Woman phenomenon, *The Cleverest Woman in England* analyses the justifications and successes of that movement as well as its excesses and errors, and works most effectively in its capacity as a tribute to Massingberd which indicates the degree of Meade's commitment both to her and her project. Others of her more prominent friends and acquaintances included Millicent Garrett Fawcett, a well-known suffragist and occasional contributor to *Atalanta*, and Lucy Toulmin Smith, who in 1894 became the first librarian of Manchester College, Oxford, and who was also Meade's sister-in-law.[26]

In the pages of *Atalanta*, Meade ran a regular column on 'Employment for Girls', included debates on the subject of women's suffrage, and provided appealing descriptions of the newly formed colleges for women at Oxford and Cambridge.[27] In 1895, in the *Strand*, she penned two articles on

'Girls Schools of To-day' in which she announced her unequivocal support for girls to be 'thoroughly educated in the broadest and fullest sense of the term' and declared the girls of her day 'able to hold their own with their brothers'.[28] This latter phenomenon she attributed to the unifying efforts of educational reformers such as Dorothea Beale, head of Cheltenham College, whose pupils, Meade asserted, 'understand one another thoroughly' and as a result 'the whole works most harmoniously', and Jane Frances Dove, head of St Leonards, whose educational ethos was to 'cultivat[e] a public spirit' at the school. Dove explained to Meade that she believed women's lives had theretofore been 'small and petty' precisely because they had lacked for so long the opportunities 'for co-operating with other girls'.[29] The outcome of a type of education based on alliances between females rather than divisions among them, Meade professed at the end of the article, would 'surely be the New Women for whom we long'.[30]

In her discussion of her childhood in the periodical *Girl's Realm* in 1900, she posited her strict and isolated upbringing in a Protestant household in the midst of an overwhelmingly Catholic region of Ireland as fundamental to her decision to advocate for women's rights and her interest in female sociality and schooling.[31] Likewise, her own education – conducted exclusively at home in strict Calvinist fashion by a series of governesses, at least one of whom inflicted regular beatings on her – left little room for close companionship with other girls. Her promotion of inclusive, transnational, and anti-sectarian education for females can also be linked to a broader Irish context during the period in which she was raised: a point at which debates surrounding the schooling of girls were particularly vehement in their denominational differences. There were vast and seemingly unbridgeable distances between the opinions of the Protestant and Catholic factions in Ireland concerning the efficacy and appropriateness of the various types of education offered to Irish girls throughout the latter half of the nineteenth century. These sectarian tensions were evidenced most notably in the ongoing demonisation of convent schools by segments of the Protestant population. High-profile forms of anti-Catholic and anti-convent propaganda deployed in the era of Meade's own young adulthood included the 'Gothic convent-as-prison' genre of polemic, highly sensationalised novels.[32] Typical of this type of text is the anonymously authored *Eveline; or, Incidents of Irish Convent Life*, published in 1861, in which the Catholic Church is imagined as a malicious entity that forces its members to remain ignorant of the spiritual 'truth' that the Bible and its rightful followers, Protestants, embody. Added to these types of fictional attacks on the convents were those publications produced by organisations such as the Convent Enquiry Society which had by the closing decades of the century embarked on a professed mission 'to influence parents against sending their children to Convent Schools'.[33] In the society's publications, which include such titles as *The Ruin of Girls in Convent Schools: Testimony of Roman Catholics and Grief-Stricken Parents* (1903), convent schools are portrayed as elaborate mechanisms for luring Protestant girls into the Roman Catholic faith. Evidencing the moral panic concerning the proliferation of convent schools both in England and on the European Continent – whose students, the society claimed, were 'nearly all from Protestant homes' – *The Ruin of Girls* launched a sustained attack on the quality of instruction that Catholic girls' schools provided.[34]

Over the course of the period 1860–1900, girls' schools in Ireland witnessed a rapid alteration in the educational priorities of their students. The post-Famine surge in emigration and an attendant decline in marriage rates had resulted in a female citizenry newly required to seek remunerative employment. Many Irish parents became wary as a result of this shift in real-world valuations of women's education of sending their daughters down the traditional route offered by convent schools – one that emphasised non-vocational attainments such as needlework, art, and music, which were designed to turn girls into more marriageable women. It was in the midst of such changes that Alexandra College, Protestant in affiliation but by and large welcoming to Catholic students, was founded in Dublin in 1866. The first Irish school outside Ulster to offer second-level education to females, Alexandra College would in the ensuing decades differ markedly from existing Catholic girls' schools by offering 'Latin, Greek, mathematics, and not a few "ologies" to its students.'[35] That convent schools were lagging behind their Protestant counterparts would be confirmed by the introduction of the Irish Intermediate Education Act in 1878, and, with it, the State-run Intermediate examinations. The result was an increase in 'controversy, unhealthy competition and dissent' between Catholic and Protestant schools.[36]

Through her promotion of homosocial bonding between females in her schoolgirl novels, Meade offers a compelling counter-narrative to the rhetoric surrounding denominational schooling that served to divide girls in her homeland. In these novels, she consistently critiques the types of factionalism that fuel such divisions either through her fictional advocacy of those school establishments whose educational policies serve to unite students, or of those students who foster inter-female alliances. With this in mind, it is relevant to consider Beth Rodgers' compelling arguments that Meade took advantage of her own transnational status as an Irish migrant to England to publicise an identity which was *both/and* rather than *either/or* and therefore to cultivate a fluid professional persona that appealed more widely than fixity could: 'Meade was perceived by the reading public as being both '"healthily English" *and* "thoroughly Irish"', Rodgers suggests, adding that her Irish characters are similarly 'complex and idiosyncratic'.[37] It would be venturing too far to suggest that a similar argument could be applied to her religious identity, yet it is evident that it is in the interests of educational reforms for all (rather than just some) girls that Meade writes, and to this end it is notable that, with very few exceptions, she is careful to avoid any overt discussion of the religious identities of her characters in either her English- or Irish-set texts for girls. During a period in which denominational debates over the schooling of girls were raging in her homeland, Meade's schoolgirl texts are admirably anti-sectarian and inclusive. What is perhaps most distinctive about them is the degree to which they emphasise the aspects of all women's existences which are shared, regardless of ethnicity, class, or religious creed, allowing these points of confluence to be recognised and acknowledged and thereby prioritising the formation not only of sororal but also of powerfully homosocial bonding systems within her educational settings. In Meade's texts, nationality, class, and religious affiliations do not matter; gender does.

In her own discussion of female homosociality, Piper Murray suggests that '[f]orming a feminist sociality has often meant, quite simply, cultivating women's capacity for "identifying" with each other: women-identified women joining other women-identified women to create a community that is not dependent on men for its constitution'.[38] Remarking on the ways in which such a configuration is far more limited and equivocal than the male equivalent first posited by Eve Kosofsky Sedgwick in *Between Men* (1985), Murray points to the degree to which female homosocial bonds continue to be portrayed as less potent than those of their male counterparts: 'any powerful community of women can and must be formed by passionate attachments to one another', Murray argues, at the same time highlighting the degree to which such attachments have been and continue to be largely unachievable in both art and life.[39] There is, she asserts, 'a fundamental – and founding – ambivalence' that surrounds female homosociality.[40] The absence of female homosocial bonds has been particularly pronounced in novels, both historical and contemporary, written about and/or for juvenile girls. Schoolgirls or school-aged girls from Charlotte Brontë's Jane Eyre, Louisa May Alcott's Jo March, and George Eliot's Maggie Tulliver to J. K. Rowling's Hermione Granger, Stephenie Meyer's Bella Swan, and Suzanne Collins' Katniss Everdeen have repeatedly been portrayed as forging few or no female friends or intrasexual alliances beyond their immediate families. When it comes to canonical or conspicuously popular fiction, the most important relationships forged by juvenile female characters have almost exclusively been with males.

For Meade's characters, however, attachments between females are both achievable and necessary to educational and personal success: the pseudo or preparatory public sphere of the school acts as a space of female alliance and allegiance, and always central to her school texts is the forming of close, even passionate, emotional bonds between females which might be advantageously translated into the larger world outside the school grounds. In considering the import and gauging the potential impact of depictions of female homosociality in her texts, it is perhaps most useful to consider those of her school-set stories that appealed widely to girl readers. Notable among these are *A World of Girls*, a book which just two years after its initial publication was already into its fourth edition and which had sold 37,000 copies by 1902, and *A Bunch of Cherries: A Story of Cherry Court School* (1898), which was reprinted at least six times in America alone.[41] Meade's texts are far less formulaic and more diverse than her popularity and copious output would seem to suggest, but both of these novels offer an insight into characteristics of her work as a whole: her portrayals of girls who prefer and prioritise the company of, and relationships with, their female peers to familial or heterosexual bonds, and the eschewing of the standard romance plot.

A World of Girls follows the careers of two students, Hester Thornton and Annie Forest, at the Lavender House boarding school. The narrative first traces the movements of Hester from her insular and not entirely happy existence at home, where she lives with her emotionally distant father and much loved younger sister Nan, to the lively environs of the school with its greater opportunities for the type of female companionship which, Meade confirms, will prove vital to her if only she can curb her separatist leanings. In the opening chapters, the pleasures of female companionship are introduced through Hester's meeting with two elderly sisters, the Misses Bruce, who set her at ease on her train journey to Lavender House by telling her of their own 'happy days at school'.[42] Once Hester arrives, however, repeated and censorious attention is drawn to the degree to which she holds herself apart from her fellow students. Her first introduction is to Annie, who, like Hester, is tomboyish, motherless, and largely unschooled. Yet instead of recognising her commonality with Annie, Hester is taken aback by the other girl's 'wild' ways and outspoken opinions and is unable to appreciate that this behaviour is due to a lack of the type of financial and familial advantages Hester herself has enjoyed. With the schoolgirl population more widely, Hester likewise remains inflexible and unfriendly: she 'has no idea of unbending or of making herself agreeable', is 'determined to be beholden to none of her schoolmates for companionship' and

> had never learned the great secret of success in all life's perplexities, the power to give and take ... As far as lessons were concerned, she was doing well; but

> the hardest lesson of all, the training of mind and character, which the daily companionship of her schoolfellows alone could give her, in this lesson she was making no way. Each day she was shutting herself up more and more from all kindly advances.[43]

Annie affords a laudable contrast to her unsociable counterpart: she may be 'wild, naughty, [and] impulsive', but she is 'the most popular girl in the school'.[44]

The comparisons which Meade encourages the reader to draw between the 'naughtiness' enacted by Annie and the ill-will inherent in Hester's snobbishness are telling in terms of her advocacy of female bonding. Annie, we are told, is 'a girl with scarcely any self-consciousness; those she loved, she loved devotedly; she threw herself with a certain feverish impetuosity into their lives, and made their interest her own. To get into mischief and trouble for the sake of a friend was an every-day occurrence with Annie.'[45] Her transgressions extend to organising midnight feasts, which gradually grow more daring in part due to Annie's own love of danger but also and primarily so that she can offer ever more exciting diversions to her schoolmates. In her descriptions of the last and most adventurous of these feasts, undertaken out of doors, Meade focuses on the revelry rather than on the disobedience of the event and thereby indicates her authorial complicity with the rule-breakers rather than the rule-makers: 'the moon riding high in the heavens looked down on the young giddy heads, and their laughter, naughty as they were, sounded sweet in the night air'.[46]

The relationship between the two schoolgirls is brought to a point of crisis first when Annie is accused of malicious pranks she did not commit and is ostracised by her fellow schoolmates and then when Hester's sister Nan comes to live at the school. Too young to attend classes, Nan becomes the ward and favourite of all the students but is particularly drawn to Annie, who in turn dotes on her. The schoolgirls are thus figured as an extended family, with Annie as the favoured 'parent'. Hester's possessive love of the little girl, however, exacerbates the existing tensions between her and Annie, who, hurt by Hester's censure, purposefully sets out to divert Nan's affections towards herself, and succeeds. Meanwhile, Hester has evidence that might exonerate Annie of the crimes she has been accused of committing and return her to favour at the school but withholds this information due to jealousy of the relationship between Annie and Nan. When Nan is kidnapped by a Gypsy, it is Annie who sets out on the dangerous (but thrilling) task of saving the little girl. Hester's repentance is brought about when Annie falls ill due to the ordeals she has undergone in facilitating the rescue, and through her contrition and the burgeoning sense of shared interests that attends it, Hester reaches the sense of mutuality to which Meade's text has been leading her all along: during Annie's illness, she confesses that she cares 'for nothing now in all the world except that Annie may live'.[47] The students who have caused or exacerbated the dissension at the school have all left Lavender House either by force or by choice by the end of the narrative, and close interpersonal ties between the schoolgirls are restored. Particularly poignant is the uniting of Hester and Annie, who have become the 'dearest and warmest' of friends by the novel's close – a near-familial relationship that leaves Annie unable to recall what loneliness means.[48]

The mimicry of familial forms of bonding between schoolgirls is echoed and developed in *A Bunch of Cherries*, which opens on a scene in which all the elder students of the Cherry Court School are communing in the midst of an orchard of cherry trees, 'which were already laden with the tempting fruit'.[49] The harmony and affection between the schoolgirls extends to their mutual excitement about and preparations for the upcoming cherry feast, which is the highlight and final event of their school year. The metaphorical resonances are clear: this is an all-female Eden before the Fall.

Discord, however, is soon introduced in two distinct forms: the (relative) poverty that comes to bear on the educational opportunities of some of the girls and the introduction of a competition for a three-year scholarship which is initiated between them. Each of the three students chosen to vie for the scholarship – Kitty Sharston, Mary Bateman, and Florence Aylmer – has a compelling financial need to win it and valid reasons to feel disadvantaged in relation to the majority of her fellow students. Conceptualised with good intentions but with a distinct taint of favouritism by the headmistress Mrs Clavering and the governor of the school, Sir John Wallis, who served with Kitty's father in Sebastopol and therefore desires her to win, the scholarship introduces dissonance to what had been an idyllic educational setting.

In this and a number of other texts, Meade makes apparent that education is not only the desire of but a requirement for females: in *A Bunch of Cherries* she explains 'that every girl cannot marry, and that the girls who do not marry … unless they have great fortunes left to them, will have to earn their own living'.[50] For the headstrong but lovable (and loving) part-Irish Kitty, whose father has suffered financial losses and who can no longer afford to pay her tuition, the scholarship affords the only opportunity to continue the education that will provide her with the means to support herself should anything happen to her father, her only immediate family. Mary Bateman, meanwhile, is the daughter of a 'very advanced, liberal-minded' clergyman who unequivocally advocates her educational priorities.[51] With modest means and eight other children to support, however, he can afford only to educate her for another three years, and the fifteen-year-old Mary knows that she will need to earn her own living once her studies are finished. The most capable student at the school in several subjects, she longs 'at the age of eighteen to [go] to a wonderful new College for women which has been established at a place called Girton'.[52] There, she will be able to 'attend the University lectures at Cambridge, and learn as much as a man learns'.[53] The scholarship will offer her the means to make this goal a reality. Of the three, it is Florence who is the most 'horribly poor' and she who is also most sorely tempted by a combination of financial and familial pressures (which Meade portrays in compelling detail) to break the rules of fair competition.[54] The daughter of a widowed mother who is uneducated and therefore lacks the skills required to earn a living, Florence craves the advantages education offers because she wants to provide her mother, to whom she is devoted, with the financial comfort she has thus far been denied.

Meade juxtaposes the unique burdens placed upon each of these girls against the petty personal animosities and one-upmanship of an older generation of females who have not formed the type of inter-female bonds the students at the boarding school enjoy. The detriments of female isolationism are exemplified most poignantly in Meade's depictions of two of these older women: Florence's mother, who the reader recognises as a spendthrift and aspirant social climber undeserving of the degree of her daughter's affection, and Florence's Aunt Susan, who in her frugality acts as the mother's opposite. Already occupying an elevated social and financial position, Aunt Susan enacts her power over Florence's mother by withholding both money and affection from her. Neither woman knows enough of the milieu in which the other lives and moves to find common ground on which to effect the most advantageous upbringing for Florence, and the results are disastrous for the young girl. Ultimately persuaded into cheating on the crucial essay portion of the competition due to the pressures placed on her by these women (both of whom desire her success so that they can bask in its reflected glory), Florence wins the competition but loses her self-respect. Realising as a result of her deception and the threat of ostracisation that accompanies it that it is only a return to the sense of camaraderie she has enjoyed with Kitty and Mary, who convey their genuine pleasure at her win, that can pull her back from the brink of moral ruin, she prays earnestly that she might be saved 'from herself' and confess her transgressions.[55] In essence a call for a return to the fold of female unity, Florence's prayer is answered in time to demonstrate her solidarity with her fellow students and to allow Kitty to take up her rightful place as the scholarship's winner. Meade's novel demonstrates that it is because Florence rejects the animosities and selfishness of the previous generation that she is able to embrace the spirit of mutuality that defines a new one. Although Florence is unable to remain at Cherry Court School, the closing pages of the book dwell on images of Kitty and Mary 'overpowered' by sadness over her fate and of Sir John recognising his own fault in placing this 'great temptation' before the girls and dividing rather than uniting them. Having thus become 'a sadder but wiser man', he helps Florence to continue her education elsewhere.[56]

Meade expressly and consistently reminds readers that the action of the novel is set not in the present day but in the 1870s, and, combined with her references to the financial difficulties her fictional students at the Cherry Court School endure, the narrative enacts a commentary on the progress that has been made in education for girls between the time in which the novel is set and the period in which it was written. Opportunities for education of a similar standard to boys had opened up increasingly from the 1860s, and London University was the first to award degrees to women in 1878 (although Oxford and Cambridge would take decades to follow suit). It was, however, largely middle-class girls whose educational horizons were broadened.[57] Lack of financial means continued to equate to a lack of access to secondary schooling. Although a 'scholarship system' through which 'poor elementary students could be offered a free place in a fee-paying secondary school' burgeoned in the final three decades of the nineteenth century, few of these types of scholarships were awarded to girls, who tended to be dissuaded by both their parents and teachers from pursuing secondary education.[58]

In drawing conspicuous attention to the financial constraints placed on the three most able students in the school, Meade's text critiques the processes that do not allow Florence, Mary, and Kitty to pursue educational opportunities to which their abilities should clearly entitle them. Similar themes appear in several of Meade's other works, most notably her 1902 novel *The Rebel of the School*, in which the Irish Kathleen O'Hara arrives at the Great Shirley School in England and witnesses inequities between pupils based on class and financial resources, which, she suggests, do not exist in her homeland. She proceeds to fight for the rights of the ill-treated foundation students who attend the school on scholarship and is proved noble in motive but mistaken in her separatist and confrontational methods. These serve to pit students against one another rather than unite them in a common cause for social equality, and Kathleen ultimately realises the detrimental effect her tactics have had and amends them.

Also important is the lack of bonds forged between female and male characters in almost all of Meade's schoolgirl texts. Heterosexual romances very rarely feature in these works, and there are few allusions to past, present, or future relationships between her adolescent schoolgirls and any males other than their fathers (who are often absent and frequently inadequate providers of emotional and/or financial support). Male characters such as Mr Everard in *A World of Girls* and Sir John Wallis in *A Bunch of Cherries* sometimes appear but are always subsidiary to the narrative action and entirely inconsequential to the day-to-day workings of the school. The relationships that matter are consistently between girls and their schoolfellows, teachers, and headmistresses, and the romances are largely confined to the 'raves' or crushes females have on other females. In the few of Meade's schoolgirl texts in which heterosexual romance plots do indeed figure, such as another of her most popular novels, *A Sweet Girl Graduate* (1891), relationships with men are shown to be secondary to the homosocial bonds which have been formed at the school and often have a devastating effect on the girls who enter into them.[59]

The messages that underlie Meade's schoolgirl texts are consistently political, and the potential for influence was vast: among her earliest readers would have been at least some of those who became the New Women of the 1890s and, later, the suffragists of the 1900s and 1910s. Through her texts, she advocates not only women's education but also equal access to and treatment within education. By promoting homosocial bonds between females and critiquing and punishing dissension, she also posits female solidarity as the most advantageous expedient to a productive and fulfilled life. In doing so, she writes not of lone females who are anomalies in society but of groups of women who are the prospective agents for change. Juxtaposed against the educational debates which were contemporaneous with them and considered in relation to women's novels that both preceded and followed them, Meade's schoolgirl texts can be recognised as progressive in message and motives not just for her time but in relation to our own. Her texts consistently portray the movement of women and girls from positions of isolation and powerlessness to spaces teeming with possibilities for alliances of (female) authority and the type of engagement she herself enjoyed as a working woman. In doing so, L. T. Meade's novels can be seen to have offered the girls of her era a literature of their own that constructed them not as the victims of their fates but as the would-be masters of them.

Notes

1 Helen Bittel, 'Required Reading for "Revolting Daughters"? The New Girl Fiction of L. T. Meade', *Nineteenth-Century Gender Studies*, 2:2 (2006), unpaginated, paragraph 5. Available at http://ncgsjournal.com/issue22/bittel.htm. Accessed 15 April 2015.

2 Vladimir Nabokov, *Speak, Memory: An Autobiography Revisited* (London: Penguin, 2015), p. 49.

3 Nabokov, *Speak, Memory*, p. 51. Julia Donaldson, author of seminal children's story *The Gruffalo*, also recommended *Beyond the Blue Mountains* to listeners during a BBC-sponsored 'Book Club Panel' at the 2013 Edinburgh Festival. Available at www.bbc.co.uk/programmes/b038h038. Accessed 15 April 2015.

4 L. T. Meade, 'How I Began', *Girl's Realm*, 3 (November 1900), 57–64, at p. 61.
5 Sally Mitchell, *The New Girl: Girls' Culture in England, 1880–1915* (New York: Columbia University Press, 1995), p. 11.
6 Letter from Katharine Tynan to Fr Matthew Russell, SJ (27 July 1889), Papers of Matthew Russell, SJ, Jesuit Archive, Dublin, Folder J27/73.
7 See Roger McHugh (ed.), *W. B. Yeats: Letters to Katharine Tynan* (Dublin: Clonmore & Reynolds, 1953), pp. 50–1.
8 Brazil's first schoolgirl novel, *The Fortunes of Philippa*, was published in 1906; her last in 1946. Meade's influence on Brazil has been acknowledged by Sally Mitchell (*The New Girl*) and Shirley Foster and Judy Simons, *What Katy Read: Feminist Re-readings of 'Classic' Stories for Girls* (Basingstoke: Palgrave Macmillan, 1995). Although direct influence is more difficult to trace in the case of Montgomery's series of *Anne of Green Gables* novels, several of Meade's plot and character devices are echoed in Montgomery's works, including the protagonist's befriending of spinster sisters who live near her school, her absent parents, ostracisation due to misbehaviour, adoration of the female headteacher, return to favour through the saving of a young girl's life (in the cases of both Anne and Annie, the younger sister of a schoolmate from whom she has been unjustly separated), and a profound love of nature that extends to a wish to sleep out of doors and ultimately leads to a transgression and punishment.
9 See 'Results of Prize Competitions: The Six Most Popular Living Writers for Girls', *Girl's Realm*, 1:4 (1899), 431; and Alice Zimmern, 'Girls' Book Lists', *The Leisure Hour: An Illustrated Magazine for Home Reading* (February 1901), 333–7, at p. 336.
10 'The Queen of Girls'-Book Makers', *Saturday Review of Politics, Literature, Science and Art*, 102:2668 (1906), 741–2, at p. 741.
11 'The Queen of Girls'-Book Makers'.
12 See Mitchell, *The New Girl*, p. 14; and Mark I. West, 'Not to Be Circulated: The Response of Children's Librarians to Dime Novels and Series Books', *Children's Literature Association Quarterly*, 10:3 (1985), 137–9.
13 See Mavis Barkman Reimer, 'Tales Out of School: L. T. Meade and the School Story' (Ph.D. dissertation, University of Calgary, 1993), p. 2; and Bittel, 'Required Reading for "Revolting Daughters" ', paragraph 1.
14 Sally Mitchell, 'Children's Reading and the Culture of Girlhood: The Case of L. T. Meade', *Browning Institute Studies*, 17 (1989), 53–63, at p. 53.
15 Bittel, 'Required Reading for "Revolting Daughters" ', paragraph 27.
16 See Tina O'Toole, *The Irish New Woman* (Basingstoke: Palgrave Macmillan, 2013); Beth Rodgers, 'Irishness, Professional Authorship and the "Wild Irish Girls" of L. T. Meade', *ELT*, 56:2 (2013), 146–66; and Whitney Standlee, *'Power to Observe': Irish Women Novelists in Britain, 1890–1916* (Oxford: Peter Lang, 2015).
17 Sarah A. Wadsworth, 'Louisa May Alcott, William T. Adams, and the Rise of Gender-Specific Series Books', *The Lion and the Unicorn*, 25:1 (2001), 17–46, at p. 18.
18 Wadsworth, 'Louisa May Alcott', p. 25.
19 L. T. Meade, 'Children Past and Present', *Parents' Review*, 6:12 (1896), 881–7, at p. 886.
20 Edward G. Salmon, 'What Girls Read', *Nineteenth Century*, 20:116 (1886), 515–29, at p. 515.
21 L. T. Meade, 'Story Writing for Girls', *Academy and Literature Fiction Supplement* (7 November 1903), p. 499.
22 Meade, 'Story Writing for Girls'.
23 Mitchell, *The New Girl*, p. 10.
24 'The Pioneer Club and Its President: A Chat with Mrs. Massingberd', *Hearth and Home* (2 February 1893), p. 339.
25 L. T. Meade, *The Cleverest Woman in England* (London: James Nisbet, 1898), pp. 340–1.
26 'Obituary: Miss Lucy Toulmin Smith', *The Times* (21 December 1911), p. 11.
27 L. T. Meade, 'Girton College', *Atalanta*, 7:77 (1894), 325–31; and 'Newnham College', *Atalanta*, 7:80 (1894), 525–9.

28 L. T. Meade, 'Girls' Schools of Today, I: Cheltenham College', *Strand*, 9 (January 1895), 283–8, at p. 283.
29 Meade, 'Girls' Schools of Today, I', p. 288; and L. T. Meade, 'Girls' Schools of Today, II: St. Leonard and Great Harrowden Hall', *Strand*, 9 (January 1895), 457–63, at p. 460.
30 Meade, 'Girls' Schools of Today, II', p. 463.
31 Meade, 'How I Began', pp. 57–64.
32 Elizabeth Butler Cullingford, '"Our Nuns Are *Not* a Nation": Politicizing the Convent in Irish Literature and Film', *Éire-Ireland*, 41:1 (2006), 9–39, at p. 15.
33 S. J. Abbott, *The Ruin of Girls in Convent Schools: Testimony of Roman Catholics and Grief-Stricken Parents* (London: Convent Enquiry Society, 1903), p. 1.
34 Abbott, *The Ruin of Girls in Convent Schools*, p. 3.
35 May Laffan, 'Convent Boarding-Schools for Young Ladies', *Fraser's Magazine*, 9:54 (1874), 778–86, at p. 786.
36 Senia Pašeta, *Before the Revolution: Nationalism, Social Change and Ireland's Catholic Elite, 1879–1922* (Cork: Cork University Press, 1999), p. 13.
37 Rodgers, 'Irishness, Professional Authorship', pp. 157, 159.
38 Piper Murray, '"They Are Well Together. Women Are Not": Productive Ambivalence and Female Hom(m)osociality in *Fefu and Her Friends*', *Modern Drama*, 44:4 (2001), 398–414, at p. 400.
39 Murray, '"They Are Well Together"', p. 412.
40 Murray, '"They Are Well Together"', p. 412.
41 Reprint and sales statistics from Reimer, 'Tales Out of School', p. 217.
42 L. T. Meade, *A World of Girls* (New York: A. L. Burt, 1886), p. 14.
43 Meade, *A World of Girls*, pp. 35, 45, and 47.
44 Meade, *A World of Girls*, p. 53.
45 Meade, *A World of Girls*, p. 83.
46 Meade, *A World of Girls*, p. 160.
47 Meade, *A World of Girls*, p. 255.
48 Meade, *A World of Girls*, p. 265.
49 L. T. Meade, *A Bunch of Cherries: A Story of Cherry Court School* (Chicago, Ill.: M. A. Donoghue, 1898), Chapter 2, paragraph 2.
50 Meade, *A Bunch of Cherries*, Chapter 13, paragraph 42.
51 Meade, *A Bunch of Cherries*, Chapter 13, paragraph 42.
52 Meade, *A Bunch of Cherries*, Chapter 13, paragraph 44.
53 Meade, *A Bunch of Cherries*, Chapter 13, paragraph 44.
54 Meade, *A Bunch of Cherries*, Chapter 13, paragraph 50.
55 Meade, *A Bunch of Cherries*, Chapter 18, paragraph 22.
56 Meade, *A Bunch of Cherries*, Epilogue, paragraph 4.
57 June Purvis, *A History of Women's Education in England* (Milton Keynes: Open University Press, 1991), p. 116.
58 Purvis, *A History of Women's Education in England*, p. 29.
59 In *A Sweet Girl Graduate* (London, Paris and Melbourne: Cassell, 1892), the death of Annabel Lee comes about due to a love rivalry with her closest friend, Maggie Oliphant. Her death leaves Maggie in an extended period of mourning and unwilling to continue her relationship with the man she loves.

5

'Breaking away': Beatrice Grimshaw and the commercial woman writer

Jane Mahony and Eve Patten

> I wanted a life of adventure – you can't tell how the longing for it used to pull at my very heartstrings! I wanted to live for myself and work out my own life; to be – well, what you would call a New Woman, I suppose. You don't need to know how the passion for absolute freedom sometimes takes hold of a girl.[1]

THESE words are voiced by the character of Eva Rivington, the young wife of 'Ireland's greatest novelist', in Beatrice Grimshaw's 1897 romantic literary thriller, *Broken Away*.[2] Such sentiments – the passionate desire for liberty and the railing against frustrated ambition – speak generally to New Woman incentives in the period and might well be read as deriving from the author's own life experience. In fact, the opposite is the case: at odds with the trammeled circumstances of her young female protagonist, Grimshaw herself carved out a life, and a career, of extraordinary expansion and range, gaining a rich international literary profile as a novelist, journalist, and travel writer and, more unusually perhaps for the first half of the twentieth century, building an enviable record of commercial success. Her situation highlights the positive role in literary history of opportunism when seen in the broader context of a select group of Irish writers who proved themselves mobile, versatile, and creative in the conditions set by the evolving publishing climate of the late nineteenth and early twentieth centuries.

In the light of her lengthy and prolific career, this essay surveys Grimshaw's writing and identifies her as one of several independent women writers of the time who successfully adapted an instinctive feminism to the increasing conservatism of the international print culture marketplace in the 1890s. In this context we touch on her first novel, *Broken Away*, as a detailed portrait of the *fin-de-siècle* commercial Irish author. We consider at the same time the novel's commentary on the pressurised concept of the 'New Woman' against the changing editorial priorities of Grimshaw's first publisher, John Lane, The Bodley Head, as the company attempted to distance itself from the decadence of Oscar Wilde and Aubrey Beardsley on the one hand and the feminism of George Egerton on the other. This initial foray can be usefully compared to a later publishing encounter, this time with the recently formed Mills & Boon, who produced Grimshaw's 1911 adventure story *When the Red Gods Call*, the tale of an Irishman's fortunes in New Guinea.[3] In this case, Grimshaw's shrewd response to the tastes of an expanding popular readership can be seen to have dovetailed with the distribution skills of her new publishers, paving the way to her status as a best-selling author. Pragmatic rather than compromised, she proved herself a successful negotiator with the major publishing houses of the period, including Cassells, Hutchinson, and Herbert Jenkins in London, and Macmillan, Doubleday, and Houghton Mifflin in America. Grimshaw emerges from this analysis as a writer working at a distinct point of tension between individual feminism and societal conservatism on the domestic front and benefiting at the same time from the new demands created abroad by fast-developing international and imperial readerships.

Born to a wealthy mercantile family in Co. Antrim in 1870, Grimshaw grew up in a conventional Belfast middle-class civic and social milieu but from an early age expressed an instinct towards independence and travel beyond the horizons of industrial Ulster.[4] She later wrote of how her family had wished her to take up a classics lectureship in a respectable women's college but that she was determined from the age of seventeen to follow her own ambitions and become a journalist.[5] 'I am a Victorian', she stated. 'I was governessed and schooled and colleged. I was taught to ride and play games. I was taught to behave.' In defiance of such traditions, she continued, she styled herself as one of the 'Revolting Daughter' figures of the era, emotionally and physically releasing herself from Victorian entrapments:

> I bought a bicycle, with difficulty. I rode it unchaperoned, miles and miles beyond the limits possible to the soberly trotting horses. The world opened before me. And as soon as my twenty-first birthday dawned, I went away from home, to see what the world might have to give to daughters who revolted. What it gave me first was the offer of a journalistic post. There were maps of far-away places, maps with tantalising blanks in them; maps of the huge Pacific, colored an entrancing blue. I swore that I would go there.[6]

In 1891, Grimshaw moved to Dublin where she became a journalist, first as a subeditor on and frequent contributor to the *Irish Cyclist*.[7] From 1895 she was editor of the *Social Review*, which regarded itself as the leading journal of society and fashion in Ireland. Here she not only reviewed new work by Irish authors such as Jane Barlow, Bram Stoker, W. B. Yeats, George Egerton, and Patrick Pearse but also penned several pseudonymous articles touching on contemporary debates around the education of women, the marriage question and the position of the woman writer. Grimshaw produced up to eight pages a week of these more substantial contributions as well as book reviews, society notes, household tips, and gossip.[8] Further writing success came with the publication of her novel *Broken Away*, and at this point in her life Grimshaw might simply have settled into the comfortable routines of Dublin's minor literati in the period. Her ambition to travel remained pressing, however, and moving on from Dublin to London she secured a position as a travel writer for the newspaper the *Daily Graphic*, for which she corresponded from several around-the-world voyages, before finally settling in Papua New Guinea. For some forty years before her death in Australia in 1953, Grimshaw's pioneering travels and adventures in the South Seas gave her global celebrity as she drew on her experiences for an extensive output of travel writing, popular cultural anthropology, more than thirty travel-based romantic adventure novels, and hundreds of short stories, published internationally.

Grimshaw's debut work *Broken Away* is set in the literary circles of young, semi-Bohemian, upper-middle-class Dublin writers to which she herself belonged after her move from Belfast. A rather heady literary romance, the novel portrays the life of a *fin-de-siècle* Irish writer and his circle and – in a parallel description of the lives of three young women – casts a jaundiced eye on the institution of marriage and the position of single women in society. The plot juxtaposes the fortunes of author Stuart Rivington with those of the previously fashionable decadent novelist, Alfred Moore, building on these foundations a closely engaged account of Dublin's writing set and its convoluted marital and emotional relationships. Much of the work's political momentum derives from the character of Rivington's astute and frequently outspoken wife, Eva, and her declarations of would-be independence, both literary and individual. When the couple moves to the Wicklow hills outside the city to escape the distraction of their urban social life, her initially enthusiastic response speaks to a broader female community of the period in her determination to gain independence, as she heralds it: 'I wanted a life of adventure … I wanted to live for myself and work out my own life; to be – well, what you would call a New Woman I suppose.'[9] Against such passions, however, Eva has spent the six years of her marriage devoted entirely to her husband and his career, losing sight of her own talents and ambitions in the process.

In conjunction with its portrait of Dublin's literati then, Grimshaw foregrounds in *Broken Away* a stringent critique of marriage and the subjugation of a woman to her husband at the expense of freedom and artistic development. In this respect, the novel is quite straightforwardly of its time, aligned with standard marital protest fiction in the period, both Irish and British. If one shifts perspective, however, from the politics of the text alone to the background and contexts of its commercial publication, the work becomes of further – and adjacent – interest, throwing into relief an ironic discrepancy between the restricted circumstances of its female protagonist, Eva, and the opportunist (and commercial) instincts of its author. *Broken Away* was published at a time of significant upheaval in the publishing market generally and issued by a young and avant-garde London publishing house at the confluence of New Woman writing, Aestheticism, and Decadence, and it was Grimshaw's proximity to this venture that laid the foundations for her successful and prolific publishing career.[10]

To appreciate fully this commercial context, it needs to be understood that British publishing for much of the nineteenth century was a deeply conservative industry, made nervous by the uncertainties of the years of the Napoleonic wars, and haunted by the bankruptcy in 1826 of Constable & Ballantyne, an innovative firm with an early vision of a mass reading public, which collapsed despite owning valuable copyrights to Walter Scott's works, the *Encyclopaedia Britannica*, and the *Edinburgh Review*.[11] Notwithstanding the Constable failure, publishers persisted with efforts to expand their market by means of six-shilling novels in library series. Richard Altick summarises their intentions: 'Between 1827 and 1832, therefore, London and Edinburgh publishers behaved as if they stood on a peak in Darien, beholding for the first time a vast sea of common readers.'[12] Such businesses had largely miscalculated the market, however. The middle classes suffered reductions in income following the stock-market collapse of 1825–26, and the library series were still too expensive for the clerks and artisans who might have fuelled market growth. In the absence of a mass market, literary-novel publishing was increasingly secured on the mammoth that was the three-decker – three volumes and 180,000 words priced at 31s and 6d, with a print run of 500 copies: the safe, profitable format affordable only for the wealthiest individual customers and the circulating libraries.

While most publishers and circulating libraries, including the dominant players Mudie and W. H. Smith, were content with the status quo for much of the nineteenth century, increasingly, booksellers and, in their turn, authors were not. Matthew Arnold had criticised the prevailing system in 1880 as 'a machinery for the multiplication and protection of bad literature, and for keeping good books dear'.[13] From the mid 1880s, younger authors, frustrated with the straitjacket of the three-decker, started to experiment with single-volume novels. Robert Louis Stevenson (a major influence on Grimshaw) was one of the authors who led the way with *Treasure Island* (1883), *Dr. Jekyll and Mr. Hyde* (1886), *Kidnapped* (1886), and other popular adventure stories published originally in the one-volume format. H. Rider Haggard published *King Solomon's Mines* in 1885 and *She* in 1887. J. M. Barrie made 'A Plea for Smaller Books' in 1893, lamenting the padding of the three-decker and urging publishers to take risks for the sake of literature.[14] Pressure mounted, and in 1894 Mudie's and W. H. Smith announced they would no longer carry the three-volume novel.[15] The impact of this volte-face was immediate and far-reaching. In the year of the announcement, 184 three-volume novels were published. In 1895, the number dropped to fifty-two and halved again to twenty-five in 1896. In 1897, when *Broken Away* appeared, only four were published.[16] The standard price of the first edition of a novel was fixed at 6s, which, although this alteration made the books more affordable for the individual consumer, was catastrophic for some authors. The assumptions and certainties of the previous seven decades disappeared almost overnight. Publishers had to rethink their publishing strategy, agreeing new terms with authors in respect of advances and copyrights. Print runs, prices, and trade discounts in the mid-1890s had no precedents, and, unsurprisingly, for the traditional firms, this led to what R. A. Gettmann has described in his history of Bentley's, one of the leading nineteenth-century publishing houses, as 'bewilderment and paralysis'.[17] This confusion in the market meanwhile provided space for the arrival of new, more flexible and fast-moving entrepreneurial publishers to set up their own companies.

In their turn, authors had to adapt to the new environment. Novel length after the demise of the three-decker was fixed at about 60,000 words, meaning that authors could effectively write three novels in the time previously taken to write one. The introduction of the Net Book Agreement in 1900, which ended trade 'underselling' of the most popular titles and firmly established the royalty structure, would permit Grimshaw and other writers who wrote primarily for entertainment to earn a good living from their work. Their predecessors, unless of the first rank, had most often sold their copyrights outright to publishers, frequently undervaluing their work and cutting off income from backlist sales. The Education Act of 1870 had created for the first time a mass reading public which from 1890 to about 1920, in the era before competition from other media, provided an ever-increasing demand for book, newspaper, and magazine publishing. Exponential growth in periodical publishing ensured that popular authors writing in English had a ready and lucrative market in newspapers and periodicals in Britain and the Empire as well as in America. In his survey of the English literary marketplace at the end of the nineteenth century, Paul Delaney notes the arrival of new writers and readers – women, newly educated lower classes – who supplanted the 'man of letters' of the high Victorian period and his relatively narrow readership. In this respect,

Delaney suggests, the opening of the literary marketplace to the energies of popular consumerism would definitively undermine nineteenth-century concepts of 'literary authority'.[18] Critically, therefore, Beatrice Grimshaw's career would start at a time of wholesale structural change in the publishing industry and benefit significantly from the accelerated evolution of commercial business in the years 1890–1914.

Broken Away was published by The Bodley Head, founded in 1887 by John Lane, a printer from Exeter, and Elkin Mathews, Yeats's first publisher. The company quickly earned a reputation as a publisher of high-art, somewhat risqué titles with limited print runs and high production values. It was at the forefront of the rise of Aestheticism as the publisher of *The Yellow Book*, illustrated by Aubrey Beardsley, whose first edition of 1 April 1894 succeeded in 'ruffling the sleek waters of bourgeois respectability and self-complacency' and rendering The Bodley Head 'infamous'.[19] The partnership between Lane and Mathews was, however, uneasy and was dissolved at the end of September 1894, allowing the former partners to follow their own interests. Lane intended to concentrate on fiction and took *The Yellow Book* with him to his new firm, John Lane, The Bodley Head, together with the new and notorious Keynotes series. This series had been inspired by *Keynotes*, a collection of short stories by the previously unknown George Egerton (Mrs Egerton Clairmonte, née Mary Chavelita Dunne, the Australian-born Irish writer) issued the year before. The book's argument on the corruptions that related to the institution of marriage rendered it an immediate success on both sides of the Atlantic. Six thousand copies sold quickly after publication, very high sales for a niche publishing house.[20] Lane published thirty-three volumes in total in the Keynotes series between 1894 and 1897: nineteen novels and fourteen volumes of short stories.

The Keynotes series included other titles also considered notorious, such as Grant Allen's *The Woman Who Did* and the riposte by Victoria Cross (Annie Sophie Cory), *The Woman Who Didn't*, both published in 1895. It was an innovative series 'which served as the vehicle through which a number of writers achieved their first real notice [and was] a valuable epitome of the kinds of fiction Lane and his staff thought new and vital at the time'.[21] Most of the volumes produced dealt extensively with the 'marriage question', often in the context of the 1890s psychological realist focus on 'irrational depths of the mind, the difficulty of being anything more than one of the minimally happy multitude, and the melancholy sense that the fates are so arranged that everything comes to one too soon or too late'.[22] The very newness of short stories as a literary form in the 1890s added to the dynamism of Keynotes.[23] The series clearly associated Lane's firm with the 'New Woman', while the contemporaneous publication of Oscar Wilde

(*Salome* in 1894, illustrated by Beardsley) and *The Yellow Book* (also between 1894 and 1897), identified it with Aestheticism and Decadence.

Publication of the Keynotes series came at a pivotal time in the campaign of sustained, hostile reaction to the New Woman undertaken by newspapers and periodicals in the late 1880s and 1890s, peaking after the 'critical uproar' that followed the publication of Blanche Alethea Crackanthorpe's article 'The Revolt of the Daughters' in *Nineteenth Century* in January 1894.[24] Crackanthorpe's article, together with Sarah Grand's (Frances Bellenden Clarke McFall) declaration, also in 1894, that 'the Woman Question is the Marriage Question', contributed to the view that the New Woman was a serious threat to the institution of marriage, the family unit, the structure of society, and, ultimately, the imperial project. Whitney Standlee has counted 350 references to the term in journals, newspapers, and periodicals in the first six months of 1895 alone but notes a steep fall in 1896 and virtually no use of the term by 1900.[25] In the same context, Sally Ledger has noted that '[c]ontemporary with the new socialism, the new imperialism, the new fiction and the new journalism, [the New Woman] was part of that concatenation of cultural novelties which manifested itself in the 1880s and 1890s'.[26] Thus, although the New Woman had little in common with Decadence,

> [T]hey were repeatedly linked in the flourishing periodical press of the 1890s. The New Woman and the decadent writers both overtly challenged the dominant sexual codes of the Victorian era ... and this association with homosexuality and perceived hostility to marriage probably underlies what was the source of panic about the New Woman, that 'she may not be at all interested in men, and could manage quite well without them'.[27]

The implications of this connection for Grimshaw's publication outlet were far-reaching. As the fictional novelist Alfred Moore's difficulties in *Broken Away* signal, the cultural climate in which John Lane and other publishers were operating changed dramatically in 1895 after the trial of Oscar Wilde.[28] According to J. Lewis May, who worked for the firm, six of their most prominent authors threatened to withdraw their books unless '[Lane] suppressed Beardsley's work in Volume V of the *Yellow Book* and omitted Oscar Wilde's name from his catalogue'.[29] Lane conceded, and, although he published nine more volumes of *The Yellow Book* after Beardsley left and remained lifelong friends with him, the magazine lost much of its previous brilliance and originality. On 27 May 1895, Wilde was convicted on eight charges of acts of gross indecency. Elkin Mathews and John Lane, among other publishers, were greatly concerned about the impact of the scandal on business and openly distanced themselves from Wilde, seeking to assure readers that steps had been taken by The Bodley Head to 'discredit

[Wilde and his associates] and to minimise their influence'.[30] These steps included a change in editorial policy causing George Egerton – writing to Lane in November 1896 – to express her reluctant agreement to changes he had demanded: 'I have had to change a good deal, out of concession to the new Bodley Head policy and this has necessitated much rewriting and rearrangement – as merely erasing would not do.'[31] Standlee suggests that:

> It reflects the decline in the fortunes not only of feminist fiction of the type that Egerton was producing at the *fin de siècle* but also of all those like Egerton and her publishers who had been associated with the Decadent movement in literature. By May of 1895, the reactions against the movement had become so pronounced that one London periodical, *The Woman's Signal*, was moved to announce exultantly, 'The Death of the Decadent.'[32]

Broken Away therefore was issued by Lane in April 1897 at a time of significant pressure on New Woman writing. Although it too treated many of the Keynotes themes, and was published in Boston by Roberts & Co., who issued all but one of the Keynotes volumes, it was consciously not presented as part of the series, which Lane abandoned only months later.[33] Perhaps tellingly, Lane did not take Grimshaw's second novel, *A Fool of Forty*, which was never published in book form but was serialised in the *Social Review* in Dublin during 1898.

Like other writers in this pressurised moral climate, Grimshaw would thus need to be politically adaptable and independent of 'New Woman material', as it were, if she wished to continue earning her living as a commercial writer. Her output, her business decisions, and her choice of publishers over the next four decades demonstrate that she was pragmatic and expedient in this respect, and she was ultimately successful in negotiating the new dispensation. Her strong personal motivation reveals itself in what can be regarded, effectively, as her second career: this time as a highly successful international travel writer.

After nearly a decade in Dublin and in order to advance her early ambitions for travel, Grimshaw moved to London in 1899 and then to Liverpool to work for the Cunard shipping line. She joined Cunard at a time when the concepts of marketing and publicity were only beginning to be developed: the transatlantic passenger trade was expanding and was the subject of fierce competition between the major shipping companies as well as from German and American shipping lines. Grimshaw was employed to write about passengers and freight, using her extensive journalistic experience in Dublin to place articles in newspapers.

At the end of 1903, she left for a round-the-world voyage on a commission for the *Daily Graphic* newspaper, having persuaded the directors of major shipping lines to underwrite her passage, in first class, provided she guarantee in return newspaper articles advertising their companies. The planned six-month voyage around the world 'expanded, like the magical tent in the *Arabian Nights*, until in the end it covered all my life'.[34] After this point, her international career took off: from 1905, newspapers around the world began to publish highly coloured accounts of Grimshaw's adventures among cannibals, lepers, pirates, and tropical storms under headlines such as 'Plucky Irish Girl on Exploring Trip in the South Seas', accompanied by a photograph of the new celebrity.[35] The author negotiated the placing of these articles directly with the press, who, in turn, prominently printed her material, quickly establishing for her a highly visible, and carefully managed, public image (see Fig. 5.1). One colourfully illustrated story, depicting Grimshaw in front of a dangerous tropical waterspout, for example, was syndicated throughout the United States in 1908 in newspapers from Los Angeles to New York, via Minnesota, Nebraska, and Kentucky, among others. Another widely distributed piece reported on the intrepid author leading a 'simple life' and learning to canoe through shark-filled waters in Tonga.[36]

Grimshaw's travels provided her with material for four books and numerous newspaper articles in the next few years. In 1904, on the strength of her reputation as a travel journalist, she was commissioned to tour and report on New Zealand for the Government Tourist Department, with a similar contract from the Governor of Fiji in 1905.[37] Meanwhile, she continued her work in fiction writing, producing an episodic novel, *Vaiti of the Islands* (1907), whose heroine – a Cook Islands princess – would feature in a series of later books and short stories. This was a major commercial success, published by the Curtis publishing company in New York and serialised almost simultaneously by their magazine the *Saturday Evening Post* in London and New York in 1906.

Grimshaw was clear about where her best interests lay, however, and her next three titles were travelogues rather than fiction. *From Fiji to the Cannibal Islands* and *In the Strange South Seas* were published in 1907. The *Daily Chronicle* listed the latter among the October 1907 list of best-sellers, and over the next four years various cheaper editions were published to maximise sales in different segments of the market.[38] By this stage, Grimshaw was a well-known figure in Australia, having been commissioned in 1908 by the Australian Liberal Prime Minister, Alfred Deakin, to write a series of articles and pamphlets aimed at attracting both capital and settlers to New Guinea. The colony's infrastructure was undeveloped, and, in a series of newspaper articles from September 1908, Grimshaw praised the opportunities for settlers, recommending the territory to 'younger sons with two or three thousand pounds' who had to make their own way in the world.[39] When asked if New Guinea

Figure 5.1 Beatrice Grimshaw on leopard-skin rug.

was a suitable place for women, she insisted that with infrastructural development it would be ideal, arguing that '[n]o country can be said to be properly settled when there are but a few white men settled here and there . . . The place wants the influence of women and society.'[40] This was a theme to which she frequently returned, criticising settler wives who removed themselves to Melbourne and Sydney because they could not, or would not, tolerate the climate or lifestyle. The articles and pamphlets from this commission were published as her third travelogue, *The New Guinea*, in 1910.[41]

Grimshaw's arrival in the South Seas could hardly have been better timed for a commercial writer with a living to make. Control of British New

Guinea had been relinquished to Australia by Britain in March 1901, and there was a politically fractious transitional period before the Australian Papua Act of September 1906. At the same time, anxieties about German ambitions, given the immediate proximity of German New Guinea in the northern half of the island, were rising in Britain and the colonies. For Australia, British New Guinea – renamed Papua – was to be its showplace 'daughter' colony, and political and public interest in the territory was intense. Fiji, a British colony since 1874, had appointed a legislative council to advise the governor in 1904. European male settlers were enfranchised for the first time, and elections to the council were held in 1905 and 1908. Grimshaw closely associated herself with the British colonial project, declaring that she had 'helped in the settlement of the tropics, in the opening up of the torrid lands to white races, and in making these places better known and understood. For this little scrap of pioneering work I am thankful.'[42]

The author's fluid adaption from the political contexts of *fin-de-siècle* Ireland to the demands of the new colony suggest a highly strategic individual, capable of managing a successful commercial career. She became a pivotal and influential figure in Papua, deciding to settle there and support herself with the sales of 'local interest' writing. At the end of 1909, she wrote to her friend, Sir Hubert Murray, the Lieutenant-General of Papua New Guinea, that she considered 'the market is ripe for New Guinea literature'.[43] She had identified a genre of romantic adventure set in the South Seas that was perfectly suited to her talent for storytelling and vivid narrative, defending the tenor of her output with defiance: 'no one should be ashamed of writing a good story', she insisted, 'that is, no author should, as so many modern authors do, consider plot and subject matter as something of no importance and concentrate solely on method and subjective interest'.[44] Sensationalism was key, and, while she maintained that her Catholicism (she had converted at the age of twenty-four) ensured that her stories were moral and without 'coarseness', as she put it, her plots frequently involved lurid love triangles (often involving an Irishman and a Briton, with the troublesome issue of miscegenation usually resolved by the tragic but honourable death of the native wife, thus permitting the marriage of her white characters). She enthusiastically included grisly accounts of murder, headhunting, and cannibalism. Grimshaw's first and perhaps most important attempt at the genre of romantic literary adventures was *When the Red Gods Call*, set in Papua New Guinea and published in 1911. With its title derived from Kipling, the story features Irishman Hugh Lynch, who, having settled in Papua, finds himself imprisoned on false charges of having killed his native wife. As with *Broken Away*, however, the novel is notable less for its content than for its publication context. It was issued by a new publisher with a reputation for launching the first books of talented young writers, particularly women. Gerald Mills and John Boon had worked together for five years at the pioneering firm of Methuen, one of the publishers that emerged in the 1890s, before deciding in 1908 to found their own house: Mills & Boon. Sir Algernon Methuen was an early publisher of cheap fiction, and Methuen was notable for publishing the book considered to be the first 'best-seller' in Britain, Marie Corelli's second novel, *The Sorrows of Satan*, in 1895.[45] At a time when a sale of 1,000 copies was considered excellent, Corelli's book sold 20,000. Boon and Mills were well trained by Methuen in new publishing methods, and, as the firm's historian, Joseph McAleer, has noted, published books 'in a form and at a price that was within the reach of a wide readership'.[46] A number of popular Methuen authors later published with Mills & Boon, including E. F. Benson, Mrs. B. M. Croker, William Le Queux, Max Pemberton, and Jack London, but the company also sought new authors essential for growth in the expanding industry of the day.

Although *When the Red Gods Call* was Grimshaw's third published novel, fourth work of fiction, and sixth published book, Mills & Boon marketed it as a first novel, cleverly allying it with recent titles they had issued. Grimshaw's novel was the third in Mills & Boon's marketing ploy of the 'June 15th Novel', heralded as 'a major discovery of a new first-time author'.[47] The first June 15th Novel in 1909 was *The Veil*, by E. S. (Ethel Stevana) Stevens. *The Rajah's People* by the Australian writer I. A. R. (Ida Alexa Ross) Wylie was 1910's offering, and *When the Red Gods Call* that of 1911. Sales figures of *When the Red Gods Call* are not extant, but, by way of comparison, *The Veil* went to seven printings or 7,000 copies, and a one-shilling paperback edition published in 1910 sold out its run of 10,000. *The Rajah's People* sold out all 14,000 copies printed over ten editions in two years.[48] Despite the fact, therefore, that *Broken Away* had been published by John Lane as far back as 1897, the combination of an exciting story and Mills & Boon's innovative marketing ensured that Beatrice Grimshaw became a 'newly discovered' best-selling popular author in 1911.[49] The novel was published the same year in America by Moffatt, Yard of New York, serialised in several newspapers including the *Sydney Morning Herald*, and translated into German, Norwegian, Swedish, and Italian.

When the Red Gods Call was followed by some thirty-three romantic adventure stories in the same vein, including *White Savage Simon* (1919), *The Terrible Island* (1920), *My South Sea Sweetheart* (1921), *The Mystery of Tumbling Reef* (1932), and *Murder in Paradise* (1940). Grimshaw moved on from Mills & Boon in the early 1920s to the popular publisher Hurst & Blackett, during a period when Mills and Boon's earlier success was compromised by difficulties experienced during the First World War and the 1920s.[50] In 1928 she moved publishers again to Cassell & Co., a company with long-established distribution branches in America and the major cities of the Empire.[51] Meanwhile she remained a prolific journalist and a prodigious writer of short stories, publishing these in leading magazines such as the *Strand*, *National Geographic*, and the *Saturday Evening Post*. One of her novels, *Conn of the Coral Seas* (1922), became the big-budget film *The Adorable Outcast* (1928), shot on location in the western Pacific with a cast of some of Hollywood's most famous silent film stars.[52] By the end of the 1920s, she was a major commercial celebrity, featuring regularly in the press up to the Second World War. Indeed, as early as 1922, when she returned to England for the first time in fifteen years, several London newspapers and periodicals dispatched reporters to Plymouth to await her arrival.[53] Interest in America was also marked on this occasion: the *Washington Times*, for example, devoted a full page to Grimshaw in its Sunday Morning section on 2 July 1922, with a report from their London correspondent on the famous 'English' novelist, 'a woman of gentle breeding and cultivation' who had escaped with her life thanks to her 'physical strength, determined presence and good luck'.[54]

Despite the attention she gained in her lifetime, Grimshaw slipped into the background after her death and, if remembered at all, is usually claimed by Australia, where she died in 1953. Her descent into literary oblivion is startling in light of her extraordinary celebrity, influence and best-selling status over the first four decades of the twentieth century and doubtless relates not only to the 'lurid' consistency of her popular romances but also to the racist texture of her work when viewed from contemporary political perspectives. The limited critical attention she *has* received from scholars based in the modern Pacific nations, Australia, and her native Ulster since the mid 1970s has tended to focus on her perceived colonial and imperial enthusiasm, racism, and assumed conversion to what has been termed 'Australianism'.[55] Earlier attempts at literary retrieval were hesitant, with critics such as Susan Gardner delving into convolutions about 'not whether Grimshaw was racist … but whether and how white women's racism differed from white men's'.[56]

What should be recognised, however, lies beyond a superficial reading of this author in terms of her proximity to any colonial or imperial mission; her profile needs to be established – in the same regard as her commercial instincts – as pragmatic and expedient in the contexts of her lifetime. As Clare McCotter has noted, 'Empire is not posited by Grimshaw as a motivating factor behind her original decision to travel to the Pacific; it only becomes a justification for travel once she is already in Oceania.'[57] Grimshaw was a pioneering figure and a confident self-publicist. She fostered and maintained her reputation in remote locations, travelled to America and onwards to Fiji, Samoa, Tonga, Australia, New Zealand, Papua New Guinea, and beyond without family or independent financial means from the age of twenty-one.[58]

In her native Ireland, meanwhile, a combination of Revivalist exclusions and distaste for the British imperial project inevitably rendered Grimshaw doubly problematic. Her publicity work for early tourism complicates her inclusion in an orthodox narrative of the woman traveller, while the unlikely stretch from a background in conservative late Victorian Ulster to the social and political climate of 1950s Australia further obscures her critical (and national) position. The contradictions continue: she was an Ulster Protestant who rebelled against her religion and converted to Catholicism; she was a 'careerist' who never married but remained a lifelong advocate of the institution of marriage (in spite of the sentiments of her female protagonist in *Broken Away*); and she was a New Woman passionately committed to female independence who nonetheless penned endless commercial romances sustaining and perpetuating a patriarchal culture – one in which women, ultimately, fall into line with their husbands. This final element – a seemingly hidebound treatment of love and marriage in her work – is perplexing. The critic John Wilson Foster in his sampling of *Irish Novels, 1890–1940* includes *When the Red Gods Call* as one novel 'among many by Irish writers that try seriously to portray the competing tides of Victorianism and modernity', and this defence goes some way to explaining the heterodox quality of Grimshaw's career as a whole.[59] In other words, it must be recognised that she published her work at a complex stage of evolution in women's writing, her fiction (much less than her travel writing) bearing the pressures and strains of those late Victorian and Edwardian political aspirations which had not yet been converted into lived or legal reality.

In support of her claims to fresh critical attention, it is necessary to address, therefore, as this discussion has attempted to do, the nature of Grimshaw's authorship – including her commercial and publication strategies – as part of her overall political context. Such an account reveals her consistency as an independent writer who not only managed to move beyond an Irish Revival cradle but who survived in her career over half a century from the 1890s to the Second World War, a period of immense social change in the position of women as well as huge structural change in the literary marketplace. Her recognition of the compromised circumstances in the period of publishers such as John Lane, her confidence in moving to new publication platforms (including an international print journalism circuit), and her willingness to adapt to the demands of a mass popular readership through the channels of a new enterprise such as Mills & Boon, all speak to her rare status as one of the very few late nineteenth-century Irish writers, female or male, fully able to capitalise on a global field of book production, distribution, and reception. In this respect, her critical reputation can begin to find a foothold, in advance of more rigorous ideological scrutiny within the contexts of Irish literary history, New Woman fiction, and imperial popular culture studies.

Notes

1 Beatrice Grimshaw, *Broken Away* (London and New York: John Lane, The Bodley Head, 1897), p. 46.
2 Grimshaw, *Broken Away*, p. 87.
3 Beatrice Grimshaw, *When the Red Gods Call* (London: Mills & Boon, 1911).
4 Grimshaw was born at Cloona House, Dunmurry, Co. Antrim, on 3 February 1870, one of six surviving children (four daughters and two sons) of Nicholas Grimshaw and Ella Newsam. Biographical information on Grimshaw is contradictory and at times incorrect. The *Oxford Dictionary of National Biography* entry for Grimshaw states that Eleanor Thomson (née Newsam) of Co. Cork was her mother, and Eugénie and Hugh Laracy refer to her mother as 'Eleanor Newson' of Co. Cork. 'Grimshaw, Beatrice Ethel (1870–1953)', *Oxford Dictionary of National Biography*, Oxford University Press (May 2009). Available at www.oxforddnb.com/view/article/54576. Accessed 29 April 2015. However, a notice in the *Morning Post* of 7 February 1861 is accurate, we believe, in the context of other information. It records the marriage in London of Nicholas William Grimshaw to Ella, only daughter of James Ramsey Newsam of Belfast and Walsall (Lancashire).
5 'About Myself: The Autobiography of a Novelist', *Register* (Adelaide) (17 September 1921), p. 4.
6 Beatrice Grimshaw, 'How I Found Adventure', *Blue Book* (April 1939). Available at http://pulprack.com/arch/2003/02/beatrice_grimsh.html. Accessed 15 September 2013.
7 The *Irish Cyclist* was a weekly magazine founded by Richard James Mecredy in 1883. There was a major expansion of the sport of cycling during the 1880s with cycling clubs established throughout Great Britain and Ireland. Before the invention of the new woman's safety cycle in 1887, the sport was largely inaccessible to women because their long skirts made cycling on the 'ordinary' or penny farthing impossible. Grimshaw, however, had been an enthusiastic cyclist since childhood and relished the physical freedom the sport afforded her. She was particularly proud of gaining the women's twenty-four-hour cycling record in the early 1890s.
8 The National Library of Ireland holds some issues of the *Social Review* in its Ephemera Collection. See also Susan M. Gardner, 'For Love and Money: Beatrice Grimshaw's Passage to Papua' (Ph.D., Rhodes University, 1986). Gardner identified sixty-six articles authored under pseudonyms such as Maev, Graphis, Orlando Lyall, Candid Jane, and Aunt Norah. The list of articles is reproduced in Peter Ruber and Victor A. Berch, 'Beatrice (Ethel) Grimshaw: A Bibliography in Progress' (2003). Available at http://pulprack.com.arch/2004/04/beatrice_ethel.html. Accessed 15 September 2013.
9 Grimshaw, *Broken Away*, p. 46.
10 For a longer discussion of John Lane in the 1890s, see Wendell V. Harris, 'John Lane's Keynotes Series and the Fiction of the 1890s', *PMLA*, 83:5 (1968), 1407–13. See also J. Lewis May, *John Lane and the Nineties* (London: John Lane, The Bodley Head, 1936).
11 John A. Sutherland, *Victorian Novelists and Publishers* (London: Athlone Press, 1976), p. 10.

12 Richard Altick, *The English Common Reader: A Social History of the Mass Reading Public, 1800–1900* (Chicago, Ill.: Chicago University Press, 1957), p. 274.
13 'Copyright', *Fortnightly Review*, 27 (1880); quoted in Philip Waller, *Writers, Readers and Reputations: Literary Life in Britain, 1870–1918* (Oxford: Oxford University Press, 2006), p. 327.
14 J. M. Barrie, 'A Plea for Smaller Books', in J. M. Barrie (ed.), *Two of Them* (New York: Lovell, Coryell & Co., 1893), pp. 192–6.
15 Troy J. Bassett, 'The Production of Three-Volume Novels in Britain, 1863–97', *Papers of the Bibliographical Society of America*, 102:1 (2008), 61–75, at p. 73.
16 Bassett, 'Three-Volume Novels in Britain', p. 65.
17 R. A. Gettman, *A Victorian Publisher: A Study of the Bentley Papers* (Cambridge: Cambridge University Press, 1960), p. 263.
18 Paul Delany, *Literature, Money, and the Market: From Trollope to Amis* (Basingstoke: Palgrave Macmillan, 2002), p. 103.
19 May, *John Lane in the Nineties*, p. 75.
20 Whitney Standlee, 'George Egerton, James Joyce, and the Irish *Künstlerroman*', *Irish Studies Review*, 18:4 (2010), 439–52, at p. 442.
21 Harris, 'John Lane's Keynotes Series', p. 1410.
22 Harris, 'John Lane's Keynotes Series', pp. 1409–10.
23 Short stories were a relatively new form in the 1890s. *Strand Magazine*, founded in 1891, was an early publisher of the form.
24 Sally Ledger, 'The New Woman and Feminist Fictions', in Gail Marshall (ed.), *The Cambridge Guide to the Fin de Siècle* (Cambridge: Cambridge University Press, 2007), pp. 153–68, at p. 154.
25 Standlee, 'George Egerton', p. 440.
26 Sally Ledger, *The New Woman: Fiction and Feminism at the Fin de Siècle* (Manchester: Manchester University Press, 1997), p. 1.
27 Ledger, *The New Woman*, p. 5.
28 When Wilde was arrested, the headlines of the Sunday papers shouted 'Arrest of Oscar Wilde, *Yellow Book* under his arm!' 'It killed *The Yellow Book* and it nearly killed me', Lane said afterwards according to his colleague. May, *John Lane and the Nineties*, p. 75.
29 May, *John Lane and the Nineties*, p. 80.
30 Standlee, 'George Egerton', p. 441. Elkin Mathews and John Lane respectively wrote letters to *The Times* on 8 April 1895 and the *New York Times* on 12 April 1895 distancing themselves from Wilde.
31 Letter from George Egerton to John Lane (10 November 1896). Selected Papers of Mary Chavelita Bright, Department of Rare Books and Special Collections, Princeton University, Box 2, Folder 17. Quoted in Standlee, 'George Egerton', p. 440.
32 Standlee, 'George Egerton', p. 442.
33 'Yesterday's New Books', *London Standard* (9 April 1897), p. 3.
34 Beatrice Grimshaw, *Isles of Adventure* (London: Herbert Jenkins, 1930), p. 20.
35 'Woman Enters Island Wilds: Plucky Irish Girl on Exploring Trip in the South Seas', *San Francisco Call* (2 July 1905), p. 3. The plucky Irish girl was then aged thirty-five. Grimshaw sent the story to the paper from Fiji.
36 Grimshaw sent these stories from the South Seas, and newspapers made few if any changes to her copy. The canoe and shark story was syndicated by several American newspapers including the *Omaha Sunday Bee* under the headline 'Authoress in Simple Life: Learning to Canoe in Tonga – Swimming Impossible Because of Sharks' (6 October 1907), p. 2.
37 Hugh Laracy and Eugénie Laracy, 'Beatrice Grimshaw: Pride and Prejudice in Papua', *Journal of Pacific History*, 12:3 (1977), 154–75, at p. 157.
38 *In The Strange South Seas* was published in London by Nelson's in 1911 in time for the summer holiday season in their 'Most Famous Books of Biography and Travel', one of their 'Popular Libraries for the Holidays' series. Hutchinson reissued it for the Christmas 1911 market as a one-shilling volume.

39 'In the Wilds of Papua: Miss Beatrice Grimshaw's Experiences', *Northern Miner* (28 September 1908), p. 2. This interview, like most with Grimshaw, was widely syndicated to other newspapers.
40 'In the Wilds of Papua'.
41 Beatrice Grimshaw, *The New New Guinea* (London: Hutchinson, 1910).
42 'About Myself: The Autobiography of a Novelist', *Register* (Adelaide) (17 September 1921), p. 4.
43 Grimshaw to Murray (23 December 1909). Murray Papers, A3138, Mitchell Library, State Library of New South Wales, Sydney. Sir Hubert Murray (1860–1940) was the son of an Irish Catholic father from Dublin and an English Anglican mother who became President of the Legislative Council of New South Wales. Like Grimshaw, he was a Catholic convert. Critics have speculated that Grimshaw and Murray were lovers, but there is no firm evidence of an affair. There are numerous photographs of Grimshaw as if in residence at Government House. See F. J. West, 'Murray, Sir (John) Hubert Plunkett (1861–1940)', *Oxford Dictionary of National Biography*, Oxford University Press, 2004. Available at www.oxforddnb.com/view/article/35168. Accessed 13 March 2013.
44 '"Southward Ho!" Adventurous Career: Miss Beatrice Grimshaw', *Sydney Morning Herald* (21 February 1935), p. 4.
45 Joseph McAleer, *Passion's Fortune: The Story of Mills & Boon* (Oxford: Oxford University Press, 1999), p. 13.
46 McAleer, *Passion's Fortune*, p. 14.
47 McAleer, *Passion's Fortune*, p. 17.
48 McAleer, *Passion's Fortune*, p. 21. There is nothing in the archive to indicate why 15 June was selected, and there is no reference to it in the history of the firm. We suggest that publishing firms had already begun to identify a summer holiday market. See note 38 above on Nelson's 'Popular Libraries for the Holidays' series.
49 McAleer, *Passion's Fortune*, p. 27. Fortuitously in terms of publicity for Grimshaw and her publishers, publication of the novel coincided with the widely reported disappearance in Papua of the Colonial Administrator and his party on an expedition in the interior in 1910, with Grimshaw herself in Papua providing newspapers with coverage of the event. The publisher understood the emerging concept of celebrity marketing, and photographs of Grimshaw appeared in several newspapers and periodicals including the *Illustrated London News* of 22 July 1911, captioned 'Miss Beatrice Grimshaw whose new novel "When the Red Gods Call" has just been published by Messrs. Mills and Boon.'
50 Gerald Mills and Charles Boon were both called up in 1916 when conscription was extended, leaving Margaret Boon, Charles's sister, to run the firm, whose fortunes declined rapidly in the period. See McAleer, *Passion's Fortune*, pp. 38, 39–41.
51 Cassell's grew rapidly after its establishment in 1848, opening offices in New York (1860), Paris (1871), Melbourne (1884), Sydney (1895), Toronto (1907), and close to Wellington, New Zealand (1920). By the late 1940s, the firm would add offices in Calcutta, Johannesburg, Karachi, and Auckland.
52 'The Adorable Outcast and Samoans', *Brisbane Courier* (29 June 1928), p. 18. The film's director was Norman Dawn and its principal actors were Edward Burns, Edith Roberts, and Walter Long. Although the film's stars were American, it was produced by Australasian films. It was retitled *Black Cargoes of the South Seas* on its American cinematic release.
53 In an article entitled 'Miss Beatrice Grimshaw to Reach Plymouth Today', the *Western Morning News* reported on 5 May 1922 that 'There is rather more than a certain activity on the part of the London Press in regard to Plymouth today. Representatives of the acme of the major papers have been for several days waiting for the arrival of the *Bhamo*, of the Henderson Line, now on her way from Rangoon. When the ship drops anchor sometime this morning she will be invaded by pressmen … The object of their search is Miss Beatrice Grimshaw … curiously enough her return synchronises with the appearance of her latest book, *Conn of the Coral Seas* (Hurst & Blackett, 7*s.* 6*d.*)'.
54 '15 Years with New Guinea Cannibals: Beatrice Grimshaw, the Daring English Writer, Nearly Eaten Up by Savages Time After Time, but She Learned a Lot of Surprising

Things for Her Next Novel'. *Washington Times* (2 July 1922), p. 3. The *Washington Times* was not alone in mistakenly attributing English nationality to Grimshaw.

55 Susan Gardner, 'A "'Vert to Australianism": Beatrice Grimshaw and the Bicentenary', Hecate Press (30 November 1987). Available at http://webcache.googleusercontent .com/search?q=cache:WuG4AvRjfvcJ:www.grimshaworigin.org/BeatriceGwHecate. htm+&cd=1&hl=en&ct=clnk&gl=ie. Accessed 9 March 2013.

56 Gardner, 'A "'Vert to Australianism" '.

57 Clare McCotter, 'Woman Traveller/Colonial Tourist: Deconstructing the Great Divide in Beatrice Grimshaw's Travel Writing', *Irish Studies Review*, 15:4 (2007), 481–506, at p. 482.

58 Her brothers Ramsey and Osborne, however, joined her in Papua when she was already established there and later moved with her to Australia.

59 John Wilson Foster, *Irish Novels, 1890–1940: New Bearings in Culture and Fiction* (Oxford: Oxford University Press, 2008), p. 62.

6

Women, ambition, and the city, 1890–1910

Ciaran O'Neill and Mai Yatani

> 'Ah! there now, Mrs Hepenstall,' cut in some one else, 'what is there new in style this time in London? It's ludicrous the way we're behind here.' 'Yes; positively we are two years behind Paris!' This from a pretty little lady, who had just come in.
>
> 'Paris! Bless us,' said the hostess, 'we don't think of Paris. London is good enough for us.'[1]

THE 'provinciality' of the Irish city is beautifully encapsulated in May Laffan's quote above. The sense of being one step behind London and two behind Paris was not unrealistic or unfair. In fiction, as in life, upward social mobility is normally achieved through a complex matrix of personal, political, and social contacts. A social climber will typically be introduced to high society by a wealthy patron, or their path to the top will be made easier by access to economic, cultural, or social capital. Ireland's provincial status was a block to this type of upward mobility. In the nineteenth century, Ireland had no capital city, and, as a result, the social and political elite were largely based in London. Smaller cities in minor polities could not compete in terms of access to social or economic capital.

Dublin, in contrast to Paris, London, or New York, had neither a very active high social circle nor a particularly buoyant local economy. Without a parliament, the city was something of a provincial sideshow, where great fortunes were made rarely, and the Dublin Castle social season was a six-week exercise in faded grandeur, ending on St Patrick's Day with a ball. The second city, Belfast, was too new a metropolis to have developed an internationally acclaimed and sophisticated social, cultural, and literary scene, despite the existence of an energetic and expanding industrial middle class.[2] The social circles of Limerick, Galway, or Cork were likewise too small and too insular to allow even the most imaginative of authors to use them as a backdrop for a society novel. Since the Act of Union, an aspirant politico, socialite, or dandy of any merit or ambition found themselves drawn inexorably to London.[3]

During the period from 1890 to 1910, Irish women writers such as Hannah Lynch, Katherine Cecil Thurston, and George Egerton frequently embedded their own authorial achievements or ambitions in their female (and male) characters. A common theme in such novels is the use of the metropole (usually London) as a site of greater personal liberty and freedom for young female characters. This instrumental use of the city as a site for either corporal or intellectual freedom during the 'Irish Ireland' or 'Revival' period offers us an opportunity to shift the focus away from Irish writers and their portrayal of the West of Ireland as a refuge from the horrors of rapidly advancing capitalism and materialism. The idea of Irish women excelling in the city continues to strike us as anachronistic in an era of apparently limited female professional upward mobility. Historians have written of the later nineteenth century as a period in which female migration from Ireland was stimulated and accelerated as a response to the rather narrow range of life opportunities available domestically.[4] The writers discussed here may be connected to this general picture, though the absence of a developed literature on most of their work has much to do with the fact that literary canons in Ireland, Britain, and elsewhere have predominantly consisted of texts by men.

For Irish women writers at the turn of the century, London was the centre of the literary world, and for those who achieved significant sales, it was the main publishing market. The conflict inherent in being an *Irish* writer in a city of global importance may not differ in general terms from the conflict inherent in being a Scottish or Cornish writer in London, or a Romanian or Hungarian writer in Paris, for that matter. Depending on the circumstances of each author, moving to a major city could be a welcome step up socially or else precipitate a state of being that could culminate in what the philosopher and critic György Lukács called 'transcendental homelessness'.[5] Not all writers felt strongly about their roots, while some felt they could never escape them. In most cases, an author felt either alienated and uprooted, or struggled to assimilate even when they desired to. This conflict provided a compelling base for their fiction.

Many of the works discussed here have either an urban focus or explicitly or implicitly reject the Western idyll, and many of them fell outside the canon of Irish literature in its creation phase. Challenging literature produced by Irish women at home or abroad has either been obscured or else bracketed within the early Modernist, Ibsenite, Decadent, or New Woman movements. In an Irish context, if these texts and their authors have been mentioned at all, it is usually through the lens of partisan politics: nationalist, unionist, or socialist.[6] These were labels that many of the writers themselves resisted, despite being surrounded and to some extent shaped by them.[7] Instead, we will concentrate on two main lines of argument, both of which relate to the idea that women's writing in this period often embedded authorial ambition in an urban context. In the first instance, this chapter focuses on a group of Irish writers who rejected, either directly or indirectly, the Western idyll propagated during the Revival period. This impulse is evident in the work of writers such as Katharine Tynan, Rosa Mulholland, and Emily Lawless. The effect of their denigration of the rural, primitive West was to privilege whatever was progressive, scientific, and urban. This tendency among Irish women writers is telling and makes an analysis of their explicitly urban stories worthwhile. Accordingly, we will then outline the utilisation of urban spaces by writers most often associated with the Decadent and New Woman novelists: Irish women making their living in Paris or London, such as George Egerton, 'Iota', and Katherine Cecil Thurston, who all created ambitious independent female characters who reflected at least some of the ideals of their authors.

The city in Irish writing

THE lack of a dynamic city was reflected in Irish writing of the *fin de siècle* and Edwardian period. The second-rate nature of Dublin is perceptible in everything from the squalor and stasis of James Joyce's *Dubliners* (1914) to the title of Mary Daly's classic history of the city in this period, *Dublin, the Deposed Capital: A Social and Economic History, 1860–1914*.[8] Deserted by its parliamentarians in the aftermath of the Act of Union, Dublin had never quite managed to regain its eighteenth-century grandeur. Its nineteenth-century experience was one of gradual depreciation as the industrial cities of northern England boomed and bustled.[9] Charles Lever captured the essence of this in his novel *Roland Cashel* (1850), in which he shows his character Mr Softly gently warning Cashel of Dublin's limitations: 'Dublin is a city which, from a great variety of causes, will always be exposed to very variable and opposing criticisms. To begin, it is provincial.'[10] The sense of being provincial, of course, was not something that was unique to Irish locations or to Ireland's literature but was just as evident in the far-flung colonies. A. A. Phillips' term 'cultural cringe', coined in the 1950s in relation to what he saw as an Australian inferiority complex with respect to native 'high' culture, is often equally evident in Irish Victorian fiction.[11]

These limitations and tensions are played out in May Laffan's *Hogan MP* (1876), where the eponymous character is a young Roman Catholic politician on the rise in Dublin and aiming for election to parliament in London. Dublin is presented as a grubby, seedy, and provincial city. It is London's lesser relation, full to the brim of publicans and builders on the lookout for an advantageous match for their convent-educated daughters. The book centres on an ill-fated romance between Hogan and Nellie Davoren, a 'slender girl of eighteen'.[12] Nellie's cosmopolitanism is a bonus to her prospects when the pair are introduced at the convent school of a mutual friend. The Mother Superior notes that Miss Davoren is difficult to place but nonetheless contrives to order her sophistication hierarchically in terms of Dublin, then England: 'Something in the young lady's tone as well as her accent, which was vastly different from that of the others, not Dublin, and yet not English of the very decided sort the reverend Mother was most accustomed to hear, struck her as remarkable.'[13] In the novel, Hogan's ambition is his downfall and a poorly paid clerkship in the colonies his eventual comeuppance. In conversation with his adviser and friend, Mr Saltasche, Hogan declares Dublin 'a drop of ditchwater under a microscope. Everybody pushing upwards on the social ladder, kicking down those behind.'[14] In Laffan's Dublin, social segregation is not of the desirable level, fashion is two years out of date, and politics and society are mere sham. 'The Chamberlains must be perfect nonentities', muses one of her characters in relation to a guest list that is too democratic for her liking, 'they allow tradespeople of all sorts in … In London you are safe not to meet that sort of mud.'[15]

The feeling that Dublin is a second-rate city runs through Irish literature in the nineteenth century, and the Irish capital seldom features as a dynamic setting for a novel written by an Irish writer.[16] This was partly rooted in the reality of cultural life in the city. Women could not take a full and active part in society for much of the nineteenth century, and even the location of a space in which to read could be challenging.[17] Many sought means to overcome intellectual restriction, whether domestic or external. Katharine Tynan remembered that although the convent school she attended as a girl worked hard to severely limit their pupils' choice of books, she and her fellow classmates invariably found ways to read those books and discuss them with their peers.[18] As previous studies have pointed out, education was one important factor that formed female reading habits, but family networks could also be utilised to source reading that might not have been recommended by a nun.[19] After leaving school, women visited libraries in pursuit of books, attending various institutions according to the type of books they required. For this to be possible, women had to be based in urban areas, and the choice was greater in proportion to the size of the city and the number of readers in it. British and French social historians have traced the growth of civic elites alongside a renewed optimism for the city as a locus for progressive association and progress from the 1840s onwards.[20] In the popular imagination at least, the city was linked with liberalism, progress, and modernity. As Patrick Joyce has noted, in the liberal worldview of the later nineteenth century the city became a natural centre of association 'in contrast to the backwardness and stupidity of the rural world'.[21]

Rejecting the West

FOCUSING her argument especially on Irish-language texts produced by Irish women writers, Ríona Nic Congáil has noted that women writers of the Revival period tended to write less romantically of the West than their male counterparts.[22] An obvious example of such an early Revival 'resistant' text in English is Emily Lawless's much-neglected *Grania: The Story of an Island* (1892).[23] Lawless was a daughter of a major landowner, the third Lord Cloncurry, the majority of whose lands were in Limerick and Kildare. She had spent portions of her youth holidaying in Connemara and by the time she came to write *Grania* had already found fame as the author of another novel based on the West, *Hurrish* (1886). Her landed background gained her notoriety in literary circles early in her career, but it also meant that her work was scrutinised more closely than that of her contemporaries for any hint of West Britishness or the kind of separatist nationalism that might set her apart from the majority of her class. Her lead character, Grania O'Malley, is largely untouched by modern and urban Ireland, thus prefiguring the Western peasants of later Abbey plays by Synge and others. Yet she is in every way the most powerful and active character in a story of frustrated ambition and desires.

The protagonist is located at the intersection of two important Irish myths rejuvenated and recast in the Revival era. The first of these myths, Diarmuid and Gráinne, provides the inspiration for the thwarted love story. The other links Lawless's Grania with the legendary pirate queen of the western seaboard, Grace O'Malley, in a way that would have been immediately obvious to contemporary readers of the novel, but Grania's tale is not one of comparable inspirational independence. She is the wealthiest girl in Inishmaan, but it is an island of very limited economic possibilities. Betrothed to Murdough Blake, a feckless Celt of the stereotypical kind in Irish literature, Grania is also characterised as feral and emotional, but she nonetheless has capital and power, and it is real and actual as opposed to ethereal and spiritual.

The outside world is represented by Murdough's increasingly frequent trips to Galway city, where he drinks and gambles against their projected future. The world also encroaches on this island world in the form of passing ships on the Atlantic, 'from the East Indies, or, maybe America, or better still, California'.[24] Lawless depicts the Irish town as a place of vice and corruption, while emigration is seen as offering hope and potential progress. There is no escape for Grania, who instead perishes on the rocks in a futile attempt to summon a priest to administer last rites to her ailing sister, Honor. The novel is a prolonged excoriation of the West as a place of no hope. J. M. Synge would later disparage *Grania* by writing that the 'real Aran spirit' was absent from the novel, but then Lawless saw the West very differently from Synge.[25]

Lawless was rather unloved by contemporary Irish critics, and James H. Murphy has recently noted the crushing pessimism of her novels of the 1880s.[26] Perhaps what is most crushing about them is that she can offer no sympathetic educated or half-educated character a way out of the barren landscape she has created. For other writers, that lack was overcome by the possibilities of the city in their fiction, but here denigration of the West ought to be seen as a mirror image of that tendency.

Katharine Tynan (1859–1931), in contrast to Lawless, was a prolific writer and self-chronicler, author of over 100 novels as well as numerous collections of short stories, poems, and reviews. In Tynan's writing, quantity sometimes triumphs over quality in an oeuvre that nevertheless reveals her as much a Revival insider-outsider as Lawless was. Her relocation to London in 1893 allowed her to critique aspects of the Revival from a safe distance. Tynan's Irish peasants tend to be unsympathetic and sometimes barbarous. Her relationship to the city is a little more positive, as befitted an author who announced in correspondence in 1884 that her 'earthly ambition' was to 'get in to a London literary circle'.[27]

Tynan published several works in her early years in London, all of which exhibit some level of fondness and respect for country life, although this is often wrapped in caustic or backhanded compliment.[28] In *The Way of a Maid* (1895), she recreates a 'typical Irish county town' she names Coolevara, in which the Catholic majority are characterised as 'hard-working' and even 'thrifty', but many of the familiar tropes remain. They are 'as quick with a blow as a kiss', they gamble, and are indecorous.[29] One could argue that there was a subtle shift in her attitude towards rural Ireland during her London years. Tynan became gradually more critical of Irish rurality from the late 1890s. The heroines of her impoverished Western gentry family in *The Handsome Brandons: A Story for Girls* (1900) are surrounded by decay and frustration, and their descent into tragedy is prevented only by a rich benefactor, Mr Desmond, returning to marry the eldest of them at the novel's end.[30] In the same year, Tynan's *A Daughter of the Fields* (1900) follows a similar pattern, when the heroine Meg O'Donoghue returns from an aristocratic education in a French convent 'unsuited to the life she must lead' and surrounded by peasants of the stereotypical sort.[31]

Tynan's relationship with London was complex. When she settled there it was not to the literary circles she had once dreamed of but to a life of suburban banality in Ealing. She wrestled with her Irish nationalism, with her anonymity, and with her lack of a supportive circle. In one of her memoirs, she notes:

> The London suburb is not exactly a friendly place ... Literary people are somewhat unclassed, if not declassed, in the London suburb ... The respectable suburb is not sure of the literary person. You may receive letters in a name which is not your married name ... Your children are imps. You do not look after your servants. Then, if you are Irish and do not go to the recognised churches – one or the other of them – things look black indeed. In London proper you may be anything you like: it is nobody's business but your own. In the suburbs, if the common formula does not apply to you, you are condemned beforehand.[32]

When Tynan wrote characters based in London, however, she tended to open out a world of possibilities that contrasted with her own suburban alienation. In *Heart o' Gold; or, The Little Princess* (1912), her orphaned heroines, Cushla and Nancy MacSweeney, are spirited away by their Irish aunt, Mrs Penrose, from their family's 'savage' Irish castle in a chaotic rural Ireland. They move to London, which Cushla finds 'cold and formal' in comparison to her home.[33] Her sister Nancy, however, has the opposite reaction, assimilating into English society with ease and disdaining her provincial origins. It is a classic Tynan text in that she was more than capable of holding two opposing views simultaneously and thus issuing a challenge to her reader and perhaps herself.[34]

Rosa Mulholland (1841–1921), later Lady Gilbert, anticipated both Lawless and Tynan in her derision of rurality and the provincial in many of her works of fiction, whether it was railing against the 'milk-and-water conventionalism' of rural Ireland in *The O'Shaughnessy Girls* (1911) late in her career or championing the city in her first novel, a *Künstlerroman* entitled *Dunmara* (1864).[35] Mulholland consistently wrote fiction with independent, strong-willed women, and her later work was mostly directed at young readers. A Belfast-born Catholic writer with a long and successful career, Mulholland was an established professional in Dublin long before she married the historian John Gilbert in 1891. The city appears as a distant but alluring figure in her early work, and, like Laffan, she acknowledges and appears to have internalised the idea that English cultural superiority was somehow genuine.

In *Cynthia's Bonnet Shop* (1901), the eponymous character emerges from an impoverished genteel background to become an independent trader in London, along with her sister Befind, who has little interest in the bonnets being traded by Cynthia but a significant interest in amateur astronomy. Befind meets her future husband, Professor Anstruther, once in Ireland and again in Paris. Her career ambitions are to work in an observatory: '"do tell me something, Professor Anstruther. They say that women are employed in some of the observatories. Could I ever learn to be clever enough for that kind of work? And how should I set about qualifying myself?" '[36] Mulholland's treatment of Befind in the novel is an enabling device for her young adult readers. Here she promotes a match that is based on intellectual curiosity and career possibilities rather than utilising the typical rescue trope in popular female-centred fiction: the appearance of an older gentleman who will provide the economic and social capital for a life of leisure and safety. Mulholland instead presents us with a businesswoman and scientist within the confines of the traditional girls' tale, a nod from a professional to the expanding credentialism of a generation of young readers with access to university qualifications that were unavailable in her own youth.

The O'Shaughnessy Girls likewise revolves around the fortunes of two sisters, Bluebell (Bell) and Lavender, the improbably named youngest daughters of Lady Sybil O'Shaughnessy, who resides by the banks of the Blackwater river in rural south Munster. The locality is described variously as 'outside of civilisation' and out of touch with 'the fashions of the present moment'.[37] Bell becomes central to the story, having left home to join her older sisters, Heliantha and Gentianella, in England. Mulholland focuses on the assimilation of both older sisters into high society:

> The two elder daughters, Heliantha and Gentianella ... had grown up to excel even their mother in beauty. The tall, slim figures, the golden hair and blue eyes, and the faultless features of these Irish maidens had excited much admiration among their English friends when they had gone visiting across the Channel, enjoying a season in London ... There was nothing Irish about them except a little touch of the unconventional, and a slight musical intonation in speech hardly to be objected to as brogue, which, it was admitted, might by some be considered even charming. The event proved the justice of this admission; for they married promptly, and were admitted with favour into aristocratic English families.[38]

In Mulholland's text, just enough 'Irishness' provides the older sisters with a useful signifier of difference on the marriage market. It is, however, ultimately a device deployed to set up the *Bildung* of their more independent-minded younger sister. Once based in London with Heliantha, Bell begins to articulate feminist sensibilities with greater regularity, rejecting high society but taking a liking to amateur dramatics.[39] 'The mere fact of her being in London', Mulholland muses, 'seemed to assure her of extraordinary probabilities, and every day brought a suggestion of something wonderful that might happen before night.'[40]

Having joined an acting troupe in a move maligned by Lady Sybil back in Ireland, Bell explains that marriage holds no allure for her and that 'it is a woman's resolution to do something with her life besides stitching embroideries, or playing golf, or tending roses. One must have some experience of life before one begins to grow old.'[41] Under her sister's patronage, Bell excels in her study of performance and becomes increasingly desirous of a career as a professional actress.[42] Alongside her training, her distaste for the conventional life grows more evident:

> What was there to withhold her, except the prejudice of a milk-and-water conventionalism? ... She could not look forward to a life of vegetation on the Blackwater, so dear to her mother and Lavender; and even more distasteful to her was the life of an establishment by marriage, as she saw it exemplified in the cases of Heliantha and Gentianella.... 'If I were a man', she said to herself, 'there would be no question about it. I should be allowed the privilege of selecting a profession for myself in accordance with my tastes and my talents.'[43]

Mulholland's treatment of the city in *Dunmara* and *The O'Shaughnessy Girls* is arguably more positive and empowering than in the work of Lawless or Tynan. All three paint unflattering portraits of rural life while urban life can offer both positive and negative possibilities. Their fiction suggests that where a man might find peace or purpose in uncivilised Ireland, a woman's path to self-actualisation will require a degree of autonomy only achieved through professional qualification or the kind of commercial opportunities afforded by a metropolitan environment. Both of these could only be achieved by using the city as an enabling space. The heroines of Lawless found the West so stifling that they could not see a path to escape, but Tynan's and Mulholland's could, and the lesson was not lost on the next generation of Irish writers.

Ambition, New Women, and the city

In their standard-bearing works on the novel in this period, both John Wilson Foster and James H. Murphy note the existence of a group of cosmopolitan female writers who moved from Ireland to England at an early age yet retained a provincial identity that had an impact on their published work, at least to some degree.[44] Writers such as Emily Lawless attempted English-based books as well – her first novel was a story of society life in London – but such enterprise frequently fared badly with an Irish market. Several other contemporaries of Lawless had gone a step further and made their art and life in London. Prominent among them were several of the earliest New Woman writers, such as the Co. Down-born novelist Frances Elizabeth Bellenden Clarke McFall (1854–1943), better known by her pen name, Sarah Grand. Like Grand, the Tipperary-born Kathleen De Vere Hunt (1852/53–1926), later Mannington Caffyn, was an avant-garde writer of the 1890s not usually considered as an Irish writer but rather as a New Woman writer. She sometimes wrote under a pen name (Iota) as did the marginally younger Mary Chavelita Dunne (1859–1945), who wrote as George Egerton and also produced her most acclaimed work in the 1890s. Egerton was born in Australia but self-identified as intensely Irish.[45] She grew up in Queen's County in the midlands of Ireland before moving to London just after the publication of her riotously successful short-story collection, *Keynotes*, in 1893.

All three women were aged thirty-five to fifty at the height of their writing careers; all succeeded as writers in London at the *fin de siècle*; and all wrote compelling feminist fiction coloured by their own provincial origins in the years before the mid-1890s conservative literary backlash against both Decadent and New Woman writing.[46] They were, naturally enough, educated to a high degree and had either studied in Germany or England (Egerton and Grand) or had been home-tutored by English and German governesses (Iota). As such, they were writing to two main audiences. The first, and most obvious, was the British market of Decadent and New Woman fiction. Second, and more speculatively, they were writing their frustration with Ireland to an Irish readership comprised of a growing strata of well-educated lower-middle-class and middle-class young women. There had been an expansion of high literacy among Irish women among the first generations to have had advanced intermediate education and university education available to them after the passing of the Intermediate Education (Ireland) Act (1878) and the University Education (Ireland) Act (1879). As Raftery and others have noted, the Intermediate Education Act of 1878 allowed public competition between the genders in open examinations, affording girls the opportunity to prove an intellectual equality for the first time. By 1900, the percentage of girls taking the exam had risen to more than a quarter of the 7,608 candidates.[47] It was a similar tale of rapid educational progress for middle-class Irish women seeking higher qualifications from 1879, when the University Act made it possible for women to be awarded degrees.[48] Most girls availing of this education were receiving it in urban contexts and emerging into adulthood in the 1890s and 1900s, in a generation much written about in Irish history.[49]

Kathleen Caffyn's first novel, *A Yellow Aster* (1894), was published under her pen name, Iota.[50] The title is a metaphor for the novel's 'unnatural' heroine: anomalies in the natural world, yellow asters can only be produced through scientific manipulation. Gwen Waring, the prototypically rational and emotionless heroine, is similarly manipulated into being, having been raised in an experimental manner by parents apparently incapable of demonstrative love. *A Yellow Aster* was received as a New Woman novel, though it was perhaps intended as a critique of the construct. A second novel, *Children of Circumstance* (1894), revolved around an amicable *ménage à trois* in London's East End, where Caffyn herself had trained to be a nurse in the 1870s.

Her fifth novel, *Poor Max: A Novel* (1898), also showcased her willingness to reverse and deconstruct gender roles in her time and again was based in London.[51] It is a relentless and progressive emasculation of the title character, Max Morland, by his circle of friends in London and his Irish wife, Judith Becher. Caffyn gradually works gender norms around to the point that by the novel's end, Morland, a temperamental and unproductive writer, exhibits stereotypically female traits. He is 'irrational' and displays a 'feminine intuition'. '[B]eautiful to look at' and 'sensitive', he is also entirely undependable.[52] His wife, in exasperation, takes control of not only the management of her own affairs but of his also. Their married life unfolds in suburban west London, in an apartment they have taken in Richmond – a far cry from the genteel, rural Irish background Judith Becher has previously known.

Modern city life gradually allows Judith to become an active agent in the direction of her own life and eventually to exert full control over both it and those surrounding her. She is a stern, man-like presence, and her creator is so keen to separate her from womanly traits that she portrays Judith as harbouring murderous rather than maternal feelings towards her family:

> 'I wonder if I could kill them – kill my own little children' – she put her fingers with a strange tenderness round each little neck in succession. 'I could – I could quite easily,' she said, turning away with a sigh. 'But women were not made to do nice easy little things – and – there's dinner, and Max said he was hungry as a hunter. I wonder if I look at all like a woman who could kill her husband and her little children? I wonder if any other women feel as I feel?'[53]

Trying to untangle the mess Max has made of their finances, she compares discussing such material matters with Max to 'wrestling with a will-o'-the-wisp … if only he had been the woman and I the man!'[54] Judith begins to write what she considers inferior but lucrative fiction, 'three horrid little books', allowing her to accrue an independent income with which she begins to cancel Max's debts.[55] Max has squandered the £3,000 he inherited and the £1,000 Judith provided on marriage, as well as running into debt with several creditors, including the lawyer Mr Graves, who would much rather deprive him of his strong-minded wife than any more of his fortune. At the end, Judith is left unencumbered by the foppish Max, who dies protesting eternal love for her, and is free to choose her own partner on more equal terms than her first, and to the material advantage of her children. Her second husband, Mr Graves, is predictable, dependable, and 'a little gouty'.[56] She marries him unromantically and rationally, and just after the failure of her last novel deprives her of what might have been total financial autonomy. Nevertheless, her compromise is on her own terms.[57] The city had given Judith a new career, a creative outlet, and the kind of leverage that was unthinkable in her previous rural existence.

Poor Max is given added spice by the autobiographical elements contained within it. Caffyn had begun her own writing career in earnest at a point when her husband, Stephen Mannington Caffyn, was experiencing serious financial strain. Stephen was a novelist, inventor, and medical doctor whose own two novels achieved critical acclaim in his lifetime, but he filed for bankruptcy in the early 1890s, citing the expense of educating their three sons at Cheltenham College.[58] The couple had settled in Australia for a time before moving back to England, when Kathleen's writing career began in earnest. Not only does the profile of Stephen match many aspects of Max, but Kathleen herself was, like Judith Becher, of a minor Irish gentry background.[59] This story of self-actualisation, we can speculate, speaks as much to the author's story as that of the lead character. The bulk of her novels were written between her husband's death and the outbreak of the First World War when she was left at liberty to write and develop as an artist in her new environment. The importance of the city to this progression impacted on her fiction in very visible ways.

Lyn Pykett has identified recurring patterns in heroines of New Woman fiction. They are very often written in the *Bildungsroman* tradition, as a *Künstlerroman*. This is certainly true of George Egerton's novel, *The Wheel of God* (1898).[60] In addition, they frequently involve a theme of sacrifice for art, an exploration of feminine interiority, a blurring of gender norms, and a critique of contemporary society. The protagonist is often exceptional, a genius even, and may or may not suffer an emotional or mental breakdown at some point in the novel. Though radically different in many aspects, the Decadents and New Woman writers were often grouped together in the public imagination as sexually explorative and deviant. Both genres are inherently urban. The city as an enabling agent has been taken for granted, even in discussions of the famous short-story collections of George Egerton, who, unlike Iota, has received consistent scholarly attention alongside Olive Schreiner and Mona Caird, researchers very often grouping her together with writers whose politics made her uncomfortable.[61] In New Woman writing, the path to financial and sexual independence was often achieved through the transformation of a 'feminine' pastime – be it painting or music – into a professional career of note. With writing careers, the transformation was more complex.

In her second short-story collection, *Discords* (1894), Egerton's emphasis shifted from the female sexual expression of *Keynotes* to an atmosphere of decay, boredom, and loneliness. In *Discords*, the importance of place is more and more prominent, and many of the stories reveal much the same derision of Dublin and exaltation of free London as we see in Laffan, Lawless, or Caffyn. In the opening story, 'A Psychological Moment at Three Periods', Egerton's protagonist is a proud woman coerced into an adulterous affair in Paris, which, having gone awry, her lover is attempting to buy his way out by offering her a pay-off via his corrupt and graceless lawyer, Aloysius Gonzaga O'Brien. It is the lawyer's manner as much as the proposal that fixates her. She maps out the reasons for his social failures. 'Neither schooling at Tullabeg, the shades of the Four Courts, nor mixing in such polite society as his success in Dublin has procured for him has deprived him of the ugliest Dublin accent.'[62] What is cosmopolitan is not uncritically preferred in her stories, however. In 'Gone Under', New York is a 'polyglot city of striking paradoxes', a 'gigantic sieve through which the surplus of the old world is silted over the new', which wearies, excites, and perplexes her working woman in equal measures.[63] The trope of the harried, lonely woman writer is evident in 'Wedlock', where her female lead is 'writing for money, writing because she must, because it is the tool given to her wherewith to carve her way'.[64]

In one of her most remarkable short stories, 'A Lost Masterpiece: A City Mood '93', Egerton captured the authorial gaze on the city. The story was published in the first issue of *The Yellow Book* alongside pieces by Henry James, George Moore, and Arthur Symons. Her unnamed, ungendered, narrator has 'come to town straight from a hillside cottage in a lonely ploughland' in a 'desire to mix with the crowd, to lay my ear once more to the heart of the world and listen to its life-throbs'.[65] They board a river steamer at Chelsea in good spirits and from that point until they step off again they chronicle the negatives of the city life around them, wondering at the tall 'giraffic' chimneys 'belching soot and smoke over the blackening city'.[66] Two musicians play a coarse music-hall ditty on a clapped-out harp and a violin. Stepping off the steamer, they reflect on their own work as it is being composed:

> I smiled benevolently at the passers-by. With their harassed business faces, and their shiny black bags bulging with the weight of common every-day documents, as I thought of the treat I would give them later on; the delicate feast I held in store for them, when I would transfer this dainty elusive birthling of my brain to paper for their benefit.[67]

This pleasant mood quickly dissipates with the appearance of a 'little woman' on a sidewalk near Chancery Lane. This woman, broad shouldered, wide of gait and tight-skirted, is in a hurry somewhere and overtakes the bus which our narrator has boarded. 'I look back at her, I criticise her, I anathematise her, I *hate* her!'[68] And then: 'What business had she, I ask, to come and thrust her white-handled umbrella into the delicate network of my nerves and untune their harmony? Does she realise what she has done?'[69] The story destabilises the reader by allowing them to see the writer travelling through the city in search of inspiration that can be converted into effective literary capital – a piece of fiction that will define the scene. The woman in a hurry is, of course, the New Woman, who has disrupted the ordinary course of things, especially for an author such as Egerton. The resentment and excitement are finely balanced as she is fascinated and infuriated by this intrusion in apparently equal measure. The New Woman will prosper in this anonymous city, and the use of two modern modes of transport by Egerton is not accidental. The vantage point of the narrator from steamer and bus is meant to show us that city life is now navigable in a way that does not discriminate by gender. Here we see the Irish writer in London, confronted by New Women and the faceless crowd, wondering where to situate themselves artistically.

The insertion of the self into fiction was a common narrative tactic for this type of Irish writer in London. Charlotte Riddell's *A Struggle for Fame* (1883) is based at least partly on her own experiences as a professional writer in London from the 1850s to the 1880s.[70] Egerton's novel *The Wheel of God* is likewise a semi-autobiographical account of the travails of a young woman in Dublin, New York, and London. Katharine Tynan chronicled her struggles in her various autobiographies much later. London looms largest in the fiction of this generation of Irish women writers, though New York also features in Egerton's work, as well as the Norwegian landscapes that evoke her own residence there in the late 1880s. Fewer Irish writers wrote of Paris, despite its European reputation as a centre of literature. One writer who did was Hannah Lynch (1859–62?–1904), born in Dublin, and an acquaintance of Katharine Tynan, who described her as one of the few people 'who eat, drink and dream books'.[71]

Imposters in Paris

LYNCH is, along with Iota, one of the least critically analysed writers in this group. Both Foster and Murphy have moved to rehabilitate her reputation in their recent surveys, and recent articles by Faith Binckes and Kathryn Laing on her best-known work, *An Autobiography of a Child* (1899), and her Parisian networks have also raised her profile.[72]

Lynch's early novels were steeped in the Parnellite and nationalist politics of her early adulthood.[73] When living in Ireland she was centrally involved in nationalist politics and, while in her twenties, was a friend of Anna Parnell. She in fact based the lead character in her third novel,

The Prince of the Glades (1891), at least partly on Anna's life story. She later moved between London, Paris, and elsewhere in Europe, either writing or working as a governess.

A stylish writer, Lynch was never a profitable one, and by 1903 she had fallen on hard times in Paris, her financial difficulties perhaps having contributed to her early death in 1904. In the interim, she produced seven more novels, several pieces of travel literature, a collection of short stories, and the impossible-to-categorise *Autobiography of a Child*. Her *Rosni Harvey* (1892) tracks the progress of an Irish female medical student and is partially set in Greece. The *Athenaeum* thought her 1897 novel *Jinny Blake* a 'very fair specimen of a modern novel' and noted how the action shifted pleasingly from Paris to London.[74] The *Academy*, on the other hand, found it a 'formless novel of manners'.[75] *Jinny Blake* features, like many of Lynch's novels, a strong central female character and is perhaps the most straightforward New Woman text in her oeuvre. A cosmopolitan figure of an altogether different nature to Rosni and Jinny is Mrs Raymond, the unlikely heroine of *An Odd Experiment* (1897). Mrs Raymond discovers her husband's infidelity with a 'passionate' young girl, Blanche, but, instead of stoic acceptance or violent rejection, she subverts the situation by adopting Blanche and inviting her into the family home for a remarkably polite domestic *ménage à trois*.

Lynch's last novels before her death were more personal affairs. A much-quoted passage from *Autobiography of a Child* posits Ireland as the most wretched land on earth for a girl to be born:

> Elsewhere boys are born in plenty. In Ireland, – the very wretchedest land on earth for woman, the one spot on the globe where no provision is made for her, and where parents consider themselves as exempt of all duty, of tenderness, of justice in her regard, where her lot as daughter, wife, and old maid bears no resemblance to the ideal of civilisation, – a dozen girls are born for one boy.[76]

The anger is palpable, delivered in breathless prose, and the assessment of the female experience not entirely unfair. Irish historians have generally agreed that the lot of women who remained in Ireland worsened in the post-Famine period, with recent work by Timothy Guinnane suggesting that low frequency of marriages in Irish society may have had as much to do with female resistance to an unattractive proposition as any other factors. The average age of marriage in this period was twenty-nine, and marriage rates were markedly lower among the better-educated and wealthier classes.[77]

This frustration with the lot of a young woman in *fin-de-siècle* Irish society is evident also in the work of Katherine Cecil Thurston (1875–1911).[78] Thurston grew up as Katherine Madden, daughter of the banker and nationalist Lord Mayor of Cork, Paul Madden. In *The Fly on the Wheel* (1908), the French-educated, cosmopolitan young female at the heart of the novel, Isabel Costello, grapples with infidelity and her return to provincial Ireland. This environment eventually asphyxiates Isabel, who commits suicide at the end of the novel in a scene drenched in religious and symbolic significance. In her final novel, *Max* (1910), a young Russian artist relocates to Paris '[i]n part to work, in part to play ... in part to learn life'.[79] Thurston's 'adventurer' is captivated by the city and its possibilities.

> But the eyes were wakeful, the soul of the adventurer was infinitely young. He looked at it all with a certain steadfastness that seemed to say, 'Yes, I see you! You are hideous, slatternly, unfriendly; but through all the disguise I recognize you. Through the mask I trace the features – subtle, alluring, fascinating. You are Paris! Paris!'[80]

The novel plays with themes of gender and provinciality throughout, with the vanities of his companions and staff at Max's three-franc hotel revolving around disguising or downplaying their disparate origins in a display of hierarchy that recalls the fiction of Balzac. Thurston's Paris is a place where Russians, Irish, Americans, and provincial French mix together in a swell of excess and romance. The novel pivots on the fact that Max is, in fact, a Russian princess, who has fled to Paris in disguise to escape the prospect of a marriage she cannot endure. The imposter features heavily across much of Thurston's fiction (including *The Circle*, *John Chilcote, MP*, *The Gambler*, and *Max*), and her central characters are flawed cosmopolitan ciphers who expose either the suffocation and cruelty of life at the provincial margins or the superficiality of metropolitan life.

Conclusion

ACROSS a broad cross-section of Irish female writers there is a consistent theme of realisable mobility and ambition in the urban environment that contrasts directly with the limited opportunities available in rural Ireland. This reveals something of the frustration of the Irish woman writer in a period more normally associated with glorification of the West and parallel dismissal of modernity and progress in Irish fiction and theatre. Many of the authors discussed in this chapter have heretofore primarily been studied for their contributions to the Decadent or New Woman movements in British fiction. While this is understandable given the radical nature of their literature, it has also had the detrimental effect of obscuring their contribution to a cosmopolitan Irish literary tradition.

No easy distinction should be made between Irish and British fiction in the first place, and we have argued that the main voices raised in opposition to the rural and the West emerged from a group of Irish women writers who were enabled to write against the dominant Revival tropes by virtue of their own residence abroad. This relocation may have been commercially motivated or independently chosen, but the distance it allowed meant that writers such as Egerton, Lynch, Iota, and Thurston could all write radically different novels than they might have had they depended on a tiny Irish market. Given the freedom afforded by their urban locations, they weaved tales of self-actualisation and upward mobility. They treated the city as a threatening, enabling, and empowering space. Their female protagonists were granted the same freedom to succeed or fail in the city as they themselves had experienced or aspired to. Elsewhere, the same writers were often willing to deliberately attack the construct of the West as the location of true Irish culture, instead depicting rural Ireland as backward and oppressive.

Later Irish women writers would replicate the process, in some cases citing the same stifling oppression of the Irish market as the main causal factor in their self-imposed exile. When Kate O'Brien felt she required space to grow as an artist, for instance, it was to the city of London she fled. Edna O'Brien, in *The Country Girls* (1960), took the idealised West to task in much the same way as Emily Lawless had done before her and did so from the safety of suburban London. In an interview for the *Paris Review* in 1984, Edna O'Brien evokes the type of urban thrill apparent in Egerton's 'A Lost Masterpiece':

> I wrote my first novel when I left Ireland and came to live in London. I had never been outside Ireland and it was November when I arrived in England. I found everything so different, so *alien*. Waterloo Station was full of people who were nameless, faceless. There were wreaths on the Cenotaph for Remembrance Sunday, and I felt bewildered and lost – an outsider. So in a sense *The Country Girls*, which I wrote in those first few weeks after my arrival, was my experience of Ireland and my farewell to it.[81]

For generations of Irish female authors, the city – whichever city – has meant some form of intellectual freedom. The traces of that freedom can be found, and are worth finding, in the novels they left behind.

Acknowledgements

THE authors would like to record their thanks to the Cambridge Group for Irish Studies, the Eighteenth and Nineteenth Century Seminar at Trinity College Dublin, and the Research Seminar in Irish Literature at Universidade de São Paulo, where versions of this paper were delivered.

Notes

1 May Laffan, *Hogan MP: A Novel*, 2nd edn (London: Macmillan, 1881), p. 99.

2 For the Belfast elite, see Jonathan Wright, *The 'Natural Leaders' and their World: Politics, Culture and Society in Belfast, c. 1801–1832* (Liverpool: Liverpool University Press, 2012); Alice Johnson, 'Middle-Class Culture and Civic Identity in Mid-Nineteenth Century Belfast' (Ph.D., Queen's University Belfast, 2009).

3 R. F. Foster and Fintan Cullen, *Conquering England: The Irish in Victorian London* (London: National Portrait Gallery, 2005).

4 Catriona Clear, *Social Change and Everyday Life in Ireland, 1850–1922* (Manchester: Manchester University Press, 2007); Joanna Bourke, *Husbandry to Housewifery: Women, Economic Change, and Housework in Ireland, 1890–1914* (Oxford: Clarendon Press, 1993).

5 For the latter, see John Neubauer and Borbála Zsuzsanna Török (eds), *The Exile and Return of Writers from East-Central Europe: A Compendium* (Berlin: De Gruyter, 2009), pp. 6–7, 20–4.

6 The classic text is perhaps C. L. Innes, *Woman and Nation in Irish Literature and Society, 1880–1935* (Athens, Ga.: University of Georgia Press, 1993). This tendency to 'politicise' the few women that are visible in Irish fiction is mirrored in Irish history. See Diane Urquhart, *A History Not Yet Told: Women in Ulster Politics, 1890–1940* (Dublin: Irish Academic Press, 2000); Linda Connolly, *The Irish Women's Movement: From Revolution to Devolution* (Dublin: Lilliput, 2003); Senia Pašeta, *Irish Nationalist Women, 1900–1918* (Cambridge: Cambridge University Press, 2013). For recent attempts to complicate the picture in literary criticism, see Heather Ingman, *Irish Women's Fiction: From Edgeworth to Enright* (Dublin: Irish Academic Press, 2013); Elke D'hoker, Raphaël Ingelbien, and Hedwig Schwall (eds), *Irish Women Writers: New Critical Perspectives* (Oxford: Peter Lang, 2011); Tina O'Toole, *The Irish New Woman* (Basingstoke: Palgrave Macmillan, 2013); Whitney Standlee, *Power to Observe: Irish Women Novelists in Britain, 1890–1916* (Oxford: Peter Lang, 2015).

7 See Anne Heilmann, *New Woman Fiction: Women Writing First-Wave Feminism* (Basingstoke: Palgrave Macmillan, 2000); and Anne Heilmann, *New Woman Strategies: Sarah Grand, Olive Schreiner, Mona Caird* (Manchester: Manchester University Press, 2004); Sally Ledger, *The New Woman: Fiction and Feminism at the Fin de Siècle* (Manchester: Manchester University Press, 1997); Jessica R. Feldman, 'Introduction', in *Victorian Modernism: Pragmatism and the Varieties of Aesthetic Experience* (Cambridge: Cambridge University Press, 2002), pp. 1–16.

8 For an ambitious re-reading of Joyce's *Dubliners* as an ode to the West, see Frank Shovlin, *Journey Westward: Joyce, Dubliners and the Literary Revival* (Liverpool: Liverpool University Press, 2012).

9 David Dickson, *Dublin: The Making of a Capital City* (London: Profile, 2014), especially Chapter 6.

10 Charles Lever, *Roland Cashel* (New York: Athenaeum, 1850), p. 26.

11 A. A. Phillips, 'The Cultural Cringe', *Meanjin*, 9:4 (1950), 299–302.

12 Laffan, *Hogan MP*, p. 11.

13 Laffan, *Hogan MP*, p. 12.

14 Laffan, *Hogan MP*, p. 82.

15 Laffan, *Hogan MP*, p. 101.

16 Declan Kiberd, 'The City in Irish Culture', *City: Analysis of Urban Trends, Culture, Theory, Policy, Action*, 6:2 (2002), 219–28; Julian Moynihan, 'The Image of the City in Nineteenth Century Irish Fiction', in Maurice Harmon (ed.), *The Irish Writer and the City* (Gerrards Cross: Colin Smythe, 1984), pp. 1–17 for an overview.

17 Frank A. Biletz, 'Women and Irish-Ireland: The Domestic Nationalism of Mary Butler', *New Hibernia Review*, 6:1 (2002), 59–72, at p. 59.

18 Katharine Tynan, *Twenty-Five Years: Reminiscences* (London: Smith, Elder, & Co., 1913), p. 40.

19 Christina de Bellaigue, '"Only What Is Pure and Exquisite": Girls' Reading at School in France, 1800–70', *French History*, 27:2 (2013), 202–22.

20 See Andrew Lees, *Cities Perceived: Urban Society in European and American Thought* (Manchester: Manchester University Press, 1985); Robert Morris, *Class, Sect and Party: The Making of the British Middle Class – Leeds, 1820–50* (Manchester: Manchester University Press, 1990).

21 Patrick Joyce, *The Rule of Freedom* (London: Verso, 2003), p. 64.

22 See Ríona Nic Congáil, '"Some of You Will Curse Her": Women's Writing During the Irish-Language Revival', *Proceedings of the Harvard Celtic Colloquium*, 29 (2009), 199–222. See also Brian Ó Conchubhair, *Fin de Siècle na Gaeilge: Darwin, an Athbheochan agus Smaointeoireacht na hEorpa* (Galway: An Clóchomhar, 2009).

23 Heather Edwards, 'The Irish New Woman and Emily Lawless's *Grania: The Story of an Island* – A Congenial Geography', *ELT*, 51:4 (2008), 421–38.

24 Emily Lawless, *Grania: The Story of an Island* (New York: Macmillan, 1892), p. 221.

25 J. M. Synge, quoted in Brendan Prunty, 'The Irish Fiction of Emily Lawless: A Narrative Analysis' (Ph.D., NUI Maynooth, 2009), p. 3.

26 James H. Murphy, *Irish Novelists and the Victorian Age* (Oxford: Oxford University Press, 2011), pp. 193–214.

27 Quoted in Whitney Standlee, '"A World of Difference": London and Ireland in the Works of Katharine Tynan', in Tom Herron (ed.), *Irish Writing London*, vol. I: *Revival to the Second World War* (London: Bloomsbury, 2013), pp. 70–83, at p. 73.

28 Several collections of short stories and sketches published in these first three years all exhibit these features and verge on twee. Katharine Tynan, *A Cluster of Nuts: Being Sketches among My Own People* (London: Lawrence & Bullen, 1894); *The Land of Mist and Mountain* (London: Catholic Truth Society, 1895); *An Isle in the Water* (London: A. & C. Black, 1895).

29 Katharine Tynan, *The Way of a Maid* (London: Lawrence & Bullen, 1895), pp. 6–9.

30 Katharine Tynan, *The Handsome Brandons: A Story for Girls* (London: Blackie & Son, 1900), p. 383.

31 Katharine Tynan, *A Daughter of the Fields* (London: Smith, Elder & Co., 1900), p. 7.

32 Katharine Tynan, *The Middle Years* (London: Constable & Co., 1916), p. 283.

33 Katharine Tynan, *Heart o' Gold; or, The Little Princess: A Story for Girls* (London: S. W. Partridge, 1912), pp. 9–10, 79.

34 Tynan repeats this formula elsewhere in *Bitha's Wonderful Year* (London: Humphrey Milford, 1921), as noted in Colette Eileen Epplé, 'Katharine Tynan's Literature for Children and the Construction of Irish Identity' (Ph.D., Catholic University of America, Washington, DC, 2010), pp. 36–46.

35 Rosa Mulholland, *The O'Shaughnessy Girls* (London: Blackie & Son, 1911), p. 137.

36 Rosa Mulholland, *Cynthia's Bonnet Shop* (London: Blackie & Son, 1901), p. 101.

37 Mulholland, *The O'Shaughnessy Girls*, pp. 10–11.

38 Mulholland, *The O'Shaughnessy Girls*, pp. 10–11.

39 Mulholland, *The O'Shaughnessy Girls*, p. 38.

40 Mulholland, *The O'Shaughnessy Girls*, p. 195.

41 Mulholland, *The O'Shaughnessy Girls*, p. 55.

42 Mulholland, *The O'Shaughnessy Girls*, p. 136.

43 Mulholland, *The O'Shaughnessy Girls*, pp. 137–8.

44 Murphy, *Irish Novelists*, pp. 193–244; John Wilson Foster, *Irish Novels, 1890–1940: New Bearings in Culture and Fiction* (Oxford: Oxford University Press, 2008), pp. 276–333, 449–95.

45 Letter from George Egerton to Ethel De Vere White (27 March 1926). Quoted in Terence De Vere White, *A Leaf from the Yellow Book* (London: Richards Press, 1958), p. 14.

46 These writers are almost always discussed in relation to the British Decadent, Ibsenite, or New Woman movements of the 1890s. See Kirsten McLeod, *Fictions of British*

Decadence: High Art, Popular Writing, and the Fin de Siècle (Basingstoke: Palgrave Macmillan, 2006) for a consideration of the movements in tandem.

47 Deirdre Raftery, Susan Parkes, and Judith Harford, 'Mapping the Terrain of Female Education in Ireland, 1830–1910', *Gender and Education*, 22:5 (2010), 565–78, at p. 569.

48 See Senia Pašeta, 'Women in the National University of Ireland', in Tom Dunne (ed.), *The National University of Ireland, 1908–2008: Centenary Essays* (Dublin: National University of Ireland, 2008), pp. 19–32.

49 R. F. Foster, *Vivid Faces: The Revolutionary Generation in Ireland, 1890–1923* (London: Allen Lane, 2014).

50 For more background on Caffyn, see Naomi Hetherington, 'Feminism, Freethought, and the Sexual Subject in Colonial New Woman Fiction: Olive Schreiner and Kathleen Mannington Caffyn', *Victorian Review*, 37:2 (2011), 47–59.

51 For one of the few extended readings of Caffyn's work, see Ingman, *Irish Women's Fiction*, pp. 34–7.

52 Kathleen Mannington Caffyn, *Poor Max: A Novel* (London: Hutchinson & Co., 1898), pp. 21, 158, 182.

53 Caffyn, *Poor Max*, p. 115.

54 Caffyn, *Poor Max*, p. 170.

55 Caffyn, *Poor Max*, p. 232.

56 Caffyn, *Poor Max*, p. 361.

57 Caffyn, *Poor Max*, p. 362.

58 These were Harold Caffyn (b. 1891), Jack (b. 1892), and Chaloner McRae (b. 1894). Jack went missing in America c. 1904 and was never heard of again. Chaloner and Harold were killed in action in the First World War. See www.cwgc.org/find-war-dead/casualty/75344/; www.cwgc.org/find-war-dead/casualty/1641365. Accessed 20 June 2014.

59 Her father was William Cecil De Vere (1823–69), a son of the romantic poet Aubrey De Vere, who retired as a commander in the Royal Navy and whose family home was in Co. Tipperary – a profile that matches Judith's background in the novel. Stephen Caffyn, like Max, had died of consumption at a relatively young age in 1896, just two years before *Poor Max* was published. Geulah Solomon, 'Caffyn, Stephen Mannington (1850–1896)', *Australian Dictionary of Biography*, National Centre of Biography, Australian National University. Available at http://adb.anu.edu.au/biography/caffyn-stephen-mannington-3137/text4677. Accessed 26 April 2015. See also Angelique Richardson noting that Caffyn is presumed (incorrectly) to have had only one child. 'Caffyn, Kathleen Mannington (1852/3–1926)', *Oxford Dictionary of National Biography*, Oxford University Press, 2004. Available at www.oxforddnb.com/view/article/55555. Accessed 25 April 2015.

60 Whitney Standlee, 'George Egerton, James Joyce and the Irish *Künstlerroman*', *Irish Studies Review*, 18:4 (2010), 439–52, at p. 445.

61 For more biographical detail on Egerton, see Margaret D. Stetz, 'George Egerton: Woman Writer of the 1890s' (Ph.D., Harvard University, 1982); Jessica March, 'Egerton, George (Mary Chavelita Dunne)', in James McGuire and James Quinn (eds), *Dictionary of Irish Biography*, 9 vols. (Cambridge: Cambridge University Press, 2009), vol. III, pp. 595–6; Jennifer Molidor, 'Violence, Silence, and Sacrifice: The Mother–Daughter Relationship in the Short Fiction of Irish Women Writers, 1890–1980' (Ph.D., University of Notre Dame, 2008), Chapter 3.

62 George Egerton, *Discords* (London: John Lane, 1894), p. 39. Tullabeg is a reference to a prominent Jesuit boarding school in Co. Offaly, operational between 1818 and 1886.

63 Egerton, *Discords*, p. 83.

64 Egerton, *Discords*, p. 123.

65 George Egerton, 'A Lost Masterpiece, A City Mood, Aug. '93', *The Yellow Book: An Illustrated Quarterly*, 1 (April 1894), 189–96, at p. 189.

66 Egerton, 'A Lost Masterpiece', p. 191. The gender of the narrator is never made clear by Egerton though most readings of the story take it for granted that the narrator is male. For

more on this, see Bryony Randall, 'George Egerton's "A Lost Masterpiece": Inspiration, Gender, and Cultural Authority at the *Fin de Siècle*', in Melissa Purdue and Stacey Floyd (eds), *New Women Writers, Authority, and the Body* (Newcastle: Cambridge Scholars, 2009), pp. 1–20; Sally Ledger, 'Wilde Women and the *Yellow Book*: The Sexual Politics of Aestheticism and Decadence', *ELT*, 50:1 (2007), 5–26; Kate Krueger Henderson, 'Mobility and Modern Consciousness in George Egerton's and Charlotte Mew's *Yellow Book* Stories', *ELT*, 54:2 (2011), 185–211.

67 Egerton, 'A Lost Masterpiece', p. 193.

68 Egerton, 'A Lost Masterpiece', p. 196.

69 Egerton, 'A Lost Masterpiece', p. 191.

70 For a full discussion of Riddell, see Margaret Kelleher, 'Charlotte Riddell's *A Struggle for Fame*: The Field of Women's Literary Production', *Colby Quarterly*, 36:2 (2000), 116–31.

71 Tynan, *Twenty-Five Years*, p. 115.

72 Foster, *Irish Novels*, pp. 276–80; Murphy, *Irish Novelists*, pp. 249–53; Faith Binckes and Kathryn Laing, 'Irish Autobiographical Fiction and Hannah Lynch's *Autobiography of a Child*', *ELT*, 55:2 (2012), 195–218; 'A Forgotten Franco-Irish Literary Network: Hannah Lynch, Arvède Barine, and Salon Culture of *Fin-de-Siécle* Paris', *Études Irlandaises*, 36:2 (2011), 157–71; 'A Vagabond's Scrutiny: Hannah Lynch in Europe', in Elke D'hoker, Raphaël Ingelbien, and Hedwig Schwall (eds), *Irish Women Writers: New Critical Perspectives* (Oxford: Peter Lang, 2011), pp. 111–32.

73 Lynch's first novel, *Through Troubled Waters* (London: Ward Lock & Co., 1885), is a Fenian story, based mostly in 1867. Faith Binckes and Kathryn Laing, '"Rival Attractions of the Season": Land War Fictions, Christmas Annuals, and the Early Writings of Hannah Lynch', in Heidi Hansson and James H. Murphy (eds), *Fictions of the Irish Land War* (Oxford: Peter Lang, 2014), pp. 57–80.

74 'Jinny Blake', *Athenaeum* (22 May 1897), pp. 675–6.

75 'Jinny Blake', *Academy* (22 May 1897), pp. 544–55.

76 Hannah Lynch, *Autobiography of a Child* (Edinburgh: Blackwood, 1901), p. 217.

77 For specific data on marriage in the period, see Timothy W. Guinnane, *The Vanishing Irish: Households, Migration, and the Rural Economy in Ireland, 1850–1914* (Princeton, NJ: Princeton University Press, 1997), pp. 160–240.

78 See Gerardine Meaney, 'Decadence, Degeneration and Revolting Aesthetics: The Fiction of Emily Lawless and Katherine Cecil Thurston', *Colby Quarterly*, 36:2 (2000), 157–75; Nicholas Allen, 'Thurston, Katherine Cecil 1875–1911', in James McGuire and James Quinn (eds), *Dictionary of Irish Biography*, 9 vols. (Cambridge: Cambridge University Press, 2009), vol. IX, pp. 364–5; Caroline Copeland, 'The Sensational Katherine Cecil Thurston: An Investigation into the Life and Publishing History of a "New Woman" Author' (Ph.D., Edinburgh Napier University, 2007).

79 Katharine Cecil Thurston, *Max* (New York: Harper & Brothers, 1910), p. 19.

80 Thurston, *Max*, p. 21.

81 Shusha Guppy, 'Edna O'Brien: The Art of Fiction No. 82', *Paris Review*, 92 (1984), 22–50, at p. 25.

7

'An Irish problem': bilingual manoeuvres in the work of Somerville and Ross

Margaret Kelleher

In August 1901, Edith Somerville and Violet Martin ('Martin Ross') attended a Petty Sessions court in Carna, Co. Galway, by invitation from the Resident Magistrate (RM), W. McDermot, and a fellow magistrate, local hotelier J. O'Loghlen. According to Martin Ross's diary for 15 August, 'Johnny O'Loghlen drove Edith and me, with three other female visitors, over to Carna, for the Petty Sessions there. There was only one case, of the drowning of a sheep, but J. O'Loghlen and W. McDermot worked it for an hour and a half for all it was worth.' Edith Somerville's diary entry for that day records going 'with three other women', driven in a wagonette, to Carna Petty Sessions: 'They are held in a sort of converted cowhouse. Only 1 case about a sheep, maliciously drowned. Our host and the R.M. the only magistrates, they stage managed the case to perfection.'[1] Over the following month, the two cousins worked their recollections of the encounter into an article entitled 'An Irish Problem', published, for a fee of twenty pounds, in the conservative journal *National Review* and soon after included in their 1903 essay collection *All of the Irish Shore*.[2] Writing of the collection in a letter to their literary agent James Pinker in 1903, Martin Ross described it as 'one of the best' stories included.[3]

Somerville and Ross's portrayal of the bilingual courtroom's social and linguistic intricacy is not only the occasion of wry humour but also a valuable instance of a still-neglected aspect of their relation to the language movement, namely the authors' representations of bilingual practice. Recent biographical and critical studies have cast light on the use of Hiberno-English dialect in Somerville and Ross's works and on their ambivalent attitudes to aspects of the Revival movement, including the Gaelic League.[4] However, a further significant consequence of the large-scale language shift in eighteenth- and nineteenth-century Ireland – the necessary existence of a societal bilingualism, however transitional in nature – is rarely made the object of thematic enquiry in readings of Somerville and

Ross, or of other Irish literature more generally. A fuller appreciation of the appearance of bilingualism in their work suggests, in turn, the need for more dynamic models of linguistic change in Irish cultural studies which can attend to the politics and practice of language use as mobile repertoires and creative manoeuvres rather than as markers of one or other monoglot ideology.

'Conversation raged on the long flanks of the mail-car': so the essay 'An Irish Problem' begins.[5] The mail-car occupants include various loquacious travellers in lively narrative combat – 'Among the swift shuttles of Irish speech the ponderous questions and pronouncements of an English fisherman drove their way' – and in their midst the two narrators 'sitting in silence, Irish wolves in the clothing of English tourists'.[6] From the outset, cultural misreadings and misinterpretations abound: 'Doubtless we were being expounded as English tourists, and our great economic value to the country was being expatiated upon.'[7] The 'privileges' and uses of a narratorial disguise as 'English tourists' are not without frustration: 'yet, to the wolf, there is something stifling in sheep's clothing; certainly, on the occasions when it was discarded by us, a sympathy and understanding with the hotels was quickly established. Possibly they also are wolves.'[8]

While awaiting a change of coach, the narrators chance upon 'Petty Sessions day in Letterbeg', held in a 'thatched and whitewashed cottage that stood askew at the top of a lane leading to the seashore'.[9] The court representatives comprise two magistrates, a clerk, an interpreter, and a district inspector of police, with the defendant and plaintiff receiving particular narrative scrutiny:

> Close to us stood the defendant, Sweeny, a tall elderly man, with a long, composed, shaven face and an all-observant grey eye: Irish in type, Irish in expression, intensely Irish in the self-possession in which he stood, playing to perfection the part of calm rectitude and unassailable integrity.
>
> Facing him, the plaintiff lounged against the partition; a man strangely improbable in appearance, with close-cropped grey hair, a young, fresh-coloured face, a bristling orange moustache, and a big, blunt nose. One could have believed him a soldier, a German, anything but what he was, a peasant from the farthest shores of western Ireland, cut off from what we call civilization by his ignorance of any language save his own ancient speech, wherein the ideas of to-day stand out in English words like telegraph-posts in a Connemara moorland.[10]

In comparison with other contemporary descriptions, Somerville and Ross's characterisation of the monoglot Darcy contains a number of distinguishing features: his apparent youth and vitality, the relativity accorded to the dominant culture, 'what we call civilization', and the vividness of the simile for cultural change, wherein the impact of modernisation retains a regional incongruity. The defendant Sweeny, in contrast, with 'a sisther married to a stationmaster and a brother in the Connaught Rangers' is keen to emphasise his lack of need for an interpreter, having 'as good English as anny man in this coort'.[11] It quickly emerges that both magistrates, 'Dochtor' Lyden and the shop-owner Heraty, are also highly competent in Irish: as Mr Byrne the local schoolteacher testifies, 'the Bench has as good Irish as I have myself, and better'.[12] In this company, the only monoglots are, thus, the Irish-speaking plaintiff Darcy and the English-speaking narrators:

> 'The law requires that the thransactions of this coort shall take place in English', the Chairman responded, 'and we have also the public to consider.'
>
> As it was pretty certain that we were the only persons in the court who did not understand Irish, it was borne upon us that we were the public, and we appreciated the consideration.[13]

In 1901, the year of Somerville and Ross's visit to the Carna court, the census figures for the province of Connaught recorded a total of 245,580 Irish speakers (38 per cent of the population of the province), of whom 12,103 were Irish-speaking only and 401,353 non-Irish speakers, the figures of Irish speakers in the county of Galway for 1901 being 108,870 or 56.5 per cent of whom 9,442 people (or 4.9 per cent) were recorded as speaking Irish only.[14] The use of an interpreter was not uncommon, or unneeded, in turn-of-the-century Ireland; as Nicholas Wolf has noted, 'in 1894 the national registrar of petty sessions clerk could report to Chief Secretary John Morley that 109 of 606 petty sessions districts in the country still made provisions for interpreters'.[15] And, 'while the language of the courts was English', as Niall Ó Ciosáin observes, 'plaintiffs, defendants and witnesses were allowed to give evidence in Irish through an interpreter, even when they were not strictly monoglot, a right confirmed by the Queen's Bench in 1856'.[16] Surviving Crown Office papers for 1893 include a series of 'interpreters papers' for Co. Mayo, detailing the applications by twelve different male individuals for the position of interpreter in Mayo County Court. The applicants' letters, with some accompanying letters of reference, indicate varying standards of literacy in English and a variety of declared competences in Irish: the sixty-year old Patrick Hughes declaring, 'I have a thorough knowledge of the Irish language and can write it down with facility as well as knowing it conversationally'; another (Luke Loftus) 'I can speak Irish since I was fourteen years of age I can also read Irish and stand an examination if required.' Writing of another applicant, twenty-five-year old John Kane, a butler's son, his referee J. F. Rutledge noted that it was 'very unusual to get a man of his age so thoroughly well up in Irish'.[17]

The case in question in 'An Irish Problem' concerns a demand by the plaintiff Darcy for compensation 'in the matter of a sheep that was drowned'.[18] As the questioning proceeds, the 'unctuous' court interpreter – 'small, old, froglike in profile, full of the dignity of the Government official' – becomes the main target of humour through his delivering of a series of imprecise translations:

> 'Now', said Mr Heraty, in a conversational tone, 'William, when ye employ the word "gorsoon," do you mean children of the male or female sex?'
>
> 'Well, yer worship', replied William, who, it may incidentally be mentioned, was himself in need of an interpreter or of a new and complete set of teeth, 'I should considher he meant ayther the one or the other.'
>
> 'They're usually one or the other', said Doctor Lyden, solemnly and in a stupendous brogue. It was the first time he had spoken; he leaned back, with his hand in his pockets, and surveyed with quiet but very bright eyes the instant grin that illumined the faces of the tapestry.[19]

And William's wavering between the use of masculine and feminine gender for the offending dog serves to further the joke: '"It appears," observed Dr Lyden serenely, "that the dog, like the gorsoons, was of both sexes."'[20]

Later misunderstandings arise from the confusion of English and Irish homonyms 'gown' and 'gamhain' (calf), while the Irish word 'ullán' – a crucial distinguishing feature of the dead sheep – defies the interpreter's powers of translation, until a formal definition is finally proffered by the teacher Byrne ('a plume or a feather that is worn on various parts of the sheep's back, for a mark, as I might say, of distinction').[21] Finally, the mistranslation of Darcy's account of his mother's injury – 'a stone fell on her and hurted her finger, and the boot preyed on it, and it has her desthroyed' – marks the comic demise of the translator's reliability:

> William's skinny hand covered his frog-mouth with all a deserving schoolboy's embarrassment at being caught out in a bad translation.
>
> 'I beg yer worships' pardon', he said, in deep confusion, 'but sure your worships know as well as meself that in Irish we have the one word for your finger or your toe.'[22]

Nor are the police representatives present exempt from judicial ridicule: the comic revelation that the sheep's 'twin sisther' had been recently sold to the police at Dhulish leads to an invitation to the two Royal Irish Constabulary men present to testify as to its 'nutritive qualities' and to the hasty escape of 'two tall and deeply embarrassed members of the RIC' from the courtroom.[23] Nearing the story's end, the narrating voice wryly remarks, 'In Ireland a point can often be better carried by sarcasm than by logic', and, proving the point, the sardonic commentary by Dr Lyden is ultimately the more successful mode of interrogation: '"We may assume, then," said Dr Lyden amiably, "that the sheep walked out into Sweeny's end of the lake and drowned herself there on account of the spite there was between the families." '[24]

When, at the essay's close, the narrators clamber into the departing mail-car to take their place 'among the inevitable tourists', their eavesdropping resumes:

> The tourists spoke of the vast loneliness, unconscious of the intricate network of social life that lay all around them, beyond their ken, far beyond their understanding. They spoke authoritatively of Irish affairs; mentioned that the Irish were 'a bit 'ot-tempered', but added that 'all they wanted was fair play'. . . .
>
> Never will it be given to them to understand the man of whom our friend Sweeny was more than a type. How can they be expected to realize that a man who is decorous in family and village life, indisputably God-fearing, kind to the poor, and reasonably honest, will enmesh himself in a tissue of sworn lies before his fellows for the sake of half a sovereign and a family feud, and that his fellows will think none the worse of him for it.
>
> These things lie somewhere near the heart of the Irish problem.[25]

An 'intricate network of social life' is indeed revealed by the preceding ethnographic study in an essay that offers to demonstrate and elucidate to its readers an Irish 'problem' beyond the ken of the occasional tourist; yet the closing judgements also serve to consolidate a narrative distance occupied by the amused but ultimately censorious (monoglot) observers.

Somerville and Ross's 1910 essay 'The Anglo-Irish Language', based on a review of Patrick Weston Joyce's *English as We Speak It in Ireland*, provides their most extensive commentary on the subject of English in Ireland. The essay opens with the identification of Ireland's complex linguistic history:

> It would be as easy to coax the stars out of the sky into your hat as to catch the heart of a language and put it in a phrase-book. Ireland has two languages; one of them is her own by birthright; the second of them is believed to be English, which is a fallacy; it is a fabric built by Irish architects with English bricks, quite unlike anything of English construction.[26]

This theory of language evolution underlines the mobility of linguistic transfer and its ability to cross (at least some) class boundaries:

> Gentlemen and peasants began to speak the same language, borrowing one from the other; the talk of the men of quality, bred in the classic tradition, enriched the vocabulary of the peasants, while the country gentlemen, themselves Irish speakers, absorbed into their English speech, something of the vigour and passion, the profuse imagery and wilful exaggeration that are inherent in the Gael.[27]

Contrastingly, the authors also recognise clearly the Anglicising force of upward social mobility: 'His [Joyce's] harvest is reaped, as is but natural, among the peasants and the poor people of the towns; each upward step in the social scale is a step further from the Irish language and its enormous influences.'[28]

Nicole Pepinster Greene's fine essay on 'Dialect and Social Identity in *The Real Charlotte*' reveals how, by 'manipulating their knowledge of social and regional Hiberno-English dialects', Somerville and Ross 'delineate subtle differences of class and personality, thus characterising language as a representation of social identity'.[29] In addition to giving close attention to Somerville and Ross's most acclaimed novel, her work also usefully returns their non-fictional commentaries on the use and abuse of Hiberno-English (in 'The Anglo-Irish Language' cited above, or in Martin's 'Children of the Captivity') to critical analysis.[30] While biographical studies of Somerville and Ross refer in passing to their learning of Irish, archival evidence provides more detailed information as to the timing and duration of their language learning.

In the early months of 1897, Edith and Violet (then on a visit to Drishane, the Somerville home) had Irish lessons taught by a Mrs Ward; the lessons were begun by Edith and her sister Hildegarde in February, and they were joined by Violet Martin on 17 March. The lessons continued regularly, on average twice a week, until May. Somerville and Ross, along with Hildegarde, occasionally describe giving 'ourselves an Irish lesson' (e.g., 26 March), using, on the advice of Douglas Hyde, the grammars written by Eugene O'Growney, Professor of Irish at St. Patrick's College, Maynooth.[31] Martin would appear to have become the more able and enthusiastic learner: on 9 April, Edith refers to a 'very difficult Irish lesson', whereas Martin on the same day records that 'we all knew our lessons very well'; Edith also records she and her sister alternately being 'put in the corner' for the poor standard of their dictation (13 and 15 April). The session of lessons ended in mid-May and would appear not to have been renewed.[32] The Queen's University archive includes a number of Irish-language exercises from the period – as Otto Rauchbauer notes, 'probably in V. M.'s handwriting', as in Figures 7.1 and 7.2 below.[33]

In late 1912, Martin, now living at Drishane, resumed learning Irish. Her diary for 30 November refers to the 'Berlitz system of learning' filling 'my head up in half an hour' and includes the following entry: 'I went down to the Castle at 3 for an Irish class held by Carrie Townshend. Miss (Jem) Barlow, May Townshend and I were the class.'[34] The classes continued on a weekly basis for the month of December, comprising 'Bock', Jem Barlow, and May Townshend as 'the other scholars' and with Martin 'importing Cameron as a *scolaire* (scholar)' in mid December.[35] On 30 December, Martin wrote: 'Cameron and I sole pupils. It lasted for two hours.' Edith Somerville did not participate in the classes and, in a diary entry for 7

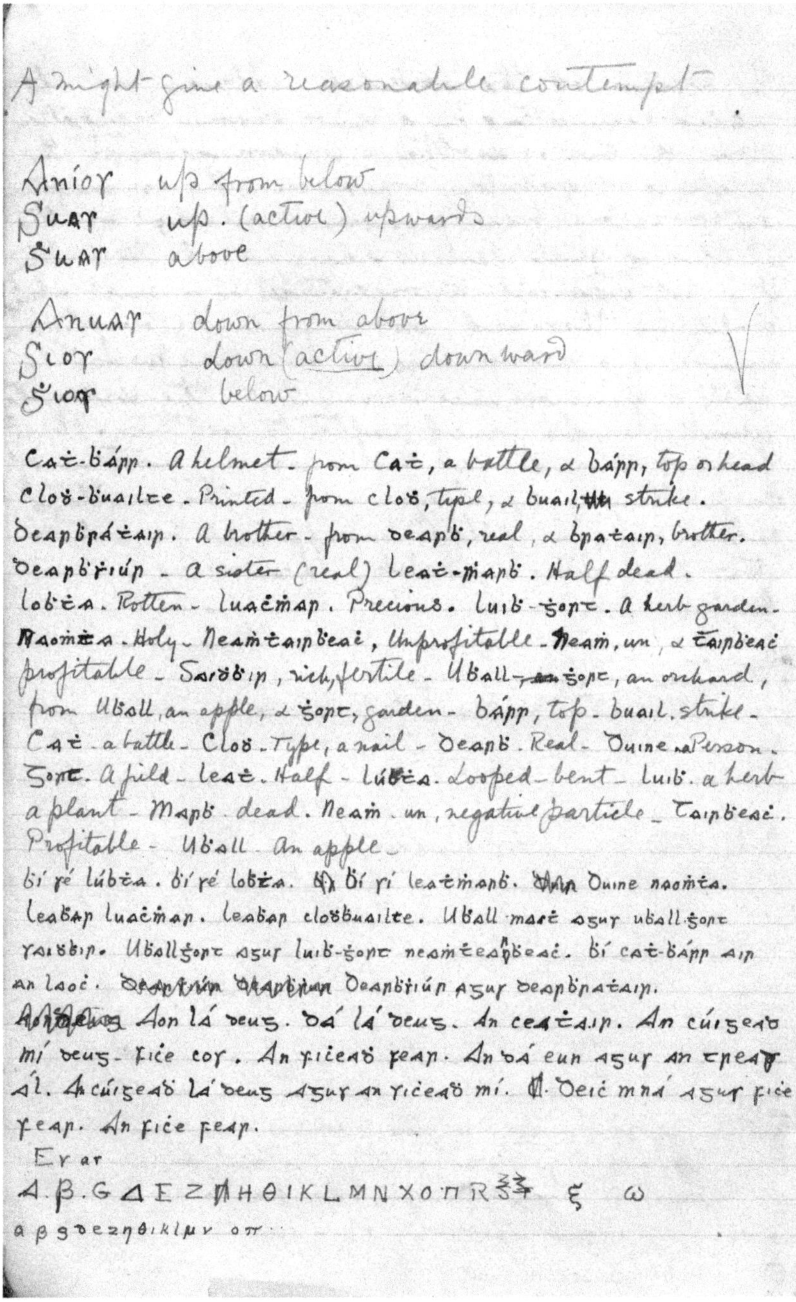

Figure 7.1 Somerville and Ross's Irish-language practice.

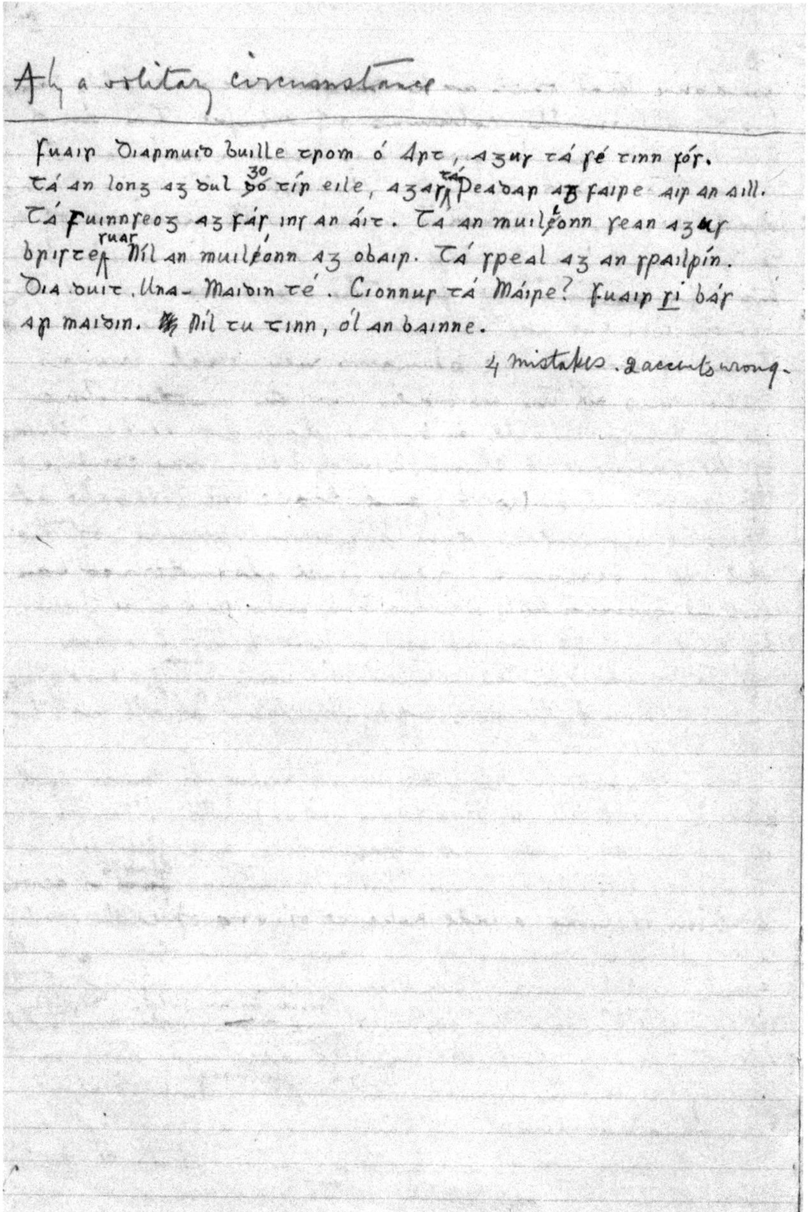

Ah, a solitary circumstance

Fuair Diarmuid buille trom ó Art, agus tá sé tinn fós.
Tá an long ag dul go tír eile, agus tá Peadar ag faire ar an aill.
Tá fuinnseog ag fás ins an áit. Tá an muileann sean agus
briste. Níl an muileann ag obair. Tá speal ag an spailpín.
Dia duit. Una – Maidin te. Cionnus tá Máire? Fuair sí bás
ar maidin. Níl tu tinn, ól an bainne.

4 mistakes. 2 accents wrong.

Figure 7.2 Irish-language corrections.

December, referred teasingly to the '*Bann Usals* (bean uasals) having their Irish class – Martin, Miss Barlow, Bock and Miss Nurse May Townshend.'[36]

The timing of Martin's resumption of her Irish-language studies was related to her involvement, along with Edith Somerville, Hildegarde (Somerville) Coghill, and Carrie Townshend, in the United Irishwomen movement (founded in 1910 by Horace Plunkett and others to improve rural women's welfare and education), and for which they received 'a castigation from the pulpit' while at church on Sunday, 19 January.[37] On 19 February, she records, 'I went to my Irish lesson with Carrie Townshend – and had the usual political discussion.' By now, however, classes were more sporadic, with Martin at times the sole member, and they appear to have come to an end by March. On Sunday 11 May, Martin records meeting '"Kendal C" [Edith's uncle, Kendal Somerville], rather on the warpath about Irish classes we imagine.'[38] It is difficult to identify precisely the proficiency in Irish gained by Somerville or Martin during these periods; unlike Augusta Gregory, there is little or no evidence in their diaries of attempts to engage in conversation with Irish-speaking neighbours, for example.[39] However, in the case of Martin, the resumption of lessons as late as 1912 suggests a continuing aspiration towards attaining some proficiency and a commitment of greater tenacity than that of her immediate social circle.

In January 1897, Douglas Hyde and Edith Somerville corresponded on the topic of regional storytelling, with Hyde exhorting Somerville to support the collection of local stories but 'not to discourage the people or shame them out of speaking Irish, for I am convinced that it is not for their moral or intellectual good to adopt – as nine tenths of the better classes do adopt – such an attitude'.[40] This comment would appear to have generated some ire in Martin Ross, as evidenced in a surviving letter fragment: 'why he should accuse you of being one of the people who discouraged the Irish language. Tell him of *The Real Charlotte* when you get a chance.'[41] Given the acclaim granted to the novel for its use of Hiberno-English, it is noteworthy that Ross views the book as evidence of their defence of Irish; on closer reading, conversations in Irish can be glimpsed on a number of occasions in the novel, mostly in the household of Julia Duffy where Charlotte encounters 'three old women ... smoking clay pipes, and holding converse in Irish that was punctuated with loud sniffs and coughs' and where conversation between Norry and Julia also takes place in Irish.[42] Bilingual communication is adroitly handled by Norry, who moves between speaking Irish to the beggar Nance the Fool and speaking English to Francie, while the inability to understand Nance's 'mouthings and mumblings of Irish' marks Francie's distance and alienation from an Irish-speaking realm which, in the novel's dramatic denouement, is also the occasion of her fatal fall.[43]

The most memorable instance of bilingual competence is, of course, that of Charlotte, where her ability to understand Irish has the additional tactical advantage of surprise (and which it is tempting to read as a form of authorial wish-fulfilment given the biographical details cited above):

> Mrs Lydon gave a laugh of polite acquiescence, and wondered inwardly whether Miss Mullen had as intimate a knowledge of everyone's affairs as she seemed to have of Shamus Bawn's.
>
> 'Oh, they say a manny a thing –' she observed with well simulated sanity. 'Arrah! *Dheen dheffeth*, Dinny! *thurrum cussoge um'na.*'
>
> 'Yes, hurry on and give me the coat, Dinny', said Charlotte, displaying that knowledge of Irish that always came as a shock to those who were uncertain as to its limitations.[44]

References to Irish elsewhere in Somerville and Ross's work are more occasional: phrases in Irish are rendered in their description of a visit to Aran in 'An Outpost of Ireland', in *Some Irish Yesterdays* (1906) and in their narrative account *Through Connemara in a Governess Cart* (1893). In the case of the latter, emphasis is placed on the narrators' discomfort in not being able to exchange the most fundamental salutations in Irish:

> Quite suddenly, out of the greyness, three men appeared, and as they passed us, one of them turned and said 'Genoong i dhieri', which, being translated, is 'God speed you.'
>
> We said feebly 'Good evening', and it was not till we were nearing the hotel that my second cousin remembered that she should have answered 'Ge moch hay ritth', which is the Irish method of saying, 'The same to you.'[45]

In these and other works, overheard conversations in Irish are marked more by noise and public torrent than secret dialogue: 'the donkey-cart, which generally contained a pig, and an old woman screaming in Irish' in *Through Connemara* or the 'storm of Irish' through which the process of disembarking takes place on Aran in 'Outpost of Ireland'.[46] Monoglots make rare appearances in their fiction and non-fiction, with the exception of the character of Darcy in 'An Irish Problem' and a fleeting reference in the RM story 'Put Down One and Carry Two'.[47] Instead, Irish-speaking characters in their writings are mostly bilingual, sometimes possessing a high level of competence in both languages deemed worthy of notice. One example is Martin's Connemara informant Anastasia in the essay 'At the River's Edge' who is illiterate and 'in all her sixty years had never been beyond the town of Galway': 'She was, of course, an Irish speaker by nature and by practice, but her English was fluent, and was set to the leisurely chant of west Galway; in time of need it could serve her purpose like slings and arrows.'[48] Responding to Anastasia's ease of translation from Irish to English, the narrator asks her 'what she thought of the Irish that was being taught now':

> Musha, I wouldn't hardly know what they'd be saying; and there's an old man that has great Irish – a wayfaring man that does be going the roads – and he says to me, 'Till yestherday comes again', says he, 'the Irish that they're teaching now will never be like the old Irish.'[49]

In *The Irish RM* stories, we are told on a number of occasions that Philippa is learning Irish, a practice which is the subject of some gentle narrative humour tinged, through the point of view of Major Yeates, by what would appear to be direct authorial experience:[50]

> During the previous winter she had had five lessons and a half in the Irish language from the National schoolmaster, and believed herself to be one of the props of the Celtic movement. My own attitude with regard to the Celtic movement was sympathetic, but a brief inspection of the grammar convinced me that my sympathies would not survive the strain of triphthongs, eclipsed consonants, and synthetic verbs, and that I should do well to refrain from embittering my declining years by an impotent and humiliating pursuit of the most elusive of pronunciations. Philippa had attained to the height of being able to greet the schoolmaster in Irish, and, if the day happened to be fine, she was capable of stating the fact; other aspects of the weather, however remarkable, she epitomized in a brilliant smile, and the schoolmaster was generally considerate enough not to press the matter.[51]

A much sharper satirical note is sounded in this story, 'The Last Day of Shraft', where the subject of Irish learning comprises its comic centre. Philippa's elderly stepbrother, Maxwell Bruce – 'tall and thin, of the famished vegetarian type of looks, with unpractical, prominent eyes, and a complexion that on the hottest day in summer imparted a chill to the beholder' – visits the Yeates household while undertaking a tour 'through the Irish-speaking counties': 'His mornings were spent in proffering Irish phrases to bewildered beggars at the hall door, or to the respectfully bored Peter Cadogan in the harness-room.'[52] A trip is ordained by Philippa to 'Hare Island', a 'place where the Irish language was still spoken with a purity worthy of the Isles of Aran'.[53] The attraction of Hare Island is also literary: 'Its folk-lore was an unworked mine, and it was moreover the home of one Shemus Ruaidh, a singer and poet' as well as smuggler 'of high local renown'.[54] Once on the island, the sounds of Irish are encountered by Yeates as 'hurling invective and personalities' or as 'howling and droning', and the absurdities of the language enthusiast become even more apparent in Bruce's conversation with islander Mrs Brickley:[55]

> I regret to say that I can neither transcribe nor translate the rolling periods in which my brother-in-law addressed himself to her. I have reason to believe that he apostrophized her as 'O worthy woman of cows!' invoking upon her and her household a comprehensive and classic blessing, dating from the time of Cuchulain.
>
> Mrs Brickley received it without a perceptible stagger.[56]

The upstaging of Bruce's expectations to record Irish 'of the purest kind', by stylograph, is finally achieved by the comic rendition of a song about Ned Flaherty's drake, recently composed, in English, and, in its ironic commentary on the assembled gathering, recognised by the narrator – though not by Bruce – as a 'startlingly appropriate requiem'.[57]

Humour, as Nicholas Wolf has recently shown in his groundbreaking study of language in nineteenth-century Ireland, is an 'unexpectedly dominant form used to express the experience of language contact in modern Ireland':

> Of at least 450 documented allusions to the Irish language that can be identified among the oral interviews collected by the Irish Folklore Commission in the 1930s and 1940s, more than half consisted of jokes and humorous short stories centering on a foolish character whose mishaps in negotiating a world of two languages provided occasion for laughter.[58]

And, as he astutely notes, 'approaching these jokes as a formal site for renegotiation and reinvention of the status of the Irish language provides a first step in resolving this seemingly incongruous and lighthearted popular response to language contact'.[59] Since, in formal terms, a key ingredient of language jokes is the deployment of 'two distinct, or incongruous, categories of understanding', verbal puns – for example, the trans-linguistic homophones of 'gown' and 'gamhain' in 'An Irish Problem' – are an 'especially efficient' example because 'they enable two scripts to emerge from a single word'.[60]

Various situations and objects of humour exist within the jokes examined by Wolf, including that of the Irish speaker in the courtroom, one of these effects being to highlight the line between 'Irish-speaking and English-speaking worlds'.[61] Yet, as he persuasively argues, the more important division staged by language humour is 'between the monoglot characters in the jokes (both English and Irish) and the bilingual audience and joke tellers':

> Ultimately, the jokes offered neither Irish nor English as the triumphant language in these instances. Rather, these nineteenth-century jokes offered both languages as a spectacle to the only observers able to discern the absurdity in both conversations: the bilingual listeners ... Only bilingualism, joke tellers argued, guaranteed immunity from being tricked or caught unaware.[62]

More unusually, in Somerville and Ross's courtroom scene, the monoglot plaintiff retains considerable dignity – and, somewhat less so, the monoglot narrators – with the immediate target of ridicule being the officious government interpreter and the graver object being the bilingual defendant's attempted manipulation of the process of law.

Writing on contemporary 'bilingual aesthetics' in the USA, Doris Sommer delivers the following powerful injunction against cultural occlusion of 'non-elite bilinguals':

> It is time we noticed that working – and also underemployed – bilinguals sparkle too, and for similar reasons to elite codeswitchers. Both know the risks of language and the magic of making contact when communication could have misfired. With an exquisite consciousness of conventions, and a keen skepticism about what can or should be said, bilinguals develop the everyday arts of manoeuvring and self-irony.[63]

Recent work in language contact, in particular by Jan Bloommaert, has argued for a new sociolinguistics of globalisation, one 'of mobile resources and not of immobile languages'.[64] Bloommaert's work brings a welcome focus on 'a sociolinguistics of *speech* and of *resources*': 'of the real bits and chunks of language that make up a repertoire, and of real ways of using this repertoire in communication'.[65] Consequently, individuals' repertoires and linguistic resources are more accurately to be understood as 'truncated' or 'unfinished', rather than as static, given languages, since 'no one knows *all* of a language'.[66]

Bloommaert's theories of changing language are positioned in the particular context of current globalisation wherein a 'monoglot ideal' (which seeks to register its constituent language as 'natural, neutral, a-contextual and non-dynamic') is defied by the 'polyglot repertoire' of contemporary migrants.[67] His observations, moreover, offer a useful conceptual vocabulary to recover the complexity, diversity, and mobility of individuals' linguistic repertoires in historical periods of language change, such as that of nineteenth-century Ireland, wherein the eventual dominance of one language can be made to seem retrospectively inevitable and where a counter-history privileges a narrative of language revival over that of bilingual continuance. Viewed from this perspective, the writings of Somerville and Ross, located towards the end of a period of large-scale language shift and near the beginning of a cultural revival, offer some especially vivid portraits of 'mobile' speech and 'truncated repertoires'. In the case of 'An Irish Problem', they show a keen understanding of the comic possibilities offered by a bilingual scene featuring its participants' 'everyday arts of manoeuvring and self-irony' and provide a valuable reminder that early twentieth-century Irish society contained many bilingual members *continuing* to use Irish.

Notes

1 Somerville and Ross's diaries record their spending three days in Cashel, Co. Galway (Wednesday, 14 August, to Friday, 16 August 1901) as the guest of 'Johnny O'Loghlen', proprietor of the Zetland Arms hotel in Cashel, having travelled by train from Ballinahinch

to Recess and then by car about five miles to Cashel. See Somerville and Ross Papers, MS 17/874, Queen's University Belfast (QUB). My grateful thanks to Maura Farrelly and colleagues at Special Collections, QUB, for their expert assistance.

2 Their diaries record their beginning the article on 9 September and sending it to editor Leopold Maxse on 9 October; it was published in the *National Review* in early November. See Somerville and Ross Papers, MS 17/874, QUB.

3 Letter from Violet Martin to James Pinker (22 February 1903), Pinker correspondence, no. 3330-1, Manuscripts Library, Trinity College Dublin; reference provided by Julie Anne Stevens, *The Irish Scene in Somerville and Ross* (Dublin: Irish Academic Press, 2007), p. 119.

4 See, in particular, Nicole Pepinster Greene, 'Dialect and Social Identity in *The Real Charlotte*', *New Hibernia Review/Iris Éireannach Nua*, 4:1 (2000), 122–37; Anne Oakman, 'Sitting on "The Outer Skin": Somerville and Ross's *Through Connemara in a Governess Cart* as a Coded Stratum of Linguistic/Feminist "Union" Ideals', *Éire-Ireland*, 39:1–2 (2004), 110–35; and Ann McClellan, 'Dialect, Gender and Colonialism in *The Real Charlotte*', *Études Irlandaises*, 31:1 (2006), 69–86.

5 E. Œ. Somerville and Martin Ross, 'An Irish Problem', in *All on the Irish Shore* (London, Calcutta, and Sydney: Harrap, 1925), pp. 177–98. For an insightful reading of the 'problem of the picturesque' in the essay, see Stevens, *The Irish Scene*, pp. 118–26.

6 Somerville and Ross, 'An Irish Problem', pp. 178, 177.

7 Somerville and Ross, 'An Irish Problem', p. 179.

8 Somerville and Ross, 'An Irish Problem', p. 179.

9 Somerville and Ross, 'An Irish Problem', p. 181.

10 Somerville and Ross, 'An Irish Problem', pp. 182–3.

11 Somerville and Ross, 'An Irish Problem', p. 186.

12 Somerville and Ross, 'An Irish Problem', p. 184.

13 Somerville and Ross, 'An Irish Problem', p. 185.

14 *The Census of Ireland for the Year 1901, Part II, General Report* (Dublin: Browne & Nolan, 1902), pp. 575–6.

15 Nicholas Wolf, *An Irish-Speaking Island: State, Religion and the Linguistic Landscape in Ireland, 1770–1870* (Madison, Wisc.: University of Wisconsin Press, 2014), p. 158.

16 Niall Ó Ciosáin, 'Gaelic Culture and Language Study', in Laurence Geary and Margaret Kelleher (eds), *Nineteenth-Century Ireland: A Guide to Recent Research* (Dublin: University College Dublin Press, 2005), pp. 136–69, at p. 150.

17 Crown Office Papers 1893, Mayo correspondence, Interpreters Papers, IC-78-51, National Archives Dublin.

18 Somerville and Ross, 'An Irish Problem', p. 183.

19 Somerville and Ross, 'An Irish Problem', pp. 183, 183–4.

20 Somerville and Ross, 'An Irish Problem', p. 185.

21 Somerville and Ross, 'An Irish Problem', pp. 186–8.

22 Somerville and Ross, 'An Irish Problem', pp. 191–2.

23 Somerville and Ross, 'An Irish Problem', p. 195.

24 Somerville and Ross, 'An Irish Problem', p. 189.

25 Somerville and Ross, 'An Irish Problem', pp. 197–8.

26 E. Œ. Somerville and Martin Ross, 'The Anglo-Irish Language', in *Stray-Aways* (London: Longmans, Green & Co., 1920), p. 184.

27 Somerville and Ross, 'The Anglo-Irish Language', p. 185.

28 Somerville and Ross, 'The Anglo-Irish Language', p. 188.

29 Greene, 'Dialect and Social Identity', p. 124.

30 See E. Œ. Somerville and Martin Ross, 'Children of the Captivity', in *Some Irish Yesterdays* (London: Nelson, 1916), pp. 237–49.

31 See Somerville and Ross Papers, MS. 17/874, QUB; and Stevens, *The Irish Scene*, p. 163.

32 See Somerville and Ross Papers, MS. 17/874, QUB. In the descriptive essay accompanying the catalogue, *The Edith Œ. Somerville Archive in Drishane* (Dublin: Irish Manuscripts

Commission, 1995), Otto Rauchbauer comments, 'It is interesting to note that E. Œ. S. and some of her relations (Hildegarde and Violet Martin) did take up the study of Irish from February to June 1897.' He also notes that 'material in the Drishane Archive and elsewhere indicates that she enjoyed learning Irish with a Mrs Ward, but that she soon discovered her own limitations and gave it up'; see p. 184, n. 51.

33 Rauchbauer, *The Edith Œ. Somerville Archive*, p. 184, n. 51; the O'Growney study books are held in the Drishane archive.

34 See Somerville and Ross Papers, MS. 17/874, QUB. 'Bock' was Edith Somerville's first cousin, Elizabeth Somerville. Jem Barlow, cousin of writer Jane Barlow, moved to Castletownshend in late 1912 and later, following the death of Violet Martin, became a central member of Edith's spiritualist circle. Carrie Townshend and her husband Charles were committed supporters of the Gaelic League and friends of its president, Ellen (Lady) Desart. Since Desart was also President of the Anti-Suffragists, Edith Somerville declined the Townshends' invitation to meet her in late 1912. See Gifford Lewis, *Edith Somerville: A Biography* (Dublin: Four Courts Press, 2005), p. 271.

35 Cameron Somerville was Edith's brother.

36 See Somerville and Ross Papers, MS. 17/874, QUB. This term, a mistranslation by Somerville into Irish of the plural form of 'noble woman', was used by her on a number of occasions to refer to the United Irishwomen; see Lewis, *Edith Somerville*, p. 265.

37 See Somerville and Ross Papers, MS. 17/874, QUB. An entry by Martin for Monday refers to a 'United Irishwomen' meeting in the Village Hall: 'Carrie T and I and five or six women there.'

38 See Somerville and Ross Papers, MS. 17/874, QUB.

39 See Maureen Murphy, 'Lady Gregory and the Gaelic League', in Ann Saddlemyer and Colin Smythe (eds), *Lady Gregory, Fifty Years After* (Gerrards Cross: Colin Smythe, 1987), pp. 143–63.

40 Letter quoted in Rauchbauer, *The Edith Œ. Somerville Archive*, p. 184.

41 Gifford Lewis (ed.), *The Selected Letters of Somerville and Ross* (London: Faber & Faber, 1989), p. 236.

42 E. Œ. Somerville and Martin Ross, *The Real Charlotte* (London: Quartet Books, 1977), pp. 59, 192.

43 Somerville and Ross, *The Real Charlotte*, pp. 109, 338.

44 Somerville and Ross, *The Real Charlotte*, p. 281.

45 E. Œ. Somerville and Martin Ross, *Through Connemara in a Governess Cart* (London: Virago, 1990), p. 122.

46 Somerville and Ross, *Through Connemara in a Governess Cart*, p. 128; E. Œ. Somerville and Martin Ross, 'Outpost of Ireland', in *Some Irish Yesterdays*, p. 15.

47 See E. Œ. Somerville and Martin Ross, *The Irish RM Complete* (London: Faber & Faber, 1928), p. 407.

48 E. Œ. Somerville and Martin Ross, 'At the River's Edge', in *Stray-Aways*, p. 4.

49 Somerville and Ross, 'At the River's Edge', p. 10.

50 See, for example, E. Œ. Somerville and Martin Ross, 'Philippa's Fox-Hunt', in *The Irish RM Complete*, p. 82.

51 E. Œ. Somerville and Martin Ross, 'The Last Days of Shraft', in *The Irish RM Complete*, p. 243.

52 Somerville and Ross, 'The Last Days of Shraft', pp. 245, 243–4.

53 Somerville and Ross, 'The Last Days of Shraft', p. 244.

54 Somerville and Ross, 'The Last Days of Shraft', p. 244.

55 Somerville and Ross, 'The Last Days of Shraft', pp. 245, 250.

56 Somerville and Ross, 'The Last Days of Shraft', p. 246.

57 Somerville and Ross, 'The Last Days of Shraft', pp. 251–2. See also the use of references to Irish as a source of comedy in 'The Whiteboys' (*The Irish RM Complete*, pp. 294–308): in the story, a character's practice of shouting in Irish to the hounds is ultimately deployed to turn the tables on Flurry Knox, who, by the story's end, having

lost the hounds in question, employs 'Jeremiah Donovan to screech in Irish down the holes in the fort, for fear O'Reilly's hounds had no English' (*The Irish RM Complete*, p. 308).

58 Wolf, *An Irish-Speaking Island*, p. 84.

59 Wolf, *An Irish-Speaking Island*, p. 89.

60 Wolf, *An Irish-Speaking Island*, pp. 95–6.

61 Wolf, *An Irish-Speaking Island*, p. 102.

62 Wolf, *An Irish-Speaking Island*, pp. 102, 107.

63 Doris Sommer, *Bilingual Aesthetics: A New Sentimental Education* (Durham, NC: Duke University Press, 2004), p. 6.

64 Jan Blommaert, *The Sociolinguistics of Globalization* (Cambridge: Cambridge University Press, 2010), p. 180.

65 Blommaert, *The Sociolinguistics of Globalization*, p. 173.

66 Blommaert, *The Sociolinguistics of Globalization*, pp. 197, 103.

67 Blommaert, *The Sociolinguistics of Globalization*, pp. 164–71.

8

'A bad master': religion, Jacobitism, and the politics of representation in Lady Gregory's *The White Cockade*

Anna Pilz

> The weakness of your position is that nearly all your writers are protestants &, so, liable to get into religious difficulties, partly through not understanding exactly what will + what will not give offence, partly because the Catholic will never quite trust your being really in sympathy with them.[1]

IN answer to their invitation for subscriptions to the proposed Irish Literary Theatre in 1897, Lady Augusta Gregory and W. B. Yeats received a cheque for £1 from a historical romance writer accompanied by a warning: 'My experience has been that any attempt at treating Irish history is a fatal handicap, not to say absolute bar, to anything in the shape of popularity.'[2] Gregory believed, however, that 'to have a real success ... one must touch a real and eternal emotion, and history comes only next to religion in our country.'[3]

In the midst of growing fervour for nationalism and a public eager to define Irishness in opposition to Englishness, the religious divide was problematic when it came to questions of representation. Following his attendance of a production of Yeats's *Where There Is Nothing* in 1904 at the Court Theatre in London, Wilfrid Scawen Blunt had issued a word of caution to Gregory: 'I am afraid the piece cannot be a success', he wrote. 'You will put this down to my "sectarian prejudice", but it is not so. The two last acts are quite impossible from my point of view, literary, dramatic or philosophical. I should despair of Ireland if they were thought good there.'[4] In the aftermath of the *Playboy* riots in 1907, Blunt again wrote a letter to Gregory that gently but firmly expressed his sympathy with the rioters: 'The weakness of your position is that nearly all your writers are protestants &, so, liable to get into religious difficulties.'[5]

Instances such as the *Playboy* riots illustrate Conor Cruise O'Brien's assertion that '[t]he story of the Irish literary revival in one of its aspects is one of Protestant and Catholic consciousness in intermittent contact, often leading to increasing mutual distrust'.[6] In order to avoid conflict, critics have argued, the Revivalists adhered to two methods: first, they retreated into folklore and pagan beliefs in order to circumvent the religious divide in contemporary society.[7] Second, as Willard Potts proposes, they avoided confrontation through 'the simple technique of populating their plays only with Catholics'.[8] This argument is weakened by its inclination to perceive the Abbey's directorate as a homogenous grouping. In that regard, it is vital to expand our knowledge of Gregory's plays to incorporate those that have, to date, received little critical attention.

Gregory wrote a number of historical dramas, subsumed under the title of *Irish Folk-History Plays*, which she published in two volumes in 1912. The first series included *Kincora*, *Dervorgilla*, and *Grania*; the second *The Canavans*, *The White Cockade*, and *The Deliverer*.[9] Her emphasis on 'Folk-History' not only chimed with her interest in oral tradition but also allowed for artistic freedom when it came to historical accuracy. The tragedies in the first series focused on legends and ancient Irish history that pre-dated Christianity. As such, the events were far removed from a contemporary context and offered her a means to evade the divide between Protestants and Catholics. William Fay, for instance, commented that *Kincora*, with its 'popular subject in historical legend', was seen as 'a safe proposition'.[10] This remoteness, however, is less of a safety valve in *The White Cockade*, set during the Williamite War (1689–91) and featuring King James II and Patrick Sarsfield, the Earl of Lucan.[11] Considering the divisiveness of the Battle of the Boyne (1 July 1690) in Irish cultural memory, Gregory's subject matter courted controversy. Its repercussions had a continued currency and interlaced history with religion.

Symbolic of the defeat of Stuart Ireland, the Battle of the Boyne stood as the end of Irish hopes to revoke the changing power structures between Catholics and Protestants in the seventeenth century. James Joyce viewed 'the fall of the Stuarts and the rise of King William as the moment in which the "unthinking cruelty" of Anglo-Saxon, Protestant domination [had taken] hold' in Ireland.[12] With the subsequent introduction of the Penal Laws from the 1690s onwards, Catholics and Nonconformists were severely restricted in social, political, and economic mobility. Although the impact of the laws varied considerably, Douglas Hyde noted in 1893 that 'Aughrim and the Boyne put an end to the dream that the Irish would ever again bear sway in their own land, and the carefully devised Penal Laws proceeded to crush all remaining independence of spirit out of them, and to grind away their very life-blood.'[13] For Protestants, however, the victory of William of Orange at the Boyne confirmed their supremacy in Ireland.

In April 1905, Gregory had her 'mind full of a play about King James – of Seumus Salach ("Dirty James") as he had been called since he ran away from the Boyne'.[14] The play was 'practically finished' three months later. In a letter to Blunt, she noted that 'James II is the broken idol which shatters all faith & belief & longing & it is comedy.'[15] Her juxtaposition of tragedy and comedy here is curious. Moreover, the play's political context added to the alienating potential of the topic. Shortly before Gregory finished *The White Cockade*, the *Irish Times* reported on the 'July Anniversary: Celebrations in Belfast':

> The 215th anniversary of the Battle of the Boyne was celebrated in Belfast yesterday by two demonstrations. [...] The procession was the largest and most imposing seen for many years. [. . .]
>
> They who lived south of the Boyne needed all the moral support they could get, for the Roman Catholics, under the malign and un-Christian influence of the priests and the Catholic Association, were getting worked up to greater intolerance, nay, hatred, of Protestants than ever, and he did not hesitate to declare his firm belief that this hatred and contempt of Protestants did not always exist, but was the product of jealousy of the independence, prosperity, and general superiority of Protestants. (Hear, hear.)[16]

Thus, the sectarian connotations of Gregory's historical subject matter could potentially have presented a 'fatal handicap' when staged at the Abbey. She was aware of the contemporary relevance, as indicated in her editorial comment in *Mr. Gregory's Letter-Box* in 1898:

> for Orangeism still flourishes, and Orange lilies, here in the West of such harmless tendency that they brilliantly deck the altars of village chapels, still unfold their petals as a declaration of war when the July sunshine falls on Ulster. The feud seems likely to last for many a long year yet, and to give lively occupation to the police and magistrates of the new century.[17]

For Catholics, it could also 'touch a real and eternal emotion' of oppression and victimhood. Most potently, the historical setting established the correlation between religion and landed wealth. James Anthony Froude estimates that by 1703 about 90 per cent of the land was 'held by Protestants of English or Scottish extraction.'[18] The playwright's families – both the Persses and the Gregorys – profited from the Jacobites' defeat in the 1690s, and their estates in Co. Galway prospered in consequence of the Penal Laws.

In focusing on James II, Gregory can be seen to interrogate and, perhaps, empathetically imagine the Catholic narrative of the Battle of the Boyne. Apart from the Captain and two Williamite soldiers, we do not encounter the iconic figure of Orangeism. Therefore, Gregory appears to have taken sides in her approach. The title of the play, *The White Cockade*, refers not only to the Jacobite emblem but also to a popular ballad by the same name. Jacobite sympathies – whether in Scotland, England, or Ireland – have been described as exhibiting cynicism, sentimentality, and nostalgia. The latter can be detected in William Ross's poem 'An Suitheans ban', or 'The White Cockade'. According to Murray Pittock, it 'displays a valedictory quality which even the most ideologically committed Jacobites could see was approaching more and more closely to what was true in reality' in which the hope for a Stuart restoration was reputed:

> Farewell to the White Cockade
> Till Doomsday he in death is laid,
> The grave has ta'en the White Cockade,
> The cold tombstone is now his shade.[19]

This air was initially associated more with Scottish Jacobitism and the failed rebellion of 1745 in particular, but it was adapted by the Irish brigades, who used it as a battle song.[20] In later centuries, Jacobite songs were also used in recruiting advertisements, testament to their efficacy as ideological instruments. The British context is further apparent in a London-based paper titled *The White Cockade: A Jacobite Journal*, founded in 1894 in the midst of the *fin-de-siècle* Jacobite revival phenomenon.[21]

The Jacobite cause inspired numerous poems and songs in the form of laments 'for the loss of her [Ireland's] Stuart lover'.[22] According to a story Richard Hayes recorded in Co. Mayo, 'The White Cockade' was played in the nineteenth century and 'considered a fitting tribute to the memory of a veteran rebel of Ninety-Eight', thus linking the Jacobite cause with the rebellion of the United Irishmen.[23] What was once specific to a particular cause gained greater symbolic currency which allowed for a narrative of continuity that connected Irish national heroes from the seventeenth to the early twentieth century.

Jacobitism, in its association with nationalism, has an inherent sectarian element in which 'James is a saviour-figure not despite his Catholicism, but because of it.'[24] The sectarian potency manifests itself when we consider that 'The White Cockade' is juxtaposed, in Gregory's play, with another ballad, 'Lilliburlero', representing allegiance to James II and William III respectively. The latter's verse is not only anti-Irish but also anti-Catholic in its satire of the Irish Jacobite Richard Talbot, Earl of Tyrconnell:

> Ho! broder Teague, dost hear de decree?
>   Lilli burlero, bullen a-la.
> Dat we shall have a new deputie,
>   Lilli burlero bullen a-la.
>   Lero lero, lilli burlero, lero lero, bullen a-la.
>   Lero lero, lilli burlero, lero lero, bullen a-la.

Ho! by shaint Tyburn, it is de Talbote:
        Lilli &c.
And he will cut de Englishen's troate.
        Lilli &c.
[. . .]
Dare was an old prophesy found in a bog,
        Lilli &c.
'Ireland shall be rul'd by an ass, and a dog.'
        Lilli &c.
And now dis prophecy is come to pass,
        Lilli &c.
For Talbot's de dog, and Ja--s is de ass.
        Lilli &c.[25]

Such sentiments and connotations would have created strong resonances among Gregory's audience, particularly considering the topicality of Jacobitism in the late nineteenth and early twentieth centuries.

Gregory tapped into this contemporary resurgence of interest in Jacobitism that spanned from the 1880s to the outbreak of the First World War.[26] Her interest in Irish Jacobitism dated from the summer of 1902 when she was 'collecting & translating Jacobite poems'.[27] Her findings were published in an article on 'Irish Jacobite Songs' in January 1903 in *The Speaker*.[28] Having come across a verse that included the line 'My heart leaps up with my bright Stuart', Gregory, surprised by such a positive memory of the Stuarts, began to enquire among the local people. She remembered the local poet Anthony Raftery (c. 1784–1835) writing: ' "James ... was the worst man for habits ... he laid chains on our bogs and mountains." '[29] James's retreat from battle was the turning point in public opinion of the Catholic king. The names of James and Charles, Gregory asserted, were likely the last to be remembered in verse, 'for ... the loyalty the poets of three hundred years have called for is loyalty to Kathleen ny Houlihan. "Have they not given her their wills and their hearts and their dreams? What have they left for any less noble Royalty?" '[30]

Indeed, the rather muted and critical attitude expressed towards the Stuart king might stand at odds with the nationalist sympathies associated with Jacobite poetry. As Daniel Corkery asserts, in the Irish *aisling* tradition, 'the place that the Stuarts themselves occupy in the Scottish poems is occupied in the Irish poems by Ireland herself'.[31] Despite the fall of the Stuarts, Jacobite poetry remained popular. The reason, Pittock proposes, is 'the *aisling*'s nationalism and not its Jacobitism'.[32] The *aisling* is a vision poem in which a woman – representing Ireland – seduces men into battle. While initially the restoration of the country was achieved through a sexual act, in the nineteenth century this erotic component was replaced by an appeal to blood sacrifice with the nation restored by death rather than sexual pleasure.

There are variations in the feminine representation of Ireland. She is generally perceived as the 'carrier of a prophetic message', originating from the *aisling*. She occurs in the form of the *spéirbhean* or sky-woman who is associated with royalty. Alternatively, she can appear as a young and beautiful woman, or an old woman, drawn from the more ancient tradition of the *Cailleach Bhéarra*.[33] It is the initial association with royalty that provides Jacobite poetry and thought with an elitist, rather than populist, framework.[34] This aristocratic elitism might account for Jacobitism's appeal to Gregory and her contemporary Protestant grandees, including Emily Lawless.

Gregory had explored the theme of 'loyalty to Kathleen ny Houlihan' in the autumn of 1901 when she was collaborating with Yeats on the writing of *Cathleen ni Houlihan*. Taking into consideration Gregory's co-authorship of the play and her familiarity with Jacobite ideology and poetry, the 'Poor Lady' in *The White Cockade* appears at first glance to be yet another representative of the *aisling* tradition who laments 'the loss of her [Ireland's] Stuart lover'.[35] Notably, the 1905 publication of the play highlights this Jacobite motif in its epigraph: 'I saw a vision through my sleep last night.'[36] Among the reviews of the play, the *Daily Express* is the only paper that picked up on the association: 'The poor lady is probably intended to represent Erin at that stirring period.'[37] Joseph Holloway noted in his diary that the actress Maire nic Shiubhlaigh as Lady Dereen 'suggested "Cathleen ni Houlihan" at almost every turn'.[38] It is she who represents – apart from Sarsfield – loyalty to the Stuart monarch. The hope in King James's victory is tied in the play to the hope of the repossession of property lost. After the Cromwellian settlement, the majority of land changed hands from Catholics to Protestants, and the Poor Lady is one of the Catholic landed aristocracy who lost their land. Her costume epitomises the shift in her status; she is dressed in '*ragged clothes that have once been handsome*'.[39]

However, there is no explicit indication that she stands as 'Lady Éire'; rather, she is given a specific name, Lady Dereen, and the lost land is specifically her property instead of the more metaphorical 'four beautiful green fields' of *Cathleen ni Houlihan*. Hopeful in the Stuart cause of the Williamite War, the old lady says: 'I lost all through Charles; I will get all back through James.'[40] Lady Dereen is concerned with her personal economic position and longs for a return to wealth and luxury as she looks forward to 'my silks and my velvets' and the 'jewels about my neck'.[41] However, she proclaims that 'James […] will bring prosperity to us all'.[42] How the other characters will profit remains unexplored. When the owner of the Inn, Matt Kelleher, returns home, he brings news from Ross that the Battle of the Boyne has been won, and James is lauded for 'raging like a lion in every gap', 'The brave Stuart!'[43] With his victory, they assume, 'We'll all get our rights' and Lady Dereen will reclaim her property: 'You'll get your estates, Lady, and your white halls!'[44] Despite this short reference to the rights of the Catholics, the emphasis throughout is on the repossession of land. Thus, the play is preoccupied with an immediate economic concern and with the realities of everyday life.

Similarly, Owen Kelleher's mother in *The White Cockade* is not lured by any romanticised idea of heroism or nationalist ideology and judges everything according to whether it would be economically viable. There is a reversal of economics in *The White Cockade* in that the emphasis is placed on Lady Dereen's economic condition as she seeks solace and shelter in the home of her former servant. Thus, rather than focusing on the rural classes, as in *Cathleen ni Houlihan*, it is the native aristocracy's decline that is put on display. The Kellehers, as representatives of the lower social order, are comparatively comfortable, pursuing their business. Mrs Kelleher's most repeated phrase, alongside her cumbersome rhetoric of proverbs, is 'it might be for profit':[45]

> MRS. KELLEHER. So long as we get it, I wouldn't mind much what King brings it. One penny weighs as good as another. [. . .]
>
> LADY. Is it nothing to you, Mary Kelleher, that the broken altars of the Faith will be built up again?
>
> MRS. KELLEHER. God grant it! Though indeed, myself I am no great bigot. I would always like to go to a Protestant funeral. You would see so many well-dressed people at it.[46]

Here, the link between religion and social and economic status becomes apparent; it is the Protestants who are 'well dressed'. However, Mrs. Kelleher's comment is devoid of a sense of envy or anger regarding inequality. There is no implication of strong political loyalties but rather an emphasis on the practicalities of everyday life that echo Bridget Gillane's in *Cathleen ni Houlihan*.

In contrast to the old woman's overt recruitment of the Gillanes' son in *Cathleen ni Houlihan*, Lady Dereen does not directly appeal to Owen's heroic ambitions but states in a manner of reportage that the 'young men are leaving the scythes in the meadows; the old men are leaving the stations and the blessed wells. Give me some white thing – some feathers – I have to make cockades for the King's men.'[47] While Michael is lured by Cathleen ni Houlihan's rhetoric, Owen sits lazily and disinterestedly in his home, daydreaming about becoming a man of action rather than actually becoming one. Yet Owen desires to be elsewhere, to be in a place where something is happening. His brief reference to 'great fighters in Ireland in the old times' is quickly rebutted by his mother: 'Believe me, if they had found as good a way of living as what you have, they would not have asked to go rambling.'[48] Mrs Kelleher's comment further suggests that the family lives a fairly comfortable life and can profit from the war by trade rather than risking their lives in battle. Owen's talk of fighting, it is implied, is nothing more than idle chatter to distract from daily work whereby the heroic ideal of the man of action is challenged.

This opens the debate between Lady Dereen and Mrs Kelleher regarding questions of loyalty and heroism. While Mrs Kelleher wishes for support in the running of the business, the old lady chastises him for not joining the battle:

> MRS. KELLEHER. I have but the one son only, and is it sending him away from me you would be?
>
> LADY. Our King has no son; he has false daughters. We must give our sons to the King!
>
> MRS. KELLEHER. It is my opinion we must keep them to mind ourselves. . . . How will Owen mind this place, and he maybe shot as full of holes as riddle?[49]

In *Cathleen ni Houlihan*, both the bride and the mother beg Michael not to enlist in service to the old woman. They rate, Joseph Valente argues, 'private interests and domestic affective concerns higher than nationalist aspirations and the good of the people, a stereotypically feminine attitude with which this particular play registers no sympathy'.[50] In *The White Cockade*, however, what Valente considers feminine attitudes are not the sole prerogative of the female characters in the play as long as Owen demonstrates an indifference to the battle. He has to decide between 'The Stuart in the field' and 'The meat in the cellar!'[51] The choice, as in *Cathleen ni Houlihan*, is between the economics of the private sphere and the politics of the country. Owen's decision, we can assume, depends on the strength of his loyalty to his country and, more specifically, the attraction of the concept of heroic action. While Lady Dereen encourages him to join the battle with her own profit in mind, it is Sarsfield who expresses the rhetoric of sacrifice.

While James II was remembered as the cowardly king who fled after the Battle of the Boyne, Patrick Sarsfield entered the Irish pantheon of nationalist heroes in ballad poetry and cultural memory. The latter's heroic status is evidenced by a nationalist monument erected in Limerick in 1881.[52] The Catholic poet Katharine Tynan pays tribute to his final fall on the battlefield in Landen in the poem 'The Flight of the Wild Geese' (1885):

> Ah! Patrick Sarsfield, when you lay,
> With your life-blood following amain,
> You looked at the dark stain on your hand,
> And 'Would it were shed for mine own dear land!'[53]

Two years later, Emily Lawless wrote about the General in *Ireland*:

> Sarsfield is the one redeeming figure upon the Jacobite side. His gallant presence sheds a ray of chivalric light upon this otherwise gloomiest and least attractive of campaigns. He could not turn defeat to victory, but he could, and did succeed in snatching honour out of that pit into which the other leaders, and especially his master, had let it drop.[54]

Considering these writers' differing denominational and political backgrounds, their portrayals illustrate Jacobitism's generic appeal which created, as Frank Shovlin writes, 'a curious bridging ground between the two main traditions in Ireland'.[55] Both Tynan's 'life-blood following amain' and Lawless's 'chivalric light' have romantic overtones with a stress on the heroic.

Gregory's play, at first glance, equally introduces Sarsfield as the one redeeming figure. The second act of *The White Cockade* presents the audience with the contrasting personalities of Sarsfield and James II as they are hiding in a wood debating war strategies. Whereas Sarsfield is a man of action willing to face danger, the King is portrayed as the fearful coward who retreats rather than attacks. When Owen – on his way to gather news of the outcome of the battle – accidentally meets James's group, he unknowingly tells them the news that the King has been defeated at the Boyne and confirms James's sense of danger; he decides to hide at the Kellehers' inn before embarking on a French ship to leave Ireland. Owen departs singing, in hope of 'James, / Our treasure and our only choice – The darling Caesar of the Gael!'[56] This is immediately followed by James's comment: 'We can go on board at once, and slip away to France. I have done with this detestable Ireland.'[57]

The King's cowardice is most potently evoked when the group hears fife and drum playing the Williamite song 'Lilliburlero', and, with the swelling of the music, James – as instructed by the stage directions – is '*clinging to* Sarsfield'.[58] This lavishly feeds into contemporary attitudes of the Stuart king. Indeed, 'Lady Gregory's presentation of that monarch on the stage does not possess any feature of attractiveness', stated the *Daily Express* following the play's opening night on 9 December 1905.[59] In contrast, the *Irish Independent* wrote, 'Mr. F. J. Fay gave a Sarsfield that appealed to the imagination – the antithesis of the king, a dashing, noble-hearted soldier and patriot.'[60] With this opposition, Gregory negates James II's place as a representative leader for Ireland whose selfish interests disregard the interest of the country. Praising the play's unity, the *Leader* highlights that the 'central idea is the contrast between the man, Sarsfield, who is by nature the leader of his people, and the poltroon, James, whom his lineage and their loyalty have unfortunately placed in that position'.[61]

Back in the inn's kitchen in the second scene of the second act, the gossip regarding the victory at the Boyne has been rectified. Just as Owen informs his family that the King is expected that evening, two Williamite soldiers arrive. Shortly thereafter, James and Sarsfield enter, and the Williamites seize their arms. As the King is threatened, Sarsfield steps forward, declaring himself to be James II, to protect his master. With the two opposing sides of the battle represented in one room, they discuss the conflict:

> SARSFIELD. I am sorry all the men of Ireland are not on the one side.
>
> FIRST WILLIAMITE. It is best to be on the winning side. [. . .]
>
> SARSFIELD. He is surely the winner who gets a great tombstone, a figured monument, cherubs blowing trumpets, angels' tears in marble – or maybe he is the winner who has none of these, who but writes his name in the book of the people. I would like my name set in clean letters in the book of the people.[62]

Sarsfield's statement is in keeping with Gregory's appreciation of Irish ballads of defeat.

The dialogue further explores the dichotomy between the sovereignty of king or country, ultimately merging the two to comply with the aesthetics of the *aisling* tradition:

> OWEN (*who has been listening eagerly*). It must be a wonderful thing to be a King!
>
> SARSFIELD. [. . .] To be a King is to be a lover – a good lover of a beautiful sweetheart.
>
> FIRST WILLIAMITE. I suppose he means the country, saying that.
>
> SECOND WILLIAMITE. I am sure he must have a heart for Ireland.[63]

Sarsfield – through his impersonation of the King – is critical of his master. James's approach to the war is undermined and lampooned, exposing him as unworthy to be 'the chosen and anointed'.[64] The reference to 'a good lover of a beautiful sweetheart' taps into the generic approach whereby the Stuart was replaced by Ireland in Jacobite thought from the eighteenth century onwards. Gregory expands on this analogy, as Sarsfield says:

> To go out, to call his men, to give out shouts because the time has come to show what her strong lover can do for her – to go hungry that she may be fed; to go tired that her dear feet may tread safely; to die, it may be, at the last for her with such glory that the name he leaves with her is better than any living love, because he has been faithful, faithful, faithful![65]

It is not, as in *Cathleen ni Houlihan*, the old woman who calls for a self-sacrifice but the general of the battle himself who speaks on her behalf.

He enacts the role James II, as Ireland's king and the saviour of Catholic rights, should have filled. This exploits the King's lack of leadership. Sarsfield's impersonation convinces even the two Williamites: 'I give up the Dutchman's pay. This man's the best', says one.[66] Owen is willing to 'follow him every hard road', and his father promises to 'never drink another drop till he has come to his rights!'[67]

Yet, when the group assembles around James II, who emerges from a barrel in which he planned to escape aboard the French ship, they abuse him as a 'traitor' who tried 'to desert the King'.[68] Once James's royal identity is clarified, there is general disbelief, as all together announce: '*That* His Majesty!'[69] As the King walks out, Owen is '*throwing off cloak and belt, and tearing cockade from his hat, throws himself down and begins to play jackstones as in First Act*'.[70] We are back where we started. James's cowardice comes to its apex; Gregory lampoons the Irish who believed in the Stuart king. Catholic Ireland's supposed saviour is unworthy of self-sacrifice, and Owen is not stirred into battle.

At the end of the play, Gregory discloses the faultiness of Jacobite – and nationalist – ideology. The two Williamites toss a coin to decide whether to follow 'the one we left or the one who left us'; the coin decides they are to abandon the white cockade and return to the service of William of Orange.[71] Even the enthusiastic Sarsfield is momentarily shocked into apathy:

> he betrayed me – he called me from the battle – he lost me my great name – he betrayed Ireland. Who is he? What is he? A King or what? (*He pulls feathers one by one from cockade.*) King or knave – soldier – sailor – tinker – tailor – beggarman – thief! (*Pulls out last feather.*) Thief, that is it, – thief. He has stolen away; he has stolen our good name; he has stolen our faith; he has stolen the pin that held loyalty to royalty! A thief, a fox – a fox of trickery! (*He sits down trembling.*)[72]

His feelings of betrayal are spoken on behalf of Catholic Ireland. For a moment, it appears as if his loyalty to the sovereign fails. However, he instantly takes up a new white cockade, putting it on his head and, thereby, embraces the ideology of self-sacrifice for a lost cause. Sarsfield turns into one of those Irish rebels Gregory had lauded in her article, 'The Felons of Our Land': by reclaiming the white cockade, he joins those 'who went out to a battle that was already lost – men who, whatever may have been their mistakes or faults, had an aim quite apart from personal greed or gain'.[73] At this point in the play, political reality succumbs to romantic nationalism.

If the play had ended with Sarsfield's speech, we could interpret it within the framework of romantic Jacobitism with Sarsfield as the hero.[74] However, Sarsfield's self-sacrifice is put under scrutiny as Mrs Kelleher asks him: 'Why would you go spending yourself for the like of *that* of a king?'[75] He makes a feeble attempt at explanation, displaying an underlying uncertainty: 'Why, why? Who can say? What is holding me? Habit, custom.... Maybe the call of some old angry father of mine, that fought two thousands years ago for a bad master!'[76] Even Lady Dereen realises the lost cause and the final words of the play are left to her: 'Poor Patrick Sarsfield is very, very mad!'[77] For some members of the audience, this was an 'unsatisfying' end, evidenced by one gentleman whispering to Dublin playgoer and diarist Joseph Holloway, 'Is it over now?'[78]

Considering Gregory's responsibility for the Gillanes' dialogue and the cottage setting, we can assume that the playwright's reservations regarding the realities of nationalist martyrology were already prevalent in *Cathleen ni Houlihan*. Michael's mother, Bridget, is aghast as she observes the transformation in her son: 'Look at him, Peter; he has the look of a man that has got the touch.'[79] This observation foreshadows Lady Dereen's and Mrs Kelleher's judgement of Sarsfield's self-sacrifice as an act of lunacy. Importantly, if we were to take Lady Dereen as the symbolic old woman of the *aisling* tradition, she withdraws from her lament to raise men into battle to fight for the restoration of her property. She accepts the lost cause; there is no renewal or rejuvenation. Coincidentally, as a representative of the Catholic aristocracy, Lady Dereen's decision to withhold her support of the Stuart cause ensures that – in contemporary terms – Gregory, as a member of the Protestant aristocracy, retains her lands (if we are to ignore the land reforms of the time). This undeniable link between religion and social status adds an element of sectarian elitism to the play.

Thus, it can be argued, *The White Cockade* challenges not only political but also romantic Jacobitism. Sarsfield – one key example of the pantheon of Irish nationalist heroes – is lampooned for his illogical willingness to follow 'a bad master' who even his fellow Catholic Irish have turned their backs on. The latter are seen to prioritise pragmatism over ideological allegiances, whether to sovereign or country. James Pethica argues in an essay on Gregory's drama that Sarsfield's 'final self-sacrifice [...] offers those around him the potential for "spiritual vision", even though they prove too debased to profit from his example'.[80] Conversely, however, the ending of the play suggests that, rather than being 'too debased' to follow Sarsfield, the Irish – of both the higher and lower social order – realise the futility of the 'spiritual vision' and declare it an act of insanity.

Once Gregory had finished the play, she sent it to Blunt in late September 1905, unsure whether he would warm to it. 'I don't know that you will like it', she remarked, 'if you still belong to the League of the White Rose.'[81] This is further confirmation of the Jacobite resurgence around the turn of the century, illustrated by a Stuart exhibition held at the

New Gallery in Regent Street in 1889. Gregory's mention of the 'League of the White Rose' might be a reference to the Order of the White Rose, established in 1886, which facilitated a renewed interest in the subject that was further explored in the society's publication, *The Royalist*, which ran from 1890 – the anniversary of the Battle of Culloden – to 1905.[82] At one time, the Order counted close to 500 members.[83] Five years after its initial foundation, a more radical grouping split from the Order calling itself the Legitimist Jacobite League of Great Britain and Ireland with a clearer defined political aim of the Stuart restoration.[84] Gregory's mixed phrase, including both 'League' and 'White Rose', could be a reference to either one of these organisations. Yet it clearly indicates her awareness of more politically inclined Jacobite ideologies prevalent at the time.

Some of the key literary figures of the 1890s had Jacobite sympathies, including McGregor Mathers and Lionel Johnson. It is in regard to the latter two, and the circle of the Rhymers Club, that Yeats was also acquainted with such sympathies, suggesting an overlap in the political, romantic, and occult aspects of Jacobitism and the diverse spectrum of groups. 'One quality such sects have in common', Fletcher argues, is 'the pursuit of power, [...] they are aristocrats whether of blood, or intellect or by ordeal'.[85] Irish Jacobite poetry was not exempt from this initial attachment to elitism as it 'was originally a conservative rhetoric imbued with the traditional values of aristocracy, hierarchy, hereditary right and social order'. However, Ó Buachalla further argues, 'it was also, potentially and eventually, a radical rhetoric in that it foretold, extolled and promoted the overthrow of the existing regime. It must accordingly be counted among the factors that contributed to the politicisation of Irish Catholics.'[86]

Although *The White Cockade* presents us with a Jacobite theme and motif, its call 'to the politicisation of Irish Catholics' fails; the Kellehers stay put, and Lady Dereen abandons her hopes for the Stuart cause, lampooning Sarsfield's continued loyalty to the sovereign. Considering the interlacing of Jacobitism with nationalism in the context of the early twentieth century, Gregory's comment to Blunt would suggest that she perceived her play to be not only anti-Jacobite but also anti-nationalist. As in Irish Jacobite thought the Irish nation was synonymous with the restoration and renewal of the Irish Catholic nation, it would also indicate that she was awake to the possibility that the play would be perceived as anti-Catholic.[87]

Following the premiere of the play, she once again wrote to Blunt, stating that 'many people were enthusiastic over it – but our audiences were small – we have not conquered the apathy of Dublin yet'.[88] The low numbers in the audience were also remarked upon by the *Leader*: 'One thing only was lacking – an audience, and that lacking with a vengeance the night I was there.'[89] This was due, the reviewer proposed, to the Abbey's adherence to high art and high class:

> They have gone about saying they do not want the public, that they do not wish to make their plays a commercial success, but they desire 'fit audience tho' few', and the like. They have also closed their doors in the face of sixpenny patrons.[90]

Despite the *Leader*'s otherwise significant praise, the review hints at the exclusivity of the theatre's approach and an administration that, the paper appears to suggest, targeted a bourgeois audience. If we are to believe D. P. Moran's assertion that those frequenting the Abbey were mainly Anglo-Irish, Gregory's angle in dealing with the Battle of the Boyne from a Catholic perspective might be seen as odd. However, if we bear in mind the outcome of the Williamite War in favour of the Protestant side, it would seem fitting. But the favourable reception among Catholics is notable.

One of *The White Cockade*'s admirers was Maud Gonne. Writing from Paris to Yeats, who had sent her a copy of the play, in December 1905, she stated:

> Lady Gregory knows the soul of our people and expresses it as no one else does. Through the surface of triviality, of selfish avarice, of folly which often jars on one, she never ceases to see and to express in her writing that deep passion which *only heroic* action or thought is able to arouse in them, & when once aroused makes them capable of sacrifice for ideals as no other people on earth are. It is a play that will live & [...] It is a play that will be popular – don't look contemptuous – such plays are needed for your work & for the public.[91]

Gonne's reference to 'the soul of our people' brings to mind an article by Maurice Joy, published only a few months previously in the *New Ireland Review*. Founded in 1894 by Fr Tom Finlay, Professor of Economics at University College Dublin, it became the 'house organ' and gave voice to Catholic militancy.[92] Joy asserted that the Revivalists' 'criticisms of life are too academic: they are not by men who have shared the struggle: they have but an external consciousness of Ireland's tragedy':

> Not one of them has been reared in Catholic tradition [. . .] These writers have broken with their own tradition. Some of them are Nationalists. [...] It is, perhaps, humanly impossible that their work should have all that sympathy which is necessary to a complete understanding of Ireland's soul.[93]

If Maud Gonne had been the only one embracing Gregory's ability to express the soul of the Irish people (despite her Protestantism), there would not be a substantial argument.

However, Alice Milligan praised the play in a very similar vein in an article on 'Yeats and the Drama', published in *Sinn Féin* in December 1906: 'I must say that nothing I have read in recent years seems so wholesome and good for national propaganda as some of [Gregory's] writing, notably *The White Cockade*.'[94] The play might have appealed to Gonne and Milligan for its Jacobite associations as they had been involved in the centenary celebrations of 1798. In this case, then, Gregory appears to have successfully tapped into the narrative of Catholic victimhood. Gonne prioritises Sarsfield's rhetoric of self-sacrifice, dismissing what she acknowledges as elements 'of selfish avarice' and 'of folly' as 'triviality'. In that regard, Gonne identified clear Jacobite ideas in the play: as Fletcher comments, 'Jacobitism always represented the triumph of an idea over reason, common sense and the tendency of events.'[95] Her prediction that the play would be a hit with the Abbey audience did not materialise. *The White Cockade* was only revived sporadically, with just forty performances between 1905 and 1932.[96]

Most significantly, however, is the positive review that appeared in the *Leader*, worth quoting at length:

> 'The White Cockade', by Lady Gregory, is one of the good things of the National Theatre Society.... A beautiful and pathetic figure is the 'Poor Lady' – a distraught and ruined wanderer in the Stuart cause, acted with admirable feeling and delicacy.... The loyal devotion of this poor female Lear, brings before us all that insane religion of Stuart loyalty which ruined our people in those days. What a terrible thing was that devotion of the many to the worthless one! No doubt, the treacherous royal figure-head was at that time in Irish eyes the palladium of their religion, their freedom, and even their nationality.... It is impossible to describe here with what subtle art the poor worn figure and the wandering mind of this withered devotee are made to express the fallacy of those principles which, in their result, annihilated our aristocracy, and gave our commons to bondage and long-continued persecution.[97]

This is an unusual source for such high praise, because, as Potts proposes, 'If any figure from the Revival could be said to speak for Irish Catholics it was Moran.'[98] As such, Moran took great pleasure in attacking Yeats and his co-Revivalists, including Æ, Gregory, and Synge.[99] Coincidentally, in 1905, he published *The Philosophy of Irish Ireland*, consisting of six essays which previously appeared in Finlay's paper. In this context, it is all the more surprising to find such a positive commentary on Gregory's play as it would have been easy to attack a Protestant landowner writing about the Catholic defeat at the Boyne. It is summarised in the *Leader* as the 'fatal [moment] when the Catholics of Ireland ruined themselves in the Stuart cause'.[100] The play's criticism of Catholic allegiance to the Stuart cause is recognised and, it appears, shared and accepted.

Gregory's approach has also been lauded by Ernest Boyd, one of the Revival's early critics, who argued that the

> treatment of one of the most delicate and dangerous subjects in Irish history indicates that Lady Gregory is able to bring considerable impartiality to the

> portrayal of national subjects. The dramatists of the Irish Theatre have broken with the tradition which demanded the patriotic idealizations of melodrama from all who essayed to dramatize the history of Ireland's struggle for freedom.[101]

The play engages in the same traditions as do the Irish political ballads in which Gregory was so interested. Her sympathy for the lost cause is romantic, yet her romanticism is not free from political criticism of 'that insane religion of Stuart loyalty'. Considering the symbolic importance of the Stuart cause in Jacobite poetry popular at the time, the *Leader*'s acceptance of – and agreement to – Gregory's representation is remarkable. It is indicative of a complex relationship between author, dramatic performance, and audience. After noting that Synge's *In the Shadow of the Glen* was attacked while Padraic Colum's lesser play, *Broken Soil*, was praised, Fay explains that Synge was 'a Protestant and a member of the "Ascendancy" class, whereas Colum was a Catholic and of the people'; 'It was a patriotic duty to haul down the one', he wrote, 'and cheer the other.'[102] In the case of *The White Cockade*, the *Leader* apparently did not adhere to such a 'patriotic duty'.

In consequence, Fay's estimation that attack and appraisal were dependent on the denominational relationship between author and audience rather than on literary merit is challenged. As the favourable response to *The White Cockade* among a Catholic audience and across the political spectrum – from the *Leader* to *Sinn Féin* and the *Daily Express* – illustrates, there was potential for dialogue and understanding between the two denominational groups, complicating the binary oppositions of the Revival which have tended to inhere. Gregory's own complex relationship with Jacobitism, both in its political and romantic incarnations, is apparent in the play and in her prose works on Irish ballad traditions. In *The White Cockade*, she brought to light the power of self-sacrificial rhetoric and, at the same time, challenged the popular concept of nationalist martyrology by presenting her audience with what is effectively a double ending that allowed for a flexibility in responses. Despite the potential divisiveness of the historical subject matter, the play's engagement with *fin-de-siècle* Irish Jacobite thought chimed well with its audiences. The contemporary acceptance of Gregory's criticism, in particular, pays tribute to her dramatic craft and complicates our understanding of the politics of representation in early twentieth-century Ireland.

Notes

1 Wilfrid Scawen Blunt to Lady Gregory (3 April 1907), Lady Gregory Collection of Papers, 1873–[1965] bulk (1873–1932), The Henry W. and Albert A. Berg Collection of English and American Literature, The New York Public Library, Astor, Lenox and Tilden Foundations, New York City. Hereafter cited as Berg.

2 Quoted in Lady Gregory, *Our Irish Theatre: A Chapter of Autobiography* (London and New York: G. P. Putnam's Sons, 1913), p. 12.
3 Gregory, *Our Irish Theatre*, p. 91.
4 Blunt to Gregory (29 June 1904), Berg.
5 Blunt to Gregory (3 April 1907), Berg.
6 Conor Cruise O'Brien, quoted in Willard Potts, *Joyce and the Two Irelands* (Austin, Tex.: University of Texas Press, 2000), p. 10.
7 Note that collecting folklore among the Irish rural poor brought religious difference to the fore. Yeats acknowledged when writing to Tynan that, 'There may be Catholic lore that would come more readily to you than to Lady Gregory or myself.' Yeats to Tynan (12 December 1915), in John Kelly (gen. ed.), *The Collected Letters of W. B. Yeats*, InteLex Electronic Edition (Oxford: Oxford University Press, 2002).
8 Potts, *Joyce and the Two Irelands*, p. 19.
9 Lady Gregory, *Irish Folk-History Plays*, First and Second Series (London and New York: G. P. Putnam's Sons, 1912).
10 W. G. Fay and Catherine Carswell, *The Fays of the Abbey Theatre: An Autobiographical Record* (New York: Harcourt, Brace & Co., 1935), p. 170.
11 Lady Gregory, *The White Cockade*, in *The Collected Plays*, vol. II: *The Tragedies and Tragic-Comedies*, ed. Ann Saddlemyer (Gerrards Cross: Colin Smythe, 1971), pp. 219–54.
12 Quoted in Frank Shovlin, *Journey Westward: Joyce, Dubliners, and the Literary Revival* (Liverpool: Liverpool University Press, 2012), p. 65.
13 Douglas Hyde, *A Literary History of Ireland: From Earliest Times to the Present Day* (New York: Charles Scribner's Sons, 1901), p. 594.
14 Gregory to Blunt (14 April 1905), Folder 34, Berg.
15 Gregory to Blunt (24 July 1905), Folder 35, Berg.
16 'July Anniversary: Celebrations in Belfast', *Irish Times* (13 July 1905), p. 6. Brian Walker notes that the 12 July parades 'enjoyed widespread support and [...] were well attended' from the 1880s onwards. See Brian Walker, *Past and Present: History, Identity and Politics in Ireland* (Belfast: The Institute of Irish Studies Queen's University Belfast, 2000), p. 80.
17 Lady Gregory (ed.), *Mr. Gregory's Letter-Box: 1813–1830* (London: Smith, Elder, & Co., 1898), p. 28.
18 Froude, quoted in Daniel Corkery, *The Hidden Ireland: A Study of Gaelic Munster in the Eighteenth Century* (Dublin: M. H. Gill & Son, 1956), p. 30.
19 Murray G. H. Pittock, *The Invention of Scotland: The Stuart Myth and the Scottish Identity, 1638 to the Present* (London and New York: Routledge, 1991), p. 70.
20 Murray G. H. Pittock, *Poetry and Jacobite Politics in Eighteenth-Century Britain and Ireland* (Cambridge: Cambridge University Press, 1994), p. 192.
21 Jonathan Clark, 'The Many Restorations of King James: A Short History of Scholarship on Jacobitism, 1688–2006', in Paul Monod, Murray Pittock, and Daniel Szechi (eds), *Loyalty and Identity: Jacobites at Home and Abroad* (Basingstoke: Palgrave Macmillan, 2010), p. 30.
22 Lady Gregory, 'Irish Jacobite Songs', *Speaker* (January 1903), 413–15, at p. 414.
23 Guy Beiner, *Remembering the Year of the French: Irish Folk History and Social Memory* (Madison, Wisc.: The University of Wisconsin Press, 2007), p. 94.
24 Pittock, *Poetry and Jacobite Politics*, p. 194.
25 'Lilli Burlero', in *Percy's Reliques of Ancient English Poetry in Two Vols.* (London: J. M. Dent & Co., 1906), vol. II, pp. 157–9.
26 Clark, 'The Many Restorations of King James', p. 29.
27 Gregory to Blunt (22 June 1902), Folder 29, Berg.
28 Gregory, 'Irish Jacobite Songs', pp. 413–15.
29 Gregory, 'Irish Jacobite Songs', p. 413.
30 Gregory, 'Irish Jacobite Songs', p. 413.
31 Corkery, *Hidden Ireland*, p. 134.
32 Pittock, *Poetry and Jacobite Politics*, p. 194.

33 Beiner, *Remembering the Year of the French*, pp. 92–3.
34 Breandán Ó Buachalla, 'Irish Jacobitism and Irish Nationalism: The Literary Evidence', in Michael O'Dea and Kevin Whelan (eds), *Nations and Nationalisms: France, Britain, Ireland and the Eighteenth-Century Context* (Oxford: Voltaire Foundation, 1995), pp. 103–16, at p. 109.
35 Gregory, 'Irish Jacobite Songs', p. 414.
36 Gregory, *The White Cockade*, quoted in Shovlin, *Journey Westward*, pp. 82–3.
37 '"The White Cockade": New Play at the Abbey Theatre', *Daily Express*, 11 December 1905, p. 6.
38 Entry for 9 December 1905, Joseph Holloway, *Joseph Holloway's Abbey Theatre: A Selection from His Unpublished Journal, Impressions of a Dublin Playgoer*, ed. Robert Hogan and Michael J. Neill, with a preface by Harry T. Moore (Carbondale, Ill.: Southern Illinois University Press, 1967), p. 63.
39 Gregory, *The White Cockade*, p. 221.
40 Gregory, *The White Cockade*, p. 221.
41 Gregory, *The White Cockade*, p. 226.
42 Gregory, *The White Cockade*, p. 222.
43 Gregory, *The White Cockade*, p. 226.
44 Gregory, *The White Cockade*, pp. 226, 222, 226.
45 Gregory, *The White Cockade*, p. 222.
46 Gregory, *The White Cockade*, p. 222.
47 Gregory, *The White Cockade*, p. 222.
48 Gregory, *The White Cockade*, p. 220.
49 Gregory, *The White Cockade*, p. 223.
50 Joseph Valente, 'The Myth of Sovereignty: Gender in the Literature of Irish Nationalism', *ELH*, 61:1 (1994), 189–210, at p. 200.
51 Gregory, *The White Cockade*, p. 224.
52 Beiner, *Remembering the Year of the French*, p. 244.
53 Katharine Tynan, *Louise de la Vallière and Other Poems* (London: Kegan Paul, 1885), p. 24.
54 Emily Lawless, *Ireland* (London: T. Fisher Unwin, 1912), pp. 289–90.
55 Frank Shovlin, 'Jacobitism and the Literary Revival', in Paddy Lyons, Willy Maley, and John Miller (eds), *Romantic Ireland: From Tone to Gonne – Fresh Perspectives on Nineteenth-Century Ireland* (Newcastle upon Tyne: Cambridge Scholars Publishing, 2013), 376–87, at p. 379.
56 Gregory, *The White Cockade*, p. 232.
57 Gregory, *The White Cockade*, p. 232.
58 Gregory, *The White Cockade*, p. 233.
59 '*The White Cockade*', *Daily Express* (11 December 1905), p. 6.
60 'The White Cockade', *Irish Independent* (11 December 1905), p. 6.
61 'A Play and a Solitude', *the Leader* (23 December 1905), p. 300.
62 Gregory, *The White Cockade*, p. 240.
63 Gregory, *The White Cockade*, pp. 241–2.
64 Gregory, *The White Cockade*, p. 241.
65 Gregory, *The White Cockade*, p. 242.
66 Gregory, *The White Cockade*, p. 242.
67 Gregory, *The White Cockade*, p. 242.
68 Gregory, *The White Cockade*, p. 251.
69 Gregory, *The White Cockade*, p. 252.
70 Gregory, *The White Cockade*, p. 252.
71 Gregory, *The White Cockade*, p. 253.
72 Gregory, *The White Cockade*, p. 253.
73 Lady Gregory, 'The Felons of Our Land', *Cornhill Magazine*, 8:47 (May 1900), 622–34, at p. 634.

74 Indeed, personally, Gregory subscribed to that discourse of perceiving Sarsfield as a romantic hero. Notably, one of her son's horses was named Sarsfield. In fact, it is probable that this was the name given to the horse Robert Gregory received as a present when he came of age in 1902, considering that his mother had been collecting Jacobite songs that summer. Gregory to Blunt (22 June 1902), Folder 29, Berg.
75 Gregory, *The White Cockade*, p. 254.
76 Gregory, *The White Cockade*, p. 254.
77 Gregory, *The White Cockade*, p. 254.
78 Entry for 9 December 1905, Holloway, *Joseph Holloway's Abbey Theatre*, p. 63.
79 W. B. Yeats, *The Hour-Glass and Other Plays: Plays for an Irish Theatre* (London and New York: Macmillan, 1904), vol. II, p. 76.
80 James Pethica, 'Lady Gregory's Abbey Theatre Drama: Ireland Real and Ideal', in Shaun Richards (ed.), *The Cambridge Companion to Twentieth-Century Irish Drama* (Cambridge: Cambridge University Press, 2004), pp. 62–78, at p. 73.
81 Gregory to Blunt (24 September 1905), Folder 35, Berg.
82 Clark, 'The Many Restorations of King James', p. 30. See also Ian Fletcher, *W. B. Yeats and His Contemporaries* (Brighton: The Harvester Press, 1987), pp. 95–6.
83 Fletcher, *W. B. Yeats and His Contemporaries*, p. 96.
84 Murray Pittock, *Spectrum of Decadence: The Literature of the 1890s* (London and New York: Routledge, 1993), pp. 98–9.
85 Fletcher, *W. B. Yeats and His Contemporaries*, pp. 112, 117.
86 Breandán Ó Buachalla, 'Irish Jacobite Poetry', *Irish Review*, 12 (spring/summer 1992), 40–9, at pp. 47–8.
87 Fletcher, *W. B. Yeats and His Contemporaries*, p. 110.
88 Gregory to Blunt (24 December 1905), Folder 35, Berg.
89 'A Play and a Solitude', p. 300.
90 'A Play and a Solitude', p. 300.
91 Gonne to Yeats (16 December 1905), in Anna MacBride White and A. Norman Jeffares (eds), *The Gonne–Yeats Letters, 1893–1938: Always Your Friend* (London: Pimlico, 1993), p. 222.
92 See Potts, *Joyce and the Two Irelands*, p. 26.
93 Maurice Joy, 'The Irish Literary Revival: Some Limitations and Possibilities', *New Ireland Review*, 32:5 (1905), 257–66, at pp. 259, 264–5.
94 Alice L. Milligan, 'Yeats and the Drama', *Sinn Féin* (31 December 1906), quoted in Robert Hogan and James Kilroy, *The Abbey Theatre: The Years of Synge, 1905–1909* (Dublin: Dolmen Press, 1978), p. 120.
95 Fletcher, *W. B. Yeats and His Contemporaries*, p. 118.
96 See http://www.abbeytheatre.ie/archives/search/plays/the%20white%20cockade. Accessed 25 May 2012.
97 'A Play and a Solitude', p. 301.
98 Potts, *Joyce and the Two Irelands*, p. 31.
99 Potts, *Joyce and the Two Irelands*, p. 34.
100 'A Play and a Solitude', p. 300.
101 Ernest A. Boyd, *The Contemporary Drama of Ireland* (Boston, Mass.: Little, Brown, & Company, 1917), p. 136.
102 Fay and Carswell, *The Fays of the Abbey Theatre*, p. 148.

9

'Old wine in new bottles'?: Katharine Tynan, Lord Edward Fitzgerald, and George Wyndham

Kieron Winterson

In 1895, Katharine Tynan (1859–1931) published a collection of short stories, *An Isle in the Water*. It included 'The Story of Father Anthony O'Toole', in which the reader learns that O'Toole is a French-born descendant of one of the Wild Geese, those who fled Ireland in the wake of Jacobite failure in the Williamite Wars. Having served as a 'colonel of French Horse', O'Toole has travelled to the country of his forebears to become clergyman of 'the Island Chapel' and 'Shepherd of his flock for thirty years' – that is, from 1780 (Tynan is quite clear on O'Toole's chronology) and, thus, during the period of Grattan's Parliament and the evolution of the United Irish Society.[1]

Tynan sets the main action of the story in 1798 when, with Wolfe Tone 'dead in the Provost Marshall's prison in Dublin and Lord Edward Fitzgerald … dying of his wounds', O'Toole sees four 'yeomen' approaching.[2] They are intent on doing away with O'Toole but, dressed now in his 'magnificent' old uniform, where the yeomanry had 'looked to find an infirm old man, stood a French colonel in his battle array'.[3] The yeomen are bloodily dispatched by O'Toole, 'and the troubles of '98 spent themselves without crossing again from the [Irish] mainland'.[4]

Modern readers of Tynan's work have not been kind, and it would be difficult to argue that 'The Story of Father Anthony O'Toole' is anything other than slight. Whatever its literary merit, though, it is representative of Tynan's political thought, for in eliding the complex political realities of one of the most turbulent periods in modern Irish history, what is revealed by 'The Story of Father Anthony O'Toole' is the ambivalence at the heart of Tynan's writing and her life. The first half of the 1890s had been of profound political significance, with the death of Charles Stewart Parnell (1891), the failure of the second Home Rule Bill (1893), and William Ewart Gladstone's retirement from politics (1894). On a personal level, Tynan had married Henry Hinkson in 1893 and moved to England where the couple remained until their return to Ireland in 1911.[5] 'The Story of Father Anthony O'Toole' thus suggests a pivot around which her life and her contribution to Irish cultural and political life might be seen to turn. Moreover, given the enormity of her literary output – more than 100 novels, eighteen poetry collections, innumerable short stories, plays, and several volumes of memoir and autobiography – and the large readership that this implies, this ambivalence is something that might have been experienced by her readership too.[6]

She was born in Clondalkin, Co. Dublin, to Andrew and Elizabeth Tynan, but for all the voluminousness of her autobiographical work, of her mother and of her siblings she says virtually nothing. It is to her father that the reader must look in order to understand something of the social, political, and literary forces that shaped her views. Andrew Tynan was 'a [tenant] farmer with three hundred acres' from which he exported cattle (some to the British Army).[7] He can thus be understood as a product of the decades following the Famine, a period which had seen a significant shift away from arable to pasture farming and which gave rise to the type of successful farmer-grazier who 'could achieve near-gentry status'.[8] Whether or not Andrew Tynan achieved that kind of status it is impossible to say, but there is no denying his daughter's awareness of social class as an element in their lives: although she doubted that her father 'was ever popular with his own class', she believed that '[w]ith the people and with a higher social class he was very much beloved and admired'.[9] Regarding his relationship with the 'people', Tynan represents her father as a benevolent employer: 'He gave a great deal of employment', she says, 'and his weekly wages bill was high, much higher than the land could repay. He made nothing from it.'[10] His benevolence at times tended towards a stern paternalism: 'The peasants, servants, tramping people, beggars, and the like, had an appreciation of him as he had of them', she says, an appreciation so keen, evidently, that '[t]hey never resented it when he was violent with them.'[11] He cuts a patrician figure in her representation, and there is, too, something Arnoldian about her perception of him. Matthew Arnold had written that the Celt was one who 'out of affection and admiration [gives] himself body and soul to some leader'.[12] She concurred with that view: her father, she wrote, 'had the feeling for rank and title – the pageantry of life which all imaginative people – at least among the Celts, have'.[13] It is an inherited mode of thought, one which unwittingly suggests something of the ideological sympathies that would inform her career, even when the surface details of her work seemed most keenly nationalistic.

That complex of thought and representation can be found in her early reading. She had been 'brought up on the dreadful churchyard stories of the Irish peasant imagination', although there was also, in the home of her youth, 'a long row, in dull chocolate covers, of Miss Edgeworth's books'.[14] She read Edgeworth's 'society' novel, *Belinda*, 'over and over and many other of Belinda's sort' – and if, as she says, such books gave her mind 'a distinct bent towards the eighteenth century', it may be that they also gave her mind a bent towards that preoccupation with the mores of the upper middle classes and the aristocracy which was to be a feature of her own fiction.[15] At the same time, her father directed her reading 'towards poetry – Irish nationalist poetry for the most part ... Davis, Duffy's *Spirit of the Nation*, D'Arcy Magee and Meagher of the Sword'.[16] These several influences are evident in the early years of her writing career. Her first collection of poetry, *Louise de la Vallière and Other Poems*, appeared in 1885, when no less a figure than Michael Davitt had written to tell her of the 'extraordinary pleasure' he had had in informing John O'Leary that the collection's author was 'a friend'.[17] In fact, Tynan had known Davitt – founder of the Land League in 1879 and the 'patron saint of Mayo radicalism' – since 1881, when she met him at the inaugural meeting of the Ladies' Land League, of which she was a member.[18]

Evidence of her early radical tendencies is more easily seen in her contribution to *Poems and Ballads of Young Ireland*, published in Dublin in 1888, a collection that has been credited with 'inaugurating the Irish Literary Revival' and which 'attempted to suggest an apostolic literary succession between the original "Young Irelanders" and the new generation of "young Ireland"': this was, arguably, Tynan's first telling contribution to Irish cultural nationalism.[19] The collection was dedicated to John O'Leary, whose involvement in the 1848 rising and membership of the Irish Republican Brotherhood were Fenian credentials of the highest order – and 'the Fenians were looked upon as stainless heroes of a lost cause' in the Tynan household.[20] According to John Kelly, Tynan was one of the 'forces behind the anthology', whose dozen contributors also included Douglas Hyde and W. B. Yeats.[21] Of her three poems in the collection, it is 'The Grave of Michael Dwyer' that makes the most obvious appeal to nationalist political sentiment. Having surrendered to the British in the wake of the failed uprisings of 1798 and 1803, Dwyer was transported to Australia where he spent the rest of his life. In Tynan's poem he is the 'chief' who 'never came home again', who spent his remaining years 'with his brave heart broken'.[22]

However, if 'The Grave of Michael Dwyer' celebrated the martyrs of those years, it was not in any sense a call to arms: rather, it is a poem that belongs to what Marianne Elliott has called the 'martyrology' that began to develop around 'the memory of the fallen United Irishmen of 1798 and 1803' and which was thriving in the late 1880s.[23] As for O'Leary's Fenianism, Tynan found it necessary to 'differentiate between Fenian and Fenian – for the Clan-na-Gael in America, which was a sort of off-shoot of Fenianism, had altogether departed from the ways of legitimate Fenianism'.[24] In Tynan's eyes, O'Leary was the epitome of such legitimacy, for she saw him as being 'almost fanatically high-minded and clean-handed ... he would have abhorred murder: and expediency was to him only another name for lying and dishonesty'.[25] Indeed, despite having been arrested in 1865 and sentenced to twenty years' imprisonment for his involvement with the Irish Republican Brotherhood newspaper, *Irish People*, perhaps O'Leary always had been 'legitimate': as Lyons notes, although 'committed' to Fenianism, 'it was characteristic of him that he refused to take the secret oath of allegiance. This was symbolic of his whole attitude towards revolution. For him the spirit of independence was the essence of nationalism, not the deeds through which men might seek to make the spirit manifest.'[26] If O'Leary represented for some a particular strain of radical politics, he also came to embody what R. F. Foster calls 'Literary Fenianism', while Kelly remarks that O'Leary was 'the acknowledged doyen of the new literary generation', a generation to which Tynan belonged at the outset of her career.[27]

Some of the contributions to *Poems and Ballads of Young Ireland* had appeared in print before 1888.[28] The collection's gestation thus seems to have been protracted, and it is not unreasonable to infer that Tynan's views in 1888 were not so different from what they had been two years earlier (not forgetting, either, her involvement with the Ladies' Land League five years earlier still). It is significant, therefore, that during the period in which she espoused radicalism she had written 'In Time of Expectation', published in *United Ireland* on 29 May 1886. The newspaper was the organ of the Land League and of the Irish Party, so that the appearance of 'In Time of Expectation' in its pages serves to contextualise Tynan's sympathies in a nexus of unambiguously nationalist but nonetheless constitutional political thought.

Over the course of twenty quatrains, the poem celebrates the illustrious Irish dead, among whom are included Hugh O'Neill, Lord Edward Fitzgerald, Wolfe Tone, and Robert Emmet. It is thus of a piece with 'The Grave of Michael Dwyer' and celebrates some of those who had fought for Irish liberty. But it is equally a poem that demands to be understood as a celebration of the Prime Minister, Gladstone. Its subject is a 'Grey Atlas of the State bearing all that burden brave, / With your years passing three score and ten' – born in 1809, Gladstone was seventy-six years old when Tynan was writing.[29] It anticipates 'your pictured face [looking] from the smoke-grimed wall[s]' of emigrants' cabins – a full-page portrait of Gladstone had appeared in *United Ireland* of 10 April.[30] And it eulogises 'our Moses ... / Leading to the lovely land for which our father prayed' – Gladstone had introduced his Home Rule Bill a month previously. Although Gladstone is not referred to by name, the circumstantial evidence is clear.

Dwyer, Davitt, Gladstone, O'Leary: they form a complex mixture of the radical, the constitutional, and the literary, a mixture that, on the surface at least, seems to be constituted from irreconcilable opposites. For one thing, after 1883, at a time when Davitt regarded Tynan as a friend, he had begun to make 'troublesome noises about land nationalisation' so that the 'middle-class leadership [of the Irish Party] quickly moved to discredit his ideas'.[31] Davitt's views must have been utterly antithetical to those of a man like Tynan's father, a strong farmer unlikely to have been won over to nationalisation of the land and a man – according to his daughter – 'more in sympathy with Isaac Butt's movement [i.e. the Home Government Association] than with anything agrarian'.[32] Yet, despite Davitt's views, both Tynan and her father visited him in Kilmainham Gaol during his imprisonment in 1882, prior to his release in the wake of the Kilmainham Treaty of that year.[33]

Looking back from the vantage point of 1913, Tynan viewed her youthful nationalism more clearly: 'The romantic force that did attract one beyond an agitation which had largely a material aspect', she wrote, 'was the personality of the leaders.'[34] Evidently, Davitt had been one of those leaders: another was Parnell. Tynan's recording of her Parnellism is short on detail, for her memoirs do not deal in specifics until the years 1890–91. The first of those years had seen the Irish Parliamentary Party split into pro- and anti-Parnellites as a consequence of Parnell's affair with Kitty O'Shea. In her diary Tynan finds 'no mention at all of events before December 2' – that is, the week of 'intense and tortured debate' that led to the split.[35] In fact, she had entertained Parnellite sympathies for nearly a decade prior to this, beginning with Parnell's release from Kilmainham in 1882: '[w]e had all been rejoicing over the Kilmainham treaty', she records, and the prospect of 'the good times that were coming'. Those good times were contingent upon the 1881 Land Act and its famous 'three Fs' (fair rent, fixity or security of tenure, and free sale of improvements), from which Andrew Tynan, as a tenant, could hardly have failed to benefit.[36]

According to T. W. Moody, the Kilmainham Treaty was 'the vital turning point in Parnell's career', when he agreed to 'damp down the land agitation and co-operate with the liberals in restoring order to Ireland'.[37] The Tynans had also reached a turning point at that time, having come to feel 'the uninspiringness of the Land League':

> Had not Mr Parnell said in one of his public speeches that if it was only the land he would never have taken off his coat for this. I imagine a good many people besides my father and myself looked beyond the Land League to that for which Mr Parnell had taken off his coat.[38]

There were many among the generation who grew up in the 'poisoned atmosphere' of Irish political life in the decade following Parnell's death who did not see 'beyond the Land League', a generation for whom, as Lyons says, 'the Parnell of the land war, or the Parnell of the last great struggle, seemed more fundamental, more real than the Parnell of the Liberal alliance or the Kilmainham "treaty" '.[39] The generation who were coming to maturity in the 1890s included Thomas MacDonagh and Patrick Pearse, but Tynan's membership in the Ladies' Land League and her other forays into a quasi-radical political life notwithstanding, it was the 'constitutional' Parnell to whom Katharine and her father looked, even as they visited Davitt in prison.

Nothing of Tynan's regard for Parnell seems to find its way into her poetry – at any rate, not explicitly. Nevertheless, it is possible to detect a Jacobite symbolism at play in certain of her poems. 'The Blackbird', for example, with whose subject no 'yellow-haired Saxon or Dane might compare', draws on the blackbird as a Jacobite symbol.[40] Likewise, 'Comfort' features a blackbird and a nightingale. The poem's speaker exhorts the blackbird to sleep and not let the song of the nocturnal bird disturb him:

> Be not troubled, golden-throat,
> He is singing, far away
> In a country dim, remote,
> Singing twixt the dark and day.[41]

But this is no simple poem of nature and sentiment, for five stanzas later the speaker explains why the bird should not be troubled:

> You've a house, and a house-mate,
> Feathered daughters and a son;
> So your duty to the State,
> As bird-citizen you have done.

Aware of the powerful symbolism of the blackbird in Irish poetry and song, Tynan appears to say that – the land agitation largely resolved – Ireland is at peace. Yet the poem's penultimate stanza poses a question:

> Therefore shall he keep you waking? –
> That brown bird of night, afar,
> Singing songs, divine, heart-rending,
> Of a bird's love for a star.

The closing couplet supplies an answer, but it is an equivocal one, its equivocation emphasised by Tynan's italics: '*Yet my blackbird may grow pale / Just to hear the nightingale*' (original italics). It is, unusually for Tynan, an enigmatic poem, and it is made more so by the fact that Parnell was 'described in popular song as the "blackbird of Avondale"' – something of which Tynan would, presumably, have been aware.[42]

Be the meaning of 'Comfort' what it may, Parnell was dead, and by the time *Cuckoo Songs* was published, the second Home Rule Bill (1893) had failed. Nevertheless, there is a sense of a continuing Gladstonian Liberal sentiment in Tynan's writing. Seemingly undaunted after the defeat of the first Home Rule Bill in 1886, Gladstone had travelled from London to Scotland on 15 June of that year when, during the course of a break in the journey at Skipton in Yorkshire, he concurred with an address presented to him in which it was insisted that 'a policy of repression [in Ireland] is no longer practicable … real union must be sought in a union of hearts of the Irish and English peoples'.[43] Later in the year, Lord Dalhousie was reported as saying, apropos the Liberal split over the matter of Home Rule, that those in the party who supported Home Rule were the 'real' Unionists because 'what they wished was to bring about a union of the hearts and wills of the peoples of England and Ireland'.[44]

Significantly, *A Union of Hearts* (1901) was to be the title of one of Tynan's novels. The chief male protagonist, Aylmer Rivers, is a member of parliament and a resident magistrate. Moreover, he is an Englishman who, in his capacity as an RM, administers the law honourably but as an outsider, and, in 'laying down the law for the benefit of those who know the country better than he will ever know it', he incurs the antagonism of the local populace.[45] Much of the plot is concerned with the tension between Rivers' plans for 'new methods of farming' on the one hand and a latent agrarian unrest on the other.[46] Slowly, Rivers demonstrates his inherent decency and overcomes the prejudices that he meets. Meanwhile, the main female protagonist, Aileen Considine, works tirelessly on behalf of the peasantry while regarding Rivers with some prejudice, for he is generally believed to have made his money rather than having inherited it and to have done so through trade as a Bradford wool-stapler.[47]

There are many twists and turns in the plot, but, eventually, Rivers overcomes all of the obstacles before him. His final challenge is to retain his parliamentary seat at the impending general election. His opponent, Sylvester Blake, tells Considine that all she needs to do in support of Blake's electoral campaign is 'look handsome, and wear a green cockade': the 'enemy' – that is, Rivers – 'has the red, white, and blue'.[48] But over time she has become increasingly aware of Rivers' fundamental goodness, and her feelings towards him have changed. Moreover, it has been discovered that his money had been made 'a generation before he was born', so that now he can be considered fit to take her hand in marriage.[49] The romantic rapprochement between the two protagonists – one Irish, one English – is mirrored in an Anglo-Irish political rapprochement, for Rivers' integrity has become increasingly widely known, and his supporters in the election now sport 'the green with the red, white, and blue of their favours'.[50] He retains his seat, and the hope now is for 'a Parliament in College Green'.[51]

Thus, the novel's title and the colour symbolism of its denouement appear to champion the cause of Home Rule. But, by the time of its publication, Tynan's political sympathies had shifted yet again, for, following the split in the Irish Parliamentary Party and her move to England, Tynan had 'lost interest' in Irish politics.[52] However, as the century was drawing to a close, her political interests began to revive and change. 'The Irish, they say, have need for a King', she would later write: 'I used to say after Mr. Parnell's death that I had emptied myself of all the hero-worship I had to give. So it was that after seven years without a hero I sent a volume of verse I had published in 1898 to Mr. Wyndham.'[53] There was more to their relationship than a shared interest in poetry, however, for she regarded Wyndham's 'great Land Act' of 1903 as 'the manumission of the Irish farmers'.[54] Moreover, Wyndham was the great-grandson of Lord Edward Fitzgerald, a fact whose significance for Tynan it would be impossible to exaggerate. 'Even then', she wrote of the years 1897–98,

> I had a feeling for the Wyndhams that there was no one else like them. Perhaps it was that I had a devotion to Lord Edward Fitzgerald to start with; that I had made a cult of him; that I was saturated in all that could be known concerning him; that he was in a sense my dream-hero; that I was writing about him when I was not writing about Mr. Parnell.[55]

It would be careless, though, to assume that, in the person of Lord Edward, Tynan had made a cult of a violent revolutionary along the lines of Father Anthony O'Toole. Recalling time spent in the Royal Dublin Society library in Leinster House, she remembered musing on the prospect of seeing a ghost, 'the radiant beloved ghost of Lord Edward himself, perhaps … up a stair, under a ceiling, by walls, stuccoed and gilt in the manner of the Irish Renaissance of the great years before the Rebellion and the Union'.[56] It is a carefully placed ghost, one that cannot be subsumed by what Foster calls 'the great myth of 1798', for it walks the corridors of Leinster House before the Rebellion and at a time, Tynan elsewhere insists, of 'great days for Ireland, days of high achievement and higher hopes'.[57]

The splendours of the late eighteenth century might have gone but now Tynan had a hero not only in George Wyndham but also in his nephews, Hugo Francis (Lord Elcho) and Ivo Alan Charteris – both of them great-great-grandchildren of Lord Edward, both of them killed in action in the Great War. The death of the former, at Katia in the Sinai Desert, was the occasion for 'The Vision' in Tynan's 1918 collection *Herb O'Grace*. The poem bears the epigraph 'Katia: Easter Sunday, 1916', and

Tynan's foregrounding of the date cannot but be understood as a tacit juxtaposition with the events that took place in Ireland on the very next day. Although Hugo Francis 'must fall', he is not alone at the hour of his death: 'St. Andrew and St. Patrick ride / Close by his side; St. George is near'.[58] He thus meets his death in the company of the patron saints of the Three Kingdoms. Tynan would later eulogise him in *Memories* (1924), where she was to write that '[h]e was one of the great losses not only to those who loved and knew him, but to the world, to England, particularly, of the War'.[59] 'Happily', she continued, 'he left his sons to England.'[60] It is a bold expression of an ideological position. Her heroic triumvirate of Lord Edward, Parnell, and Wyndham constitutes a political lineage that links the quasi-autonomy of Grattan's Parliament with Ireland in the early twentieth century, and, through the loss of Wyndham's nephews as soldiers in the British Army, Lord Edward – thanks to a remarkable sleight of hand – is enlisted by Tynan in the cause of Empire. That complex set of linkages and associations is the stuff of her creative life and of a body of work that, whatever its literary merits, gave expression to a vision of Ireland. Moreover, her work found a wide readership: to fail to take this into account is to overlook the extent to which Tynan gave voice to a significant body of opinion in Ireland and, indeed, England.

Another of Tynan's poems of the Great War, 'The Watchers', has Ireland protected by Irish saints – Saints Patrick, Brigid, Brendan, Kevin, and Colum – but it is not only they, along with 'men-at-arms in white and gold' who 'Glide swiftly by the outer wall' and see Ireland safe from 'the evil beast': beyond Ireland's shores the war effort demanded more than these five saints for its successful prosecution.[61] It needed the 'Millions of men' who were 'coming up from the edge of the world' in 'The Call': the 'White men, black men, men of the tawny gold', who came 'from the ice-floes … from the jungles'.[62] Those men were, of course, the men of the Empire (although Tynan does not use that word), and they inform another of her war poems, 'The Colonists'. The men of this poem owe their allegiance to England, the 'Queen of every loyalty', their 'secret garden rose', that 'little garden place', that 'Paradise', 'Hedged with the sweet-briar of the sea'.[63] The men of 'The Colonists' are 'dwellers 'mid the ice and snow', 'toilers 'mid the sultry plain', who, even if they 'never knew' England at first hand are nonetheless 'of her blood and race'.[64]

It is a vision of harmony that was echoed on the Home Front as well as the Western Front, as was made clear by John Redmond's Woodenbridge speech in September 1914, when he offered the Irish Volunteers to the war effort. During his visit to the Western Front in November of the following year, he told the 2nd Battalion of the Royal Irish Rifles that he was sure that 'their harmony and unity in the great cause in which they were fighting was a happy omen of the relationship which would exist between all Ireland after the war'.[65] For her part, Tynan would recall her own perception of those events, and the brief optimism they engendered, in *Memories*. The Irish Volunteers were at first 'taken as representing ... extremists', she wrote – referring, presumably, to the period following their formation in November 1913.[66] But later, she noted, 'there was a genuine rapprochement. All classes met in the Volunteers and all creeds.'[67] Here, she refers to the period between August and September 1914, when Redmond offered the Volunteers first for the defence of Ireland and then for active service in the British Army, and the consequent split in the Volunteer movement. 'Rapprochement', 'all classes', 'all creeds': these words form a key to Tynan's thought, implying as they do something of her support for the status quo, socially and politically.

Yet if the rapprochement that Tynan wished for was indeed taking place, it was doing so against a background of continuing turbulence. The complex realities of Irish political life exposed inconsistencies in Tynan's thinking, for in the year before Redmond made his offer, and in the same year that Wyndham died, James Larkin had taken up the cause of agricultural labourers in Co. Dublin: now unionised, at harvest-time 'they were able to hold the farmers to ransom'.[68] If the immediate consequence was simply that 'farmers and their wives and daughters ... had to turn out to fodder and bed the horses and cattle and milk the cows', the longer-term consequence was more profound: strong farmers – the class from which Tynan herself had come – 'were as grieved and angry as the families of the good landlords when *their* social order came tumbling about their heads. It was the beginning of the revolution.'[69]

Irish farmers might have been manumitted, thanks to Wyndham, but other potential changes in Irish social relationships were not so easily accommodated. Concerned for her own class though she may have been, Tynan was nevertheless aware of the appalling conditions in which the Dublin poor lived – 'They cry to Heaven for vengeance' – and she came to see the Dublin Lockout of 1913 as the 'genesis of the Easter Week, 1916, Rebellion'.[70] Connolly, she thought, had had no choice but to resort to 'something violent' in order 'to win justice for the people, to draw attention to their evil case, to frighten good comfortable folk'.[71] The Rising was 'a counsel of despair'.[72]

Neither had she been unaware of the material condition of the rural poor, some of them her father's labourers. She knew about their living conditions well enough to describe them in detail: the puddles on the clay floor of their leaking cottage, the acrid smoke of the fire where they burnt 'green sticks', the family of nine sleeping in one room. Of some things, however, she confessed her ignorance: 'I don't know what they lived on', she said, but supposed that it was 'White bread and tea and potatoes and American bacon, with an occasional dole from the house' (that is, her father's house). Despite that, she was confident that they 'never thought of hardship, or that they might have been better treated'.[73]

They had conducted the revolution differently in France, Tynan observed, 'where the aristocrats went in tumbrils to the guillotine': in England 'after the war, it was only that Mr Selfridge went to Landsdowne House'.[74] Before the war, and in 1916, things had been different. It had been 'ill-paid schoolteachers' who had 'largely kept alive' Irish disaffection towards England, and the Rising 'had a good many of the ill-paid civil servants in its ranks', but now the *ancien régime* was being brought low by commerce.[75] In England, she complained, the days of 'supplicating tradesmen, hat in hand', competing for the custom of their social superiors, had been superseded by 'paying on the nail and carrying home your own purchases'.[76] She recalled her early experience of 'post-war manners', when the 'indifference, the almost contempt of those who served, were appalling to one accustomed to shopping as a gay and ever-fresh adventure, as it is in Ireland'.[77] The manners of Irish shop assistants were better than those of their English counterparts, but in the years following the Great War – specifically, during the Anglo-Irish War – in their out-of-hours activities those 'softly spoken and anxiously polite shop-assistants who served you yesterday' had acquired a 'strange new ruthlessness', something that had been 'missing from the old Irish warfare'.[78] The ill-paid teachers and civil servants of the Rising had been upstaged by tradespeople and – in the personage of Mr Selfridge – shopkeepers.

Perhaps by the time of the War of Independence, Tynan, now in her sixtieth year, had become weary of the still-unresolved turbulence in Irish political life. Her engagement with political change had seen her allegiance given first to the Ladies' Land League, Davitt, and O'Leary; then to Gladstone and Parnell; then to Wyndham. Yet still, in 1920, there had been a recurrence of agrarianism in the West. She observed in *The Wandering Years*, the final instalment of her autobiographical writings, that the Sinn Féin courts had 'killed' the outbreak: '[t]he ruthlessness of Sinn Féin in its police-work is all to the good'.[79] It is difficult to take at face value this apparent support for such ruthlessness: in her early years she had distinguished between legitimate and illegitimate Fenianism in favour of the former, and there is nothing in her work produced in the intervening period to suggest anything remotely other than a constitutional nationalism in support of Home Rule.

A poem published in September 1920 but not included in any of her late collections of verse sheds some light on the position Tynan had reached vis-à-vis Irish liberty. 'The Prisoner' was published in the Jesuit-run quarterly, *Studies*.[80] The prisoner of the title is visited in his prison yard by the vision of his 'dear Black Rose': her 'beauty and glamour blind his wondering eyes, / For whom so many men made sacrifice / Flinging their lives down with a jest and song'.[81] She is the means by which he is able to transcend his circumstances: 'What matter for the gyves upon his hands!' – and she 'understands'.[82] Moreover, 'she is worth it all, his Lady who knows / There is no beauty like to hers, Dark Rose'.[83] Is this a gesture of support for those Volunteers who had been imprisoned after the Rising or during the ongoing War of Independence? In the same edition of *Studies* appeared an article by P. J. Gannon, SJ, on 'The Ethical Aspect of the Hunger Strike' which considered the morality of the action of Terence MacSwiney, Lord Mayor of Cork City and a member of the Volunteers, then on hunger strike in Brixton prison.[84] The problem, Father Gannon explained, was whether or not the hunger strike violated 'the divine precept of self-preservation, that is to say, whether it invokes the guilt of suicide'.[85] His conclusion was predicated on a distinction between political and divine law: 'on what grounds', he asked rhetorically, 'should any moral obloquy attach to the hunger protest of Irish political prisoners?'[86]

There is no evidence to suggest that Tynan was writing about MacSwiney or any of the hunger-strikers in prison in Cork, nor that she was addressing the ethical problems of the hunger strike: 'The Prisoner' is not a theological or political enquiry. Nevertheless, the publication of 'The Prisoner' in the same edition of *Studies* as Father Gannon's Jesuitical essay points to the nuanced position of Tynan's poem. It is a nationalist poem, one that invokes Ireland's 'fields of honey-grass', the 'silver' rain and 'grey mist', and the cattle that feed 'knee-deep in grass', and whose 'liquid eyes give praise'.[87] It is also a poem about a man who has been imprisoned for Ireland's sake. However, despite its invocation of the Black Rose, it does not follow Joseph Plunkett's apocalyptic 'The Little Black Rose Shall Be Red At Last', with its 'trumpets and the noise of battle', but instead echoes Aubrey de Vere's 'The Little Black Rose':

> The Silk of the Kine shall rest at last;
>   What drove her forth but the dragon-fly?
> In the golden vale she shall feed full fast,
>   With her mild gold horn and her slow dark eye.[88]

Like de Vere's, Tynan's poem is a kind of pastoral nationalism, one that eschews direct political comment. In *Lord Edward: A Study in Romance*, published in 1916, Tynan had made clear her sympathy with the frustrations of certain among her fellow nationalists. There, she quotes from a letter written in 1797 by one Lady Sarah Napier to Lady Sophia Fitzgerald (Lord Edward's sister): 'I really do think that to try to promote our shaking off the yoke of England by means of the French at this moment of danger, is cruel to poor Ireland ... for it is egging on the poor deluded people to dash into certain misery and destruction.'[89] Just as Tynan's rhetorical question, 'Was not the old wine [of the 1790s] in new bottles in the Dublin rising of 1916?', avoids passing judgement on her revolutionary contemporaries, so 'The Prisoner' makes no judgement.[90] Although the man in prison is not legally innocent (the poem does not claim that he has been wrongly convicted), neither is he morally guilty (there is no criticism of him for whatever it is that he has been convicted of): instead, like the Black Rose herself, the poem simply 'understands'.

The equilibrium of 'The Prisoner' would not easily be maintained, and, over the next two years, Tynan's mood changed with the changing state of Ireland. By the time of her near-completion of *The Wandering Years* it must have seemed to her as if a resolution to Ireland's difficulties had been achieved, albeit not the Home Rule that she favoured: 'On the happy days of the Truce I end my tale', she wrote at the beginning of what had been intended as the final paragraph.[91] Those words were written towards the end of 1921, in the wake of July's truce between the Irish Republican Army and the British Army. In May 1922, six months after the book was finished – but, evidently, before it went to the press – she added an Afterword: Ireland, she said, was 'more than ever in the melting-pot, and what is to emerge from it God only knows'.[92] By April, the anti-Treaty forces had occupied the Four Courts; in June, the Civil War began.

End dates might be convenient for literary scholars and for historians, but for the lived experience of individuals, as for nations, they are not necessarily neat resolutions. Tynan was sixty-six years old in 1927, the year that saw the publication of her final collection of poetry, *Twilight Songs*. Its mood is in equal measure elegiac and bitter, personal and political. 'Ireland Long Ago' is a lament for the past; the title is also a refrain, occurring no fewer than twelve times in the poem's thirty-two lines. It celebrates the land, as many of Tynan's earlier poems had done – its mists and streams, flowers and birds, its mountains and its 'emerald plain' – but it is no longer the land of agrarianism, Land Acts, the blackbird of Avondale, or the Dark Rose. It is not a political or even a geographical place. It is, rather, a prelapsarian land of childhood. The poet longs 'to be a child again beside my father's knees, / And coming home of evening to his fond smile and his kiss, / In darling Ireland long ago'.[93] Similarly, 'The Unemployed' is a dialogue between past and present:

> The dead men to the living call:
>   Brothers of old, how goes the day?
> Is there ripe fruit on the Southern wall
>   Rich with our blood that rot in clay?[94]

Whoever these 'dead men' were and whenever it was they died, they have been spared the knowledge won by the 'Victors', the unemployed who 'stand in the market place', where 'no man gives them wine or bread': 'Would that we too had won that race / And earned the clay-cold rest! they said':

> But to the dead, who lie alone,
> They answered; it is well; go sleep,
> Never to know what we have known;
> With dreams to keep; with dreams to keep![95]

What was it that those ironically titled 'Victors' had won and what terrible knowledge had they acquired in achieving their victory? If Tynan had specific historical detail in mind when she wrote the poem, she chose not to include it; it is enough that the dead can cling to their dreams.

For the living, dreams had been superseded by bitter knowledge. 'The Fifes and Drums' evokes the 'Days when we dreamt great dreams', the early days of the Great War, when the public schools and the universities provided the men who would save Ireland, England, and Empire:

> Sudden in the grey day
> Feet of the marching men,
> Music gallant and gay,
> Bring the great days again.[96]

For as long as the men march past, 'The old dream', 'The old glamour' can reawaken 'joy' and 'hope'.[97] Yet as the marching men pass by and the music fades away, so 'Hope and faith are as lies'.[98] The final stanza is Yeatsian in its cadences and its elegiac yet almost disinterested final judgement:

> Never, never again great dreams
> Shall we dream as of old,
> Let be! The dreams were in vain,
> The days drenched and a-cold.[99]

It is the final response of one for whom the past is dead and for whom there is no future.

A period of nearly forty-five years had elapsed between the publication of *Louise de la Vallière* and the appearance of *Twilight Songs*. Was Tynan, as Foster insists, a 'high-class hack', guilty of 'over-productive drudgery'?[100] Was it the case, as Ann Connerton Fallon suggests, that 'throughout her life', she was 'unsophisticated and emotional' in her political views?[101] Certainly she was to look back at her early years in a spirit of reappraisal: joining the Ladies' Land League, she was to say, made a 'great change' to what had hitherto been a dull life, but, although she describes herself as having been taken up with 'active politics', she nevertheless 'had not the cause very much to heart' and was 'a most unserious member'.[102] If a lack of enthusiasm characterises her involvement with the League, mere fickleness seems to have informed her later forays into the political world: 'I was so busy about [decorating] my room that I think the Home Rule Bill of 1886 must have passed by me without affecting me much.'[103] Perhaps Foster's and Fallon's views each contain some truth, and one might indeed understand some of her earlier work as expressing the as-yet-unformed, unfixed views of a developing mind.

However, neither value judgements such as those offered by Foster and Fallon nor the suggestion that in her earlier years her political thinking was as yet only partially formed quite do justice to a life and work that embraced so much. The period between the first Home Rule Bill and the Anglo-Irish and Civil Wars, which saw the evolution of physical-force unionism and nationalism, was a time of such drastic transition that it is hard to imagine any individual maintaining an unchanging, unequivocal belief in what the prospect of Irish liberty should entail. Indeed, the post-Civil War reality of a divided Ireland would hardly have been foreseeable. Instead of viewing Tynan's career through the prism of value judgement or accusations of political dilettantism it is more productive of a reasoned understanding of her work if it is seen as it evolved: namely, as a continuing and changing response to what were the continually, and unpredictably, altering circumstances of Irish political life. If, in the final analysis, Tynan does not always seem to have known exactly what kind of Irish liberty she was striving for, nor from whom it was to be won, that in itself is indicative of her times. Moreover, the popularity of her innumerable novels, poetry collections, short story collections, and the rest suggests that her readership to some degree shared her equivocations and uncertainties. Whatever the value of her contribution to Irish literary culture, her oeuvre is of significance for what it implies about the political tenor of Ireland at the most formative period in the country's recent history.

Notes

1 Katharine Tynan, *An Isle in the Water* (London: A. & C. Black, 1895), pp. 12–27.

2 In fact, Tynan's chronology is wrong: Lord Edward died in June 1798, Tone in November of the same year. See Thomas Pakenham, *The Year of Liberty* (London: Orion Books Limited, 1992), pp. 235, 346.

3 Tynan, *An Isle in the Water*, pp. 16, 23.

4 Tynan, *An Isle in the Water*, pp. 19, 21, 23, 26.

5 She generally wrote under the name 'Katharine Tynan', except for her journalistic and religious works, which were published under the name 'Katharine Tynan Hinkson'. I would like to thank Whitney Standlee for reminding me of this.

6 For Tynan's output, see Ann Owens Weekes, *Unveiling Treasures: The Attic Guide to the Published Works of Irish Women Literary Writers* (Dublin: Attic Press, 1993), p. 347.

7 Douglas Hyde, quoted in Ann Connerton Fallon, *Katharine Tynan* (Boston, Mass.: Twayne Publishers, 1979), p. 25. For a brief account of Andrew Tynan's exports, see Fallon, *Katharine Tynan*, p. 20.
8 R. F. Foster, *Modern Ireland, 1600–1972* (Harmondsworth: Penguin, 1989), pp. 378–9.
9 Katharine Tynan, *Twenty-Five Years: Reminiscences* (London: Smith, Elder & Co., 1913), p. 16.
10 Katharine Tynan, *The Years of the Shadow* (London: Constable, 1919), p. 7.
11 Tynan, *Twenty-Five Years*, p. 16.
12 Matthew Arnold, *Poetry and Prose* (London: Rupert Hart-Davis, 1954), p. 474.
13 Tynan, *Twenty-Five Years*, p. 14.
14 Tynan, *Twenty-Five Years*, pp. 24, 41.
15 Tynan, *Twenty-Five Years*, p. 41.
16 Tynan, *Twenty-Five Years*, p. 41.
17 Tynan, *Twenty-Five Years*, p. 150. Tynan does not give the letter's date.
18 Foster, *Modern Ireland*, p. 404.
19 John Kelly (ed.), *Poems and Ballads of Young Ireland* (Otley: Woodstock Books, 2000). There are no page numbers in the Introduction. Kelly suggests that claims for *Poems and Ballads of Young Ireland* inaugurating the Revival are 'over-enthusiastic' but 'not absurd'. The volume was originally published in Ireland, rather than England.
20 Tynan, *Twenty-Five Years*, p. 40.
21 Kelly, *Poems and Ballads of Young Ireland*, n.p. Hyde's contributions appeared under the pen name An Chraoibhin Aoibhinn (more usually spelt An Craoibhín Aoibhinn), the 'pleasant little branch'.
22 Kelly, *Poems and Ballads of Young Ireland*, pp. 9–10.
23 Marianne Elliott, *Robert Emmet: The Making of a Legend* (London: Profile, 2003), p. 104.
24 Tynan, *Twenty-Five Years*, p. 131.
25 Tynan, *Twenty-Five Years*, p. 131.
26 F. S. L. Lyons, *Ireland Since the Famine* (London: Fontana, 1973), p. 129.
27 Foster, *Modern Ireland*, p. 393; 'Introduction', *Poems and Ballads of Young Ireland*, n.p.
28 For example, Douglas Hyde's 'Marching Song of the Gaelic Athletes' had been published in the *Gael* in October 1887.
29 Quotations from the poem in this paragraph are taken from the fourteenth, nineteenth, and fourth stanzas, respectively.
30 Katharine Tynan, 'In Time of Expectation', *United Ireland* (29 May 1886), pp. 5–6.
31 Alan O'Day, *Irish Home Rule, 1867–1921* (Manchester: Manchester University Press, 1998), p. 86.
32 Tynan, *Twenty-Five Years*, pp. 72–3.
33 Tynan, *Twenty-Five Years*, pp. 71–2, 99.
34 Tynan, *Twenty-Five Years*, p. 72.
35 Tynan, *Twenty-Five Years*, p. 324.
36 Tynan, *Twenty-Five Years*, p. 91.
37 T. W. Moody, *Leaders and Workers* (Cork: Mercier Press, 1978), p. 50.
38 Tynan, *Twenty-Five Years*, p. 81.
39 Lyons, *Ireland Since the Famine*, p. 201.
40 Katharine Tynan, *Ballads and Lyrics* (London: Kegan Paul, Trench, Trübner & Co., 1891). '"The Blackbird" is a Jacobite song', Padraic Colum says in his introduction to *'Broad Sheet Ballads' Being a Collection of Irish Popular Songs with an Introduction by Padraic Colum* (Dublin and London: Maunsel & Co. n.d. [stamped 1 January 1914 by the British Library]), n.p.
41 Katharine Tynan, *Cuckoo Songs* (London: Elkin Matthews, 1894), pp. 96–7.
42 Michael Davitt, *Jottings in Solitary*, ed. Carla King (Dublin: University College Dublin Press, 2003), p. xxvii. Avondale was the name of Parnell's estate in Co. Wicklow.
43 *The Times* (18 June 1886), p. 10.
44 *The Times* (29 September 1886), p. 6. Lord Dalhousie, Sir John William Ramsay, was Liberal MP for Liverpool in 1880 and Secretary for Scotland. The quotation is from a speech made at Broughty Ferry, Dundee.
45 Katharine Tynan, *A Union of Hearts* (London: James Nisbett & Co., 1901), p. 46.

46 Tynan, *A Union of Hearts*, p. 272.
47 Tynan, *A Union of Hearts*, p. 2.
48 Tynan, *A Union of Hearts*, p. 132.
49 Tynan, *A Union of Hearts*, p. 84.
50 Tynan, *A Union of Hearts*, p. 277.
51 Tynan, *A Union of Hearts*, p. 276.
52 Katharine Tynan, *Memories* (London: Eveleigh Nash and Grayson, 1924), p. 66.
53 Katharine Tynan, *The Middle Years* (London: Constable & Co., 1916), p. 226.
54 Tynan, *The Middle Years*, p. 235.
55 Tynan, *The Middle Years*, p. 184.
56 Tynan, *Twenty-Five Years*, pp. 84–5.
57 R. F. Foster, 'Ascendancy and Union', in R. F. Foster (ed.), *The Oxford Illustrated History of Ireland* (London: Guild Publishing, 1989), pp. 161–212, at p. 183. Katharine Tynan, *Katharine Tynan's Book of Irish History* (Dublin and Belfast: The Educational Company of Ireland Limited, n.d. [stamped 25 November 1918 by the British Museum), pp. 153–4. The book's internal evidence shows that it was written during the First World War.
58 Tynan, *Katharine Tynan's Book of Irish History*, p. 61.
59 Tynan, *Memories*, p. 231.
60 Tynan, *Memories*, p. 232.
61 Katharine Tynan, *Flower of Youth* (London: Sidgwick & Jackson, 1915), p. 19.
62 Tynan, *Flower of Youth*, pp. 12–13.
63 Katharine Tynan, *The Holy War* (London: Sidgwick & Jackson, 1916), pp. 37–8. To those of her readers who knew their Shakespeare, the correspondences with John of Gaunt's panegyric in *Richard the Second* (Act II, Scene 1, line 42 ff.).
64 Tynan, *The Holy War*, pp. 37–8.
65 Quoted in Timothy Bowman, *The Irish Regiments in the Great War: Discipline and Morale* (Manchester: Manchester University Press, 2003), p. 25.
66 Tynan, *Memories*, p. 70.
67 Tynan, *Memories*, p. 72.
68 Lyons, *Ireland Since the Famine*, p. 282.
69 Tynan, *The Years of the Shadow*, p. 8. Italics in original.
70 Tynan, *The Years of the Shadow*, p. 74.
71 Tynan, *The Years of the Shadow*, pp. 78–9.
72 Tynan, *The Years of the Shadow*, p. 78.
73 Tynan, *The Years of the Shadow*, p. 7.
74 Katharine Tynan, *The Wandering Years* (London: Constable, 1922), p. 333. The allusion is to Harry Gordon Selfridge (1858–1947), who had opened London's first branch of Selfridges in 1909. He lived at Lansdowne House, Berkeley Square, from 1921 to 1929.
75 Tynan, *The Wandering Years*, p. 34.
76 Tynan, *The Wandering Years*, p. 88.
77 Tynan, *The Wandering Years*, p. 88.
78 Tynan, *The Wandering Years*, p. 198.
79 Tynan, *The Wandering Years*, pp. 206–7. In fact, *Memories*, published in 1924, post-dates *The Wandering Years*. However, unlike her four volumes of autobiography, which deal with her life and times in chronological order, *Memories* ranges freely, its topics including the South African war, the Ladies' Land League, and Parnell. It is not, therefore, a contemporary record of her response to events as they unfolded in the same way as the other four volumes.
80 Katharine Tynan, 'The Prisoner', *Studies: An Irish Quarterly Review*, 9:35 (1920), 413.
81 Tynan, 'The Prisoner'.
82 Tynan, 'The Prisoner'.
83 Tynan, 'The Prisoner'.
84 P. J. Gannon, 'The Ethical Aspect of the Hunger Strike', *Studies: An Irish Quarterly Review*, 9:35 (1920), 448–56.

85 Gannon, 'The Ethical Aspect of the Hunger Strike', p. 449.
86 Gannon, 'The Ethical Aspect of the Hunger Strike', p. 449.
87 Tynan, 'The Prisoner'.
88 Joseph Plunkett, 'The Little Black Rose Shall Be Red At Last', in Desmond Ryan (ed.), *The 1916 Poets* (Dublin: Gill & Macmillan, 1995), p. 160; Aubrey de Vere, 'The Little Black Rose', in W. B. Yeats (ed.), *A Book of Irish Verse* (London and New York: Routledge, 2002), pp. 78–9.
89 Katharine Tynan, *Lord Edward: A Study in Romance* (London: Smith, Elder & Co., 1916), p. 218.
90 Tynan, *Lord Edward*, p. 243.
91 Tynan, *The Wandering Years*, p. 386.
92 Tynan, *The Wandering Years*, p. 387.
93 Katharine Tynan, *Twilight Songs* (Oxford: Basil Blackwell, 1927), p. 23.
94 Tynan, *Twilight Songs*, p. 41.
95 Tynan, *Twilight Songs*, p. 41.
96 Tynan, *Twilight Songs*, p. 42.
97 Tynan, *Twilight Songs*, p. 42.
98 Tynan, *Twilight Songs*, p. 42.
99 Tynan, *Twilight Songs*, pp. 42–3.
100 R. F. Foster, *W. B. Yeats: A Life*, vol. I: *The Apprentice Mage* (Oxford: Oxford University Press, 1997), p. 72.
101 Fallon, *Katharine Tynan*, p. 102.
102 Tynan, *Twenty-Five Years*, pp. 75, 71, 99.
103 Tynan, *Twenty-Five Years*, p. 183.

10

'The blind side of the heart': Protestants, politics, and patriarchy in the novels of F. E. Crichton

Naomi Doak

The absence of Ulster women writers, particularly Ulster Protestant women novelists, from the annals of Irish literary history is a phenomenon which has recently achieved some degree of critical attention.[1] Due to these recent efforts at recovering alternative Irish literary traditions, it has become apparent that this absence is not attributable to the fact that such women did not write books. On the contrary, archive research has uncovered more than twenty Ulster Protestant women writers who published one or more novels between the years 1900 and 1960.[2] This chapter focuses on the life and works of just one of these hitherto forgotten woman novelists, F. E. Crichton of Belfast. Through close readings of her first and last works of adult fiction, it will open a critical window onto an author who, it will be argued, is deserving of a place in Irish literary history.[3]

Crichton was born Frances Elizabeth Sinclair at her family's substantial residence, Hopefield House, on the Antrim Road in Belfast in 1877. She was the eldest daughter of a large family which included a brother, stepbrothers and stepsisters. Her birth mother, Mary Sinclair (née Duffin), passed away when her brother was an infant and Crichton herself was just two years old. Less than four years later, Crichton's father married his second wife, Elizabeth Lecky Richardson, who brought with her into the Sinclair fold another four children.[4] Census records suggest that, by 1901, Hopefield House was a bustling gentleman's residence, with five family members (including a then twenty-three-year-old Crichton), and a complement of eight domestic servants, which included a governess and sick nurse on the evening that the records were captured.[5] The domestic servants were shown to have come from a variety of denominations – Lutheran, Church of Ireland, Methodist, and Presbyterian – and hint at the multifarious nature of Protestantism which then existed and continues to mark the religious landscape of the North of Ireland. By 1911, census records identify one young man of the household as a Roman Catholic manservant residing with the family. It is fair to say that Hopefield House and its inhabitants represent a melting pot of identities: predominantly Protestant, but diverse enough to embody a microcosm of Ulster society at the turn of the twentieth century. This is important given that Crichton's father was the Right Hon. Thomas Sinclair, DL, one of Ulster's contemporary leading Liberal Presbyterian Unionists and author of the 1912 Ulster Covenant.[6]

When research into her life and work was first being undertaken, the connection between Crichton and her celebrated father was not immediately apparent. While archive research uncovered several works penned by 'F. E. Crichton', only one version of her novella, *The Precepts of Andy Saul*, which was discovered in Belfast's Linen Hall Library, detailed the author as 'F. E. Sinclair Crichton'. This 1908 publication by the Belfast house M'Caw, Stevenson & Orr unlocked the door to the remarkable family history that lay behind this modest book. Originally published after her marriage in 1906 and subsequent relocation to Hoylake near Liverpool, the novel itself offers no evidence through which to discern whether Crichton chose to include her maiden name (which was also her husband's middle name) in an attempt to ride on the coat-tails of her father's reputation, or as a nostalgic nod to the family that she had left behind.[7] What is certain is that after this publication, the name Sinclair no longer formed part of her pen name. It is a telling clue to her literary motives at this juncture, however, that a 1908 review in the *Irish Independent* describes Crichton as a 'gifted authoress' who had captured 'the shrewd, practical wisdom typical of hardy Northerners with the most genial and captivating humour', suggesting that she had by then already made a name for herself outside the Sinclair sphere of influence.[8]

This is remarkable given the prominence of the Sinclair family in Belfast. Sinclair involvement with the Presbyterian Church in the North of Ireland stretched back at least two generations. In the aftermath of the evangelical Protestant Revival that swept Ulster in the late 1800s, Crichton's grandfather (Thomas Sinclair Senior) erected both Duncairn Presbyterian Church on Belfast's Antrim Road and the maritime-themed Sinclair Seaman's Presbyterian Church in the dockland area of the city.[9] Crichton's father followed her grandfather's record of service to the church as a Sabbath officer and a clerk of session at Duncairn Church at the age of twenty-nine.[10] Later in life he would become a seminal figure not just in Presbyterian church life in Belfast but also in politics, as his involvement with the unionist campaign would see him partially responsible for the unification of Ulster's denominationally disparate Protestants in their fight against Home Rule.

In late nineteenth- and early twentieth-century Ulster, active participation in church life and politics were almost hand in glove. As a Presbyterian, Sinclair supported Disestablishment, opposing the privileges conferred by the state upon the Church of Ireland. Participating in public debates on the issue, he held an attitude which was representative of a strain of Liberal dissenting politics that historically associated closely with Ulster Presbyterianism. Described by Graham Walker as 'the leading Presbyterian layman of his generation', Sinclair was an important figure in a movement that stressed Ulster Presbyterianism as a separate ethnic identity not just from Irish Catholics, but also from Anglican Protestants.[11] Although initially an admirer of Gladstone, Sinclair came to view Gladstone's intention to introduce Home Rule for Ireland as a betrayal. In 1886, he declared that '[w]e shall show the world that come what may Ulster will never consent to yield up her citizenship, or be expelled from the Imperial Parliament to be degraded to a junior partnership in a subordinate colony'.[12] For Sinclair, this was not just empty rhetoric. In 1912 he drafted the text for the Solemn League and Covenant that was signed on Ulster Day of the same year by almost half a million unionists both in Ulster and throughout Britain.

One such signature was provided by his daughter, F. E. Crichton, while she was living at her new marital home near Liverpool. More accurately, Crichton's signature can be found on the separate women's declaration (the wording of which was also penned by her father), due to the fact that in the pre-franchise era women were not permitted to sign the Ulster Covenant. In her own research into the subject, Diane Urquhart has pointed out that the Ulster Unionist Council had forbidden women from signing the original covenant, and women therefore had to negotiate in order to have a separate declaration drawn up.[13] It has been well documented that this shorter declaration noted women's desire to 'associate' themselves with the men of Ulster in their uncompromising opposition to the Home Rule Bill and that 228,999 women and 218,206 men in Ulster are recorded as signatories.[14] Urquhart has comprehensively detailed the active, albeit auxiliary, role that unionist women assumed in the early twentieth century. Legitimised in many ways by the more politically engaged part that aristocratic women such as Lady Londonderry or the second Duchess of Abercorn held, many women engaged in petitioning and mobilising sympathy for the unionist cause as an extension of their familial duty to support the political movements espoused by the male head of the family.[15] In both Catholic and Protestant homes, the domestic sphere was a sacred one, sanctified through religious teachings that extended into political life. To engage with the unionist (or nationalist) cause offered an opportunity to extend maternal and commonly 'domestic' traits into the realm of the political. Although Crichton's father was a privy councillor – an elite status in contemporary Ireland – the Sinclair family were merchants and not landed gentry in the sense that a family such as the Londonderrys were. In the absence of documentary evidence, such as the diaries and letters of Lady Londonderry, which have been preserved in public archives, it is difficult to discern the level of power or influence that Crichton may have had had she stayed in Ireland. What is slightly easier to suggest is that the unionist strain running through her novels – all written once she left Belfast and one specifically dedicated to her father – indicates that, for Crichton, familial ties were strong and political sympathies shared.

The remainder of this chapter will read two of Crichton's works in the light of these political and personal circumstances, contextualising them and their relatively unknown author within the cultural and political framework of the era. Although the two works under scrutiny are extremely different in stylistic accomplishment, they provide evidence of a female author who was actively contributing to the evolution of a sort of provincial or regional self-consciousness for Ulster, and specifically for Ulster Protestants, during the pre-Partition era.

The Precepts of Andy Saul (1908)

CONSISTING of five chapters spanning just fifty-two pages, Crichton's first publication, *The Precepts of Andy Saul* (hereafter referred to as *The Precepts*), is a novella rather than a full-length novel.[16] First published in 1908 and reissued in 1912 and 1913, Crichton's slim volume is nevertheless a remarkable literary artefact with its republication hinting at some degree of success.

The storyline in the novella is simple: the first-person narrator of the tale, Miss Hazel, has come back to Fiddlerstown, a fictional country house in Ulster, to visit her cousins after many years. She spends her time walking around the gardens and conversing with the elderly gardener, Andy Saul. It does not take her long to realise that very little has changed since her last visit to the house, not least the strong opinions of the gardener himself. Miss Hazel's experiences and conversations with Andy are recorded in what could be described as a diarised, anecdotal style, with Andy's Ulster-Scots dialect reproduced verbatim. Filtering Andy's lower-class voice through the consciousness of an upper-class Protestant woman's mind, Crichton uses her character's voice to explore, record, and gently satirise her own community from within, a daring step for the daughter of one of the leading Ulster unionists of the time.

Stylistically, the novella's narrative technique has its origins in Maria Edgeworth's *Castle Rackrent*.[17] However, while the main story in *Castle Rackrent* is told in colloquial dialect through the voice of the Catholic servant Thady Quirk, the narrative voices in *The Precepts* alternate between the first-person voice of the female narrator, Miss Hazel, and her second-hand recording of the main character, Andy Saul's, direct speech. Although Miss Hazel is the primary recorder of the narrative, as with Thady Quirk in *Castle Rackrent*, it is Andy's speech that dominates the text. However, whereas Edgeworth's text contains footnotes and a glossary to interpret her Irish character's colloquial dialect to non-Irish audiences, Crichton uses a woman from a higher social class to translate Andy's assorted array of Ulster-Scots vernacular phrases and malapropisms to her readers. Using a form of 'reverse anthropology', as Declan Kiberd has described Edgeworth's technique, Crichton's position as the author of *The Precepts* allows her to act as a kind of native informant who uses the character of Andy to both document and criticise aspects of the Ulster Protestant community in and with its own words, as it were.[18]

A crucial distinction between Crichton's narrative and that of her literary predecessor is that where Thady Quirk is a Catholic servant working for the Irish Protestant Ascendancy, Andy is a Protestant servant working in a Protestant Big House. Thus, from the very outset of the novella, post-colonial binaries which tend to perpetrate straightforward divisions between the Protestant colonisers and the Catholic colonised are deconstructed. While Kiberd's reading of Edgeworth is couched in post-colonial ideology, Crichton's work is arguably best interpreted in terms of class and gender relations.

To reiterate, the story is set in Fiddlerstown, an imaginary country house estate in Co. Down with just a hint of stage Irishness in its name, indicative of the tone of the piece as a whole. Andy is an elderly gardener who works on the land and is regarded by his employer to be as much a part of the estate as the Big House itself. The opening line of the story states that, 'The nature of Andy's position at Fiddlerstown had never been closely defined, but no one who knew the place could well imagine it without him.'[19] The reader is also told that the owner of the house, Colonel Moore, '[w]ould no more have thought of parting with Andy than he would of selling the gaunt old house itself!'[20] On a more figurative level, Andy can be seen as representative of a certain type of Ulster Scotsman who had also yet to be defined in the literary consciousness of Ireland in 1908. With its concentration on Andy's unique characteristics as an Ulsterman, Crichton's novella is an attempt to formulate and contribute towards this evolving identity. Whereas at this early point in her career Crichton ridicules as outmoded the sexist 'precepts' by which Andy lives, as shall be demonstrated, by the end of her career, all traces of New Woman sympathies are sidelined in favour of unionist politics. As the second half of this chapter will show, the daring glimpses of satirical humour evident throughout *The Precepts* are notably absent in *The Blind Side of the Heart*.

From a feminist perspective, what makes this novella so interesting is its playful take on Victorian attitudes towards women's traditional roles. For example, despite his position as a kind of servant at Fiddlerstown, Andy asserts his control over the 'improvements' that one of the ladies of the house, Miss Charlotte, has proposed for their garden:

> 'Nothin' will do her only thry ivery new thing. Some day A'll just let her commit herself wi' som o' them English seeds, an' learn her the risks she runs. For, mind you, there's very few improvements is for the betther, an' we done rightly wi' the owl' seeds up to now.'[21]

In keeping with contemporary colonial stereotypes of the Irish as backward or irrational, Crichton here gently derides Andy's position as both a servant and a gardener who does not particularly want to cultivate or work in the garden. Significantly, where traditional Irish stereotypes have tended to be Catholic and 'native', Andy Saul's characterisation as a Protestant Ulster Scot complicates this construction. On a more metaphorical level, if Andy does not want to change the garden in a literal sense, neither does he want to improve or alter his ideas regarding the status quo. Andy threatens to let Miss Charlotte plant 'English seeds', which, he suggests, will ruin the garden. These disparaged 'English seeds' are arguably representative of modern ideas, perhaps even New Woman ideas, imported from Britain. Later in the narrative, when Andy takes Miss Hazel to see the small improvements that Miss Charlotte has managed to make (improvements colloquially dismissed as 'capers' by the gardener), Miss Hazel is moved by their paucity: 'How she [Miss Charlotte] had battled to this extent against Andy's inertia I could hardly imagine. The beds were still a trifle new, and sparsely furnished: there they were, however, with the small fountain trickling sullenly in the midst.'[22] Despite Andy's obstructive nature, Miss Charlotte has persevered with her ideas for the garden, the small 'sullen' fountain representing a meagre and seemingly hard won victory.

Miss Hazel records remarks made by her cousin, Miss Charlotte, which demonstrate the latter's inability to effect change on her own land: 'It's intolerable that I should feel a culprit in my own garden … but still I do.'[23] The reality of the situation is that, despite her class, Miss Charlotte is regarded in Andy's eyes as a woman and thereby as necessarily subject to traditional patriarchal rules. Indeed, Miss Charlotte's comment hints not only at the restrictive nature of women's position in Ulster society but also at the potential feeling of betrayal that those women who do not wish to conform to the dictates of their community might experience. Although Andy's speeches are filtered through colloquial dialect and often interspersed with malapropisms (including references to the Sabbath Day 'Absurdities' instead of 'Observances' and the

'Bonesuckers' instead of the Sisters of 'Bon Secours') which are used for comic effect, behind his superficially humorous words are actions that have serious repercussions for women that are not altogether comedic. Bearing in mind the Colonel's unwavering loyalty to Andy, Crichton's Fiddlerstown is a patriarchal regime that surpasses class divisions and upholds the respect for tradition as its main sanctioning device. In so far as Fiddlerstown is a microcosm of Ulster society, the precepts by which Andy lives, as recorded in his own words by Miss Hazel, are, from a feminist perspective, a subtle attempt by Crichton to indict traditional, class-transcending male attitudes towards women.

Andy's unabashed sexism is again lampooned in a later conversation with Miss Hazel when he comments that 'ye need the quare firm hand wi' women! ... Ye want to be aisy with them, but at the same time to show them ye'll stand no capers. There's no bounds to the way a wumman'll carry on without some man conthrols her.'[24] As Andy's own character is controlled by both the voice of the female narrator of the story and by Crichton's own authorial voice, the gardener's comments are humorously ironic. Apparently oblivious to his own chauvinism, and much to the reader's entertainment, Andy then advises Miss Hazel to get married herself. Taken aback, Miss Hazel tells him that she 'seem[s] to get on very well as it is', to which Andy replies:

> 'If ye'll excuse me sayin' it, then, Miss Hazel, thon's a big mistake. A've no weesh to be presumptious, but the genthry an' werselves is alike in this, an A know rightly what A'm sayin'. A wumman has no call to be too independent. If she can do things too well, sure there's no man'll be wantin' to do them for her. The wise one'll let a man help her, even if he's only in her road, an' herself wishin' him far enough.'[25]

In Andy's world, too much female independence is a bad thing, not just for men but for women themselves. In this respect, in terms of the themes of class and gender, Crichton's novella shares much in common with the work of novelists like Kate O'Brien and George Moore. For example, where a novel such as Moore's *A Drama in Muslin* (1886) critiques the charade of Victorian propriety as a cover for a capitalistic marriage market, and, almost fifty years later, Kate O'Brien's *Without My Cloak* (1931) maintains this theme, so too does Crichton assess, critically, the Victorian value system where feminine weakness and passivity have more currency for women than independence and talent. Here we have male and female, Catholic and Protestant, northern and southern writers whose novels are ideologically comparable.

The parodying thrust of *The Precepts* comes from the fact that Andy's precepts have been recorded and ordered by a capable and independent woman writer, one of those very ladies whose autonomy the gardener suggests would be better curbed for their own good. Yet despite the underlying element of stage Irishness at work in this tale, the gardener is by no means dim-witted when it comes to understanding the superficial nature of gender performance. Indeed, it could be said that what appear to be Andy's sexist views on women are not simply the result of chauvinism or ignorance on his part but have been learned through first-hand observation of the pantomimic antics of the upper classes themselves. The juxtaposition of what Andy perceives to be Miss Charlotte's failed courtship, beside her sister Miss Geraldine's successful one, provides anecdotal evidence of this. Of the former's courtship he says:

> A mind as well as if it was yestherday how oncet a young gentleman come here till stay – a fine, sthrong young man he was, – an' the whole talk o' the place was that he was afther Miss Charl't. He followed her round from stable to yard, an' back again, an' asked nothin' but till help her an' do for her. A mind one day here she had him helpin' wi' the prunin' – an' mind you Miss Hazel, he was the quare bad hand at it, and slow as a slug. An' Miss Charl't, she watched him to she cud thole it no longer, an' at last she whipped the shears from him, an' says she: 'A can do it betther meself.' . . . A think he was cut like, for he quit Fiddlerstown the day afther, an' niver come back no more. He's marrit now till a wee timid wumman that let on she cudn't live without he showed her how![26]

On the other hand, of the courtship of Miss Geraldine – now Mrs Beresford of Broadwater – he recalls that:

> [She] wud be rompin' all over the place when she was her lone here, leppin' all before her like a boy. But when Captain Beresford come to stay there was the big change. He'd be handin' her over the wee sthream that careful, an' pickin' the best stones for her till set her fut, an' warnin' her off the coggly ones. An all the while A cud ha' choked meself laughin', knowin' that Miss Geraldine cud up the sthream rightly her lone – aye, an' done it too ivery day in life.[27]

Filtered through the medium of this working-class man's colloquial dialect, the reader laughs with Andy at the absurdities of the Victorian gentry rather than at him. Exposing the charade of gender performance, Andy's straight-talking gives him the upper hand here, while the author makes use of him to point a mocking finger at the upper classes.

In his study *Catholic Fiction and Social Reality in Ireland, 1873–1922*, James H. Murphy suggests that upper-class Catholic novelists publishing at the end of the nineteenth century wrote fiction that presented their own class as conforming to the social mores of Victorian English society for two reasons: first, in order to acknowledge a British aspect to their identity, and, second, in order to separate themselves from the British national stereotypes of the Irish as feckless idiots.[28] Similarly, but for different reasons, in *The Precepts*, Crichton creates a fiction that seeks not only to acknowledge but also to specify certain aspects of her and her character's Irish identity. In other words, rather than trying to create an identity entirely separate from the British colonial categorisation of the stage Irishman, Crichton attempts to create a space for an Ulster-Scots Protestant version of Irishness. Rather than reproducing the colonial construction of the feckless, drunken Paddy, Crichton modifies and expands elements of this notion to include another type – that of the stereotypical Ulsterman. Andy is described as a 'dogged Ulster Protestant ... with a certain dignity of rectitude in his hard, bronzed face, and a gleam of grudging humour in his light blue eyes'.[29] Although he admits that '[i]t's the quare pity that Protestants an' Catholics should spite each other the way they do', Andy's understanding of religion is steeped in hearsay and what could be described as folklore. For instance, he tells Miss Hazel a story about a man from Belfast who believed that one of his legs was a Catholic and the other one a Protestant: 'D'ye know, he hated the Catholic leg, Miss Hazel, so he did. He gave it the quare abuse, an' had it stickin' out o' bed in the cowld, an' knocked it about all sorts to he died.'[30] If Andy showed intelligence in his understanding of gender performance, clearly his comprehension of religious differences owes less to empirical rationale and more to the folklore tradition of legend and storytelling. Although Crichton exploits certain commercial aspects of the stage Irishman (such as his verbosity and unusual turn of phrase), her impulse towards creating a 'new' version of the stereotype simultaneously deconstructs the very notion of national typecasts, as religious, regional, and linguistic differences indicate the inherent danger in homogenous grand narratives.

The Precepts is remarkable in terms of the careful balancing act that the author treads between creating a sympathetic character in Andy Saul and presenting a critique of all that this character represents. There is much self-reflexive irony in Crichton's work as the author allows her leading male protagonist to expose the sexism in his community while simultaneously trying to present a shared understanding of the dynamics of that community to her English and Irish audiences through the vehicle of satire. As with Edgeworth's relation to her character, Thady Quirk, Crichton's position in relation to Andy is ambiguous: he can be both the object and architect of social caricature, ridiculed and vindicated, castigated for his intransigence or praised for forthrightness. Also like Edgeworth, Crichton here crosses gender lines by assuming the voice of a male servant to invoke her own animus as a source of creativity.[31]

The Blind Side of the Heart (1915)

If, from a feminist perspective, Crichton's feelings of loyalty towards her sex filtered through *The Precepts* in the form of gentle satire, by the time her final novel, *The Blind Side of the Heart* (hereafter referred to as *The Blind*

Side), appeared in 1915, any inklings of New Woman sympathies had all but disappeared. Politically in Ireland, Home Rule had been put on the statute books for implementation at the end of the war but without any provision being made for the exclusion of Ulster. Published the year before the 1916 Easter Rising, which would change the course of Irish history forever, Crichton's novel crudely but daringly challenges what she sees as the threat of political nationalism emanating from the Irish Literary Revival. The tone and overt political propaganda in *The Blind Side* represents an increasingly 'Ulsterised' sense of unionist identity in Ireland.[32] The novel should not, however, be read in isolation from Crichton's personal circumstances. In February 1914, Crichton's father passed away at the age of seventy-six. Commenting on the death of Sinclair, an article in the *Spectator* stated that 'Ulster unionism has lost one of its ablest and most respected champions ... He was among the first to sign the Ulster Covenant in 1912, and, after Sir Edward Carson, no other leader exerted greater influence or inspired more confidence.'[33] In the light of the deeply personal mourning that accompanied the death of her father, whose passing was also understood as a great political loss for the liberal unionist cause in Ireland, Crichton's *The Blind Side* can be read as a grieving daughter's filial commitment to the family cause.[34] Where her father's strengths lay in political leadership, however, his daughter's engagement was literary. As shall be demonstrated, Crichton's final novel critiques the Romanticism of the Celtic Twilight and its Ascendancy advocates, in its place presenting a pragmatic vision of an Ireland that firmly maintains its links to Britain.

The plot of *The Blind Side* is straightforward: an English engineer, Dick Sandford, finds himself travelling to the fictional village of Loughnashee in Ireland in order to work on the construction of a dam. While in Ireland, Sandford has many unusual encounters with the local inhabitants and begins to fall in love with a beautiful woman, Eithne Blake, who resides at the local Big House, Ardsollus. Eithne has a reputation as a sort of 'visionary' and has a spiritual connection to the Celtic lore of the region, rendered through her ability to recite ancient Celtic tales as well as her apparently unwavering belief in fairy lore. Following Sandford's decision to cut down a fairy thorn tree, the local people begin to turn against him. At the same time, he realises that Eithne is not the love of his life, and he travels to Scotland, where Betty Oliphant, the woman to whom he was betrothed before he made the trip to Ireland, awaits his return.

In terms of genre, *The Blind Side* could be viewed as part of the subgenre of Irish Gothic. All the key elements of the Gothic tale are visible in the text: a foreigner's (Sandford's) journey through an unknown land, a dilapidated stately home (Ardsollus), an ephemeral female figure (Eithne), and a sprinkling of supernatural activities. Certainly a reader familiar with Irish Gothic will be instantly reminded of Jonathan Harker's journey through Transylvania in Bram Stoker's *Dracula* (1897) as they turn the pages that describe Sandford's journey to Ardsollus. On this journey, he observes 'white clay pipes jostling with little leaden rosaries, scapulars and shells for Holy Water' in windows; the text is also peppered with anecdotal examples of the locals talking in a stage-Irish brogue.[35] Sandford is constructed as an alien 'Other' travelling through a foreign land where even the place names require interpretation (for example Loughnashee is interpreted as meaning the 'Hill-Ridge-of-Melody').[36] Although Crichton's novel lacks the literary finesse of Stoker's classic, what makes this novel interesting is not Crichton's use of the genre per se but her subversion of some of the class and political expectations associated with it. Terry Eagleton has famously summarised Irish Gothic as a genre where a cast of remote aristocrats preside over an atavistic peasantry who act as allegorical representations of the political plight of a colonial Ireland which has been subjected to the Protestant Ascendancy.[37] Aristocrats and peasants do exist in Crichton's novel, but they are not portrayed in accordance with Eagleton's theory.

In the first instance, there is Crichton's characterisation of Eithne. Described in the novel as 'an enthusiast about fairy lore', Eithne is loved by the local people for her good nature and supposed supernatural powers.[38] A resident of the Big House, she is an aristocrat who enjoys spending her time wandering through the countryside with her hound, Aengus; she has a keen knowledge of Irish myth and legend (at one point in the novel she relates the story of Deirdre and Naoise to Sandford); and during one of her brief appearances she sings a song which 'just came' to her 'like the idea of the ancient runes'.[39] Sandford's fascination with Eithne is described as 'open[ing] a byway into fairyland'.[40] Crichton's references to the Yeatsian Revivalist movement are obvious here. Indeed, the imagination need not be stretched far to see in the character of Eithne a crude caricature of one of Yeats's high-profile contemporaries, Lady Gregory. Take, for example, the comments of the local priest, Father Connolly, regarding Eithne:

> I think there is a great difference between Miss Blake's beliefs and those of the peasants. With the poor people, I believe they are like the wall-paper in the rooms where they are born, their natural, inevitable surroundings, but hers are like pictures, deliberately chosen and hung up with her own hands ... I don't think she's consciously insincere, but she's full of romance, and she worships what's picturesque. I haven't much patience with it myself. To be born in the dim, limited world of the peasants, is one thing, but to walk with open eyes into the twilight, and hide there with a lot of dreams, is quite another.[41]

This short paragraph is crucial in terms of understanding Crichton's class, political, and counter-Revivalist sympathies. Through the mouthpiece of a Catholic authority figure, Crichton compares and contrasts the so-called 'limited' understanding of the peasantry (Eagleton's atavism), with the high-brow, self-conscious artistry of Revivalists such as Lady Gregory. Crichton's horror is not of an Ireland where the peasantry rise to prominence but one where the folly, as she depicts it, is a type of Irish nationalism led by Anglo-Irish aristocrats that leads people into a state of twilight reverie rather than a pragmatic present or future. Use of the character of the priest to articulate this view permits the author to cross religious and class divides without any accusation of anti-Catholic bias while simultaneously critiquing the Ascendancy. Although the story trades on a colonial idea of the Irish as mysterious Others in a land where it is apparently quite normal to see such things as a 'host of fairy drifting down the hollow from Loughnashee', the 'Others' who are criticised in Crichton's work are not Irish Catholics but specifically Anglo-Irish Revivalists, epitomised and parodied in the persona of Eithne.[42] From a commercial point of view, the author has infused her own novel with just enough of the mysticism of the Celtic Twilight to render it marketable to an Irish readership. Crichton's engagement with this version of Ireland, however, has a peculiar Ulster, Presbyterian, and Dissenter inflection: Irish Catholics are not the enemy, Anglo-Irish artists are.

In the novel, Sandford is forced to cut down a fairy thorn tree believed to have supernatural powers and especially loved by Eithne in order to complete the dam that he is in Ireland to construct. Shortly after this tree is felled, one of the local foremen on the site dies in his sleep. The death is presumed to be the result of a curse unleashed by Sandford's cutting of the sacred tree. This event loses him favour both with people in the village more generally and with Eithne. As a result of insurmountable differences (which are never fully clarified), Eithne and Sandford break off their affair, and he travels to Scotland to stay with the Oliphant family to whose daughter he appears to have already been betrothed. During his stay in Edinburgh, Sandford realises that Betty Oliphant is in fact the true love of his life, and he leaves all thoughts of Eithne behind.

The political allegory at the end of the novel is clear, albeit rather crudely rendered: England's (Sandford's) union with Scotland or the Ulster Scots (Betty) is more desirable than a union with Ireland and, more specifically, the Anglo-Irish nationalist movement (Eithne). Writing as early as 1915, Crichton seems to be propagating a brand of partitionism where Presbyterians in particular have a separate ethnic identity, a type of partitionism which was not yet part of the political landscape in Ireland. Crichton's novel could be dismissed as a piece of crude political propaganda and in many respects it is unapologetic in its unionist overtones. However, in terms of the history of Irish women's writing from the North of Ireland, this work is a rare example of a non-Ascendancy writer who had a strong unionist ideology and was not afraid to air it.

From a feminist perspective, the credibility of Crichton's story and the ultimate failure of the novel as a piece of fiction lies in her portrayal – or inability to portray – Betty Oliphant, Sandford's love interest. Where the reader is informed that Eithne inspired in Sandford 'a vague, ineffable sense of poetry and loveliness', Betty, on the other hand, is 'neat', 'simple', 'upright', and blessed with an ability to 'see life steadily'.[43] Where Eithne has a tendency towards romance and supernaturalism, Betty is described as having 'an almost boyish sense of rectitude'.[44] These stress points in the novel, where the author struggles to convince us of the virtues of her rather manly heroine, are arguably examples of the difficulty that gendered representations of historical relations have for women writers who want to explore their female characters' subjectivities. In an Irish context, cultural nationalists and Revivalists were appropriating female icons and feminine traits to inspire allegiance to the nationalist cause: Mother Erin, the *Shan Van Vocht*, and famously in Lady Gregory and Yeats's 1902 play, *Cathleen ni Houlihan*, are celebrated examples of this phenomenon. Writing from an anti-Revivalist and pro-Union perspective, Crichton is unable to depict her heroine in too feminine a guise in case her story is politically misinterpreted. Indeed, as Betty only makes an appearance in the novel through second-hand descriptions or letters that she has written to Sandford, it would appear that the author encountered so much difficulty with the portrayal of this character that she decided to leave her out of the story as much as possible. There is some irony in a daringly vocal female writer whose own political voice has not been acknowledged in historical accounts of Irish women's writing silencing the voice of the character who arguably most closely resembles her own subject position. As a writer, Crichton is not unaware of this difficulty and makes some effort to depict the relationship between Sandford and Betty as a plausible one, for example in a section where she highlights the idea that '[i]t really was most unromantic to have fallen in love with a person who had slapped one's face in the nursery but on the other hand, where could one find a comrade like the one who understood everything, and shared all'.[45] Here, Crichton is rewriting a national marriage plot, the happy-ever-after being a pragmatic – and decidedly unromantic – union between the English and Ulster Scots. Betty's father also tells Sandford that, 'Betty's the sort of woman to attract manly men. These strong-minded, over-capable females only appeal to weaklings. Betty does most things well, I imagine, but not too well for people to want to help her.'[46] If Betty can be interpreted at this point as a rare female personification of unionism, her feminine 'weakness' is a call to arms for 'manly' suitors such as Sandford to rescue her. Capable of slapping one's face and doing most things well, Betty has her own strengths and is an unconventional choice of partner for a romance novel.

Betty's silence and the stress points in this novel are most apparent during sequences where the author would like to give her character a voice but cannot imagine how to do so without betraying her overriding political ideology. In some ways, this silence symbolises the absence of Ulster Protestant women writers from canonical accounts of writing from the North of Ireland; it is also indicative of the problem that a unionist writer had in 'imagining' female characters outside the emerging national narratives of the era. Although this chapter has concentrated on a unionist author, as many critics have pointed out, gendered narratives of nation have impacted upon the creative lives of all Irish women, from whatever their cultural or political background. Much critical attention has been focused on deconstructing female tropes of Irish nationhood associated with cultural revivalism; much work remains to be done on reconstructing the voices of those female writers who did not live within this gendered narrative but had their own unionist or other 'nationhoods' to contend with.

This chapter's main aim has been to give a brief insight into the life and work of one author who has emerged as an interesting voice amidst a plethora of voices, as part of a larger project of cultural retrieval. Although it is acknowledged that Crichton lived in England for the duration of her publishing career, her virtual erasure from the cultural and political history of the era is intriguing, especially given her father's prominent role in Ulster society. It is an oversimplification to suggest that Crichton's work has been forgotten solely because she was a popular (and therefore minor) writer of the period. It is also untrue to suggest that her books were somehow 'bad' novels. As *The Precepts* demonstrates, Crichton's work enjoyed several reprints, and her mocking humour and representation of Ulster Scots are both entertaining and well written. As recently as 1960, an article in the *Irish Times* laments the disappearance of Crichton's novels, thanking her for 'adding sweetness to our Irish heritage' and suggesting that two of her novels (*The Soundless Tide* and *Tinker's Hollow*) are worthy of inclusion in the World Classics Series alongside Somerville and Ross.[47] Her children's fiction was also extremely popular, with *Peep-In-The-World* enjoying several reprints between the years 1908 and 1929, some eleven years after her sudden and untimely death at the age of just forty-one.

Although unionist politics dominated her last work at the expense of the credibility of the story, it would also be unfair to suggest that Crichton's politics made her unpopular or somehow subverted the ideals of cultural nationalism to such an extent that it may have disconcerted the reader of popular fiction who simply hoped to enjoy a good 'Irish' novel. Although no figures have been discovered to indicate the exact number of novels that she sold, the reprints of all of her books were considerable, with publishers in Belfast, London, and New York suggesting that her works were globally popular. Part of the reason she has been forgotten may lie in her non-Revival or (towards the end of her career) anti-Revivalist status. Irish Literary Revivalism was, and to a large extent still is, the dominant force in studies of Irish literary history. Those contemporary writers or writers of popular fiction who did not fit readily into this literary mould have been somewhat waylaid – Protestant and Catholic, male and female alike. Understood in this context, Crichton should be viewed as one of many writers whose works have yet to be uncovered and explored.

Jane Austen was famously criticised by another wartime novelist, Virginia Woolf, for supposedly ignoring the political landscape against which she was writing: specifically, the course of the Napoleonic War and its consequences for England.[48] In Crichton we have an example of a female author who was doing the opposite by ultimately choosing to make political engagement the *raison d'être* for her work, setting aside the cause of her own sex in favour of the principles of a brand of political unionism that would evince an increasingly masculine identity after Partition in 1922. Excepting those unionist women from an aristocratic background whom Urquhart demonstrates had considerable political influence over contemporary leading male politicians within their social sphere, here is an example of an upper-middle-class Presbyterian writer publishing in the pre-franchise era who self-consciously engaged in the 'Ulsterisation' of political unionism. A comparison of the two works chosen here may seem a peculiar juxtaposition not just to readers who may be familiar with Crichton's work but to those coming to the subject of fiction written by Protestant women from Ulster for the first time. It is hoped that this analysis of *The Precepts of Andy Saul* and *The Blind Side of the Heart* has demonstrated that Crichton's fiction provides evidence of her considerable talent, determination, and political conviction. In this Decade of Centenaries, as recently as 2012, 30,000 people took to the streets of Belfast to commemorate the signing of the Ulster Covenant just over 100 years after it was written by Crichton's father. In 2014, a plaque commemorating Thomas Sinclair was unveiled at the newly refurbished Duncairn Centre for Arts and Culture on Belfast's Antrim Road. To this day, there are no such memorials for his daughter, a daring counter-Revivalist who is arguably one of unionism's leading literary ladies from the North. History, it would seem, has indeed preferred *his* story. One cannot help but wonder if Crichton herself would have approved.

Notes

1 See John Wilson Foster, *Irish Novels, 1890–1940: New Bearings in Culture and Fiction* (Oxford: Oxford University Press, 2008).

2 Naomi Doak, 'Assessing an Absence: Ulster Protestant Women Authors, 1900–1960', in Mervyn Busteed, Frank Neal, and Jonathan Tonge (eds), *Irish Protestant Identities* (Manchester: Manchester University Press, 2008), pp. 126–37.

3 A full list of Crichton's publications includes: *The Precepts of Andy Saul* (London: M'Caw, Stevenson & Orr, 1908); *The Soundless Tide* (London: Edward Arnold, 1911); *Tinker's Hollow* (London: Edward Arnold, 1912); and *The Blind Side of the Heart* (Dublin and London: Maunsel & Co., 1915). Crichton also produced books of juvenile fiction, including *Peep-in-the World* (London: Edward Arnold, 1908) and *The Little Wizard of White Cloud Hill* (London: Edward Arnold, 1910).

4 See http://records.ancestry.co.uk. Accessed 10 February 2015.

5 Irish Census Records, The National Archives of Ireland. See www.census.nationalarchives.ie. Accessed 15 February 2015.

6 Sinclair's second wife (Crichton's stepmother) is documented on the census record as being a member of the Society of Friends.

7 Crichton married William Sinclair Crichton, a merchant from Liverpool, by way of special license at Hopefield House on 9 April 1906. Crichton is not present in the Sinclair household on the 1911 census record, but her signature appears on the Ulster Covenant in 1912 with an address in Liverpool. Source: Certified Copy of an Entry in Marriage Registration Records, Registrar's District of Belfast; PRONI http://applications.proni.gov.uk/UlsterCovenant/SearchResults.aspx. Accessed 10 February 2015.

8 'The Precepts of Andy Saul', *Irish Independent* (25 May 1908), p. 8.

9 Simon Walker, *Historic Ulster Churches* (Belfast: Queen's University Belfast Press, 2000), p. 118.

10 North Belfast Partnership Board, *The Famous Faces of North Belfast*, www.northbelfastpartnership.com/north-belfast/famous-faces-of-north-belfast. Accessed 10 February 2015.

11 Graham Walker, 'Thomas Sinclair: Presbyterian and Liberal Unionist', in Richard English and Graham Walker (eds), *Unionism in Modern Ireland: New Perspectives on Politics and Culture* (Basingstoke: Palgrave Macmillan, 1996), pp. 19–40, at p. 20.

12 Ulster-Scots Community Network, *Understanding the Ulster Covenant* (Belfast: Arts Council of Northern Ireland) www.ulster-scots.com. Accessed 15 February 2015. Rather oddly, until recently Thomas Sinclair has been a largely forgotten figure in Ulster history. Born in 1838, Sinclair was educated at Belfast Royal Academy and went on to attend the Queen's College (now Queen's University) in Belfast as a scholar of mathematics. Graduating with a first-class-honours degree, he was regarded as one of the best students the college had ever seen and received an honorary D.Litt. in 1882. For all his academic promise, Sinclair chose to enter the family business, J. & T. Sinclair Provendar Merchants, acting as head of the firm until his death in 1914.

13 Diane Urquhart, 'Ulster Covenant: Women's Signature Role in the Fight against Home Rule', *Belfast Telegraph* (25 September 2012). See www.belfasttelegraph.co.uk/opinion/news-analysis/ulster-covenant-womens-signature-role-in-the-fight-against-home-rule-28866873.html. Accessed 28 February 2015.

14 Urquhart, 'Ulster Covenant'.

15 For further reference, see Diane Urquhart, *The Ladies of Londonderry: Women and Political Patronage, 1800–1959* (London and New York: I. B. Tauris & Co., 2007).

16 This novel was republished in 1912 and 1913.

17 Maria Edgeworth, *Castle Rackrent: A Hibernian Tale* (London: J. Johnson, 1800).

18 Declan Kiberd, *Irish Classics* (London: Granta, 2000), p. 26.

19 Crichton, *The Precepts of Andy Saul*, p. 1.

20 Crichton, *The Precepts of Andy Saul*, p. 1.

21 Crichton, *The Precepts of Andy Saul*, p. 2.

22 Crichton, *The Precepts of Andy Saul*, pp. 10–11.
23 Crichton, *The Precepts of Andy Saul*, p. 32.
24 Crichton, *The Precepts of Andy Saul*, p. 14.
25 Crichton, *The Precepts of Andy Saul*, p. 19.
26 Crichton, *The Precepts of Andy Saul*, pp. 19–20.
27 Crichton, *The Precepts of Andy Saul*, pp. 20–1.
28 See James H. Murphy, *Catholic Fiction and Social Reality in Ireland, 1873–1922* (Westport, Conn.: Greenwood Press, 1997).
29 Crichton, *The Blind Side*, pp. 1–2.
30 Crichton, *The Blind Side*, p. 25.
31 Kiberd, *Irish Classics*, p. 26.
32 The term 'Ulsterisation' is used by Andrew Holmes, in 'The Development of Unionism before 1912', Irish History Live. Available at www.qub.ac.uk/sites/irishhistorylive/IrishHistoryResources/Articlesandlecturesbyourteachingstaff/ThedevelopmentofUnionismbefore1912. Accessed 15 February 2015.
33 *Spectator* (21 February 1914), p. 3.
34 Records accessed at http://records.ancestry.fr/frances_elizabeth_sinclair_records.ashx?pid=57279255 also indicate that Crichton gave birth to three children during the height of her publishing career: Colin, Nancy, and Marion. These records suggest that her infant son, Colin, died in 1914. Accessed 20 February 2015.
35 Crichton, *The Blind Side*, p. 14.
36 Crichton, *The Blind Side*, p. 2.
37 Terry Eagleton, *Heathcliff and the Great Hunger* (New York: Verso, 1995), p. 188.
38 Crichton, *The Blind Side*, p. 12.
39 Crichton, *The Blind Side*, p. 94.
40 Crichton, *The Blind Side*, p. 95.
41 Crichton, *The Blind Side*, p. 230.
42 Crichton, *The Blind Side*, p. 2.
43 Crichton, *The Blind Side*, pp. 192, 286, 37, 7, 269.
44 Crichton, *The Blind Side*, p. 191.
45 Crichton, *The Blind Side*, p. 289.
46 Crichton, *The Blind Side*, p. 279.
47 D. M. Hartford, 'Tinker's Hollow: The Books of Mrs. F. E. Crichton', *Irish Times* (2 July 1960), p. 7.
48 Virginia Woolf, 'The Leaning Tower', in *The Moment and Other Essays* (New York: Harcourt Brace & Co., 1975), pp. 130–1.

11

'The Red Sunrise': gender, violence, and nation in Ella Young's vision of a new Ireland

Aurelia Annat

UNTIL recently, Ella Young's part in the transformation of Irish politics and culture between 1891 and 1922 had been largely forgotten. This is unsurprising as, despite her integration into *fin-de-siècle* nationalist and Revivalist circles and close association with some of the most well documented personalities of early twentieth-century Irish history, only a faint impression of her life has remained in the written record, particularly for the years before 1900. Recently, however, works such as Rose Murphy's popular biography, Dorothea McDowell's book on Young's work, and an edition of Young's collected writings edited by John Matthews and Denise Sallee demonstrate resurgent interest in her life and literature.[1] Furthermore, the growing body of scholarly research on the 1916 generation increasingly acknowledges the significance of marginal and marginalised individuals, including Irish women and their writings.[2] This chapter indicates the possibilities inherent in close examination of texts produced by Young between 1900 and 1925. It focuses on how she absorbed and adapted contemporary discourses of gender, violence, and nation in her reworking of Irish myth and mysticism in order to generate a vision of a new Ireland that was both particular and powerful: particular, because it was characteristic of Young's singular politics and spirituality; powerful, because it influenced Young's immediate social milieu and, through notable friends such as Maud Gonne, would find wider audiences.

Ella Young was born in 1867 in the Presbyterian parish of Ahogill, in Co. Antrim, on the northern coast of Ireland, but spent the latter part of her childhood and education in Dublin, eventually studying history, jurisprudence, and political economy at the Dublin Royal University.[3] By the early 1900s she was integrated into the prominent intellectual and political nationalist circles of Dublin. She actively bonded elements of this broad movement together, hosting regular open evenings, and engineering introductions.[4] These years saw her emerge as a writer, encouraged and supported by key literary figures including Standish O'Grady, George Russell ('Æ'), Padraic Colum, and Seamus O'Sullivan. By 1900 her work was appearing in O'Grady's journal, the *All Ireland Review*, and in 1904 five of her poems were included in Æ's important collection, *New Songs*.[5]

Young's writings in the early twentieth century were integral to her construction of a personal identity that rejected her Protestant unionist northern background and reflected her association with Dublin's exciting subcultures and the alternative Ireland that they seemed to promise. In particular, her poetry and prose are evocative expressions of her immersion in the Irish Literary Revival, particularly in its Celtic Twilight aspect. Young's resistance to the modernist and realist literary trends that came to supplant the Celtic Twilight as the twentieth century progressed are part of the explanation for the limited success of her literary career, and she experienced some difficulty finding publishers for her later poetry.[6] She was also unfortunate in her publisher, Maunsel & Company of Dublin. Although it played a central part in the Irish Renaissance, and her association with it affirmed her position among leading Irish authors, she endured a fraught relationship with its director, George Roberts.[7] Nonetheless, Young won sufficient literary acclaim in Ireland to enable her to survive, albeit frugally, as a writer and lecturer for the rest of her life. It was her reputation in Ireland that carried her to America on a lecture tour in 1925 and later gained her the Phelan Lectureship in Celtic Mythology and Literature at the University of California, Berkeley. Although she remained in America until her death in 1956, her literary output, which mostly consisted of children's tales based on Celtic myths, remained rooted in visions of Ireland, its history, and its landscape.

As evidence of her political activity, Young's writings reveal something of the more opaque agents shaping early Irish nationalism. This is because Young's perspective reflects the unconventionality of the woman herself. Her standards, as one friend put it, differed 'widely from the average'.[8] As well as being a poetess and a republican, she was an occultist and probably a lesbian. Young did not operate within the confines of political, cultural, or social consensus. She consequently gives us access to radical aspects of early twentieth-century Irish nationalism that have been displaced by subsequent historical narratives. Through her we are given a glimpse of how dominant discourses were internalised and repurposed to meet both personal and wider political agendas by those who worked on the fringes of the nationalist movement. This chapter explores her appropriation of concepts of gender and nationalism in her writings by analysing the unorthodox roles she adapted for herself from her vision of an ancient Celtic pagan past: druidess, poet, and warrior. It will be argued that, while elements of Young's construction of Ireland appear emulative, taken as a whole they amount to a strikingly coherent and particular projection of the spirit of the land. This is because her writings were shaped not only by contemporary conventions of feminised and nationalist imagery but also by her personal imperatives. In Young's texts, what emerges is a consistent and lucid image of Ireland that is given substance and purpose by her spiritual practice.

Druidess

YOUNG's spirituality was the bedrock of her politics. In the years between 1900 and 1925, she was actively engaged in esoteric activities that were intended to reawaken Ireland and bring about its sovereignty. We cannot fully understand the significance of Young's writing without recognising this other side of her work; the two were different aspects of the same impulse, expressive of her fusion of gender, mysticism, and nationalism.

Young had originally become interested in the esoteric through theosophy. The Theosophical Society, founded in 1875, had gained thousands of converts worldwide, especially in India, by the time a Dublin branch was established in 1889. But the society had specific significance for late-nineteenth-century Ireland. Selina Guinness has argued persuasively that in *fin-de-siècle* Ireland, theosophy seems to have offered a spiritual escape from sectarianism and the opportunity to construct a nationhood unconstrained by religious difference.[9] Young conforms to this model, and it is likely that theosophy secured her flight from her northern Protestant background. She joined the Dublin branch in the 1890s, having been impressed by Æ, who was one of the leading figures in Dublin theosophy.[10] Later, she followed him into his Hermetic Society.[11] By the turn of the century, Young was knowledgeable about various esoteric doctrines and was a practised occultist. Yeats respected her sufficiently to engage in correspondence in 1903 on arcane subjects, although his relationship with her deteriorated subsequently.[12] By 1906 he was referring to her as one of the 'imitative and subjective and sentimental' group that surrounded Æ, and in *Autobiographies* he represented her as the ridiculous 'Miss A- B-', the epitome of Æ's 'fluid, tenuous, flimsy-minded' Dublin Theosophists.[13]

Yet it would seem that at this time Young was no mere theosophist acolyte. Instead, she was intent on creating a distinctly different esoteric group along the lines of Yeats's own Celtic Mystical Order. In the 1890s, Yeats, Gonne, and Æ, among others, had planned a 'Druidic' Order for the 'revitalisation of the Western religious tradition' by synthesising paganism and Christianity.[14] Gonne later remembered that she and Yeats had hoped to help free Ireland by making 'contact with the hidden forces of the land' through this Celtic Mystical Order.[15] If not familiar with the Order itself, Young would have been indirectly influenced by it through her friendships with Æ and Gonne. According to Gonne, Young left the Hermetic Society, 'feeling that Eastern mysticism was not suitable for Ireland's needs', and founded her own company, called the Fine, in 1900.[16] Gonne records that Young's aim for this group was 'to draw together for the freeing of Ireland the wills of the living and of the dead in association with the earth and the elements which to her seemed living entities'.[17] It was therefore a means of using occult practice to awaken both Ireland's landscape and people (living and historical) in order to effect a political and cultural transformation of Ireland that would liberate its true identity. The group appears to have been made up of women and to have been active well into the twentieth century, for Gonne was writing about it to Yeats as late as 1915.[18] While ostensibly the aims of the Fine appear to have been consistent with Yeats's Celtic Mystical Order, Young's magical work was made distinctive through its female emphasis.

There is little substantial evidence of Young's Fine, although accounts of visualisations undertaken on Young's instruction by various female friends in the early 1900s may be records of its activities.[19] Even if they are not, they provide further evidence that she worked collaboratively with a predominantly female company, using a form of magic in sympathy with natural forces. Other manuscript sources may be more reliable evidence of the membership of the Fine. An intriguing letter to the Jewish nationalist artist (and later wife of Seamus O'Sullivan), Estella Solomons, in which a piece of folded paper referred to as 'the open membership' has been inserted, might be interpreted as confirmation of her initiation into the company. The tiny package contains the remains of a plant.[20] This may be heather, as in 1920 Young sent a similar package to Diarmuid Coffey telling him that it contained, 'some heather from Slieve Gullion the Founder & Protector of the Fellowship'. She instructed him not to open it. 'If at any time you wish to resign return the packet to me.'[21] Diarmuid's acceptance into the group may indicate the integration of male membership, or an exception marking friendship and loss, for Diarmuid had married Young's friend, the nationalist artist Cesca Trench, in 1917, only to be made a widower when she succumbed to the Spanish flu on 30 October 1918.[22]

By the time of Young's 1925 American lecture tour, she had cultivated an exoticised appearance and demeanour that advertised her immersion in Celtic mysticism. She wore robes rather than clothes and was, according to Edward Alden Jewell in the *New York Times Magazine*, 'a woman whose quiet intensity and power, you immediately feel'.[23] This persona had been carefully cultivated during her years in Dublin. In a derisive diary entry written by Cesca Trench eleven years earlier, she described Young as 'very

Celtic Twilighty' after one of their initial meetings. Trench was later influenced by Young's esoteric beliefs, and, like other close friends, including Colum, came to see Young as a 'druidess' belonging to 'the ancient Celtic world'.[24]

Young's persona as a druidess is significant. On the one hand, her self-conscious identification with something approximating Gaelic paganism was consistent with the contemporary mood of Revivalism, which looked back to Ireland's heritage to inspire cultural and hence national regeneration. In that sense, it positions Young's work within a context of established cultural nationalist discourses. On the other hand, it emphasises a pattern of spiritual heterodoxy that reveals less conventional aspects of cultural nationalism, enabling a more complex appreciation of the diversity of that movement. Ultimately, Young's unorthodox spirituality articulates an intimate bond between religion and politics in her construction of a new Ireland. In Young's conception of a sovereign Ireland, it was not only British authority that would be overthrown but the supremacy of institutionalised Christianity also.

Poet

A FURTHER radical aspect of Young's heterodox religiosity is its construction of femininity. Both her apprehension of a mystical spirituality and her work as a practising occultist were defined around gendered discourses and contexts. This is made explicit in her writings and develops our understanding of how Young's work drew on cultural conventions and literary tropes while simultaneously reflecting an original and personal conception of a feminised Ireland.

This is evident in her literary accounts of her spiritual awakening. In her memoirs, published in 1945 as *Flowering Dusk*, Young recorded her rejection of the staunch unionist Presbyterianism of her parents and renunciation of God at an early age, despite her belief that this would lead to her damnation.[25] Her friend, the American lesbian poet Elsa Gidlow, later interpreted these actions in feminist terms: 'Brought up a Presbyterian and compelled to sit on Sundays with her family in a church ... the child Ella was filled with rebellion. Early there was revolt against what now we call patriarchy.'[26] In Gidlow's account, this repudiation of the male God was simultaneous with Young's turn to female objects of sexual and spiritual devotion. In two autobiographical accounts, Young demonstrates how her spirituality was released from the strictures of the Presbyterian Church by female agency when a religious revelation was prompted by her first encounter with Brysanthe, a young girl, during a service: 'I had eyes for nothing else in the church save that child. She was like the first sunlight on a day of Winter. The ice in my heart broke up. All my ideas about God and the Universe surged and tumbled to destruction.'[27] Her short story of 1911, 'The Rose Queen', likewise hints at the centrality of this experience. In it, the young protagonist is startled from her resentment of attending services ('Church was hateful, but I had to go there') by the appearance of the Rose Queen. Following the Queen to her garden gate, the child is given a rose.[28] This withers, but the 'virtue of it' remains, and the story culminates in mystical allegory:[29]

> I am not a child outside the gate any longer. I can go in now [. . .] The Rose-Queen is there faintly smiling, ivory-white, subtle as flame. She is as wise as the tallest of the queens in Avalon and in her hands which so many lovers have kissed she holds the million-petalled Rose of Dreams.[30]

The language of the 'The Rose Queen' is overtly Arthurian. But the significance of the narrative is complex. It may be interpreted as religious revelation, sexual awakening, or a visionary encounter with Ireland. The association of the rose with passion and the female may be read in political as well as religious terms. In addition to being identified with the Virgin Mary and other pagan and Oriental female divinities, the rose also symbolises the female personification of Ireland and had been made popular in that context by the nationalist poet James Clarence Mangan, whose ballad 'Dark Rosaleen' (1846) drew on the earlier folk song 'Roisin Dubh' (Little Black Rose) as well as the tradition of the *aisling*, which personified Ireland as a beautiful maiden.[31] More contemporaneously, Yeats had drawn on this symbolism, as well as the alchemical meanings of the flower in various stories collected into *The Secret Rose* (1897), and in the rose poems of the 1890s, written while he was immersed in the ascetic cult of beauty.[32] In 1920, Young would also publish a series of rose poems, full of religious and Arthurian imagery.[33] This links her work to existing nationalist discourses but also reflects the distinctively personal nature of Young's work. In her 1922 poem 'The Black Rose', Ireland is identified as a divine female force, the 'Virgin', compelling revelation and reverence. This echoes 'The Rose Queen', yet by 1922 Young had witnessed years of conflict and death, and her image of Ireland had changed. Now the feminine divinity inspires violence and sacrifice and is herself imagined in violent as well as sublime terms: 'O Sword, O flame, O Light . . . '

> The Black Rose.
> For thee the thorn-pierced centuries
> bleed and die –
> O Sword, O flame, O Light that
> durst endure

> The murk of Hell, thyself unchanged
> and pure,
> Supernal Love that dost our hopes
> deny,
> Giving thyself to us, Virgin most high
> Branch of White Silver, Blossom
> that dost lure
> Our hearts to death when life sits
> most secure
> In the world's mart beneath a cloud-
> less sky.
> Eire we stretch our hands to thee –
> The dead,
> Thou hast burned our lives away, O
> Quenchless Flame,
> Our years are but thy petals spent
> and shed:
> So with thy splendour now our
> honour grows
> We are free of earthly praise or
> blame,
> White with thy Whiteness, carmined
> with thy Rose.

The poem was dedicated, as Young explained on a handwritten copy, to 'Erskine Childers, Rory O'Connor Liam Mellowes & those other noble comrades who died with them'.[34] It was published on a commemorative sheet priced two pence, with the names of 'soldiers of the Republic who gave their lives in this second War of Independence'.[35] These, Young told Erskine's widow Molly, were 'names to be remembered for ever'.[36]

Young's use of the trope of a feminised Ireland in 'The Black Rose' represents another recurrent and derivative feature of her early writings. However, it also conveys Young's intense and personal identification with the concept of the Motherland.[37] In an article for the *All Ireland Review* in 1901, she addressed Ireland in the spirit of invocation:

> O Eire, queen of the sacred hills, kindle once more the old heroism in the hearts of thy children … Enchantress, whose reward is the death-gift, call us again from the mart, from the sordid life of the hour, from the fire-light of home to the quest from which none of thy lovers turn back.[38]

If this was a prayer to the spirit of Ireland, it was also an injunction to readers of the *All Ireland Review* to shake off British influence and awaken to a consciousness of the 'eternal' nation and to a sense of devotion to the land itself. Of course, this aim was not unique to Young. Yeats famously was doing the same thing when he and Lady Gregory co-wrote *Cathleen ni Houlihan*, the 1902 play performed by Inghinidhe na hÉireann (Daughters of Ireland), a politico-cultural society founded by Maud Gonne in 1900.[39] Gonne herself played the title role in the production, representing the spirit of Ireland and inspiring the generation that took up arms in Easter 1916. The character of Cathleen belonged to a wider project in which Yeats, drawing upon theosophy and the pre-Raphaelites, had used the symbol of the goddess to discover religious and political power.[40] Young knew the play well since she was involved with the Inghinidhe in rehearsals for this production.[41] Young's construction of a feminised and spiritual Ireland was therefore not unique. However, it was undoubtedly internalised, particular, and consistent. There is striking continuity between the language of Young's 1901 invocation in the *All Ireland Review* and her tribute in 'The Black Rose' to republicans who, by 1922, had answered the 'lure' of Éire, abandoning security in 'the world's mart' for her cause.

We can develop our understanding of the particularity of Young's writings if we further explore the wider cultural constructs that informed her fusion of empowerment, femininity, and heterodoxy. The association of the arcane with transgressive femininity was an idea entrenched in later Victorian popular fiction, in the archetype of what Diana Basham has termed the 'Occult Mother'. This was a monstrous figure, presiding over a psychic or geographical borderland rather than the familiar domestic sphere. She was Ayesha in Bulwer Lytton's *A Strange Story* (1862) and 'She Who Must Be Obeyed' in Rider Haggard's *She* (1887). For Basham, this trope held political ramifications for late-nineteenth-century women in the fabrication of the New Woman.[42] Both Young's poetry and prose borrow from this genre in describing mysterious and powerful women who inhabit spaces removed from the comfort of home. In 'The Wood-Queen', published in *Poems* (1906), we follow the music of the 'May-time' deep into the 'dim recesses' of a forest world, where, through 'oak-boughs parted', we at last witness 'the Queen who holds the woods in sway'. The language of the poem emphasises a sense of awe and reverie.[43]

However, for Young, the disturbing quality of her female characters is creative rather than degenerative and opens the opportunity for revelation and growth. This is explicit in 'My Lady of Dreams':

> One night the beauty of the stars
> Made magic for me white and still,
> I climbed the road above the hill
> The road no waking footstep mars.
> I met my Lady in the wood
> The black pine wood above the hill,
> Dream-fair her beauty, white and still;
> I knelt as one before the Rood.
> White Dream that makes my life a war

Of wild desires and baffled will
Once more my soul with beauty fill
Rise through the darkness, O my Star.[44]

Key elements of Young's poetry, including the conceptualisation of an inner journey that draws the writer through darkness to inspiration and the wood as a symbolic setting, recur in Young's short story 'Lilith'. The title itself, as a name with complex cultural associations that include Jewish as well as Arthurian folklore, foregrounds the unsettling, seductive, and degenerative quality of female power. This is explicit in a draft copy of this story, where the character Fionn comes upon a wood where he is overwhelmed by She whom he accosts: 'She stood. Her beauty was terrible. It penetrated through every pore of his body: it loosed sinew & joint: it dried the marrow in his bones. Her beauty was like a sword that twisted in his heart. There was no strength in him.'[45] This passage is not included in 'Lilith: A Story', which was printed in the *Dublin Magazine* in 1924. However, while the published version similarly narrates Lilith's disruptive power, she is also projected as an agent of rebirth. Here, Lilith offers to kiss the eyes of the unnamed man who encounters her, making him forget the earth. Although he admits that he desires her, and indeed confesses, 'I have called you all my life', he rejects her. His lack of courage prevented him from transcending material comfort and answering an inner imperative to embrace the spirit of the land and (by implication) Ireland's sovereignty. Lilith goes and leaves him in a cold grey wood which is now seemingly dull after the glamour she had temporarily brought it.[46] There is obvious continuity between this prose piece and Young's invocation to Ireland in 1901. In both writings, Young imagines the eternal feminine energy of the land startling those who encounter it, answering to deep desire, and awakening the possibility for change. But while in 1901 Young anticipated the men of Ireland waking up and rising to the call of the land, by 1924 she was recoiling from what she saw as the betrayal of Ireland in the aftermath of the Civil War and the victory of the Irish Free State forces. Young's story narrates the failure of Ireland's men to answer her call. In Lilith's departure and the bleakness that is left, we can sense Young's hopelessness. It is not surprising that she would choose to leave Ireland for good in 1925.

Warrior

THE evolution of Young's vision of Ireland can be further explored by analysing her in the role of 'warrior' and the texts, both her published poetry and her private correspondence, which expressed her militancy. Between 1900 and 1925, Young perceived herself to be engaged in the battle for Irish sovereignty through her literary and mystical work. As is implicit in her accounts of a feminised Ireland, her concept of this conflict was consistently defined in archetypal and esoteric terms that conceived of Ireland's rebirth as a violent rupture that would necessitate the loss of certainties that had structured individuals' lives under British rule. By the early 1920s, as that violence was realised in the Anglo-Irish and Civil Wars, Young more explicitly and urgently assumed the role of warrior.

The character of Young's politics before 1916 was informed by her association with nationalist organisations, including Inghinidhe na hÉireann from the early 1900s and later Cumann na mBan (Irishwomen's Council), founded in 1914.[47] Her fellowship with these women's groups was connected to her mystical work through republican friends including Gonne, Constance Markievicz, and Helena Molony, and reinforced the distinctly female context of her esoteric activity. Her intervention in these institutions was cultural; she saw this work as a vital aspect of nationalist resistance to British rule, especially in the absence of a viable campaign of physical force. In *Flowering Dusk* she would retrospectively figure cultural nationalism as an active and aggressive agent in securing political change. Her text uses the present tense to recapture the immediacy of the past she recalled: 'It is true that we have no hope of an armed thrust at the might of England, but we can tear to pieces the calumnies with which she strives to hide her exploitation. We can retrieve our ancient culture and our language.'[48] Crediting the work of Celtic Language specialist Kuno Meyer as well as the stories of Patrick Pearse, Thomas Clarke, and Whitley Stokes, she imagined the dynamic impact of their work: 'The sagas and hero-tales even now are spreading amongst us as oil spreads upon water, iridescent and unescapable ... these are building up our nationhood: these and the Gaelic language.'[49] Young's own contribution was through writing and teaching. For Inghinidhe na hÉireann, she taught history by retelling 'sagas and hero-tales' to a class of about eighty children from the Dublin poor, 'eager-eyed ... adding new names to the hero-names that they have cherished ever since they could put names together'.[50]

This underlines the explicitly nationalistic purpose behind her publications of juvenile literature in these years. In fact, publication of the *Gubbaun Saor* tales in the *Dublin Magazine* (a journal aimed at adults) indicates that Young's stories were not exclusively intended for young readers.[51] Yet a letter to Starkey from about 1907 shows it was her intention to write Celtic stories in a form 'suitable for children'.[52] Significantly, Gonne's involvement as illustrator was already settled by that time, demonstrating that these women were collaborating in their cultural endeavours, as well as in their political and mystical activities in the 1900s. Gonne produced the art-work for both Young's *The Coming of Lugh* (1909) and *Celtic Wonder Tales*

Figure 11.1 'Ethlinn with Lugh', by Maud Gonne.

(1910). The illustrations were sufficiently distinctive for reviewers to comment, not always sympathetically, on their esoteric character.[53] However, they advanced Young's spiritual vision of mythic Ireland, employing occult symbolism and evoking the mystical art of Æ as well as the Rider-Waite tarot which was used by the Golden Dawn, an occult order that Gonne had joined in 1891 through Yeats's influence.[54] The image of 'Ethlinn with Lugh' in *The Celtic Wonder Tales* is a case in point, as it bears striking affinities with the 'High Priestess' card in the Rider-Waite deck.[55] Here, the beautiful Ethlinn, daughter of 'Balor of the Evil Eye', presents the child she has conceived secretly with the hero Cian, despite being shut away in a dun by her father (see Fig. 11.1).[56] Her robe, and the crescent within which she cradles her son, emphasise that she represents the night from which day is born. It is also allegorically significant, in Irish nationalist terms, that the infant Lugh holds a sword. This image indicates the birth of hope out of oppression and anticipates the tale of how Lugh the Sun-God will grow up to defeat Balor and acquire the Sword of Tethra which will allow him to scatter the darkness. This had obvious relevance for nationalists' imagining of Irelands' liberation from British dominance.

An earlier collaboration between Young and Gonne represents a more explicit expression of their fusion of femininity, politics, mysticism, and art. Two of Young's poems were included in Gonne's one-act propaganda play *Dawn*, published in the *United Irishman* in 1904. Like Yeats and Lady Gregory's *Cathleen ni Houlihan*, this play self-consciously used allegory to arouse patriotism, but it was also, Nancy Cardozo has argued, a feminist statement.[57] One of the poems was 'The Red Sunrise', also called Moraig's song, an invocation of change, an unashamed call to battle, written from the sidelines, in a mother's voice:

> O, it's dark the land is, and it's dark my heart
> is, but the Red Sun rises when the hour
> is come.
> O, the Red Sun rises, and the dead rise: I can
> see them, and it's glad they are and proud.
> White Oscur's with them, and my own boy,
> and Conn, who won the battles, and the
> lads who lost.
> They have bright swords with them that clash
> the battle-welcome: a welcome to the Red
> Sun that rises with our luck.[58]

The 'Red Sun' is a symbol Young later used in her narration of the Celtic saga of Fionn, *The Tangle-Coated Horse* (1929). In this later work, it is a red sunset that signifies a violent turn of fortune that brings darkness, but also the hope of a new dawn in the future.[59] The red of dawn that she depicts represents the painful birth of a new era *following* darkness. As Gonne had written in her play, the red dawn meant that 'the river of blood must flow, but there is freedom on the other side of it, and the Strangers are driven away like clouds before the sun'.[60] As with Young's visions of a feminised Ireland, Moraig's song acknowledges and invites the inevitable violence of change.

By 1914, with the spread of militarism and the arming of Volunteers across Ireland, physical force was becoming a practical possibility for the nationalist cause. Women played an important part in defining and promoting an uncompromising separatist attitude. Young was one of the many women involved in acquiring, hiding, moving, and manufacturing arms for the Irish Volunteers in the lead-up to the Rising in 1916.[61] In 1914, at her Dublin home in Temple Hill, she stored and distributed guns for the Irish Volunteers who would eventually hold Dublin against the British in Easter week.[62] However, although Young possessed a pistol and ammunition at this time, she did not participate in the Rising.[63]

For Young, a battle waged on cultural and mystical terms was as important as one with guns, and here she played an ongoing part. In September 1920, 'The Red Sunrise' was reprinted as the sally for the first edition of the *Red Hand Magazine*, a nationalist journal of northern Revivalism. The editor described Young's poem as hailing 'the breaking of to-morrow upon the land'.[64] It is difficult to assess exactly what Young envisioned that nationalist tomorrow to look like politically. She was acquainted with James Connolly and was close to Helena Molony, who, by 1911, had embraced a republican ideal that united the causes of labour, women, and Ireland, and who would become the general secretary to the Irish Women Workers' Union in 1915.[65] In 1920, Young would ask Solomons, 'aren't you glad of the Bolshevik successes?'[66] Yet, while retrospective accounts of republican nationalism marry its socialist dimensions with an acceptable democratic aim, Lyman's portrait of Young represents her leaning towards totalitarianism:

> In her social attitudes, Ella Young was anti-democratic. She believed in an elite group who should lead in thought and culture. She believed that the common man should follow these leaders and not try to impose his own inferior point of view on society. Thus Ella Young could have been either a Communist or a Fascist.[67]

If W. W. Lyman's account of her elitism is credible, then it would seem that, as in other respects, her philosophy was aligned with that of her contemporary, the IRA intellectual Ernie O'Malley, who would come to know Young after her emigration to America.[68] Richard English has suggested that O'Malley's 'political violence during the 1916–24 Irish revolution was founded on Republican *faith* and not on extended political *analysis*', and these ideas might be applied to Young also.[69]

Her commitment to violence is more explicit and less complicated than is the nature of her republican belief. She was fired by a conviction that only through rupture could the Irish nation be reborn. Her ideal for Ireland was a sympathetic fusion of ancient myth and radical modernity. Rejecting the liberal imperialist world in which she was raised, she embraced instead the reactionary politics of the emerging modern era. She sought a 'New Order' – a cultural, spiritual, and political revolution that would 'restore' authentic nationhood – and rejected the Anglo-Irish Treaty of 6 December 1921. For her, as for other republicans, it sold cheap an ideal made costly through self-sacrifice. She looked to guerrilla Gaelicism to maintain the struggle for Ireland's independence, believing the revolution had to be effected metaphysically before it could be enacted physically. Burning with spiritual militancy and a powerful sense of the centrality of cultural nationalism within the fight for Ireland's liberation, she wrote to the northern nationalist poet Joseph Campbell in 1922, only a couple of days before civil war was initiated by the Provisional Government. It is worth quoting her at length.

> I fully agree with what you say about the neglect shown to our National Culture & those who have worked for it. This is really the False Dawn – I hope the true one will not be too long delayed. I see that we must overthrow this civilization and this social system … Let us draw the sword upon it and never cease from warfare till we have slain the Unclean Thing. We are strong enough & only we the Poets and Makers the worshippers of the Holy Earth which these things defile. All things are destroyed first in the mind & spirit before they decay in the body and we can destroy these things. Preach the gospel of it & enlist recruits everywhere. It is not the Republic or the Dáil we are now fighting for, it is the 'New Order' the 'New Age'.[70]

With civil war under way, her consciousness of fighting a moral and cultural battle was heightened. Her language when writing to Seamus O'Sullivan in November that year was unreservedly militant. 'We are here to fight & to endure', she told him.[71] De Valera's capitulation on 24 May 1923 concluded the Civil War but did not reconcile Young and other intransigent republicans with the Free State government. In 1924 she was one of a party of republicans calling themselves 'the Optimists' who were brought together by Gonne 'with heart and commitment and vision'.[72] This was also the year that she published 'Lilith', with its bleak conclusion. But it would be wrong to read this, and Young's emigration the following year, as evidence that she gave up her battle.

The strength of Young's vision of Ireland is evidenced by the fact that it continued to animate her writing even after she moved to America. While exile weakened her political and social connections to Ireland, the literature she produced in the USA affirmed her identity as an Irish republican nationalist and her identification with Gaelic Revivalism. She published three volumes of children's Celtic tales in the years following her emigration. Together with the Celtic tales she brought out in Ireland, these may be interpreted as a development of the teaching she undertook for Inghinidhe na hÉireann; collectively, they demonstrate the importance she attached to storytelling and to children as an audience. In 1922, she told Joseph Campbell's wife, Nancy, about the influence that Irish myth could exert over children. Hoping the Campbells would bring their son up 'on Irish & all the old stories', she added, 'if he is going to be one of the great ones you must train him for it because a Great One has so heavy a burden to lift & so big a sword to swing that he needs to be hero-nurtured from the cradle'.[73] Young's 'New Order' was not realised in her lifetime, but in her juvenile literature we see her ongoing commitment to it. Colum recognised this when he described these later works as 'part of a sacred history'.[74] By addressing her vision to children, Young assumed a maternal role, nurturing a new generation who would perhaps bring into being the new Ireland which she had anticipated in 'The Red Sunrise'.

While she never had children, her literature was her legacy. As with her militancy, it was through her visions and writings that she sought to influence the future generation. As a poet and storyteller, Young, like the mother Moraig in 'The Red Sunrise', viewed the unfolding events that culminated in Irish independence from a marginal position. Yet it is precisely Young's position on the sidelines, self-consciously set apart from the fray, that makes her and her intervention worthy of study. This vantage point afforded her agency in the roles she adopted in the struggle for a new and independent Ireland: those of a druidess, a poet, and a warrior, using metaphysical means to effect physical change. Her subjectivity is valid; her perspective is valuable. While it was informed by contemporary political, social, and spiritual movements, as well as cultural discourses and literary tropes, it was also distinctly conceptualised, personally motivated, and constant. Young's importance as a female writer in twentieth-century Irish history lies in her radical vision for Ireland and the range of unconventional mechanisms that she employed to bring this into being. These are particularly relevant because they challenge modern stereotypes of republican nationalism by flouting the conventional Catholic democratic mould and extending our understanding of less conventional contexts in which feminism and nationalism were operating at the start of the twentieth century. She fused cultural, esoteric, and militant activity into a highly feminised and idiosyncratic pagan-Republicanism. Through this distinctive approach we can see Young's vision of nation, one that blended gender and violence in its hopes for a new dawn: the Red Sunrise.

Notes

1 Rose Murphy, *Ella Young: Irish Mystic and Rebel – From Literary Dublin to the American West* (Dublin: The Liffey Press, 2008); Dorothea McDowell, *Ella Young and Her World: Celtic Mythology, the Irish Revival and the California Avant-Garde* (Palo Alto, Calif.: Academica Press, 2014); John Matthews and Denise Sallee (eds), *At the Gates of Dawn: A Collection of Writings by Ella Young* (Cheltenham: Skylight Press, 2011).

2 R. F. Foster, *Vivid Faces: The Revolutionary Generation in Ireland, 1890–1923* (London: Allen Lane, 2014); Senia Pašeta, *Irish Nationalist Women, 1900–1918* (Cambridge: Cambridge University Press, 2013).

3 Murphy, *Ella Young*, p. 10; Deirdre Toomey, 'Young, Ella (1867–1956)', *Oxford Dictionary of National Biography*, Oxford University Press, 2004. Available at www.oxforddnb.com/view/article/59452. Accessed 26 April 2015; Anne T. Eaton, 'Ella Young's Unicorns and Kyelins', *Horn Magazine: Books and Reading for Young People*, 9:3 (1933), 115–20, at p. 115.

4 W. W. Lyman, 'Ella Young: A Memoir by W. W. Lyman', *Éire-Ireland*, 8:3 (1973), 65–9, at p. 67; Mary Colum, *Life and the Dream* (London: Macmillan, 1947), p. 185.

5 Ella Young, 'A Sunflower', *All Ireland Review*, 1:19 (1900), 6; 'The Celtic Renaissance in Poetry', *All Ireland Review*, 2:19 (1901), 142–3 and 2:20 (1901), 150–1; George Russell, *New Songs: A Lyric Selection made by Æ* (Dublin and London: O'Donoghue & Co. and A. H. Bullen, 1904).

6 Ella Young to Joseph McGarrity (18 June 1930), Joseph McGarrity Papers, MS 17,492, National Library of Ireland, Dublin (hereafter NLI).

7 David Gardiner (ed.), *The Maunsel Poets, 1905–1926* (Bethesda, Md.: Academica Press, 2003), p. 3; J. D. O'Bolger to Ella Young (30 November 1914); and J. D. O'Bolger to Ella Young (12 April 1917), Ella Young Papers, Reel 1 MS.402/4 (4) UCLA; Talbot Press Limited to Ella Young (30 April 1938), Ella Young Papers, Reel 1 MS.402/4 (7) UCLA, Ballymena Central Branch Library, Ballymena (hereafter BCBL), microfilm copies of MSS held by the Department of Special Collections, University of California, Los Angeles Library. For Roberts, see Padraic Colum and Mary Colum, *Our Friend James Joyce* (London: Gollancz, 1959), p. 89; and Clare Hutton, '"Yogibogeybox in Dawson Chambers": The Beginnings of Maunsel and Company', in Clare Hutton (ed.), *The Irish Book in the Twentieth Century* (Dublin: Irish Academic Press, 2004), pp. 36–46.

8 Lyman, 'Ella Young', p. 66.

9 Selina Guinness, '"Protestant Magic" Reappraised: Evangelicalism, Dissent, and Theosophy', *Irish Studies Review*, 33:1 (2003), 14–27; 'Ireland through the Stereoscope: Reading the Cultural Politics of Theosophy in the Irish Literary Revival', in E. A. Taylor FitzSimon and James H. Murphy (eds), *The Irish Revival Reappraised* (Dublin: Four Courts Press, 2004), pp. 19–32, at pp. 25–6.

10 Ella Young, *Flowering Dusk* (New York: Longmans, 1945), pp. 28–34.

11 Young, *Flowering Dusk*, p. 34.

12 W. B. Yeats, *The Collected Letters of W. B. Yeats*, vol. III: *1901–1904*, ed. J. Kelly and R. Schuchard (Oxford: Clarendon Press, 1994), pp. 381–2.

13 W. B. Yeats, *The Collected Letters of W. B. Yeats*, vol. IV: *1905–1907*, ed. J. Kelly and R. Schuchard (Oxford: Clarendon Press, 2005), p. 488; W. B. Yeats, *Autobiographies* (London: Macmillan, 1955), pp. 467, 469, 470.

14 The term 'Druidic' is in Elizabeth A. Sharp, *William Sharp (Fiona Macleod): A Memoir Compiled by His Wife* (London: Heinemann, 1910), p. 277; see also George Mills Harper, *Yeats's Golden Dawn* (New York: Macmillan, 1974), pp. 5–6; Yeats, *Autobiographies*, p. 254.

15 Maud Gonne, 'Yeats and Ireland', in Stephen Gwynn (ed.), *Scattering Branches: Tributes to the Memory of W. B. Yeats* (London: Macmillan, 1940), p. 22.

16 Maud Gonne, *A Servant of the Queen*, ed. A. Norman Jeffares and Anna MacBride White (Gerrards Cross: Colin Smythe, 1994), p. 334.

17 Gonne, *A Servant of the Queen*, p. 335.

18 Anna MacBride White and A. Norman Jeffares (eds), *The Gonne–Yeats Letters, 1893–1938: Always Your Friend* (London: Pimlico, 1993), Letter 276 from Gonne to Yeats, n.d. (June 1913?), p. 321; Letter 283 from Gonne to Yeats (n.d., November 1913), p. 329; Letter 312 from Gonne to Yeats (10 November 1915), p. 361. See also p. 510 note 8; Gonne, *A Servant of the Queen*, p. 8.

19 Handwritten notes by Ella Young (dated 1903), Reel 5, Ella Young Papers, BCBL, microfilm copy of MS.303 held at Department of Special Collections UCLA Library.

20 Ella Young to E. Solomons (n.d.), O'Sullivan/Solomons Collection, MSS 4630-9/4695, Trinity College Dublin (hereafter TCD).

21 Ella Young to D. Coffey (18 January 1920), Coffey and Chenevix Trench Papers, MS 46,307/16, NLI.

22 Anthony Fletcher, 'Cesca: A Young Nationalist in the Easter Rising', *History Today*, 56:4 (2006), 30–8, at p. 38.

23 E. Riehle, 'The Shining Land of Ella Young', *Dublin Magazine*, 33:2 (1958), 17–22, at p. 17; E. A. Jewell, 'Elfland Sends an Ambassadress to Us', *New York Times Magazine* (18 October 1925), p. 12.

24 Hilary Pyle, *Cesca's Diary, 1913–1916: Where Art and Nationalism Meet* (Dublin: Woodfield, 2005), pp. 158–9, 243–50; Padraic Colum, *Ella Young: An Appreciation* (London: Longmans & Co., 1931), p. 3.
25 Young, *Flowering Dusk*, p. 10.
26 Elsa Gidlow, *Elsa: I Come With My Songs – The Autobiography of Elsa Gidlow* (San Francisco, Calif.: Bootlegger Press & Druid Heights Books, 1986), pp. 312–13.
27 Young, *Flowering Dusk*, p. 12.
28 Ella Young, 'The Rose Queen', *Irish Review*, 1:4 (1911), 187–9, at p. 187.
29 Young, 'The Rose Queen', p. 188.
30 Young, 'The Rose Queen', p. 189.
31 Frank Kinahan, *Yeats, Folklore and Occultism: Contexts of the Early Work and Thought* (London: Unwin Hyman, 1988), pp. 129–38; M. H. Thuente, 'The Folklore of Irish Nationalism', in Thomas E. Hachey and Lawrence John McCaffrey (eds), *Perspectives on Irish Nationalism* (Lexington, Ky.: University Press of Kentucky, 1989), p. 54; see also C. L. Innes, *Woman and Nation in Irish Literature and Society, 1880–1935* (Athens, Ga.: University of Georgia, 1993), p. 21.
32 Richard Ellmann, *Yeats: The Man and the Masks* (London: Faber & Faber, 1969), p. 97; Marjorie Howes, *Yeats's Nations: Gender, Class and Irishness* (Cambridge: Cambridge University Press, 1998), pp. 29–30, 72–4.
33 Ella Young, *The Rose of Heaven: Poems by Ella Young, Decorated by Maud Gonne* (Dublin: The Candle Press, 1920).
34 Ella Young to M. Childers (n.d.), Erskine Childers Papers, MSS. 7851/ 1331, TCD.
35 Printed sheet 'In Memoriam', Ella Young Papers, Reel 3, MS. 303 UCLA, BCBL, microfilm copies of MSS held by the Department of Special Collections, University of California, Los Angeles Library.
36 Ella Young to M. Childers (n.d.), Erskine Childers Papers, MSS. 7851/ 1335, TCD.
37 There is a vast literature on the use of female imagery to represent Ireland and the idea of the motherland. See, for instance, Innes, *Woman and Nation*; Scott Brewster, Virginia Crossman, Fiona Becket, and David Alderson (eds), *Ireland in Proximity: History, Gender, Space* (London and New York: Routledge, 1999); Richard Kearney, *Myth and Motherland* (Derry: Field Day Theatre Company, 1984). For comparative work on France, see Joan B. Landes, *Visualising the Nation: Gender, Representation, and Revolution in Eighteenth-Century France* (Ithaca, NY: Cornell University Press, 2001).
38 Ella Young, 'Three Mountains', *All Ireland Review*, 2:42 (1901), 352.
39 Maire Nic Shiubhlaigh, *The Splendid Years: Recollections of Maire Nic Shiubhlaigh as Told to Edward Kenny with Appendices and Lists of Irish Theatre Plays, 1899–1916* (Dublin: James Duffy, 1955), p. 2.
40 Elizabeth Butler Cullingford, 'At the Feet of the Goddess: Yeats's Love Poetry and the Feminist Occult', in Deirdre Toomey (ed.), *Yeats and Women, Yeats Annual No. 9* (London: Macmillan, 1992), pp. 31–59, at p. 42.
41 Gonne to Yeats (March 1902), in White and Jeffares, *The Gonne–Yeats Letters*, p. 150.
42 Diana Basham, 'Through the Looking Glass: Madame Blavatsky and the Occult Mother', in D. Basham (ed.), *The Trial of Woman: Feminism and the Occult Sciences in Victorian Literature and Society* (Basingstoke: Macmillan, 1992), pp. 178–214.
43 Ella Young, *Poems by Ella Young* (Dublin: Maunsel & Co., 1906), p. 25.
44 Young, *Poems by Ella Young*, p. 9.
45 'Lilith', Young Papers, The Huntington Library, California.
46 Ella Young, 'Lilith: A Story', *Dublin Magazine*, 2 (1924), 136–7.
47 Gonne, *A Servant of the Queen*, p. 366.
48 Young, *Flowering Dusk*, p. 65.
49 Young, *Flowering Dusk*, pp. 65–6.
50 Margaret Ward, *Maud Gonne: Ireland's Joan of Arc* (London: Pandora, 1990), p. 66; Young, *Flowering Dusk*, pp. 70–1.
51 Ella Young, 'The Adventures of the Gubbaun Saor and His Son', *Dublin Magazine*, 1 (August 1923/January 1924), 41–4, 513–19.

52 Ella Young to James Starkey (1907?), O'Sullivan/Solomons Collection, MSS 4630-49/4674, TCD.
53 E. G. Davidson, 'Two Books of Wonder Tales', *The New Ireland Review*, 34:6 (1911), 370–2, at p. 372; 'Celtic Wonder Tales', *Irish Review*, 1:1 (1911), 50–1, at p. 51.
54 R. A. Gilbert, *The Golden Dawn Companion: A Guide to the History, Structure, and Workings of the Hermetic Order of the Golden Dawn* (Wellingborough: Aquarian, 1986), p. 147.
55 Maud Gonne, 'Ethlinn with Lugh', in Ella Young, *Celtic Wonder Tales* (New York: Dover, 1995); 'The High Priestess' in A. E. Waite, *The Pictorial Key to the Tarot* (New York: Samuel Weiser Inc., 1973), p. 77; Henry Summerfield, *That Myriad Minded Man: A Biography of George William Russell 'Æ', 1867–1935* (Gerrards Cross: Colin Smythe, 1975).
56 Young, *Celtic Wonder Tales*, p. 60.
57 Nancy Cardozo, *Lucky Eyes and a High Heart: The Life of Maud Gonne* (New York: The Bobbs-Merrill Company, 1978), pp. 245–6.
58 This version is from Young, *Poems*, p. 22. See also Ella Young, 'The Red Sunrise (Moraig's Song)', *Red Hand Magazine*, 1:1 (1920), 5.
59 Ella Young, *The Tangle-Coated Horse* (Edinburgh: Floris Books, 1991), p. 15.
60 Maud Gonne, *Dawn*, in Karen Steele (ed.), *Maud Gonne's Irish Nationalist Writings, 1895–1946* (Dublin: Irish Academic Press, 2004), p. 210.
61 For women's activity, see Pašeta, *Irish Nationalist Women*, pp. 128–69; Sinéad McCoole, *No Ordinary Women: Irish Female Activists in the Revolutionary Years, 1900–1923* (Dublin: The O'Brien Press, 2003); Ruth Taillon, *When History Was Made: The Women of 1916* (Belfast: Beyond the Pale Publications, 1996), pp. 14–20.
62 Young, *Flowering Dusk*, p. 116.
63 Young, *Flowering Dusk*, pp. 123–7.
64 Editorial, *Red Hand Magazine*, 1:1 (1920), 4; Young, 'The Red Sunrise (Moraig's Song)',p. 5.
65 Nell Regan, 'Helena Molony (1883–1967)', in Mary Cullen and Maria Luddy (eds), *Female Activists: Irish Women and Change, 1900–1960* (Dublin: The Woodfield Press, 2001), pp. 147, 150–1.
66 Ella Young to E. Solomons (30 January 1920), O'Sullivan/Solomons Collection, MSS 4630-49/493, TCD.
67 Lyman, 'Ella Young', p. 67.
68 Richard English, *Ernie O'Malley: IRA Intellectual* (Oxford: Clarendon Press, 1998), p. 148.
69 Richard English, 'Green on Red: Two Case Studies in Early Twentieth-Century Irish Republican Thought', in D. George Boyce, Robert Eccleshall, and Vincent Geohagen (eds), *Political Thought in Ireland since the Seventeenth Century* (London and New York: Routledge, 1993), pp. 161–89, at p. 161.
70 Ella Young to Joseph Campbell (13 June 1922), Joseph Campbell Papers, MSS 10171/1271, TCD.
71 Ella Young to S. O'Sullivan (James Starkie) (25 November 1922), O'Sullivan/Solomons Collection, MSS 4630-49/533, TCD.
72 Margaret Ward, *Hanna Sheehy Skeffington: A Life* (Cork: Attic Press, 1997), p. 262.
73 Ella Young to Nancy Campbell (5 January 1922), Joseph Campbell Papers, MSS 10171/1270, TCD.
74 Colum, *Ella Young*, p. 5.

12

Liberté, égalité, sororité: the poetics of suffrage in the work of Eva Gore-Booth and Constance Markievicz

Lauren Arrington

On 18 December 1896, men and women from Sligo town and the surrounding countryside gathered at the village of Drumcliffe to hear the Gore-Booth sisters speak about suffrage.[1] Just two days prior, Constance, twenty-eight years old and the eldest daughter of Sir Henry, landlord of the Lissadell estate, had been elected president of a new local suffrage organisation. Eva, twenty-six, was its honorable secretary, and their youngest sister, Mabel, twenty-two, served on the committee alongside other local men and women. The Gore-Booth sisters were inspired by private relationships and public reforms. Earlier the same year, when Eva was convalescing from a respiratory illness in Bordighera, Italy, she met the British suffrage campaigner Esther Roper, who would become her lifelong partner.[2] Roper's involvement in suffrage campaigns on a local level in Manchester and on a national level in England inspired Eva Gore-Booth to initiate a local branch of the Irish Women's Suffrage and Local Government Association.[3]

British and Irish suffragists believed that the United Kingdom was on the cusp of radical change. The Local Government Act of 1894 increased certain women's power in the public sphere, permitting those who met specific property qualifications to serve as Poor Law guardians. In Ireland, the Dublin Women's Suffrage Association declared the act to be a landmark in the women's movement: 'There is nothing which has happened in our time that has imparted so powerful a stimulus ... to our fellow countrywomen ... a stimulus [which] will be powerfully strengthened when in addition, they obtain the County and the Municipal.'[4] The Gore-Booth sisters seized upon this sense of promise. Their Sligo suffrage campaign was the first public political act of two women who would shape the history of twentieth-century Britain and Ireland. Constance, who married the Polish painter and playwright Casimir Markievicz in 1900, would become a leading figure in Irish republicanism and in 1918 would be the first female elected to the British Parliament. Eva would lead the fight for social reform in Britain, focusing her attention on improving the lives of working-class women including barmaids and female factory workers. Both sisters wrote poetry and plays that articulated their individual attitudes to Irish nationality and their shared battle for sexual equality.

The suffrage meeting in Drumcliffe gives a foretaste of the poetics that Constance and Eva developed over the following three decades. The meeting hall was 'packed to the doors' with an audience that consisted primarily of men – most of whom had come to object to women's right to vote. However, the suffragists had prepared to meet their opponents with the full force of a rich and subversive discourse. Alongside the Christmas evergreen that decorated the hall, they hung banners proclaiming, 'No taxation without representation' and 'Liberality, justice, and equality'.[5] These slogans from the American and French revolutions placed Irish women's suffrage on equal footing with those national movements, and – implicitly – the Irish national movement that was inspired by eighteenth-century republicanism in France and the United States. Another banner, 'Who would be free themselves must strike the blow', proclaimed a line from Byron that had been appropriated by the abolitionist Frederick Douglass in his argument that the emancipation of black slaves and Daniel O'Connell's campaign for Catholic Emancipation in Ireland were analogous.[6] Douglass was committed to universal suffrage and championed the women's rights movement in the USA. The discourses of liberty that were evoked in these slogans were expounded in Constance and Eva Gore-Booth's speeches, which demonstrate the way in which the sisters manipulated radical social and national discourses in their attempt to appeal to the various sympathies of the audience.

In her brief speech, Constance Gore-Booth used a range of rhetorical techniques. She first played to the audience's sense of nationality, declaring:

> It seems to me an extraordinary thing that this our country of Ireland which has ever been so much to the fore in the battle for liberty, should as yet be so far behind England in this joint struggle for the representation in Parliament of so large a member of its inhabitants.[7]

Her words were calculated to appeal to a spectrum of political identities: to republicans, Home Rulers, and even loyalists. She simultaneously appealed to reason, drawing from the enlightenment discourse of John Stuart Mill, who had supported Irish suffrage societies. In his landmark essay, 'The Subjection of Women', Mill had argued that the 'testimony of experience' should be the basis of any law; since men and women had never been equals in civil society, present-day inequality was based on feeling rather than fact. Constance Gore-Booth followed on from Mill's principle, glossing her logic with a wry allusion to the forthcoming celebration of Victoria's

Diamond Jubilee: 'If women are so incompetent, why has there never been [an] outcry against clerks, accountants, or our woman Queen?'[8] Her speech moved swiftly from reason to emotion, concluding on an evangelical note that mimics some of Douglass's most renowned speeches: 'Many of our ablest teachers are gone, they saw the Promised Land from the mountain top, then died like Moses in the wilderness, having had their glimpse of the land of Canaan, dim and faint in the distance.'[9]

Eva Gore-Booth's remarks received less coverage in the local press but were equally rousing. She called on 'Irishwomen to follow the example of the farmers at Drumcliffe, and to insist in spite of opposition in taking their affairs into their own hands (cheers).'[10] This may have been an allusion to the Gore-Booth family's support of Horace Plunkett's Irish Agricultural Organisation Society, which aimed to give tenant farmers a greater share of profits through cooperative enterprises such as the Drumcliffe Creamery. Yet Co. Sligo had also been a prominent battleground in the Land Wars. The founder of the Land League, Michael Davitt, had urged the tenant farmers of Sligo to withhold their rents in an act of civil disobedience. By not specifying to which 'example of the farmers' she was referring, Eva created a range of potential interpretations for her audience, depending on an individual's political allegiance.

Passive resistance was the foundation from which all of Eva's activism would proceed. By contrast, Constance's work combined staunchly rationalist arguments with emotionally charged propaganda. This rationalism has obscured the extent of Constance's feminism. Whereas Eva moved in identifiably feminist circles throughout her life, it is a widely held misconception that Constance – if she were ever a feminist at all – abandoned feminism for nationalism. However, as a discussion of the Gore-Booth sisters' writing about suffrage will demonstrate, Constance's vision of Ireland was of a state that embodied complete social equality, of the classes and the sexes, and, to her mind, the emancipation of women was implicit in the emancipation of the Irish nation.

The divergence of the sisters' politics can be credited to fundamental differences in personality as well as to the influence of the social circles in which they moved after they left Lissadell. Constance first studied at the Slade School of Art in London, where she briefly encountered Fabian socialism; her next important move was to the Académie Julian in Paris where she lived a bohemian life that was politically on the fringe but was essentially non-activist. When she returned to Dublin as Countess Markievicz in 1903, she began to move in radical nationalist networks, which she encountered through friendships forged in Dublin's avant-garde art and theatre scenes and through the radical periodical culture of Revivalist Dublin. Eva moved from Sligo to Manchester, where she lived with Roper and became a leader in the radical suffrage movement in Britain. She was a committed pacifist and therefore a suffragist *not* a suffragette. Nonetheless, Eva was an important mentor to Christabel Pankhurst, who went on to co-found the militant Women's Social and Political Union. Eva Gore-Booth became increasingly involved with sexual radicalism, co-founding in 1912 the Aëthnic Union, a society devoted to the abolition of gender distinctions. In 1913, she moved with Roper to London, where their first residence was in Bloomsbury in the same house as Roger Fry and the Omega Workshop. Prior to the outbreak of the First World War, Eva Gore-Booth's political writing focused on suffrage and trade unionism, and this was also a major theme of her poetry. The war precipitated a shift in her preoccupations; in her political writing, she focused on pacifism while her poetry grew increasingly esoteric. Constance wrote poetry occasionally, most of which is highly propagandistic in tone. Her most prolific work was her journalism for radical magazines and newspapers, in which she frequently codifies women's suffrage in Republican discourse.

The revolutionary ideals that were so prominent at the Sligo suffrage meeting are at the forefront of Eva Gore-Booth's first volume of poetry, *Poems* (1898). The quality of the selections is uneven, yet *Poems* is nonetheless important for understanding the linguistic codes and images through which Gore-Booth addressed suffrage. The French Revolution is a major trope. 'In Praise of Liberty', the second poem in the volume, uses simplistic rhyming couplets and a series of clichés to weigh the merits of love, life, and liberty against one another. The refrain asserts, 'I know that Liberty is best, / And no man sadder than a slave'.[11] Slavery recurs throughout the volume. It is implicit in 'Prayer of the Modern Greek', which introduces a rare tone of militancy as the poet beckons ancient heroes out of the Elysian fields to join 'A fight as glorious' as the epic victory at the battle of Salamis.[12] The object of the present-day battle is undisclosed, but the poet's petition, 'Let each man take his victor's crown / And fling it down [. . .] Let Liberty's course cap of red / Flame out athwart your brows instead', provides an important conceptual link to Gore-Booth's discourse on suffrage. Freedmen in Rome wore the red Phrygian cap as a symbol of their emancipation, and the cap was adopted by French Revolutionary partisans to signify liberation.[13] The cap in the poem connects the setting in antiquity with the historical moment that was for Eva Gore-Booth representative of the triumph of class and sexual equality.

The reality of the French Revolution was problematic for a dedicated pacifist. A pair of poems placed almost forty pages later indicates Gore-Booth's attempt to reconcile history with her politics. 'Song of the Fair Exile' and 'The Exile's Return' are in the voice of a French exile to Scotland who cannot repatriate for fear of being killed. The first poem is a lament for France, with very little to suggest historical specificity beyond the recurrence of the colour gold, an emphasis on the sun ('sunshine' and 'Sun-gilded'), and the image of 'golden lilies', which hint at the fleur-de-lis.[14] These images are more prominent in the second poem, 'The Exile's Return', which celebrates the end of suffering: 'Let us laugh and sing and dance / Though all flowers are dead in France: / Yet the day of death is done, / For the Children of the Sun'.[15] Gore-Booth's elision of the political dissidence that plagued the Bourbon Restoration enables her to critique revolutionary violence and present an image of a peaceful and equal society. Similarly, her short poem 'Tricolor' omits any hint of the barricades:

> In liberty of thought,
>   Equality of life,
> The generations sought
>   A rest from hate and strife.
> Hard work on common ground,
>   Strong arms and spirits free,
> In these at last they found
>   Fraternity.

By writing out the bloodshed, Gore-Booth codifies her belief that women's suffrage was a battle that should be conducted through a peaceful parliamentary campaign. Even so, the didacticism of *Poems* was objectionable to several reviewers. The *Academy* cautioned, 'Miss Gore-Booth has a trick of pulpiteering, which should be checked'; W. B. Yeats agreed, advising her to 'avoid every touch of rhetoric every tendency to teach'.[16]

One way of avoiding didacticism was to turn to more flexible scenarios than the historical tropes and female icons, such as Joan of Arc and the biblical Eve, which have a heavy presence in *Poems*. The Revival's focus on retelling, or inventing, myth and legend offered an ideal cast of characters which Gore-Booth could adapt to her purposes. The Gore-Booth family's introduction to Irish mythology seems to have been through W. B. Yeats, who visited Lissadell in December 1894 on one of his folklore-collecting expeditions.[17] However, Yeats was not a singular influence. George Russell (Æ) took note of *Poems* and invited Gore-Booth to contribute to the *Irish Homestead* and to his edition *New Songs: A Lyric Selection made by Æ* (1904). The volume includes poets who would become some of the most notable voices of the Revival, including Padraic Colum, Alice Milligan, Susan Mitchell, Seamus O'Sullivan, and Ella Young. Among them, Eva Gore-Booth was the only poet to have previously published a volume of poems.[18] In *New Songs*, Gore-Booth's work is distinctively feminist. In Susan Mitchell's 'The Living Chalice', 'the mother' is merely a conduit for the 'Master of Life', whereas Gore-Booth's 'The Revolt Against Art' has a female deity: 'the earth bends to her dream'.[19]

Gore-Booth's one-act play *Unseen Kings*, also published in 1904, builds upon Revivalist themes. The plot is almost certainly based on Lady Gregory's *Cuchulain of Muirthemne* (1902). In Cathy Leeney's study, *Irish Women Playwrights*, she notes Gregory and Gore-Booth's common construction of a spatial binary in their texts: 'an inner, protected space where Cuculain is encircled by women, poets, music, and feasting' and the external space where violence threatens the interior sanctum.[20] Gore-Booth's drama also differs in important ways. *Unseen Kings* is ostensibly about Cúchulainn, but the agency in the play is given to the two female characters: Niamh, a prophetess who has the power to control Cúchulainn's actions, and the Stranger who enchants Niamh and returns in her guise to send Cúchulainn out to battle where he is killed. In *Cuchulain of Muirthemne*, Niamh is not a mystic and is simply the hero's lover, but in *Unseen Kings*, Niamh's pacifism is not driven by a romantic desire to protect Cúchulainn's life but by an esoteric vision: she believes that the world is an illusion that cannot be penetrated by violence.[21]

Niamh in *Unseen Kings* stands as an important counterpoint to Queen Maeve, whose tomb, according to legend, crests Knocknarea, the mountain that presides over the Lissadell estate. Eva Gore-Booth would later invent another history for the warrior queen, but in the poems that follow the play in *Unseen Kings*, she seeks simply to establish Maeve's neglect. In 'A Hermit's Lament for Maeve', she is described as lying in a 'lonely grave' of 'gray stones', compared to the 'earth-encrusted gold' of the High King's dun.[22] 'To Maeve' focuses on the slander of Maeve's reputation after her death, which Gore-Booth suggests was driven by jealousy.[23]

One of the most important poems in the volume is 'Lament of the Daughters of Ireland'. It begins with an epigraph from Sophocles' *Electra*: Orestes' reminder to his sister, 'in women, too dwells the Spirit of Battle'.[24] Importantly, this was not a literal call to combat; Gore-Booth's representation of violence here is as nuanced as in *Poems*. While 'Lament of the Daughters of Ireland' proclaims the daughters' origins in violence, this violence is located in the ancient past, not modernity.[25] This is reinforced by the poem's footnote referring readers to Douglas Hyde's *A Literary History of Ireland from Earliest Times to the Present Day*. Gore-Booth cites Hyde's discussion of the Council of Drumceat of the year 590 at which, he notes, 'women were exempted from military service'.[26] The episode is indexed in Hyde's book as 'women … tardily exempted from service', but for Eva Gore-Booth, Irish women's role in combat was evidence of their social and legal equality with men in ancient Ireland. Gore-Booth is not calling for a renewal of violence but for a restoration of the equality that she believed characterised antiquity.

In Gore-Booth's play *The Triumph of Maeve: A Romance*, published in 1905, Maeve, the High Queen of Connaught, is explicitly pacifist. All of the principal parts are female apart from Nera, a harpist in Maeve's court, and Fergus, the Chief of the Ultonian exiles. Both of these characters are portrayed negatively. Fergus protests, 'I would not obey a woman', and Nera bewitches Maeve, forcing her to 'storm the city of the magic fire'.[27] In both plays, Gore-Booth's drama is not simply feminist in its recasting of female characters in the lead. Rather, she rewrites the very nature of the heroic in order to reinforce her pacifist convictions. Acts of violence are the result of sinister interference, not heroism, and the heroic character is reimagined as a strong leader who holds the affections of the people but who refrains from conflict.

Gore-Booth returns to didacticism in the *Egyptian Pillar* (1907), but her polemic is tempered by greater poetic skill.[28] The titular image is taken from the poem 'Women's Trades on the Embankment', which is set at the Egyptian obelisk that stands on London's Victoria Embankment. The suffragist theme is emphasised in the poem's dedication to Constance, in memory of 'some dreams we hold in common'. Furthermore, the epigraph – ' "Have Patience!" – The Prime Minister to the Franchise Deputation, May 19th, 1906' – refers directly to Gore-Booth's activism and is a stark contrast to the codifications of her other suffrage poetry. 'Women's Trades' opens with London's 'sad-eyed workers' passing by the obelisk, an object that creates a temporal fulcrum between the contemporary oppression of the working-class and the slavery of the ancient Israelites. The analogy is sustained throughout the poem, with the last stanza referring back to the epigraph: 'Long has submission played a traitor's part— / Oh human soul, no patience any more / Shall break your wings and harden Pharaoh's heart, / And keep you lingering on the Red Sea shore'.

Egyptian imagery is important to Gore-Booth's poetry for several reasons. While the slavery of the Israelites was a common trope in abolitionism as well as in the women's suffrage movement, Egyptian texts were also taken as the foundation of the modern theosophical movement. In 1877, the founder of the Theosophical Society, Helena Petrovna Blavatsky, published her influential book *Isis Unveiled*, which claimed to be, as Matthew Beaumont summarises, 'a vast repository of all those ancient occultist insights inaccessible to contemporary, positivistic science'.[29] Beaumont's essay discusses the elective affinity between socialism and occultism at the *fin de siècle*; similarly, occultism was closely tied to the women's suffrage movement. One of the tenets of theosophy was the belief in the duality of humanity: the presence of 'masculine and feminine principles at the cosmic level'.[30] In Joy Dixon's *Divine Feminism*, she explains that the emphasis was not on sexual difference but on sexual equality: 'men and women were so different precisely because, in essence, they were only different aspects of the same thing'.[31]

In 1907, the year that the *Egyptian Pillar* was published, the Irish suffragist and theosophist Charlotte Despard published 'The Case for Women's Suffrage'. Despard's essay opened with the subject of 'the "great woman principle" in ancient cosmogonies', including 'the mysterious Isis of Egypt'.[32] Although Gore-Booth did not formally join the Theosophical Society until 1919, theosophical ideas are present in her writing more than a decade earlier. *The Sorrowful Princess*, also published in 1907, is set in 'a wood in Egypt before the shrine of Isis'.[33] The theosophical idea of the duality of humanity is suggested by the stage directions, with Isis' shrine on one side of the stage and a 'tree Sacred to Osiris' on the other.[34]

In Egyptian mythology, Isis is the goddess of the natural world as well as the goddess of magic. Here, Gore-Booth's interests in esoteric religion, Irish mythology, and women's suffrage coalesce. 'Women's Rights' which follows 'Women's Trades' in the *Egyptian Pillar*, is set by Glencar waterfall on the border of counties Sligo and Leitrim. The poem equates the natural world with springtime, peace, the spiritual, and the feminine, in contrast to a male, industrial, urban environment: 'where men in office sit / Winter holds the human wit [. . .] Frozen, frozen everywhere / Are the springs of thought and prayer'.[35] The poem evokes the early poetry of W. B. Yeats, particularly 'The Stolen Child' from *Crossways* (1889) and the opening line of 'The Lake Isle of Innisfree' from *The Rose* (1893).[36] However, by creating a gendered contrast between the natural world and the material world, Gore-Booth transmutes the anti-materialist impulse characteristic of Irish Revivalist writing into a poetics of suffrage: 'Men have got their pomp and pride— / All the green world is on our side'.[37]

In three of the poems that follow 'Women's Rights' in the *Egyptian Pillar*, the masculine and feminine binary is complicated by the gender-neutral term 'comrade'. The poem 'Comrades' begins with a sympathetic image of 'Men who are born to die whose dreams are soiled by the dust', but the poet asserts that while truth and justice may be the shared pursuit of some men and women, 'only the gods in heaven are true enough to be just'.[38] The word 'comrades' is used to similar effect in 'The Visionary', where fellowship, 'a dream of comrades', is the preserve of the other world. These poems mark a transition from poetry that is directly engaged with the fight for women's suffrage to an esoteric verse that challenges the very notions of gender. 'The Anti-suffragist' in *The Agate Lamp* is an exception in which the overtly political impulse lingers. Even here Eva Gore-Booth maintains a mythical artifice. The subject of the poem is a princess who is held prisoner in a tower without any contact with the natural world: 'They brought her forth at last when she was old; / The sunlight on her blanchèd hair was shed / too late to turn its silver into gold'.[39] For Gore-Booth, sexual equality is the natural and spiritual state of humanity.

Eva worked towards abstraction, but Constance became a consummate propagandist. She adopted popular forms and later in her career even used gender stereotypes in order to achieve her desired effect. The most extreme examples of this are her plays and cartoons from the Irish Civil War that depict Irishwomen as wives and mothers who sacrifice their husbands and sons for the nation. Yet Markievicz's earlier work hints at the intricate relationship between nationalism, socialism, and feminism which is obscured by her later choice of form. In 1908, Markievicz travelled to Manchester and London to participate in large-scale suffrage rallies organised by Eva and Esther Roper. She was given a prominent place on the platform; at one rally in Trafalgar Square where she and Eva both spoke, the *Irish Times* presciently reported that 'as in most other political agitations, the voice of Ireland was not silent'.[40] The friendships that Markievicz formed in Dublin's theatres and salons combined with her suffrage work in Sligo, Manchester, and London to effect a new political commitment: to an Irish republic in which men and women of all classes would enjoy the same liberty.

The issue of women's suffrage divided Irish nationalists. The Irish Women's Franchise League, founded in November 1908, was open to women of any political persuasion. Both Arthur Griffith, founder and President of Sinn Féin, and Maud Gonne, founder of Inghinidhe na hÉireann (the Daughters of Ireland), supported the league and stated unequivocally that suffrage was not a party question.[41] Markievicz vehemently disagreed. She argued in *Sinn Féin*:

> Let Irishwomen who are not admitted to the rights of British citizens rather glory in the fact and organise over here and join with those men who believe in Liberty in making Ireland ungovernable; let them fan the flame of Rebellion and Revolution, helping to intensify the aspirations of the whole people in the councils of their nation, that England daily more harassed and perplexed through the effects of her iniquitous foreign policy, towards free nations and towards nations subjected by her, will have to capitulate and accede to their demands.[42]

Markievicz alluded to the most famous quotation from the life of Wolfe Tone, the founder of Irish republicanism and leader of the 1798 Rising whose goal was 'To unite the whole people of Ireland'.[43] After his death in the rising, Tone fell into obscurity, but his legacy was resurrected by the poets of Young Ireland who found in the United Irishmen a model for Protestant nationalism.[44] Tone played a similar role for Markievicz, but for her he did not simply signify the leadership of the Anglo-Irish and cooperation across sectarian lines; she fully espoused Tone's vision of a republic. Markievicz adapts his republican discourse to encode Irishwomen's suffrage in eighteenth-century political thought.

The Rising of 1798 is the subject of Constance and Casimir Markievicz's first major success for the Dublin theatres: *The Memory of the Dead* (1910). It was not the first of their collaborations to have a strong female role. *The Dilettante*, staged in 1908, has a feminist plot: an aristocratic widow (Constance Markievicz) and the daughter of the family's steward (Máire nic Shuibhlaigh) turn against the poet and cad Archibald Longhurst (J. M. Carré) who has been playing them both. At its core, *The Dilettante* is a society farce in which the female characters bridge class divides in order to overthrow the patriarchal figure, but the sexual politics of the play are diffused by other less defined ideas such as the question of the value of art over life. The *Irish Independent* recognised an Ibsenite tendency in the play but criticised, 'In thesis-drama, it is a serious blemish to have no revelation of the thesis.'[45] The *Memory of the Dead* is far more accomplished, but even here one thesis – national liberation – obscures the concomitant idea of female emancipation.

The Memory of the Dead opens with Colonel Charort (J. M. Carré) arriving at the Doyle family's cottage to request a guide to Donegal, where he will meet Napper Tandy, an actual historical figure who facilitated collaboration with the French in the 1798 Rising. All of the able-bodied young men have already left the village to join the uprising, so Norah Doyle (Constance Markievicz) disguises herself in male clothing and offers to assist him. The radical potential of this transvestitism is offset by Norah's assumption of conventional gender roles during the course of the action. When she and Charort meet a wounded soldier, Norah's former suitor James McGowan, Norah stays behind to nurse him. Similarly, the conclusion of the play follows gender norms. Norah's husband, Dermod O'Dowd, is killed; she throws herself between his body and the British Army officer and declares: 'My husband, you have not died in vain … I swear that I will bring up your child to take your place, to live as you lived, to die as you died – a hero for our country!'[46] Importantly, Norah's revenge is not through militancy but through raising their child to follow his father's example. This may seem like a mixed message, but, in fact, it suggests that Norah is free to take on a conventionally male role and to function in society as a wife and mother. The feminist aspect of the plot was undermined by the play's setting in such an iconic historical event, which had been reinvigorated in the public imagination by the centenary commemorations just a decade before. It is unsurprising perhaps that the reception of the play focused exclusively on it as a nationalist melodrama.[47]

The Markieviczes may have also deliberately disclosed the gender politics of the play. Constance Markievicz was keenly aware that her support for suffrage was oppositional to the majority view of the Sinn Féin party. In February 1909, an anonymous article in the party organ asserted that there was no time to waste 'suffragetting': 'If we must contend let it be in seeing who'll be the most Irish.'[48] Markievicz published a rejoinder in the *Irish Nation* in which she conceded that a woman who lived by the national ideal 'will know that for Ireland's sake she must make her home life beautiful and ideal too'.[49] In a lecture to a Dublin branch of Sinn Féin, she made her views clearer: while there was a great deal of national work to be carried out in the home, 'she would rather see women working for the nation as comrades with men, each according to her own abilities and power'.[50] In light of her prominent statements on suffrage in *Bean na hÉireann* and the *Irish Nation*, when the National Literary Society invited Markievicz to speak in spring 1909, the audience expected that she would address suffrage overtly. Instead, she negotiated the tension between women's suffrage and the national question by again drawing from an Irish republican discourse of liberty.

Markievicz's speech was published in instalments as 'Irishwomen's Duty at the Present Time' and then by the Daughters of Ireland as the pamphlet, *Women, Ideals and the Nation*.[51] She situated Ireland in a broader imperial context alongside India, Egypt, and South Africa, but the greater part of her argument was dedicated to a discussion of Russia and Poland:

> In Ireland the women seem to have taken less part in public life, and to have had less share in the struggle for liberty, than in other nations. In Russia, amongst the people who are working to overthrow the tyrannical and unjust government of the Czar and his officials, and in Poland where, to be a nationalist, men and women must take their lives in their hands, women work as comrades, shoulder to shoulder with their men.[52]

Her anti-imperialist argument then took a surprising turn:

> Catholicism is an integral part of a Pole's nationality, the Orthodox religion an integral part of a Russian's, for all Poles are Catholic, all Russians Orthodox – and a Pole of the Orthodox religion would even now be regarded with suspicion in Poland and could not possibly enter any Polish National Movement; while a Russian who was a Catholic would find it difficult even to live in his country.[53]

Markievicz would convert to Catholicism in 1916, but in 1909 she did not believe that either Protestantism or atheism were incompatible with Irish nationalism, as the importance of 1798 to her political thought shows. Rather, religion serves to codify her suffrage politics in a discourse that is less polarising for her audience. She argues that suffrage and nationalism, like the Polish national identity and Catholicism, go hand in hand.

The allusion was clear to her audience; in the questions afterward, a representative of the Irish Women's Franchise League rose in objection, demanding that the vote was the most important political weapon and should be prioritised.

The Home Rule Bill brought the Daughters of Ireland and the Irish Women's Franchise League in alliance, along with other national women's organisations including the Irish Suffrage Federation and the Irish Women Workers' Union. The societies held a coalition meeting on 1 June 1912 to demand the emancipation of women in the Home Rule Bill.[54] In what appears to be a volte-face, Markievicz supported the coalition, but her support seems to have been a delicate political manoeuvre. Like Eva, Constance's suffrage politics were intertwined with a socialist commitment. By 1912, Markievicz endorsed James Connolly as leader of the Irish labour left and publicly espoused the socialism that he advocated. Connolly sent a message to the suffrage coalition in which he stated his opposition to Home Rule in principle, while allowing that 'A Home Rule Bill that excluded half of the people of Ireland from the franchise would be an anomaly in this age of progress and would be a poor recompense to the women of Ireland for all they have done and suffered in the past for the freedom of Ireland.'[55] Connolly and Markievicz were both aware that the Irish Parliamentary Party would never concede to the enfranchisement of women in the Home Rule Bill. By advocating the inclusion of suffrage in Irish Home Rule, they were implicitly discrediting any Bill that did not include suffrage. Therefore, Connolly and Markievicz's support of the suffrage coalition can be seen as part of their campaign to unite competing factions in the common cause of independence, as will be seen from the alliance of the Irish Citizen Army and the Irish Volunteers discussed further below. In the end, the failure of Home Rule to address the concerns of both suffragists and the labour left contributed to the radicalisation of Irish nationalism and the rise of militant separatism.

During this period of rapid widespread radicalisation, suffrage ostensibly disappears from Markievicz's writing. Yet, in fact, it becomes more deeply encoded. Key to recovering Markievicz's attitude to suffrage is her belief about the social construction of gender, which is very similar to Eva's idea of the dual nature of humanity. In her speech 'The Future of Irishwomen', delivered to the Irish Women's Franchise League in October 1915 and printed in the *Irish Citizen*, Markievicz argued that the Catholic and Protestant churches 'foster the tradition of the segregation of the sexes', and she stated, 'It would be well to aim at bringing out, as it were, the masculine side of women's souls as well as the feminine side of men's souls.'[56] In the same speech, she referred to the Council of Drumceat. Markievicz proclaimed that 'Ancient Ireland bred warrior women, and women played a heroic part in those days. To-day we are in danger of being civilised by men out of existence.'[57] She asserted that the women in the labour movement and the suffragists embodied the ancient ideal. Auxiliary committees merely 'demoralise women, set them up in separate camps, and deprive them of all initiative and independence'.[58] Women must reject the notion that 'woman is merely sex and an excuse for a drink':

> Don't trust to your 'feminine charm' and your capacity for getting on the soft side of men, but take up your responsibilities and be prepared to go your own way depending for safety on your own courage, your own truth, and your own common sense, and not on the problematic chivalry of the men you may meet on the way.[59]

This is very similar to the ideas in Eva Gore-Booth's 'Comrades'.

Just as 'comrade' appears in Eva Gore-Booth's poetry as a substitute for gendered pronouns, it arises in Markievicz's propaganda. 'To the Citizen Army', published in the *Workers' Republic* in June 1915, is doggerel but is nonetheless enlightening for the way that it creates a collage of images that bring together facets of Markievicz's political thought. Although she uses the gendered cliché, 'keep your powder dry, my boys', this phrase is followed in the next stanza by, 'When comrade by comrade we stand on the day'.[60] The poem was published under the pseudonym 'Maca', the same name under which Markievicz published pro-suffrage essays in *Bean na hÉireann* and *The Irish Nation and the Irish Peasant*. The female authorship signified by the pseudonym changes the tone of a poem that would otherwise be read as masculine and hints at Markievicz's vision of men and women fighting together as comrades against the British Empire.

Similarly, 'The Call', published under Markievicz's own name in the *Workers' Republic* the week prior to the Easter Rising, is addressed to 'men of the Gael' and 'men of Irish blood', but the last stanza uses the collective pronoun 'we': 'We answer the call with a ringing cheer / With bayonets fixed we stand'.[61] Again, the female authorship is essential to reading the poem. Furthermore, the bayonets in the poem explicitly link the 1798 Rising with the Easter Rising that is about to unfold. This is more than simple use of a popular image. It evokes a historical event that is foundational to Markievicz's political thought and is essential to her vision for the role of women in the imagined republic.

Markievicz wrote prolifically for the *Irish Citizen* in 1915. One of her series of essays was 'The Women of '98' in which she writes short biographies of women from the whole of Ireland who took an active role in the Rebellion. The series emphasised the unity of social classes in the national struggle with lengthy anecdotes of well-educated women and the daughters of peasants fighting alongside the men. In her story of the peasant woman

Mary Doyle, who supplied cartridges to the rebels at the battle of New Ross, Markievicz imagines Doyle saying 'Boys, I will stay behind, no matter what happens to me, unless you take my dear little gun too.'[62] This essay informs Markievicz's use of 'boys' in 'To the Citizen Army' and the ostensibly male subjects of 'The Call'. She is not excluding women from the national struggle, nor is she privileging the national over the feminist. Helena Molony, Markievicz's friend and comrade in the Irish Citizen Army, believed that the ICA 'promoted an "idea of freedom [that] was the widest of its kind, the abolition of domination of nation over nation, class over class, sex over sex".'[63] Her emphasis reinforces this reading of Markievicz's codification of sexual equality in these poems.

Whereas Eva drew parallels between women from classical antiquity and the Irish past, Constance suggested that the stories of female combatants in ancient Ireland were exceptional. She manipulates suffragist icons in order to conjoin nationalist and feminist discourse, principally the figure of Joan of Arc. Molly Weston, who fought in the Rising, is described as

> Mounted on a spirited grey pony, dressed in green habit, and with the United Irishmen's cockade in her hat, she galloped up to the insurgents, and at once joined in the battle. There being no capable leader among the rebels, the girl, a farmer's daughter, placed herself at their head, and, with no weapon but a riding whip, led the patriots to the charge, not seeming to mind any danger, provided that she could rally the insurgents each time they were driven back, and lead them to the charge again and again.[64]

Markievicz allowed that it was not necessary for all women to become militants, but the tonality of her essays privileged the women who took up arms or who sacrificed their life in the struggle.[65]

Throughout 'The Women of '98', Markievicz argued that the 'rebel ranks' respected women and offered them greater opportunities than the British Army. This was another implicit argument that a free Ireland would offer female liberty while an Ireland joined to the Empire would lead to further oppression. There is a similar anti-imperialist argument at work in her series, 'Experience of a Woman Patrol', which ran simultaneously to 'The Women of '98'. In 'Woman Patrol', Markievicz modelled an active role for women in the public sphere, including the responsibility for policing, since, she implied, the Dublin Metropolitan Police did not act in the benefit of Irish society. She describes walking a 'beat' around the north city centre, where she saw the effects of Dublin's extreme poverty: drunkenness, vagrancy, and prostitution. She encourages her readers to reject the imperial war work that was now available to them and instead turn their attentions to the 'open sore' in their own city.[66] Just as the First World War was facilitating Irish separatism, Markievicz also believed that the war was 'shaking women out of old grooves and forcing responsibilities on them'.[67] Her articles for the *Irish Citizen* are agitation-propaganda pieces, aimed at preparing Irish women for positions of leadership in the new Ireland that she imagined would liberate all classes and sexes. She demands, 'We have got to get rid of the last vestige of the Harem before woman is [as] free as our dream of the future would have her.'[68]

Markievicz thought that the Proclamation of the Republic declared at Easter 1916 was a fulfilment of the ambitions of the United Irishmen in 1798. This commitment to the Proclamation was the basis for her intransigent republicanism and the cause of her bitter disillusionment during the Irish Civil War and in its aftermath. In March 1922, Cumann na mBan member and anti-Treaty Sinn Féin TD (*teachta dála*, member of parliament) Kathleen O'Callaghan addressed the vote on women's franchise in which she declared, 'The brave men who put their names to the proclamation of the Irish Republic in Easter Week wanted to put the men and women on the same footing in the voting register.'[69] She proposed a Bill that would admit women to the parliamentary franchise on the same basis as Irish men. Markievicz rose in support:

> My first realization of tyranny came from some chance words spoken in favour of women's suffrage and it raised a question of the tyranny it was intended to prevent women voicing their opinions publicly in the ordinary and simple manner of registering their vote at the polling booth. This was my first bite, you may say, at the apple of freedom and soon I got on to the other freedoms, freedom to the nation, freedom to the workers ... I have a vote myself now to send men and women to the Dáil, and I wish to have that privilege extended to the young women of Ireland, whom I count in every way as my superiors ... Today, I would appeal here to the men of the IRA more than to any of the other men to see that justice is done to these young women and young girls who took a man's part in the Terror.[70]

Not only does Markievicz state unequivocally that the origins of her anti-imperialist politics were in the women's suffrage movement, she also repeats the phrase 'the Terror' in which she equates the 1916 Easter Rising with the French Revolution.

In an article for *Bean na hÉireann*, again written under the pseudonym 'Maca', Markievicz described Irish women as being 'double enslaved, and with a double battle to fight'.[71] This discourse of enslavement is part of a wider discourse of suffrage, from which Constance Markievicz and Eva Gore-Booth both drew. Similarly, both sisters looked to republican discourse for a language in which to address suffrage: the language of Revolutionary France and of the United Irishmen Rebellion of 1798. The sisters also addressed gender similarly; while Eva Gore-Booth's theosophical pursuits led her to the dual nature of humanity, Constance Markievicz's writing reflects a belief in the flexibility of gender, epitomised in her ambition to cultivate the 'masculine side of women's souls' and the 'feminine side of men's souls'.[72] These principles are essential to understanding the way in which both sisters develop a poetics of suffrage that complements their political activism.

Notes

1 'Women's Suffrage', *Sligo Champion* (19 December 1896), p. 8.
2 Sonja Tiernan, *Eva Gore-Booth: An Image of Such Politics* (Manchester: Manchester University Press, 2012), pp. 28–44.
3 The Irish Women's Suffrage and Local Government Association was founded in 1876; see Carmel Quinlan, *Genteel Revolutionaries: Anna and Thomas Haslam and the Irish Women's Movement* (Cork: Cork University Press, 2002).
4 Rosemary Cullen Owens, *A Social History of Women in Ireland, 1870–1970* (Dublin: Gill & Macmillan, 2005), p. 13.
5 'Women's Suffrage', *Sligo Champion* (19 December 1896), p. 8.
6 Frederick Douglass, 'Men of Color, to Arms!', *Broadside* (Rochester) (21 March 1863).
7 'Women's Suffrage', *Sligo Champion* (19 December 1896), p. 8.
8 Sophia A. van Wingerden, *The Women's Suffrage Movement in Britain* (Basingstoke: Palgrave Macmillan, 1999), p. 69.
9 Frederick Douglass, 'What to the Slave Is the Fourth of July?' in Philip S. Foner (ed.), *Frederick Douglass: Selected Speeches and Writings* (Chicago, Ill.: Lawrence Hill, 1999), pp. 188–206.
10 'Woman's Suffrage Movement', *Sligo Champion* (26 December 1896), p. 8.
11 Eva Gore-Booth, 'In Praise of Liberty', in *Poems* (London: Longmans, Green & Co, 1898), pp. 4–5.
12 Gore-Booth, 'Prayer of the Modern Greek', in *Poems*, pp. 9–10.
13 Jennifer Harris, 'The Red Cap of Liberty: A Study of Dress Worn by French Revolutionary Partisans, 1789–94', *Eighteenth-Century Studies*, 14:3 (1981), 283–312.
14 Gore-Booth, 'Song of the Fair Exile', in *Poems*, pp. 52–4.
15 Gore-Booth, 'The Exile's Return', in *Poems*, pp. 55–7.
16 Tiernan, *Eva Gore-Booth*, p. 51.
17 W. B. Yeats to Susan Mary Yeats (16 December 1894), in *The Collected Letters of W. B. Yeats*, vol. I: *1865–1895*, ed. John Kelly and Eric Domville (Oxford: Clarendon Press, 1986), p. 418.
18 David Gardiner (ed.), *The Maunsel Poets, 1905–1926* (Bethesda, Md.: Academica, 2003), p. 4.
19 Susan Mitchell, 'The Living Chalice', and Eva Gore-Booth, 'The Revolt Against Art' in George Russell (ed.), *New Songs: A Lyric Selection Made by Æ* (Dublin and London: O'Donoghue & Co. and A. H. Bullen, 1904), pp. 25 and 23 respectively.
20 Cathy Leeney, *Irish Women Playwrights, 1900–1939: Gender and Violence on Stage* (Oxford: Peter Lang, 2010), pp. 71–2. Gore-Booth uses the spelling Cuculain in *Unseen Kings*, while Gregory spells it Cuchulain in *Cuchulain of Muirthemne*.
21 Eva Gore-Booth, *Unseen Kings: A Play in One Act and in Verse with Other Poems* (London: Longmans & Co., 1904), p. 20. Casimir Markievicz's Independent Theatre Company produced *Unseen Kings* in 1912, and Constance Markievicz played the part of the Stranger.
22 Gore-Booth, 'A Hermit's Lament for Maeve', in *Unseen Kings*, pp. 57–9.

23 Gore-Booth, 'To Maeve', in *Unseen Kings*, pp. 60–2.
24 Sophocles, *The Electra*, ed. R. C. Jebb (London: Rivingtons, 1867).
25 Gore-Booth, 'Lament of the Daughters of Ireland', in *Unseen Kings*, p. 68.
26 Douglas Hyde, *A Literary History of Ireland: From Earliest Times to the Present Day* (New York: Charles Scribner's Sons, 1901), p. 234.
27 Eva Gore-Booth, *The Triumph of Maeve: A Romance*, in *The Three Resurrections and the Triumph of Maeve* (London: Longmans, 1905), pp. 142, 145.
28 Eva Gore-Booth, *The Egyptian Pillar* (Dublin: Tower Press, 1907).
29 Matthew Beaumont, 'Socialism and Occultism at the *Fin de Siècle*: Elective Affinities', *Victorian Review*, 36:1 (2010), 217–32, at p. 221.
30 Beaumont, 'Socialism and Occultism', p. 221.
31 Joy Dixon, *Divine Feminism: Theosophy and Feminism in England* (Baltimore, Md.: Johns Hopkins University Press, 2001), p. 182.
32 Dixon, *Divine Feminism*, p. 186.
33 Eva Gore-Booth, *The Sorrowful Princess* (London: Longmans, Green, & Co., 1907), p. 11.
34 Gore-Booth, *The Sorrowful Princess*, p. 11.
35 Gore-Booth, 'Women's Rights', in *The Egyptian Pillar*, pp. 29–30, 29.
36 W. B. Yeats, 'The Stolen Child', in *The Poems*, ed. Daniel Albright (London: Everyman, 1994), p. 44; and 'The Lake Isle of Inisfree', p. 60.
37 Gore-Booth, 'Women's Rights', in *The Egyptian Pillar*, p. 30.
38 Gore-Booth, 'Comrades', in *The Egyptian Pillar*, pp. 32–3, at p. 32.
39 Eva Gore-Booth, 'The Anti-Suffragist', in *The Agate Lamp* (London: Longmans, Green, & Co., 1912), p. 93.
40 'Lancashire Suffragists', *Manchester Guardian* (15 June 1908), p. 8; and 'London Correspondence', *Irish Times* (15 June 1908), p. 6.
41 'M.G.', 'Sinn Féin and the Suffragettes', *Irish Nation and the Peasant* (30 January 1909), p. 8.
42 'Irishwomen and the Suffrage', *Sinn Féin* (27 March 1909), p. 4.
43 Wolfe Tone, quoted in James Quinn, 'Theobald Wolfe Tone and the Historians', *Irish Historical Studies*, 32:125 (2000), 113–23, at p. 121.
44 See Quinn, 'Theobald Wolfe Tone and the Historians', p. 114.
45 J. H. Cox, 'Two New Plays', *Irish Independent* (4 December 1908), p. 4.
46 *The Memory of the Dead* (Dublin, 1910), Act III, p. 10.
47 'A Drama of '98', *Irish Independent* (15 April 1910), p. 6.
48 'Irishwomen's Duties', *Sinn Féin* (27 December 1909), p. 4.
49 Maca, 'Irish Women's Duty: A Rejoinder', *Irish Nation and the Irish Peasant* (15 May 1909), p. 5.
50 'Irishwomen in the Nation: Lecture by Countess Markievicz in Drumcondra', *Irish Nation and the Irish Peasant* (27 May 1909), p. 7.
51 Constance de Markievicz, *Women, Ideals and the Nation: A Lecture Delivered to the Students' National Literary Society, Dublin* (Dublin: Inghinidhe na hÉireann, 1909).
52 Markievicz, *Women, Ideals, and the Nation*, p. 6.
53 Markievicz, *Women, Ideals, and the Nation*, p. 6.
54 'Tonight's Mass Meeting', *Irish Citizen* (1 June 1912), p. 12.
55 'The Recent Mass Meeting', *Irish Citizen* (15 June 1912), p. 29.
56 Constance Markievicz, 'The Future of Irishwomen', *Irish Citizen* (23 October 1915), p. 137.
57 Markievicz, 'The Future of Irishwomen', p. 137.
58 Markievicz, 'The Future of Irishwomen', p. 137.
59 Markievicz, 'The Future of Irishwomen', p. 137.
60 'To the Citizen Army', *Workers' Republic* (26 June 1915), p. 1.
61 C. de Markievicz, 'The Call', *Workers' Republic* (15 April 1916), p. 8.
62 'Women of Ninety-Eight', *Irish Citizen* (13 November 1915), p. 161.
63 Molony also represents Connolly as unbound by gender norms: 'Connolly was a good suffragist himself you know and he was very keen on absolute equality between men

and women. If a girl could handle a gun, she was given a gun. If a man could cook a meal, he was not made to feel in anyway degraded by it.' See Helena Molony, 'Women of the Rising', Raidio Telefís Éireann radio interview, 16 April 1963, RTÉ Sound Archive, Dublin. Quoted in Karen Steele, 'When Female Activists Say "I": Veiled Rebels and the Counterhistory of Irish Independence', in Gillian McIntosh and Diane Urquhart (eds), *Irish Women at War: The Twentieth-Century* (Dublin: Irish Academic Press, 2010), p. 55.

64 McIntosh and Urquhart, *Irish Women at War.*

65 Constance de Marcievicz [*sic*], 'The Women of '98', *Irish Citizen* (6 November 1915), pp. 150–1; see also 13 November 1915, p. 161; 20 November 1915, pp. 168–9; 27 November 1915, pp. 77–8; 4 December 1915, p. 183.

66 C. M., 'Experience of a Woman Patrol: Part II', *Irish Citizen* (23 October 1915), p. 137; see also 9 October 1915, p. 122.

67 Markievicz, 'Experience of a Woman Patrol: Part II', p. 137.

68 Markievicz, 'The Future of Irishwomen', p. 137.

69 'Irishwomen and the Franchise', Dáil Éireann, vol. II (2 March 1922). See http://historical-debates.oireachtas.ie/D/DT/D.S.192203020023.html. Accessed 3 November 2014.

70 'Irishwomen and the Franchise'.

71 Maca, 'To Miss Nora Cassidy and the Young Girls of Ireland', *Bean na hÉireann* (July 1909), p. 14.

72 Markievicz, 'The Future of Irishwomen', p. 137.

Bibliography

ARCHIVES

Coffey and Chenevix Trench Papers, National Library of Ireland, Dublin
Crown Office Papers, National Archives, Dublin
Ella Young Papers, microfilm copies of manuscripts held by the Department of Special Collections, University of California Los Angeles Library
Erskine Childers Papers, Trinity College Dublin
Joseph Campbell Papers, Trinity College Dublin
Joseph McGarrity Papers, National Library of Ireland, Dublin
Lady Gregory Collection of Papers, The Berg Collection of English and American Literature, The New York Public Library, New York City
Matthew Russell Papers, SJ, Jesuit Archive, Dublin
Murray Papers, Mitchell Library, Sydney
O'Sullivan/Solomons Collection, Trinity College Dublin
Selected Papers of Mary Chavelita Bright, Department of Rare Books and Special Collections, Princeton University
Somerville and Ross Papers, Special Collections, Queen's University Belfast
Young Papers, The Huntington Library, California

ELECTRONIC DATABASES

Australian Dictionary of Biography, National Centre of Biography, Australian National University. Available at http://adb.anu.edu.au/biography.
Irish Census Records, The National Archives of Ireland, www.census.nationalarchives.ie
Marriage Registration Records, Registrar's District of Belfast; Public Records Office, Northern Ireland, http://applications.proni.gov.uk/UlsterCovenant/SearchResults.aspx
Oxford Dictionary of National Biography http://www.oxforddnb.com

NEWSPAPERS AND PERIODICALS

Academy and Literature Fiction Supplement
All Ireland Review

Atalanta
Athenaeum
Cornhill Magazine
Dublin Magazine
Entomologist's Monthly Magazine
Fraser's Magazine
Freeman's Journal
Gael
The Gentleman's Magazine
Girl's Realm
Hearth and Home
Horn Magazine: Books and Reading for Young People
Illustrated London News
Irish Citizen
Irish Cyclist
Irish Independent
Irish Nation and Peasant
Irish Review
Ladies' Realm
The Leader
The Leisure Hour: An Illustrated Magazine for Home Reading
London Standard
Manchester Courier and Lancashire General Advertiser
Manchester Guardian
Morning Post
National Review
New Ireland Review
New York Times
New York Times Magazine
Nineteenth Century: A Monthly Review
Northern Miner
Omaha Sunday Bee
Parents' Review
Red Hand Magazine
Register (Adelaide)
San Francisco Call
Saturday Review of Politics, Literature, Science and Art
Sinn Féin
Sligo Champion
Social Review
The Speaker
Strand Magazine
Studies: An Irish Quarterly Review
Sydney Morning Herald
The Times
The Times Literary Supplement
United Ireland
Western Morning News
Western Times

Westminster Review
Workers' Republic
Yellow Book

PRINTED SOURCES

Abbott, S. J., *The Ruin of Girls in Convent Schools: Testimony of Roman Catholics and Grief-Stricken Parents* (London: Convent Enquiry Society, 1903).

Allen, Nicholas, 'Thurston, Katherine Cecil 1875–1911', in James McGuire and James Quinn (eds), *Dictionary of Irish Biography*, 9 vols. (Cambridge: Cambridge University Press, 2009), vol. IX, pp. 364–5.

Altick, Richard, *The English Common Reader: A Social History of the Mass Reading Public, 1800–1900* (Chicago, Ill.: Chicago University Press, 1957).

Arnold, Matthew, *Poetry and Prose* (London: Rupert Hart-Davis, 1954).

Backus, Margot Gayle, '"The Children of the Nation?" Representations of Poor Children in Mainstream Nationalist Journalism, 1882 and 1913', *Éire-Ireland*, 44:1–2 (2009), 118–46.

Barrie, J. M., 'A Plea for Smaller Books', in J. M. Barrie (ed.), *Two of Them* (New York: Lovell, Coryell & Co., 1893), pp. 192–6.

Basham, Diana, 'Through the Looking Glass: Madame Blavatsky and the Occult Mother', in D. Basham (ed.), *The Trial of Woman: Feminism and the Occult Sciences in Victorian Literature and Society* (Basingstoke: Macmillan, 1992), pp. 178–214.

Beaumont, Matthew, 'Socialism and Occultism at the *Fin de Siècle*: Elective Affinities', *Victorian Review*, 36:1 (2010), 217–32.

Beiner, Guy, *Remembering the Year of the French: Irish Folk History and Social Memory* (Madison, Wisc.: The University of Wisconsin Press, 2007).

Bellaigue, Christine de, '"Only What Is Pure and Exquisite": Girls' Reading at School in France, 1800–70', *French History*, 27:2 (2013), 202–22.

Biletz, Frank A., 'Women and Irish-Ireland: The Domestic Nationalism of Mary Butler', *New Hibernia Review*, 6:1 (2002), 59–72.

Binckes, Faith, and Kathryn Laing, 'A Forgotten Franco-Irish Literary Network: Hannah Lynch, Arvède Barine, and Salon Culture of *Fin-de-Siècle* Paris', *Études Irlandaises*, 36:2 (2011), 157–71.

——'Irish Autobiographical Fiction and Hannah Lynch's Autobiography of a Child', *English Literature in Transition*, 55:2 (2012), 195–218.

——'"Rival Attractions of the Season": Land War Fictions, Christmas Annuals, and the Early Writings of Hannah Lynch', in Heidi Hansson and James H. Murphy (eds), *Fictions of the Irish Land War* (Oxford: Peter Lang, 2014), pp. 57–80.

——'A Vagabond's Scrutiny: Hannah Lynch in Europe', in Elke D'hoker, Raphaël Ingelbien, and Hedwig Schwall (eds), *Irish Women Writers: New Critical Perspectives* (Oxford: Peter Lang, 2011), pp. 111–32.

Bittel, Helen, 'Required Reading for "Revolting Daughters"? The New Girl Fiction of L. T. Meade', *Nineteenth-Century Gender Studies*, 2:2 (2006), unpaginated. Available at http://ncgsjournal.com/issue22/bittel.htm. Accessed 15 April 2015.

Bleiler, E. F., 'Introduction', in E. F. Bleiler (ed.), *The Collected Ghost Stories of Mrs J. H. Riddell* (New York: Dover Press, 1977), pp. v–xxii.

Blommaert, Jan, *The Sociolinguistics of Globalization* (Cambridge: Cambridge University Press, 2010).

Bowman, Timothy, *The Irish Regiments in the Great War: Discipline and Morale* (Manchester: Manchester University Press, 2003).

Boyd, Ernest A., *The Contemporary Drama of Ireland* (Boston, Mass.: Little, Brown, & Company, 1917).

Brewster, Scott, Virginia Crossman, Fiona Becket and David Alderson (eds), *Ireland in Proximity: History, Gender, Space* (London and New York: Routledge, 1999).

Brown, Stephen J., SJ, *Ireland in Fiction: A Guide to Irish Novels, Tales, Romances, and Folk-lore* (Dublin and London: Maunsel & Co., 1916).

Bourke, Joanna, *Husbandry to Housewifery: Women, Economic Change, and Housework in Ireland, 1890–1914* (Oxford: Clarendon Press, 1993).

Caffyn, Kathleen Mannington, *Poor Max: A Novel* (London: Hutchinson & Co., 1898).

Cardozo, Nancy, *Lucky Eyes and a High Heart: The Life of Maud Gonne* (New York: The Bobbs-Merrill Company, 1978).

Clark, Jonathan, 'The Many Restorations of King James: A Short History of Scholarship on Jacobitism, 1688–2006', in Paul Monod, Murray Pittock, and Daniel Szechi (eds), *Loyalty and Identity: Jacobites at Home and Abroad* (Basingstoke: Palgrave Macmillan, 2010), pp. 9–56.

Clear, Catriona, *Social Change and Everyday Life in Ireland, 1850–1922* (Manchester: Manchester University Press, 2007).

Colum, Mary, *Life and the Dream* (London: Macmillan, 1947).

Colum, Padraic, *Ella Young: An Appreciation* (London: Longmans & Co., 1931).

——'Introduction', in *'Broad Sheet Ballads' Being a Collection of Irish Popular Songs with an Introduction by Padraic Colum* (Dublin and London: Maunsel & Co., n.d. [stamped 1 January 1914 by the British Library]).

Colum, Padraic and Mary Colum, *Our Friend James Joyce* (London: Gollancz, 1959).

Connolly, Linda, *The Irish Women's Movement: From Revolution to Devolution* (Dublin: Lilliput, 2003).

Copeland, Caroline, 'The Sensational Katherine Cecil Thurston: An Investigation into the Life and Publishing History of a "New Woman" Author' (Ph.D., Edinburgh Napier University, 2007).

Corkery, Daniel, *The Hidden Ireland: A Study of Gaelic Munster in the Eighteenth Century* (Dublin: M. H. Gill & Son, 1956).

Coughlan, Patricia and Tina O'Toole (eds), *Irish Literature: Feminist Perspectives* (Dublin: Carysfort Press, 2008).

Crichton, F. E., *The Blind Side of the Heart* (Dublin and London: Maunsel, 1915).

——*The Little Wizard of White Cloud Hill* (London: Edward Arnold, 1910).

——*Peep-in-the-World* (London: Edward Arnold, 1908).

——*The Soundless Tide* (London: Edward Arnold, 1911).

——*Tinker's Hollow* (London: Edward Arnold, 1912).

Crichton, F. E. Sinclair, *The Precepts of Andy Saul* (London: M'Caw, Stevenson & Orr, 1908).

Crossley, A. C., *The Eton College Hunt: A Short History of Beagling at Eton* (Eton: Spottiswoode, Ballantyne, 1922).

Crouch, Marcus, *The Nesbit Tradition: The Children's Novel, 1945–1970* (London: Ernest Benn, 1972).

Cullen Owens, Rosemary, *A Social History of Women in Ireland, 1870–1970* (Dublin: Gill & Macmillan, 2005).

Cullingford, Elizabeth Butler, 'At the Feet of the Goddess: Yeats's Love Poetry and the Feminist Occult', in Deirdre Toomey (ed.), *Yeats and Women: Yeats Annual No. 9* (London: Macmillan, 1992), pp. 31–59.

——'"Our Nuns Are *Not* a Nation": Politicizing the Convent in Irish Literature and Film', *Éire-Ireland*, 41:1 (2006), 9–39.

Dale, Emma, 'Irish Stories Are Quite Gone Out', in Charlotte Riddell, *A Struggle for Fame* (Dublin: Tramp Press, 2014), pp. v–viii.

Davidson, E. G., 'Two Books of Wonder Tales', *The New Ireland Review*, 34:6 (1911), 370–2.

Davitt, Michael, *Jottings in Solitary*, ed. Carla King (Dublin: University College Dublin Press, 2003).

Delany, Paul, *Literature, Money, and the Market: From Trollope to Amis* (Basingstoke: Palgrave Macmillan, 2002).

De Vere White, Terence, *A Leaf from the Yellow Book* (London: Richards Press, 1958).

D'hoker, Elke, Raphaël Ingelbien, and Hedwig Schwall (eds), *Irish Women Writers: New Critical Perspectives* (Oxford: Peter Lang, 2011).

Dickson, David, *Dublin: The Making of a Capital City* (London: Profile, 2014).

Dixon, Joy, *Divine Feminism: Theosophy and Feminism in England* (Baltimore, Md.: Johns Hopkins University Press, 2001).

Doak, Naomi, 'Assessing an Absence: Ulster Protestant Women Authors, 1900–1960', in Mervyn Busteed, Frank Neal, and Jonathan Tonge (eds), *Irish Protestant Identities* (Manchester: Manchester University Press, 2008), pp. 126–37.

Douglass, Frederick, 'Men of Color, to Arms!', *Broadside* (Rochester) (21 March 1863).

——'What to the Slave Is the Fourth of July?' in Philip S. Foner (ed.), *Frederick Douglass: Selected Speeches and Writings* (Chicago, Ill.: Lawrence Hill, 1999), pp. 188–206.

Eagleton, Terry, *Heathcliff and the Great Hunger* (New York: Verso, 1995).

Eaton, Anne T., 'Ella Young's Unicorns and Kyelins', *Horn Magazine: Books and Reading for Young People*, 9:3 (1933), 115–20.

Edgeworth, Maria, *Castle Rackrent: A Hibernian Tale* (London: J. Johnson, 1800).

Edwards, Heather, 'The Irish New Woman and Emily Lawless's *Grania: The Story of an Island* – A Congenial Geography', *ELT*, 51:4 (2008), 421–38.

Egerton, George, *Discords* (London: John Lane, 1894).

——'A Lost Masterpiece: A City Mood, Aug. '93', *The Yellow Book: An Illustrated Quarterly*, 1 (April 1894), 189–96.

Elliott, Marianne, *Robert Emmet: The Making of a Legend* (London: Profile, 2003).

Ellis, S. M., 'Mrs. J. H. Riddell: The Novelist of the City and of Middlesex', in S. M. Ellis (ed.), *Wilkie Collins, Le Fanu and Others* (London: Constable, 1931), pp. 266–335.

Ellmann, Richard, *Yeats: The Man and the Masks* (London: Faber & Faber, 1969).

English, Richard, *Ernie O'Malley: IRA Intellectual* (Oxford: Clarendon Press, 1998).

——'Green on Red: Two Case Studies in Early Twentieth-Century Irish Republican Thought', in D. George Boyce, Robert Eccleshall, and Vincent Geohagen (eds), *Political Thought in Ireland since the Seventeenth Century* (London and New York: Routledge, 1993), pp. 161–89.

Fallon, Ann Connerton, *Katharine Tynan* (Boston, Mass.: Twayne Publishers, 1979).

Fay, W. G. and Catherine Carswell, *The Fays of the Abbey Theatre: An Autobiographical Record* (New York: Harcourt, Brace & Co., 1935).

Feldman, Jessica R., *Victorian Modernism: Pragmatism and the Varieties of Aesthetic Experience* (Cambridge: Cambridge University Press, 2002).

Fitzpatrick, David, *Irish Emigration, 1801–1921* (Dublin: The Economic and Social History of Ireland, 1985).

Fletcher, Anthony, 'Cesca: A Young Nationalist in the Easter Rising', *History Today*, 56:4 (2006), 30–8.

Fletcher, Ian, *W. B. Yeats and His Contemporaries* (Brighton: The Harvester Press, 1987).

Foster, John Wilson, *Irish Novels, 1890–1940: New Bearings in Culture and Fiction* (Oxford: Oxford University Press, 2008).

Foster, R. F., 'Ascendancy and Union', in R. F. Foster (ed.), *The Oxford Illustrated History of Ireland* (London: Guild Publishing, 1989), pp. 161–212.

——*Modern Ireland, 1600–1972* (Harmondsworth: Penguin, 1989).

——*Vivid Faces: The Revolutionary Generation in Ireland, 1890–1923* (London: Allen Lane, 2014).

——*W. B. Yeats: A Life*, vol. I: *Apprentice Mage* (Oxford: Oxford University Press, 1997).

Foster, R. F. and Fintan Cullen, *Conquering England: The Irish in Victorian London* (London: National Portrait Gallery, 2005).

Foster, Shirley and Judy Simons, *What Katy Read: Feminist Re-readings of 'Classic' Stories for Girls* (Basingstoke: Palgrave Macmillan, 1995).

Francis, M. E., *The Story of Mary Dunne* (London: John Murray, 1913).

Gannon, P. J., 'The Ethical Aspect of the Hunger Strike', *Studies: An Irish Quarterly Review*, 9:35 (1920), 448–56.

Gardiner, David (ed.), *The Maunsel Poets, 1905–1926* (Bethesda, Md.: Academica Press, 2003).

Gardner, Susan M., 'For Love and Money: Beatrice Grimshaw's Passage to Papua' (Ph.D., Rhodes University, 1986).

——'A "'Vert to Australianism": Beatrice Grimshaw and the Bicentenary', Hecate Press, 30 November 1987. Available at http://www.grimshaworigin.org/BeatriceGwHecate.htm. Accessed 9 March 2013.

Gettman, R. A., *A Victorian Publisher: A Study of the Bentley Papers* (Cambridge: Cambridge University Press, 1960).

Gidlow, Elsa, *Elsa: I Come with My Songs – The Autobiography of Elsa Gidlow* (San Francisco, Calif.: Bootlegger Press & Druid Heights Books, 1986).

Gilbert, R. A., *The Golden Dawn Companion: A Guide to the History, Structure, and Workings of the Hermetic Order of the Golden Dawn* (Wellingborough: Aquarian, 1 986).

Gonne, Maud, 'Ethlinn with Lugh', in Ella Young, *Celtic Wonder Tales* (New York: Dover, 1995).

——'The High Priestess', in A. E. Waite, *The Pictorial Key to the Tarot* (New York: Samuel Weiser Inc., 1973).

——*A Servant of the Queen*, ed. A. Norman Jeffares and Anna MacBride White (Gerrards Cross: Colin Smythe, 1994).

——'Yeats and Ireland', in Stephen Gwynn (ed.), *Scattering Branches: Tributes to the Memory of W. B. Yeats* (London: Macmillan, 1940), pp. 15–34.

Gonzalez, Alexander G., *Irish Women Writers: An A-to-Z Guide* (Westport, Conn.: Greenwood Press, 2005).

Gore-Booth, Eva, *The Agate Lamp* (London: Longmans, Green & Co., 1912).

——*The Egyptian Pillar* (Dublin: Tower Press, 1907).

——*Poems* (London: Longmans, Green & Co., 1898).

——*The Sorrowful Princess* (London: Longmans, Green & Co., 1907).

——*The Three Resurrections and the Triumph of Maeve* (London: Longmans, 1905).

——*Unseen Kings: A Play in One Act and in Verse with Other Poems* (London: Longmans & Co., 1904).

Gregory, Lady Augusta, 'The Felons of Our Land', *Cornhill Magazine*, 8:47 (May 1900), 622–34.

——*Irish Folk-History Plays*, First and Second Series (London and New York: G. P. Putnam's Sons, 1912).

——'Irish Jacobite Songs', *Speaker* (January 1903), 413–15.

——(ed.), *Mr. Gregory's Letter-Box: 1813–1830* (London: Smith, Elder, & Co., 1898).

——*Our Irish Theatre: A Chapter of Autobiography* (London and New York: G. P. Putnam's Sons, 1913).

——*The White Cockade*, in *The Collected Plays, II, The Tragedies and Tragic-Comedies*, ed. Ann Saddlemyer (Gerrards Cross: Colin Smythe, 1971), pp. 219–54.

Gregory, James, 'Rev. of Guilty Money: The City of London in Victorian and Edwardian Culture, 1815–1914'. Available at www.history.ac.uk/reviews/review/771#author-response. Accessed 21 April 2015.

Grimshaw, Beatrice, *Broken Away* (London and New York: John Lane, The Bodley Head, 1897).

——*Isles of Adventure* (London: Herbert Jenkins, 1930).

——*The New New Guinea* (London: Hutchinson, 1910).

——*In the Strange South Seas* (London: Nelson, 1911).

——*When the Red Gods Call* (London: Mills & Boon, 1911).

Guinnane, Timothy, *The Vanishing Irish: Households, Migration and the Rural Economy in Ireland, 1850–1914* (Princeton, NJ: Princeton University Press, 1997).

Guinness, Selina, 'Ireland through the Stereoscope: Reading the Cultural Politics of Theosophy in the Irish Literary Revival', in E. A. Taylor FitzSimon and James H. Murphy (eds), *The Irish Revival Reappraised* (Dublin: Four Courts Press, 2004), pp. 19–32.

——'"Protestant Magic" Reappraised: Evangelicalism, Dissent, and Theosophy', *Irish Studies Review*, 33:1 (2003), 14–27.

Guppy, Shusha, 'Edna O'Brien, The Art of Fiction No. 82', *Paris Review*, 92 (1984), 22–50.

Haberstroh, Patricia Boyle and Christine St Peter (eds), *Opening the Field: Irish Women: Texts and Contexts* (Cork: Cork University Press, 2007).

Hansson, Heidi, 'From Reformer to Sufferer: The Returning Exile in Rosa Mulholland's Fiction', in Michael Böss, Irene Gilsenan Nordin, and Britta Olinder (eds), *Re-mapping Exile: Realities and Metaphors in Irish Literature and History* (Aarhus: Aarhus University Press, 2005), pp. 89–106.

——'Introduction: Out of Context', in Heidi Hansson (ed.), *New Contexts: Re-framing Nineteenth-Century Irish Women's Prose* (Cork: Cork University Press, 2008), pp. 1–15.

——(ed.), *New Contexts: Re-framing Nineteenth-Century Irish Women's Prose* (Cork: Cork University Press, 2008).

Harper, George Mills, *Yeats's Golden Dawn* (New York: Macmillan, 1974).

Harris, Jennifer, 'The Red Cap of Liberty: A Study of Dress Worn by French Revolutionary Partisans, 1789–94', *Eighteenth-Century Studies*, 14:3 (1981), 283–312.

Harris, Wendell V., 'John Lane's Keynotes Series and the Fiction of the 1890s', *PMLA*, 83:5 (1968), 1407–13.

Heilmann, Anne, *New Woman Fiction: Women Writing First-Wave Feminism* (Basingstoke: Palgrave Macmillan, 2000).

——*New Woman Strategies: Sarah Grand, Olive Schreiner, Mona Caird* (Manchester: Manchester University Press, 2004).

Henderson, Kate Krueger, 'Mobility and Modern Consciousness in George Egerton's and Charlotte Mew's *Yellow Book* Stories', *ELT*, 54:2 (2011), 185–211.

Hetherington, Naomi, 'Feminism, Freethought, and the Sexual Subject in Colonial New Woman Fiction: Olive Schreiner and Kathleen Mannington Caffyn', *Victorian Review*, 37:2 (2011), 47–59.

Hillan, Sophia, *May, Lou and Cass: Jane Austen's Nieces in Ireland* (Belfast: Blackstaff Press, 2011).

Hogan, Robert and James Kilroy, *The Abbey Theatre: The Years of Synge, 1905–1909* (Dublin: Dolmen Press, 1978).

Holloway, Joseph, *Joseph Holloway's Abbey Theatre: A Selection from His Unpublished Journal Impressions of a Dublin Playgoer*, ed. Robert Hogan and Michael J. Neill, with a preface by Harry T. Moore (Carbondale, Ill.: Southern Illinois University Press, 1967).

Holmes, Andrew, 'The Development of Unionism before 1912', Irish History Live. Available at www.qub.ac.uk/sites/irishhistorylive/IrishHistoryResources/Articlesandlecturesbyourteachingstaff/ThedevelopmentofUnionismbefore1912. Accessed 15 February 2015.

Howes, Marjorie, *Yeats's Nations: Gender, Class and Irishness* (Cambridge: Cambridge University Press, 1998).

Hutton, Clare, '"Yogibogeybox in Dawson Chambers": The Beginnings of Maunsel and Company', in Clare Hutton (ed.), *The Irish Book in the Twentieth-Century* (Dublin: Irish Academic Press, 2004), pp. 36–46.

Hyde, Douglas, *A Literary History of Ireland: From Earliest Times to the Present Day* (New York: Charles Scribner's Sons, 1901).

Ingman, Heather, *Irish Women's Fiction: From Edgeworth to Enright* (Dublin: Irish Academic Press, 2013).

Innes, C. L., *Woman and Nation in Irish Literature and Society, 1880–1935* (Athens, Ga.: University of Georgia, 1993).

James, Henry, 'Preface', in *The Tragic Muse*, 3 vols. (New York: Charles Scribner's Sons, 1908).

Jewell, E. A., 'Elfland Sends an Ambassadress to Us', *New York Times Magazine*, 18 October 1925, p. 12.

Johnson, Alice, 'Middle-Class Culture and Civic Identity in Mid Nineteenth Century Belfast' (Ph.D., Queen's University Belfast, 2009).

Joy, Maurice, 'The Irish Literary Revival: Some Limitations and Possibilities', *New Ireland Review*, 32:5 (1905), 257–66.

Joyce, Patrick, *The Rule of Freedom* (London: Verso, 2003).

Kearney, Richard, *Myth and Motherland* (Derry: Field Day Theatre Company, 1984).

Kelleher, Margaret, 'Charlotte Riddell's *A Struggle for Fame*: The Field of Women's Literary Production', *Colby Quarterly*, 36:2 (2000), 116–31.

Kelly, John (ed.), *Poems and Ballads of Young Ireland* (Otley: Woodstock Books, 2000).

——(gen. ed.), *The Collected Letters of W. B. Yeats*, InteLex Electronic Edition (Oxford: Oxford University Press, 2002).

Kiberd, Declan, 'The City in Irish Culture', *City: Analysis of Urban Trends, Culture, Theory, Policy, Action*, 6:2 (2002), 219–28.

——*Irish Classics* (London: Granta, 2000).

Kickham, Lisbet, *Protestant Women Novelists and Irish Society, 1879–1922* (Helgonabacken: Lund University, 2004).

Kinahan, Frank, *Yeats, Folklore and Occultism: Contexts of the Early Work and Thought* (London: Unwin Hyman, 1988).

Kirkpatrick, Kathryn (ed.), *Border Crossings: Irish Women Writers and National Identities* (Tuscaloosa, Ala.: University of Alabama Press, 2000).

Laffan, May, 'Convent Boarding-Schools for Young Ladies', *Fraser's Magazine*, 9:54 (1874), 778–86.

——*Hogan MP: A Novel*, 2nd edn (London: Macmillan, 1881).

Landes, Joan B., *Visualising the Nation: Gender, Representation, and Revolution in Eighteenth-Century France* (Ithaca, NY: Cornell University Press, 2001).

Laracy, Hugh and Eugénie Laracy, 'Beatrice Grimshaw: Pride and Prejudice in Papua', *Journal of Pacific History*, 12:3 (1977), 154–75.

Lawless, Emily, 'An Addition to Mr. Birchall's List of "The Lepidoptera of Ireland"', *Entomologist's Monthly Magazine* (3 January 1867), 187.

——*The Book of Gilly: Four Months Out of a Life* (London: Smith, Elder, 1906).

——'A Dredging Ground', *Nineteenth Century: A Monthly Review*, 10:53 (1881), 131–41.

——*Grania: The Story of an Island* (New York: Macmillan, 1892).

——'Iar-Connaught: A Sketch', *Cornhill Magazine*, 45:267 (1882), 319–33.

——*Ireland* (London: T. Fisher Unwin, 1912). First published 1887.

——'In the Kingdom of Kerry', *Gentleman's Magazine*, 252:1817 (1882), 540–53.

——'Notes in the Morbihan', *National Review*, 4:22 (1884), 492–503.

Ledger, Sally, 'The New Woman and Feminist Fictions', in Gail Marshall (ed.), *The Cambridge Guide to the Fin de Siècle* (Cambridge: Cambridge University Press, 2007), pp. 153–68.

——*The New Woman: Fiction and Feminism at the Fin de Siècle* (Manchester: Manchester University Press, 1997).

——'Wilde Women and the *Yellow Book*: The Sexual Politics of Aestheticism and Decadence', *ELT*, 50:1 (2007), 5–26.

Leeney, Cathy, *Irish Women Playwrights, 1900–1939: Gender and Violence on Stage* (Oxford: Peter Lang, 2010).

Lees, Andrew, *Cities Perceived: Urban Society in European and American Thought* (Manchester: Manchester University Press, 1985).

Lennon, Mary, Marie McAdam, and Joanne O'Brien, *Across the Water: Irish Women's Lives in Britain* (London: Virago, 1988).

Lever, Charles, *Roland Cashel* (New York: Athenaeum, 1850).

Lewis, Gifford, *Edith Somerville: A Biography* (Dublin: Four Courts Press, 2005).

——(ed.), *The Selected Letters of Somerville and Ross* (London: Faber & Faber, 1989).

Loeber, Rolf, Magda Loeber, and Anne Mullin Burnham, *A Guide to Irish Fiction, 1650–1900* (Dublin: Four Courts Press, 2006).

Lyman, W. W., 'Ella Young: A Memoir by W. W. Lyman', *Éire-Ireland*, 8:3 (1973), 65–9.

Lynch, Hannah, *Autobiography of a Child* (Edinburgh: Blackwood, 1901).

——*Through Troubled Waters* (London: Ward Lock & Co., 1885).

Lyons, F. S. L., *Ireland Since the Famine* (London: Fontana, 1973).

McAleer, Joseph, *Passion's Fortune: The Story of Mills and Boon* (Oxford: Oxford University Press, 1999).

McClellan, Ann, 'Dialect, Gender and Colonialism in *The Real Charlotte*', *Études Irlandaises*, 31:1 (2006), 69–86.

McCoole, Sinéad, *No Ordinary Women: Irish Female Activists in the Revolutionary Years, 1900–1923* (Dublin: The O'Brien Press, 2003).

McCotter, Clare, 'Woman Traveller/Colonial Tourist: Deconstructing the Great Divide in Beatrice Grimshaw's Travel Writing', *Irish Studies Review*, 15:4 (2007), 481–506.

McDowell, Dorothea, *Ella Young and Her World: Celtic Mythology, the Irish Revival and the California Avant-Garde* (Palo Alto, Calif.: Academica Press, 2014).

McHugh, Roger (ed.), *W. B. Yeats: Letters to Katharine Tynan* (Dublin: Clonmore & Reynolds, 1953).

McLeod, Kirsten, *Fictions of British Decadence: High Art, Popular Writing, and the Fin de Siècle* (Basingstoke: Palgrave Macmillan, 2006).

Mac Suibhne, Breandán, 'Agrarian Improvement and Social Unrest: Lord George Hill and the Gaoth Dobhair Sheep War, 1856–60', in William Nolan, Liam Ronayne, and Mairead Dunlevy (eds), *Donegal: History and Society* (Dublin: Geography Publications, 1995), pp. 547–82.

——'Soggarth Aroon and Gombeen-Priest: Canon James MacFadden (1842–1917)', in Gerard Moran (ed.), *Radical Irish Priests, 1600–1970* (Dublin: Four Courts Press, 1998), pp. 149–84.

Maguire, W. A., *Living like a Lord: The Second Marquess of Donegall* (Belfast: Appletree Press, 1984).

Malcolmson, A. P. W., *Virtues of a Wicked Earl: The Life and Legend of William Sydney Clements, Third Earl of Leitrim* (Dublin: Four Courts Press, 2008).

Mangan, J. A. and C. McKenzie, 'Privileged Education, Hunting and the Making of Martial Masculinity', *International Journal of the History of Sport*, 25:9 (2008), 1106–31.

March, Jessica, 'Egerton, George (Mary Chavelita Dunne)', in James McGuire and James Quinn (eds), *Dictionary of Irish Biography*, 9 vols. (Cambridge: Cambridge University Press, 2009), vol. III, pp. 595–6.

Markievicz, Constance, *Women, Ideals and the Nation: A Lecture Delivered to the Students' National Literary Society, Dublin* (Dublin: Inghinidhe na hÉireann, 1909).

Markievicz, Constance and Casimir Markievicz, *The Memory of the Dead* (Dublin, 1910).

Matthews, John and Denise Sallee (eds), *At the Gates of Dawn: A Collection of Writings by Ella Young* (Cheltenham: Skylight Press, 2011).

Maume, Patrick, 'Containing Granuaile: Grace O'Malley in Two Nineteenth-Century Novels', *New Hibernia Review*, 19:1 (2015), 98–114.

——'Music-Hall Unionism: Robert Martin and the Politics of the Stage-Irishman', in Peter Gray (ed.), *Victoria's Ireland: Irishness and Britishness, 1837–1901* (Dublin: Four Courts Press, 2004), pp. 69–80.

May, J. Lewis, *John Lane and the Nineties* (London: John Lane, The Bodley Head, 1936).

Meade, L. T., *A Bunch of Cherries: A Story of Cherry Court School* (Chicago, Ill.: M. A. Donoghue, 1898).

——'Children Past and Present', *Parents' Review*, 6:12 (1896), 881–7.

——*The Cleverest Woman in England* (London: James Nisbet, 1898).

——'Girls' Schools of Today, I: Cheltenham College', *Strand*, 9 (January 1895), 283–8.

——'Girls' Schools of Today, II: St. Leonard and Great Harrowden Hall', *Strand*, 9 (January 1895), 457–63.

——'Girton College', *Atalanta*, 7:77 (1894), 325–31.

——'How I Began', *Girl's Realm*, 3 (November 1900), 57–64.

——'Newnham College', *Atalanta*, 7:80 (1894), 525–9.

——'Story Writing for Girls', *Academy and Literature Fiction Supplement*, 7 November 1903, p. 499.

——*A Sweet Girl Graduate* (London, Paris and Melbourne: Cassell, 1892).

——*A World of Girls* (New York: A. L. Burt, 1886).

Meaney, Gerardine, 'Decadence, Degeneration and Revolting Aesthetics: The Fiction of Emily Lawless and Katherine Cecil Thurston', *Colby Quarterly*, 36:2 (2000), 157–75.

Mitchell, Sally, 'Children's Reading and the Culture of Girlhood: The Case of L. T. Meade', *Browning Institute Studies*, 17 (1989), 53–63.

——*The New Girl: Girls' Culture in England, 1880–1915* (New York: Columbia University Press, 1995).

Molidor, Jennifer, 'Violence, Silence, and Sacrifice: The Mother–Daughter Relationship in the Short Fiction of Irish Women Writers, 1890–1980' (Ph.D., University of Notre Dame, 2008).

Moody, T. W., *Leaders and Workers* (Cork: Mercier Press, 1978).

Morris, Robert, *Class, Sect and Party: The Making of the British Middle Class – Leeds, 1820–50* (Manchester: Manchester University Press, 1990).

Moynihan, Julian, 'The Image of the City in Nineteenth Century Irish Fiction', in Maurice Harmon (ed.), *The Irish Writer and the City* (Gerrards Cross: Colin Smythe, 1984), pp. 1–17.

Mulholland, Rosa (Lady Gilbert, Ruth Murray), *Cynthia's Bonnet Shop* (London: Blackie & Son, 1901).

——*Dunmara*, 3 vols. (London: Smith, Elder, 1864).

——*Marcella Grace: An Irish Novel*, ed. James H. Murphy (Washington, DC: Maunsel, 2001).

——*Norah of Waterford* (New York: P. J. Kenedy, 1915).

——*The O'Shaughnessy Girls* (London: Blackie & Son, 1911).

——*The Return of Mary O'Murrough* (London: Sands, 1909).

Murphy, James H., *Catholic Fiction and Social Reality in Ireland, 1873–1922* (Westport, Conn.: Greenwood, 1997).

——*Ireland: A Social, Cultural and Literary History, 1791–1891* (Dublin: Four Courts Press, 2003).

——*Irish Novelists and the Victorian Age* (Oxford: Oxford University Press, 2011).

Murphy, Maureen, 'Lady Gregory and the Gaelic League', in Ann Saddlemyer and Colin Smythe (eds), *Lady Gregory, Fifty Years After* (Gerrards Cross: Colin Smythe, 1987), pp. 143–63.

Murphy, Rose, *Ella Young: Irish Mystic and Rebel – From Literary Dublin to the American West* (Dublin: The Liffey Press, 2008).

Murray, Piper, '"They Are Well Together. Women Are Not": Productive Ambivalence and Female Hom(m)osociality in *Fefu and Her Friends*', *Modern Drama*, 44:4 (2001), 398–414.

Nabokov, Vladimir, *Speak, Memory: An Autobiography Revisited* (London: Penguin, 2015). First published 1946.

Neubauer, John and Borbála Zsuzsanna Török (eds), *The Exile and Return of Writers from East-Central Europe: A Compendium* (Berlin: De Gruyter, 2009).

Nic Congáil, Ríona, '"Fiction, Amusement, Instruction": The Irish Fireside Club and the Educational Ideology of the Gaelic League', *Éire-Ireland*, 44:1–2 (2009), 91–117.

——'"Some of You Will Curse Her": Women's Writing During the Irish-Language Revival', *Proceedings of the Harvard Celtic Colloquium* 29 (2009), 199–222.

Nic Shiubhlaigh, Maire, *The Splendid Years: Recollections of Maire Nic Shiubhlaigh as told to Edward Kenny with Appendices and Lists of Irish Theatre Plays, 1899–1916* (Dublin: James Duffy, 1955).

Oakman, Anne, 'Sitting on "The Outer Skin": Somerville and Ross's *Through Connemara in a Governess Cart* as a Coded Stratum of Linguistic/Feminist "Union" Ideals', *Éire-Ireland*, 39:1–2 (2004), 110–35.

Ó Buachalla, Breandán, 'Irish Jacobite Poetry', *Irish Review*, 12 (spring/summer 1992), 40–9.

——'Irish Jacobitism and Irish Nationalism: The Literary Evidence', in Michael O'Dea and Kevin Whelan (eds), *Nations and Nationalisms: France, Britain, Ireland and the Eighteenth-Century Context* (Oxford: Voltaire Foundation, 1995), pp. 103–16.

Ó Ciosáin, Niall, 'Gaelic Culture and Language Study', in Laurence Geary and Margaret Kelleher (eds), *Nineteenth-Century Ireland: A Guide to Recent Research* (Dublin: University College Dublin Press, 2005), pp. 136–69.

Ó Conchubhair, Brian, *Fin de Siècle na Gaeilge: Darwin, an Athbheochan agus Smaointeoireacht na hEorpa* (Galway: An Clóchomhar, 2009).

O'Connor, Theresa (ed.), *The Comic Tradition in Irish Women Writers* (Gainesville, Fla.: University Press of Florida, 1996).

O'Day, Alan, *Irish Home Rule, 1867–1921* (Manchester: Manchester University Press, 1998).

Ogilvie, John (ed.), *The Imperial Dictionary: English, Technological and Scientific*, 2 vols. (Glasgow, London, and Edinburgh: Blackie & Son, 1859).

O'Neill, Ciaran, *Catholics of Consequence: Transnational Education, Social Mobility, and the Irish Catholic Elite, 1850–1900* (Oxford: Oxford University Press, 2014).

——'The Irish Schoolboy Novel', *Éire-Ireland*, 44:1–2 (2009), 147–68.

O'Toole, Tina, *The Irish New Woman* (Basingstoke: Palgrave Macmillan, 2013).

Pakenham, Thomas, *The Year of Liberty* (London: Orion Books Limited, 1992).

Pašeta, Senia, *Before the Revolution: Nationalism, Social Change and Ireland's Catholic Elite, 1879–1922* (Cork: Cork University Press, 1999).

——*Irish Nationalist Women, 1900–1918* (Cambridge: Cambridge University Press, 2013).

——'Women in the National University of Ireland', in Tom Dunne (ed.), *The National University of Ireland, 1908–2008, Centenary Essays* (Dublin: National University of Ireland, 2008), pp. 19–32.

Pepinster Greene, Nicole, 'Dialect and Social Identity in *The Real Charlotte*', *New Hibernia Review/Iris Éireannach Nua*, 4:1 (2000), 122–37.

Pethica, James 'Lady Gregory's Abbey Theatre Drama: Ireland Real and Ideal', in Shaun Richards (ed.), *The Cambridge Companion to Twentieth-Century Irish Drama* (Cambridge: Cambridge University Press, 2004), pp. 62–78.

——(ed.), *Lady Gregory's Diaries, 1892–1902* (Gerrards Cross: Colin Smythe, 1996).

Petzold, Dieter, 'A Race Apart: Children in Late Victorian and Edwardian Children's Books', *Children's Literature Association Quarterly*, 17:3 (1992), 33–6.

Phillips, A. A., 'The Cultural Cringe', *Meanjin*, 9:4 (1950), 299–302.

Pittock, Murray, *The Invention of Scotland: The Stuart Myth and the Scottish Identity, 1638 to the Present* (London and New York: Routledge, 1991).

——*Poetry and Jacobite Politics in Eighteenth-Century Britain and Ireland* (Cambridge: Cambridge University Press, 1994).

——*Spectrum of Decadence: The Literature of the 1890s* (London and New York: Routledge, 1993).

Potts, Willard, *Joyce and the Two Irelands* (Austin, Tex.: University of Texas Press, 2000).

Prunty, Brendan, 'The Irish Fiction of Emily Lawless: A Narrative Analysis' (Ph.D., National University Ireland Maynooth, 2009).

Purvis, June, *A History of Women's Education in England* (Milton Keynes: Open University Press, 1991).

Pyle, Hilary, *Cesca's Diary, 1913–1916: Where Art and Nationalism Meet* (Dublin: Woodfield, 2005).

Quinlan, Carmel, *Genteel Revolutionaries: Anna and Thomas Haslam and the Irish Women's Movement* (Cork: Cork University Press, 2002).

Quinn, James, 'Clements, William Sydney', in James McGuire and James Quinn (eds), *Dictionary of Irish Biography*, 9 vols. (Cambridge: Cambridge University Press, 2009), vol. II, pp. 579–80.

——'Theobald Wolfe Tone and the Historians', *Irish Historical Studies*, 32:125 (2000), 113–28.

Raftery, Deirdre, Susan Parkes, and Judith Harford, 'Mapping the Terrain of Female Education in Ireland, 1830–1910', *Gender and Education*, 22:5 (2010), 565–78.

Randall, Bryony, 'George Egerton's "A Lost Masterpiece": Inspiration, Gender, and Cultural Authority at the *Fin de Siècle*', in Melissa Purdue and Stacey Floyd (eds), *New Women Writers, Authority, and the Body* (Newcastle: Cambridge Scholars, 2009), pp. 1–20.

Rauchbauer, Otto, *The Edith Œ Somerville Archive in Drishane* (Dublin: Irish Manuscripts Commission, 1995).

Regan, Nell, 'Helena Molony (1883–1967)', in Mary Cullen and Maria Luddy (eds), *Female Activists: Irish Women and Change, 1900–1960* (Dublin: The Woodfield Press, 2001), pp. 141–68.

Reimer, Mavis Barkman, 'Tales Out of School: L. T. Meade and the School Story' (Ph.D., University of Calgary, 1993).

Riddell, Charlotte, *Austin Friars* (London: Tinsley Brothers, 1870).

——*Berna Boyle: A Love Story of the County Down* (London: Macmillan & Co., 1900).

——*The Earl's Promise: A Novel* (London: Hutchinson, n.d).

——*The Nun's Curse*, 3 vols. (New York: Garland Press, 1979).

——*A Rich Man's Daughter* (London: F. V. White, 1897).

——*A Struggle for Fame* (Dublin: Tramp Press, 2014).

Riehle, E., 'The Shining Land of Ella Young', *Dublin Magazine*, 33:2 (1958), 17–22.

Rodgers, Beth, 'Irishness, Professional Authorship and the "Wild Irish Girls" of L. T. Meade', *English Literature in Transition, 1880–1920*, 56:2 (2013), 146–66.

Ruber, Peter and Victor A. Berch, 'Beatrice (Ethel) Grimshaw: A Bibliography in Progress' (2003). Available at http://pulprack.com.arch/2004/04/beatrice_ethel.html. Accessed 15 September 2013.

Russell, George, *New Songs: A Lyric Selection made by Æ* (Dublin and London: O'Donoghue & Co. and A. H. Bullen, 1904).

Russell, Matthew, 'Irish Writers of the Nineteenth Century', *Irish Monthly*, 27:314 (1899), 423–6.

Ryan, Desmond (ed.), *The 1916 Poets* (Dublin: Gill & Macmillan, 1995).

Salmon, Edward G., 'What Girls Read', *Nineteenth Century*, 20:116 (1886), 515–29.

Sharp, Elizabeth A., *William Sharp (Fiona Macleod) A Memoir Compiled by His Wife* (London: Heinemann, 1910).

Shovlin, Frank, 'Jacobitism and the Literary Revival', in Paddy Lyons, Willy Maley, and John Miller (eds), *Romantic Ireland: From Tone to Gonne – Fresh Perspectives on Nineteenth-Century Ireland* (Newcastle upon Tyne: Cambridge Scholars Publishing, 2013), pp. 376–87.

——*Journey Westward: Joyce, Dubliners and the Literary Revival* (Liverpool: Liverpool University Press, 2012).

Sichel, Edith, 'Emily Lawless', *Nineteenth Century and After: A Monthly Review*, 76:449 (1914), 80–100.

Somerville, E. Œ. and Martin Ross, *All on the Irish Shore* (London, Calcutta, Sydney: Harrap, 1925). First published 1903.

——*The Irish R. M. Complete* (London: Faber & Faber, 1928).

——*The Real Charlotte* (London: Quartet Books, 1977). First published 1894.

——*Through Connemara in a Governess Cart* (London: Virago, 1990). First published 1893.

——*Some Irish Yesterdays* (London: Nelson, 1916). First published 1906.

——*Stray-Aways* (London: Longmans, Green & Co., 1920).

Sommer, Doris, *Bilingual Aesthetics: A New Sentimental Education* (Durham, NC: Duke University Press, 2004).

Standlee, Whitney, 'George Egerton, James Joyce, and the Irish *Künstlerroman*', *Irish Studies Review*, 18:4 (2010), 439–52.

——*'Power to Observe': Irish Women Novelists in Britain, 1890–1916* (Oxford: Peter Lang, 2015).

——'"A World of Difference": London and Ireland in the Works of Katharine Tynan', in Tom Herron (ed.), *Irish Writing London*, vol. I: *Revival to the Second World War* (London: Bloomsbury, 2013), pp. 70–83.

Steele, Karen (ed.), *Maud Gonne's Irish Nationalist Writings, 1895–1946* (Dublin: Irish Academic Press, 2004).

——'When Female Activists Say "I": Veiled Rebels and the Counterhistory of Irish Independence', in Gillian McIntosh and Diane Urquhart (eds), *Irish Women at War: The Twentieth-Century* (Dublin: Irish Academic Press, 2010), pp. 51–68.

Stetz, Margaret D., 'George Egerton: Woman Writer of the 1890s' (Ph.D., Harvard University, 1982).

Stevens, Julie Anne, *The Irish Scene in Somerville and Ross* (Dublin: Irish Academic Press, 2007).

Summerfield, Henry, *That Myriad Minded Man: A Biography of George William Russell 'Æ', 1867–1935* (Gerrards Cross: Colin Smythe, 1975).

Sutherland, John A., *Victorian Novelists and Publishers* (London: Athlone Press, 1976).

Taillon, Ruth, *When History Was Made: The Women of 1916* (Belfast: Beyond the Pale Publications, 1996).

Thuente, M. H., 'The Folklore of Irish Nationalism', in Thomas E. Hachey and Lawrence John McCaffrey (eds), *Perspectives on Irish Nationalism* (Lexington, Ky.: University Press of Kentucky, 1989), pp. 42–60.

Thurston, Katherine Cecil, *The Fly on the Wheel* (New York: Grosset & Dunlap, 1908).

——*Max* (London and New York: Harper & Brothers, 1910).

Tiernan, Sonja, *Eva Gore-Booth: An Image of Such Politics* (Manchester: Manchester University Press, 2012).

Toomey, Deirdre, 'Young, Ella (1867–1956)', *Oxford Dictionary of National Biography*, Oxford University Press, 2004. Available at www.oxforddnb.com/view/article/59452. Accessed 26 April 2015.

Tynan, Katharine, *Ballads and Lyrics* (London: Kegan Paul, Trench, Trübner & Co., 1891).

——*Bitha's Wonderful Year* (London: Humphrey Milford, 1921).

——*A Cluster of Nuts: Being Sketches among My Own People* (London: Lawrence & Bullen, 1894).

——*Cuckoo Songs* (London: Elkin Matthews, 1894).

——*A Daughter of the Fields* (London: Smith, Elder & Co., 1900).

——*Flower of Youth* (London: Sidgwick & Jackson, 1915).

——*The Handsome Brandons: A Story for Girls* (London: Blackie & Son, 1900).

——*Heart o' Gold; or, The Little Princess: A Story for Girls* (London: S. W. Partridge, 1912).

——*The Holy War* (London: Sidgwick & Jackson, 1916).

——*An Isle in the Water* (London: A. & C. Black, 1895).

——*Katharine Tynan's Book of Irish History* (Dublin and Belfast: The Educational Company of Ireland Limited, n.d. [stamped 25 November 1918 by the British Museum]).

——*The Land of Mist and Mountain* (London: Catholic Truth Society, 1895).
——*Lord Edward: A Study in Romance* (London. Smith, Elder & Co., 1916).
——*Louise de la Vallière and other Poems* (London: Kegan Paul, 1885).
——*Memories* (London: Eveleigh Nash and Grayson, 1924).
——*The Middle Years* (London: Constable & Co., 1916).
——'The Prisoner', *Studies: An Irish Quarterly Review*, 9:35 (1920), 413.
——'In Time of Expectation', *United Ireland*, 29 May 1886, pp. 5–6.
——*Twenty-Five Years: Reminiscences* (London: Smith Elder & Co., 1913).
——*Twilight Songs* (Oxford: Basil Blackwell, 1927).
——*A Union of Hearts* (London: James Nisbett & Co., 1901).
——*The Wandering Years* (London: Constable, 1922).
——*The Way of a Maid* (London: Lawrence & Bullen, 1895).
——*The Years of the Shadow* (London: Constable, 1919).

Ulster-Scots Community Network, *Understanding the Ulster Covenant* (Belfast: Arts Council of Northern Ireland). Available at www.ulster-scots.com. Accessed 15 February 2015.

Urquhart, Diane, *A History Not Yet Told: Women in Ulster Politics, 1890–1940* (Dublin: Irish Academic Press, 2000).
——*The Ladies of Londonderry: Women and Political Patronage, 1800–1959* (London and New York: I. B. Tauris & Co., 2007).
——'Ulster Covenant: Women's Signature Role in the Fight against Home Rule', *Belfast Telegraph* (25 September 2012). Available at www.belfasttelegraph.co.uk/opinion/news-analysis/ulster-covenant-womens-signature-role-in-the-fight-against-home-rule-28866873.html. Accessed 28 February 2015.

Valente, Joseph, 'The Myth of Sovereignty: Gender in the Literature of Irish Nationalism', *ELH*, 61:1 (1994), 189–210.

Vaughan, W. E., *Sin, Sheep and Scotsmen: John George Adair and the Derryveagh Evictions* (Belfast: Ulster Historical Foundation, 1983).

Wadsworth, Sarah A., 'Louisa May Alcott, William T. Adams, and the Rise of Gender-Specific Series Books', *The Lion and the Unicorn*, 25:1 (2001), 17–46.

Walker, Brian, *Past and Present: History, Identity and Politics in Ireland* (Belfast: The Institute of Irish Studies Queen's University Belfast, 2000).

Walker, Graham, 'Thomas Sinclair: Presbyterian and Liberal Unionist', in Richard English and Graham Walker (eds), *Unionism in Modern Ireland: New Perspectives on Politics and Culture* (Basingstoke: Palgrave Macmillan, 1996), pp. 19–40.

Walker, Simon, *Historic Ulster Churches* (Belfast: Queen's University Belfast Press, 2000).

Waller, Philip, *Writers, Readers and Reputations: Literary Life in Britain, 1870–1918* (Oxford: Oxford University Press, 2006).

Ward, Margaret, *Hanna Sheehy Skeffington: A Life* (Cork: Attic Press, 1997).
——*Maud Gonne: Ireland's Joan of Arc* (London: Pandora, 1990).

Webb, Jean, 'Conceptualising Childhood: Robert Louis Stevenson's *A Child's Garden of Verses*', *Cambridge Journal of Education*, 32:3 (2002), 359–65.

Weekes, Ann Owens, *Irish Women Writers: An Uncharted Tradition* (Lexington, Ky.: The University Press of Kentucky, 1990).
——*Unveiling Treasures: The Attic Guide to the Published Works of Irish Women Literary Writers* (Dublin: Attic Press, 1993).

West, Mark I., 'Not to Be Circulated: The Response of Children's Librarians to Dime Novels and Series Books', *Children's Literature Association Quarterly*, 10:3 (1984), 137–9.

White, Anna MacBride and A. Norman Jeffares (eds), *The Gonne–Yeats Letters, 1893–1938: Always Your Friend* (London: Pimlico, 1993).

Wingerden, Sophia A. van, *The Women's Suffrage Movement in Britain* (Basingstoke: Palgrave Macmillan, 1999).

Wolf, Nicholas, *An Irish-Speaking Island: State, Religion and the Linguistic Landscape in Ireland, 1770–1870* (Madison, Wisc.: University of Wisconsin Press, 2014).

Wolff, Robert Lee, 'Two Irish Novels by Mrs. J. H. Riddell', in Charlotte Riddell, *Maxwell Drewitt*, 3 vols. (New York: Garland, 1979), vol. I, pp. v–ix.

Woolf, Virginia, *The Moment and Other Essays* (New York: Harcourt Brace & Co, 1975).

Wright, Jonathan, *The 'Natural Leaders' and Their World: Politics, Culture and Society in Belfast, c. 1801–1832* (Liverpool: Liverpool University Press, 2012).

Yeats, W. B., *Autobiographies* (London: Macmillan, 1955).

——(ed.), *A Book of Irish Verse* (London and New York: Routledge, 2002). First published 1895.

——*The Collected Letters of W. B. Yeats*, vol. III: *1901–1904*, ed. J. Kelly and R. Schuchard (Oxford: Clarendon Press, 1994).

——*The Collected Letters of W. B. Yeats*, vol. IV: *1905–1907*, eds. J. Kelly and R. Schuchard (Oxford: Clarendon Press, 2005).

——*The Hour-Glass and Other Plays: Plays for an Irish Theatre*, 5 vols. (London and New York: Macmillan, 1904).

——*The Poems*, ed. Daniel Albright (London: Everyman, 1994).

Young, Ella, 'The Adventures of the Gubbaun Saor and His Son', *Dublin Magazine*, 1 (August 1923/January 1924), 41–4, 513–19.

——'The Celtic Renaissance in Poetry', *All Ireland Review* 2:19 (1901), 142–3; 2:20 (1901), 150–1.

——*Celtic Wonder Tales* (New York: Dover, 1995).

——*Flowering Dusk* (New York: Longmans, 1945).

——'Lilith: A Story', *Dublin Magazine*, 2 (1924), 136–7.

——*Poems by Ella Young* (Dublin: Maunsel & Co., 1906).

——'The Red Sunrise (Moraig's Song)', *Red Hand Magazine*, 1:1 (1920), 5.

——*The Rose of Heaven: Poems by Ella Young, Decorated by Maud Gonne* (Dublin: The Candle Press, 1920).

——'The Rose Queen', *Irish Review*, 1:4 (1911), 187–9.

——'A Sunflower', *All Ireland Review*, 1:19 (1900), 6.

——*The Tangle-Coated Horse* (Edinburgh: Floris Books, 1991).

——'Three Mountains', *All Ireland Review*, 2:42 (1901), 352.

Index

Note: page numbers in *italic* refer to illustrations.